PROCREATIVE RIGHTS IN INTERNATIONAL LAW

Draghici contends that the advent of assisted reproductive technologies has given rise to new claims to fundamental, albeit not unqualified, rights. They include the right to use medically assisted procreation (e.g. artificial insemination, in vitro fertilisation, potentially gamete donation, posthumous conception or surrogacy) in order to become a parent (typically where natural procreation is hindered by infertility, sexual orientation, relationship status or adverse life events); the recognition of intention-based parenthood in relation to donor-conceived children jointly planned and raised with the genetic parent; and the right to pursue the conception of a healthy child (e.g. through recourse to pre-implantation genetic diagnosis and embryo selection to avoid severe illness in future offspring). To substantiate this assertion, the book relies on a comprehensive analysis of international case law on procreative autonomy, contextualised by a discussion of highly divisive bioethical controversies, from the status of embryos to the morality of genetic screening and third-party reproduction. This title is part of the Flip it Open Programme and may also be available Open Access. Check our website Cambridge Core for details.

Carmen Draghici is Professor of Law at City, University of London, a Senior Fellow of the UK's Higher Education Academy, an Honorary Member and former academic fellow of the Inner Temple, a member of the Network of UNESCO Chairs in Communication (Orbicom), and a former visiting fellow at the Harvard Law School's Human Rights Program and Tufts' Fletcher School of Law and Diplomacy. She has authored the monograph *The Legitimacy of Family Rights in Strasbourg Case Law: 'Living Instrument' or Extinguished Sovereignty?* (2017).

Procreative Rights in International Law

INSIGHTS FROM THE EUROPEAN COURT OF HUMAN RIGHTS

CARMEN DRAGHICI
City, University of London

CAMBRIDGE
UNIVERSITY PRESS

CAMBRIDGE
UNIVERSITY PRESS

Shaftesbury Road, Cambridge CB2 8EA, United Kingdom

One Liberty Plaza, 20th Floor, New York, NY 10006, USA

477 Williamstown Road, Port Melbourne, VIC 3207, Australia

314–321, 3rd Floor, Plot 3, Splendor Forum, Jasola District Centre, New Delhi – 110025, India

103 Penang Road, #05-06/07, Visioncrest Commercial, Singapore 238467

Cambridge University Press is part of Cambridge University Press & Assessment, a department of the University of Cambridge.

We share the University's mission to contribute to society through the pursuit of education, learning and research at the highest international levels of excellence.

www.cambridge.org
Information on this title: www.cambridge.org/9781009443951

DOI: 10.1017/9781009443982

When citing this work, please include a reference to the DOI 10.1017/9781009443982

First published 2024

A catalogue record for this publication is available from the British Library

Library of Congress Cataloging-in-Publication Data
NAMES: Draghici, Carmen, author.
TITLE: Procreative rights in international law : insights from the European Court of Human Rights / Carmen Draghici, City University London.
DESCRIPTION: Cambridge, United Kingdom ; New York, NY : Cambridge University Press, 2024. | Includes bibliographical references and index.
IDENTIFIERS: LCCN 2023041701 (print) | LCCN 2023041702 (ebook) | ISBN 9781009443951 (hardback) | ISBN 9781009443937 (paperback) | ISBN 9781009443982 (ebook)
SUBJECTS: LCSH: Reproductive rights–Europe. | Human reproduction–Law and legislation–Europe. | Artificial insemination, Human–Law and legislation–Europe. | Human reproductive technology–Law and legislation–Europe. | International law and human rights–Europe. | European Court of Human Rights. | Reproductive rights.
CLASSIFICATION: LCC KJC3575 .D73 2024 (print) | LCC KJC3575 (ebook) | DDC 342.08/5–dc23/eng/20231003
LC record available at https://lccn.loc.gov/2023041701
LC ebook record available at https://lccn.loc.gov/2023041702

ISBN 978-1-009-44395-1 Hardback
ISBN 978-1-009-44393-7 Paperback

To my parents

Contents

Table of International Cases

EUROPEAN COURT OF HUMAN RIGHTS

A, B and C v. *Ireland* [GC], App. No. 25579/05, 16 December 2010.
A.K. v. *Latvia*, App. No. 33011/08, 24 June 2014.
A.L. v. *France*, App. No. 13344/20, 7 April 2022.
A.M. v. *Norway*, App. No. 30254/18, 24 March 2022.
Abdulaziz, Cabales and Balkandali v. *The United Kingdom*, App. Nos. 9214/80; 9473/81; 9474/81, 28 May 1985.
Ahrens v. *Germany*, App. No. 45071/09, 22 March 2012.
Akdeniz v. *Turkey*, App. No. 20877/10, 11 March 2014.
Anayo v. *Germany*, App. No. 20578/07, 21 December 2010.
Animal Defenders International v. *The United Kingdom* [GC], App. No. 48876/08, 22 April 2013.
Arslan and Bingöl v. *Turkey*, App. Nos. 47121/06; 13988/07; 34750/07, 18 June 2019.
Aspisi v. *Italy*, App. No. 44453/19, 14 February 2023.
B. and L. v. *The United Kingdom*, App. No. 36536/02, 13 September 2005.
B.B. v. *Poland*, App. No. 67171/17, 18 October 2022.
Baghli v. *France*, App. No. 34374/97, 30 November 1999.
Biao v. *Denmark* [GC], App. No. 38590/10, 24 May 2016.
Bonnaud and Lecoq v. *France*, App. No. 6190/11, 1 March 2018.
Bortolato v. *Italy*, App. No. 35967, 10 January 2023.
Boso v. *Italy*, App. No. 50490/99, 5 September 2002.
Bruggeman and Scheuten v. *Germany*, App. No. 6959/75, 12 July 1977.
Budayeva and Others v. *Russia*, App. No. 15339/02, 20 March 2008.
Burghartz v. *Switzerland*, App. No. 16213/90, 22 February 1994.
C. and E. v. *France*, App. Nos. 1462/18; 17348/18, 19 November 2019.
C.E. and Others v. *France*, App. Nos. 29775/18; 29693/19, 24 March 2022.

Callamand v. *France*, App. No. 2338/20, 7 April 2022.
Carbonai v. *Italy*, App. No. 9825/21, 29 November 2022.
Case 'relating to certain aspects of the laws on the use of languages in education in Belgium' (Belgian Linguistics Case), App. Nos. 1474/62; 1677/62; 1691/62; 1769/63; 1994/63; 2126/64, 23 July 1968.
Cengiz Kılıç v. *Turkey*, App. No. 16192/06, 6 December 2011.
Centre for Legal Resources on Behalf of Valentin Câmpeanu v. *Romania*, App. No. 47848/08, 17 July 2014.
Charron and Merle-Montet v. *France*, App. No. 22612/15, 16 January 2018.
Christine Goodwin v. *The United Kingdom* [GC], App. No. 28957/95, 11 July 2002.
Codarcea v. *Romania*, App. No. 31675/04, 2 June 2009.
Cossey v. *The United Kingdom*, App. No. 10843/84, 27 September 1990.
Costa and Pavan v. *Italy*, App. No. 54270/10, 28 August 2012.
Courten v. *The United Kingdom*, App. No. 4479/06, 4 November 2008.
Csoma v. *Romania*, App. No. 8759/05, 15 January 2013.
D. and B. v. *Austria*, App. No. 40597/12, 31 October 2017.
D. and Others v. *Belgium*, App. No. 29176/13, 8 July 2014.
D. v. *France*, App. No. 11288/18, 16 July 2004.
D. v. *The United Kingdom*, App. No. 30240/96, 2 May 1997.
D.B. and Others v. *Switzerland*, App. Nos. 58817/15; 58252/15, 22 November 2022.
Dalia v. *France*, App. No. 26102/95, 19 February 1998.
Denisov v. *Ukraine* [GC], App. No. 76639/11, 25 September 2018.
Dickson v. *The United Kingdom* [GC], App. No. 44362/04, 4 December 2007.
Draon v. *France* [GC], App. No. 1513/03, 6 October 2005.
E.B. v. *France* [GC], App. No. 43546/02, 22 January 2008.
Emonet v. *Switzerland*, App. No. 39051/03, 13 December 2007.
Eryiğit v. *Turkey*, App. No. 18356/11, 10 April 2018.
Evans v. *The United Kingdom* [GC], App. No. 6339/05, 10 April 2007.
Fedotova and Others v. *Russia* [GC], App. Nos. 40792/10; 30538/14; 43439/14, 17 January 2023.
Foulon and Bouvet v. *France*, App. Nos. 9063/14; 10410/14, 21 July 2016.
G.B. and R.B. v. *The Republic of Moldova*, App. No. 16761/09, 18 December 2012.
G.M. and Others v. *The Republic of Moldova*, App. No. 44394/15, 22 November 2022.
Gas and Dubois v. *France*, App. No. 25951/07, 15 March 2012.
Gaskin v. *The United Kingdom*, App. No. 10454/83, 7 July 1989.
Gudrun Hansen v. *Turkey*, App. No. 36141/97, 23 September 2003.
H. v. *The United Kingdom*, App. No. 32185/20, 31 May 2022.

H.N. v. *Poland*, App. No. 77710/01, 13 September 2005.
Hirst v. *The United Kingdom (No. 2)* [GC], App. No. 74025/01, 6 October 2005.
Hokkanen v. *Finland*, App. No. 19823/92, 23 September 1994.
Honner v. *France*, App. No. 19511/16, 12 November 2020.
Hugh Jordan v. *The United Kingdom*, App. No. 24746/94, 4 May 2001.
I. v. *The United Kingdom* [GC], App. No. 25680/94, 11 July 2002.
I.G. and M.K. v. *Slovakia*, App. No. 15966/04, 13 November 2012.
J.M. v. *The United Kingdom*, App. No. 37060/06, 28 September 2010.
Jäggi v. *Switzerland*, App. No. 58757/00, 13 July 2006.
Jeunesse v. *The Netherlands* [GC], App. No. 12738/10, 3 October 2014.
Jurčić v. *Croatia*, App. No. 54711/15, 4 February 2021.
K.K. and Others v. *Denmark*, App. No. 25212/21, 6 December 2022.
Kalda v. *Estonia*, App. No. 17429/10, 19 January 2016.
Karner v. *Austria*, App. No. 40016/98, 24 July 2003.
Keegan v. *Ireland*, App. No. 16969/90, 26 May 1994.
Keenan v. *The United Kingdom*, App. No. 27229/95, 3 April 2001.
Knecht v. *Romania*, App. No. 10048/10, 2 October 2012.
Konstantin Markin v. *Russia* [GC], App. No. 30078/06, 22 March 2012.
Kopf and Liberda v. *Austria*, App. No. 1598/06, 17 January 2012.
Kozak v. *Poland*, App. No. 13102/02, 2 March 2010.
Kroon v. *The Netherlands*, App. No. 18535/91, 27 October 1994.
Kuppinger v. *Germany*, App. No. 62198/11, 15 January 2015.
Kurt v. *Turkey*, App. No. 24276/94, 25 May 1998.
L. v. *The Netherlands*, App. No. 45582/99, 1 June 2004.
Labassee v. *France*, App. No. 65941/11, 26 June 2014.
Laborie v. *France*, App. No. 44024/13, 19 January 2017.
Lautsi and Others v. *Italy* [Chamber], App. No. 30814/06, 3 November 2009.
Lautsi and Others v. *Italy* [GC], App. No. 30814/06, 18 March 2011.
Lia v. *Malta*, App. No. 8709/20, 5 May 2022.
Lukács v. *Hungary*, App. No. 61924/15, 16 December 2020.
Lyubenova v. *Bulgaria*, App. No. 13786/04, 18 October 2011.
M.P. and Others v. *Romania*, App. No. 39974/10, 15 April 2014.
M.S. v. *Croatia (No. 2)*, App. No. 75450/12, 19 February 2015.
Mandet v. *France*, App. No. 30955/12, 14 January 2016.
Manenc v. *France*, App. No. 66686/09, 21 September 2010.
Marckx v. *Belgium*, App. No. 6833/74, 13 June 1979.
Maurice v. *France* [GC], App. No. 11810/03, 6 October 2005.
McCann and Others v. *The United Kingdom* [GC], App. No. 18984/91, 27 September 1995.
Mennesson v. *France*, App. No. 65192/11, 26 June 2014.

Mikulić v. *Croatia*, App. No. 53176/99, 7 February 2002.
Moretti and Benedetti v. *Italy*, App. No. 16318/07, 27 April 2010.
N.B. v. *Slovakia*, App. No. 29518/10, 12 June 2012.
N.M. and Others v. *France*, App. No. 66328/14, 3 February 2022.
Nazarenko v. *Russia*, App. No. 39438/13, 16 July 2015.
Nedescu v. *Romania*, App. No. 70035/10, 16 January 2018.
Nitecki v. *Poland*, App. No. 65653/01, 21 March 2002.
Odièvre v. *France* [GC], App. No. 42326/98, 13 February 2003.
Okpisz v. *Germany*, App. No. 59140/00, 25 October 2005.
Oliari and Others v. *Italy*, App. Nos. 18766/11; 36030/11, 21 July 2015.
Omoregie and Others v. *Norway*, App. No. 265/07, 31 July 2008.
Open Door Counselling and Others v. *Ireland*, App. Nos. 14234/88; 14235/88, 29 October 1992.
Ostace v. *Romania*, App. No. 12547/06, 25 February 2014.
P.B. and J.S. v. *Austria*, App. No. 18984/02, 22 July 2010.
Panaitescu v. *Romania*, App. No. 30909/06, 10 April 2012.
Paradiso and Campanelli v. *Italy* [Chamber], App. No. 25358/12, 27 January 2015.
Paradiso and Campanelli v. *Italy* [GC], App. No. 25358/12, 24 January 2017.
Parrillo v. *Italy* [GC], App. No. 46470/11, 27 August 2015.
Pejřilová v. *The Czech Republic*, App. No. 14889/19, 8 December 2022.
Pentiacova and Others v. *The Republic of Moldova*, App. No. 14462/03, 4 January 2005.
Petithory Lanzmann v. *France*, App. No. 23038/19, 12 November 2019.
Petrovic v. *Austria*, App. No. 20458/92, 27 March 1998.
Pini and Bertani & Manera and Atripaldi v. *Romania*, App. Nos. 78028/01; 78030/01, 22 June 2004.
Pretty v. *The United Kingdom*, App. No. 2346/02, 29 April 2002.
R.R. v. *Poland*, App. No. 27617/04, 26 May 2011.
Rantsev v. *Cyprus and Russia*, App. No. 25965/04, 7 January 2010.
Rees v. *The United Kingdom*, App. No. 9532/81, 17 October 1986.
Ristevska and Ristevski v. *Former Yugoslav Republic of Macedonia*, App. No. 54344/07, 2 July 2013.
Rodrigues da Silva and Hoogkamer v. *The Netherlands*, App. No. 50435/99, 31 January 2006.
S.F.K. v. *Russia*, App. No. 5578/12, 11 October 2022.
S.H. and Others v. *Austria* [Chamber], App. No. 57813/00, 1 April 2010.
S.H. and Others v. *Austria* [GC], App. No. 57813/00, 3 November 2011.
S.-H. v. *Poland*, App. Nos. 56846/15; 56849/15, 16 November 2021.
S.W. and Others v. *Austria*, App. No. 1928/19, 6 September 2022.
Salman v. *Turkey* [GC], App. No. 21986/93, 27 June 2000.

Santos Nunes v. *Portugal*, App. No. 61173/08, 22 May 2012.
Schalk and Kopf v. *Austria*, App. No. 30141/04, 24 June 2010.
Schneider v. *Germany*, App. No. 17080/07, 15 September 2011.
Schwizgebel v. *Switzerland*, App. No. 25762/07, 10 June 2010.
Söderbäck v. *Sweden*, App. No. 24484/94, 28 October 1998.
Thlimmenos v. *Greece* [GC], App. No. 34369/97, 6 April 2000.
Timurtaş v. *Turkey*, App. No. 23531/94, 13 June 2000.
Tóth v. *Hungary*, App. No. 48494/06, 12 February 2013.
Tysiąc v. *Poland*, App. No. 5410/03, 20 March 2007.
Useinov v. *The Netherlands*, App. No. 61292/00, 11 April 2006.
V.C. v. *Slovakia*, App. No. 18968/07, 8 November 2011.
Valdís Fjölnisdóttir and Others v. *Iceland*, App. No. 71552/17, 18 May 2021.
Vallianatos and Others v. *Greece* [GC], App. Nos. 29381/09; 32684/09, 7 November 2013.
Van der Heijden v. *The Netherlands* [GC], App. No. 42857/05, 3 April 2012.
Vo v. *France* [GC], App. No. 53924/00, 8 July 2004.
Wagner and J. M. W. L. v. *Luxembourg*, App. No. 76240/01, 28 June 2007.
X and Others v. *Austria* [GC], App. No. 19010/07, 19 February 2013.
X and Y v. *The Netherlands*, App. No. 8978/80, 26 March 1985.
X, Y and Z v. *The United Kingdom* [GC], App. No. 21830/93, 22 April 1997.

EUROPEAN COMMISSION ON HUMAN RIGHTS

Brüggemann and Scheuten v. *Federal Republic of Germany*, App. No. 6959/75, 12 July 1977.
E.L.H. and P.B.H. v. *The United Kingdom*, App. Nos. 32094/96; 32568/96, 22 October 1997.
Hendricks v. *The Netherlands*, App. No. 8427/78, 8 March 1982.
J.R.M. v. *The Netherlands*, App. No. 16944/90, 8 February 1993.
Jonsson v. *Sweden*, App. No. 12495/86, 7 December 1987.
Kerkhoven and Hinke v. *The Netherlands*, App. No. 15666/89, 19 May 1992.
Lavisse v. *France*, App. No. 14223/88, 5 June 1991.
M. v. *Federal Republic of Germany*, App. No. 10995/84, 13 December 1984.
M.B. v. *The United Kingdom*, App. No. 22920/93, 6 April 1994.
Paton v. *The United Kingdom*, App. No. 8416/78, 13 May 1980.
R.H. v. *Norway*, App. No. 17004/90, 19 May 1992.
Röösli v. *Germany*, App. No. 28318/95, 15 May 1996.

X v. *Belgium and The Netherlands*, App. No. 6482/74, 10 July 1975.
X v. *France*, App. No. 9993/82, 5 October 1982.
X v. *The United Kingdom*, App. No. 6564/74, 21 May 1975.

UN HUMAN RIGHTS COMMITTEE

Althammer v. *Austria*, Communication No. 998/2001, 8 August 2003.
C. v. *Australia*, Communication No. 2216/2012, 28 March 2017.
Joslin and Others v. *New Zealand*, Communication No. 902/1999, 30 July 2002.
Llantoy Huamán v. *Peru*, Communication No. 1153/2003, 24 October 2005.
Mellet v. *Ireland*, Communication No. 2324/2013, 31 March 2016.
Whelan v. *Ireland*, Communication No. 2425/2014, 17 March 2017.
X v. *Colombia*, Communication No. 1361/2005, 30 March 2007.
X.Q.H. v. *New Zealand*, Communication No. 2197/2012, 29 April 2014.
Young v. *Australia*, Communication No. 941/2000, 6 August 2003.

INTER-AMERICAN COURT OF HUMAN RIGHTS

Artavia Murillo et al. ('In Vitro Fertilisation') v. *Costa Rica*, Case No. 12.361, 28 November 2012.
Gómez Murillo and Others v. *Costa Rica*, Case No. 12.798, 29 November 2016.
I.V. v. *Bolivia*, Case No. 329, 30 November 2016.

INTER-AMERICAN COMMISSION ON HUMAN RIGHTS

Alvarez Giraldo v. *Colombia*, Report No. 122/18, Case No. 11.656 (Merits), 5 October 2018.
Beatriz v. *El Salvador*, Report No. 9/20, Case No. 13.378 (Merits), 3 March 2020.
Duque v. *Colombia*, Report No. 5/14, Case No. 12.841 (Merits), 2 April 2014.
Gómez Murillo and Others v. *Costa Rica*, Report No. 1/15, Case No. 12.798 (Merits), 29 January 2015.
Henry and Edwards v. *Jamaica*, Report No. 400/20, Case 13.637 (Merits), 31 December 2020.
T.B. and S.H. v. *Jamaica*, Report No. 401/20, Case 13.095 (Merits), 31 December 2020.

Table of International Instruments

Additional Protocol to the American Convention in the Area of Economic, Social and Cultural Rights, San Salvador, 17 November 1988, in force 16 November 1999.

African Charter on Human and Peoples' Rights, Banjul, 27 June 1981, in force 21 October 1986, O.A.U. Doc. CAB/LEG/67/3/Rev. 5.

American Convention on Human Rights, San José, 22 November 1969, in force 18 July 1978.

Charter of Fundamental Rights of the European Union, 14 December 2007, in force 1 December 2009, 2007/C 303/01.

Committee on Economic, Social and Cultural Rights, General Comment No. 22 (2016) on the Right to Sexual and Reproductive Health (Article 12 of the International Covenant on Economic, Social and Cultural Rights), E/C.12/GC/22, 2 May 2016.

Convention on the Rights of Persons with Disabilities, New York, 13 December 2006, in force 3 May 2008, UNTS vol. 2515 (p. 3).

Convention on the Rights of the Child, New York, 20 November 1989, in force 2 September 1990, UNTS vol. 1577 (p. 3).

Council of Europe, Convention for the Protection of Human Rights and Dignity of the Human Being with Regard to the Application of Biology and Medicine, Oviedo, 4 April 1997, in force 1 December 1999, ETS No. 164.

Council of Europe, Recommendation No. R(90)13 of the Committee of Ministers to Member States on Prenatal Genetic Screening, Prenatal Genetic Diagnosis and Associated Genetic Counselling.

European Convention on Human Rights and Fundamental Freedoms, Rome, 4 November 1950, in force 3 September 1953, ETS No. 5.

Geneva Convention I for the Amelioration of the Condition of the Wounded and Sick in Armed Forces in the Field, Geneva, 12 August 1949, in force 21 October 1950, UNTS 75 (p. 31).

Geneva Convention II for the Amelioration of the Condition of the Wounded, Sick and Shipwrecked Members of the Armed Forces at Sea, Geneva, 12 August 1949, in force 21 October 1950, UNTS 75 (p. 85).

Geneva Convention III Relative to the Treatment of Prisoners of War, 12 August 1949, Geneva, in force 21 October 1950, UNTS 75 (p. 135).

Geneva Convention IV Relative to the Protection of Civilian Persons in Time of War, Geneva, 12 August 1949, in force 21 October 1950, UNTS 75 (p. 287).

Inter-American Convention for the Elimination of All Forms of Discrimination against Persons with Disabilities, Guatemala City, 8 June 1999, in force 14 September 2001.

Inter-American Convention on the Prevention, Punishment and Eradication of Violence against Women, Belém do Pará, 6 September 1994, in force 3 May 1995.

International Covenant on Civil and Political Rights, New York, 16 December 1966, in force 23 March 1976, UNTS vol. 999 (p. 171).

International Covenant on Economic, Social and Cultural Rights, New York, 16 December 1966, in force 3 January 1976, UNTS vol. 993 (p. 3).

Optional Protocol to the Convention on the Rights of the Child on the Sale of Children, Child Prostitution and Child Pornography, New York, 25 May 2000, in force 18 January 2002, UNTS vol. 2171 (p. 227).

Protocol 1 to the European Convention on Human Rights and Fundamental Freedoms, Paris, 20 March 1952, in force 18 May 1954, ETS No. 009.

Protocol 12 to the European Convention on Human Rights and Fundamental Freedoms, Rome, 4 November 2000, in force 1 April 2005, ETS No. 177.

Protocol Additional to the Geneva Conventions of 12 August 1949 and Relating to the Protection of Victims of International Armed Conflicts (Protocol I), Geneva, 8 June 1977, 7 December 1978, UNTS 1125 (p. 3).

Protocol Additional to the Geneva Conventions of 12 August 1949 and Relating to the Protection of Victims of Non-international Armed Conflicts (Protocol II), Geneva, 8 June 1977, 7 December 1978, UNTS 1125 (p. 609).

Report of the Special Rapporteur on the Sale and Sexual Exploitation of Children, Including Child Prostitution, Child Pornography and Other Child Sexual Abuse Material, A/HRC/37/60, 15 January 2018.

Rome Statute of the International Criminal Court, Rome, 17 July 1998, in force 1 July 2002, UNTS 2187 (p. 3).

UN General Assembly, Declaration on Social Progress and Development, Resolution 2542 (XXIV), 11 December 1969.

UNESCO General Conference, Universal Declaration on Bioethics and Human Rights, Paris, 19 October 2005, SHS/EST/BIO/06/1.

UNESCO General Conference, Universal Declaration on the Human Genome and Human Rights, Paris, 11 November 1997, BR/2001/PI/H/1.

Vienna Convention on the Law of Treaties, Vienna, 23 May 1969, in force 27 January 1980, UNTS vol. 1155 (p. 331).

Introduction

In modern times, technology has proffered humanity an ally and a foe, bringing about tremendous progress but also unforeseen destruction. Rather unsurprisingly, new technologies tend to inspire both enthusiasm and apprehension. This book embraces the view that, in the field of biomedicine, with adequate regulation, technology has the potential to greatly improve human experience in its relational dimension. In fact, for couples unable to conceive naturally, technology means access to biological parenthood. Since the birth in England in 1978 of Louise Brown, the first child in the world to be conceived via in vitro fertilisation (IVF),[1] reproductive technologies have become less exceptional and their capabilities have expanded. Only six years later, the first IVF pregnancy achieved with donor oocytes was reported;[2] by overcoming the intended mother's inability to produce viable oocytes, this technique permits a man to procreate with an infertile partner, as well as giving the woman the opportunity to experience pregnancy and form a prenatal bond with the baby. The novelty of third-party reproduction was followed by the advent of preimplantation genetic diagnosis (PGD), first successfully used in humans in 1989; designed as an alternative to prenatal diagnosis, it enables known carriers of serious hereditary conditions to have a biological child without that condition while avoiding a clinical termination of pregnancy.[3] Conception outside the human body also paved the way for gestational

[1] See Amel Alghrani, *Regulating Assisted Reproductive Technologies: New Horizons* (Cambridge: Cambridge University Press, 2018) 22.

[2] See Lorna Marshall, 'Ethical Issues in the Evolving Realm of Egg Donation', in Leslie Francis (ed.), *The Oxford Handbook of Reproductive Ethics* (Oxford: Oxford University Press, 2017) 478–498, at 478.

[3] See Lisa Rubin and Aliza Phillips, 'Infertility and Assisted Reproduction Technologies: Matters of Reproductive Justice', in Joan Chrisler (ed.), *Reproductive Justice: A Global Concern* (Santa Barbara: Praeger, 2012) 173–199, at 186; Karen Sermon, André Van Steirteghem and Inge

surrogacy.[4] Unlike the less sophisticated traditional surrogacy (involving the use of the intended father's gametes to inseminate the surrogate), this collaborative reproductive method allows a woman who cannot sustain a pregnancy to become a genetic mother.[5] All these scientific developments have prompted new questions about what the law ought to prohibit, permit or facilitate in the regulation of assisted reproduction technologies (ARTs).

The overarching question, however, is whether the law should permit only treatment analogous to natural procreation – such as the woman's artificial insemination with her husband's gametes, or IVF procedures using the gametes of the couple – or whether it should go beyond the realm of biological possibility: (a) by allowing third-party reproduction, that is, the donation of gametes or embryos and surrogacy services, and/or (b) by allowing parents to predetermine, to a certain degree and in certain circumstances, the genetic make-up of the future child through embryo diagnosis and selection. Admittedly, third-party reproduction raises complex questions about the identity of the resulting child and possible exploitative elements of ova donation and surrogacy. While those questions invite further reflection, it would be oversimplistic to suggest that medically assisted reproduction should only emulate what is naturally achievable. Indeed, medical treatment regularly seeks to improve on nature, and even fight it, rather than copying it. It can also be conceded that PGD may raise ethical concerns if it is not confined to selection against serious genetically transmissible illnesses. At the same time, eugenic alarmism would be a reductive approach to a problem that affects certain core individual interests.

The book will argue that the availability of modern technologies for medically assisted reproduction has given rise to a set of new fundamental (albeit qualified) rights. Such is the right to have recourse to reproductive treatment (artificial insemination; IVF; potentially, in the future, gamete donation and

Liebaers, 'Preimplantation Genetic Diagnosis' (2004) 363 (9421) *The Lancet* 1633–1641, at 1633.

4 Surrogacy first captured the attention of the legal scholarship with the decision *In the Matter of Baby M*, 109 N.J. 396, 537A.2d 1227 (N.J. 1988), concerning a traditional surrogacy contract concluded in New Jersey in 1985, followed by *Johnson* v. *Calvert*, 5 Cal. 4th 84 (1993), a case of gestational surrogacy. For a comparative discussion, see Leslie Francis, 'Is Surrogacy Ethically Problematic?', in Leslie Francis (ed.), *The Oxford Handbook of Reproductive Ethics* (Oxford: Oxford University Press, 2017) 388–406, at 389–391.

5 For a snapshot of legal responses to surrogacy worldwide along a spectrum, including prohibition, non-regulation, permissive approach on an altruistic basis and legalisation of commercial surrogacy, see Sonia Allan, 'The Surrogate in Commercial Surrogacy: Legal and Ethical Considerations', in Paula Gerber and Katie O'Byrne (eds.), *Surrogacy, Law and Human Rights* (London: Routledge, 2015) 113–143, at 130–132.

surrogacy) in order to experience biological parenthood when natural procreation is hindered by infertility, gender reassignment, sexual orientation or the lack of a partner. Additionally, the infertile member of a couple can claim a right to the recognition of intention-based parenthood in relation to the partner's donor-conceived or surrogate-born children when they were jointly planned and cared for as a family. This new array of procreative rights further encompasses the right to pursue the birth of a healthy child, to the extent that genetic diagnosis and selection of embryos for implantation can avoid disease and disability at the conception stage; like prenatal testing (upon which the option of therapeutic abortion depends), embryo selection gives prospective parents control over the outcome of the reproductive process. In a distant future, procreative autonomy could conceivably include aspiring parents' right to choose certain traits in their offspring, irrespective of medical needs.

Procreative claims have emerged at the intersection between reproductive health concerns and the right to respect for privacy and family life. It is estimated that '48 million couples and 186 million individuals worldwide live with infertility'.[6] However, the inability to procreate is not merely a health issue; it touches upon important sociopsychological dimensions of personal identity and family life. In fact, parenthood is also a matter of self-fulfilment, which is comprised within the broader right to respect for private and family life.[7] Lisa Rubin and Aliza Phillips have noted the particularly strong link between motherhood and self-fulfilment: 'Although, at least in the West, women have an increasing array of choices other than motherhood as a path through adulthood, the "mandate" for motherhood, or the idea that motherhood is key to fulfilling a woman's adult identity, remains strong.'[8] Advances in medical technology have made the resigned acceptance of infertility more difficult and have elevated parenthood expectations, including the possibility to influence the genetic constitution of the future child. Gillian Douglas recalled the case of an American sperm bank set up in the 1970s to store the gametes of academically inclined high achievers, to be used by women with a high IQ, an initiative criticised by some for its 'overtly eugenic

6 'Infertility: Why the Silence?' (2022) 10(6) *Lancet Global Health* e773, at e773.

7 See *Fernández Martínez* v. *Spain* [GC], App. No. 56030/07, 12 June 2014, [126]: 'The Court stresses the importance for individuals to be able to decide freely how to conduct their private and family life. In this connection, it reiterates that Article 8 also protects the right to self-fulfilment, whether in the form of personal development . . ., or from the point of view of the right to establish and develop relationships with other human beings and the outside world, the notion of personal autonomy being an important principle underlying the interpretation of the guarantees laid down in that provision.'

8 Rubin and Phillips, 'Infertility and Assisted Reproduction Technologies', 178.

motivation'; Douglas rightfully queried whether, as long as this is a voluntary enterprise for all those involved, the desire of some people to use such a facility in the hope of having more intelligent children is necessarily problematic.[9] Indeed, the choice of a mating partner whose characteristics the woman hopes to see replicated in her offspring also occurs in natural procreation, albeit less clinically, and it needs to be respected as a matter of autonomy. Other aspects of collaborative assisted reproduction may, nevertheless, warrant or require State regulation.

A legal framework for the regulation of access to medical assistance to procreate cannot develop without proper analysis of the human rights engaged. Despite a degree of scepticism in the scholarly literature over the role of human rights methodology in bioethical debates,[10] there is a growing body of international jurisprudence in the area of assisted reproduction, in particular under the European Convention on Human Rights (ECHR).[11] More than any other treaty-based human rights body, the European Court of Human Rights (ECtHR) has been faced with numerous controversies regarding procreative rights, such as the ban on certain ARTs (e.g. heterologous fertilisation and IVF, ova donation, posthumous use of frozen gametes/ embryos, embryo preimplantation screening for healthy carriers of serious genetic disorders), the recognition of legal effects arising from foreign surrogacy arrangements, and the subject of transgender or same-sex parenthood for children born through assisted insemination with donor sperm. By necessity, the book will therefore focus on ECHR practice, although references to other international instruments will be made where relevant material is available. Other human rights–monitoring bodies such as the Inter-American Commission and Court set up by the American Convention on Human Rights (ACHR)[12] and the UN Human Rights Committee (HRC) established under the International Covenant on Civil and Political Rights (ICCPR)[13] have not had the same opportunity to pronounce on more detailed aspects of

9 Gillian Douglas, *Law, Fertility and Reproduction* (London: Sweet and Maxwell, 1991) 202–203.

10 See Elizabeth Fenton, 'Genetic Enhancement – A Threat to Human Rights?' (2008) 22(1) *Bioethics* 1–7, at 7: 'The call for human rights to serve as the foundation and *lingua franca* of the new bioethics is misguided. Human rights form only a part of morality, and so should form only a part of bioethics.'

11 European Convention on Human Rights and Fundamental Freedoms, Rome, 4 November 1950, in force 3 September 1953, ETS No. 5. The book follows the Court's case law up until the end of March 2023.

12 American Convention on Human Rights, San José, 22 November 1969, in force 18 July 1978.

13 International Covenant on Civil and Political Rights, New York, 16 December 1966, in force 23 March 1976, UNTS vol. 999 (p. 171).

the regulation of procreative rights. Indeed, the volume of cases decided by other treaty-based human rights bodies is only a fraction of the hundreds of thousands of applications examined in Strasbourg.[14] The prevailing human rights concerns evidenced by the complaints brought elsewhere are also different. For example, a large proportion of applications under the ACHR concentrate on forced disappearances, extrajudicial killings, torture and the death penalty; freedom from torture and fair trial guarantees are frequently the subject of communications under the ICCPR. Thus, the use of ARTs features in an exiguous number of decisions outside the ECHR system.[15]

In light of this emerging jurisprudence, the book sets out to demonstrate that individual claims to assisted procreation can be resolved through human rights analysis rather than being deferred to the value-laden policy choices of deliberative majorities. It further contends that procreative rights, viewed as an extension of the rights to decisional autonomy, privacy (including identity) and respect for family life, should be restricted only inasmuch as they demonstrably harm equally important rights of others or societal interests. Thus, any restrictions on the pursuit of parenthood aspirations through ARTs must satisfy the well-established tests for State interferences with the exercise of fundamental rights: a pressing social need (not merely speculative fears or moral unease with novel practices) and recourse to the minimum interference necessary to achieve legitimate objectives.

Chapter 1 argues that parenthood aspirations have started to evolve into justiciable rights and sets the background for the discussion of such rights in the chapters that follow. First, it examines the rise of new human rights claims in international litigation and in the scholarly literature as a result of the development of reproductive technologies. On the one hand, individual reproductive decisions are seen to lie at the very core of privacy and physical self-determination rights. Elizabeth Wicks has powerfully suggested that 'few exercises of autonomy are more private, more fundamental, or more embodied, than those surrounding reproduction'.[16] On the other hand, the allocation of legal parenthood is a public matter, and public policy objections

[14] For statistical data, see European Court of Human Rights, Public Relations Unit, 'Overview 1959–2021' (February 2022), available at www.echr.coe.int/documents/d/echr/Overview_19592021_ENG.

[15] The Inter-American Court of Human Rights has condemned the absolute prohibition on IVF, the denial of access to therapeutic abortion and the use of involuntary sterilisation. The HRC has also pronounced on the prohibition of abortion on grounds of fatal foetal abnormality. See Chapter 1 (Section 1.2.1), Chapter 2 (Section 2.1.1) and Chapter 4 (Section 4.2.1).

[16] Elizabeth Wicks, *The State and the Body: Legal Regulation of Bodily Autonomy* (Oxford: Hart, 2016) 61.

may be adduced to reproductive techniques involving third-party reproduction. As Robin Mackenzie aptly noted, 'under most countries' family law, parental rights and responsibility may not be simply transferred or waived as a matter of private ordering'.[17] Therefore, the State's cooperation is necessary to ratify the effects of gamete donation and surrogacy arrangements through the legal recognition of social parenthood. The chapter acknowledges the challenges to the development of reproductive rights stemming from the distinction between negative and positive obligations in international law and, in particular, the difficulties in placing positive duties on State authorities. The chapter identifies a number of potential negative and positive obligations in relation to human procreation as put forward in international litigation. It examines the ECtHR's justifications for treating a claim as engaging negative or positive obligations, and it considers whether that classification has any impact on the outcome of the case.

Chapter 2 inquires whether a person has the right to a genetically related child, understood as the right to have recourse to the available ARTs in order to become a biological parent. Any obstacles to an individual's endeavour to have genetically related children will affect their core interests. In fact, as Michael Boucai has noted, the right to procreate 'could be thought to serve a number of human interests, among them species survival, bodily integrity, sexual autonomy, and personal longings for genetic immortality'.[18] The chapter considers the right to make reproductive decisions – for example, resorting to artificial insemination or using frozen embryos created with one's gametes for the purposes of generating a pregnancy – including, potentially, the decision to use the genetic material of a deceased spouse or child for posthumous procreation. The right to make autonomous reproductive decisions may conflict with the rights of other private parties, in particular the other gamete contributor – for example, a former partner no longer consenting to the use of joint embryos following the breakdown of the parties' relationship, or a deceased spouse whose consent to the posthumous use of his genetic material cannot be verified. It can also collide with State interests: safeguarding public order by limiting prisoners' procreative activities, ensuring the lawful operation of assisted reproduction clinics, or protecting embryos no longer intended for a pregnancy (e.g. against donation for scientific research).

17 Robin Mackenzie, 'Beyond Genetic and Gestational Dualities: Surrogacy Agreements, Legal Parenthood and Choice in Family Formation', in Kirsty Horsey and Hazel Biggs (eds.), *Human Fertilisation and Embryology: Reproducing Regulation* (London: Routledge-Cavendish, 2007) 181–203, at 194.

18 Michael Boucai, 'Is Assisted Procreation an LGBT Right?' (2016) *Wisconsin Law Review* 1065–1125, at 1117.

The right to a genetic child in cases of partial infertility also occupies an important place in this chapter. In fact, for individuals living with an infertile spouse, 'collaborative' reproduction, that is, the use of sperm/ova donated by a third party or surrogacy services, is the only route to achieving genetic parenthood without forgoing the marriage. The refusal to treat such couples with donated gametes requires the fertile member of the couple to choose between parenthood aspirations and the continuance of their family life with the infertile spouse; it thus affects not only prospective but also existing family life and requires justification. A related claim discussed in this chapter is the right to respect for the reality of biological parentage in surrogacy cases. This includes the right of genetic fathers whose children were born through surrogacy abroad to be recognised as legal parents in the State of residence, even if that jurisdiction does not permit surrogacy, as well as the right of genetic fathers having used domestic surrogacy arrangements (whether or not lawful or enforceable) to rebut presumptions of paternity benefitting others, for example, the surrogate's husband.

Chapter 3 shifts the perspective towards a putative right to the protection of intention-based parenthood in the absence of genetic ties to the child. Two situations are foregrounded here: social parenthood in relation to the child born to a (same-sex or opposite-sex) partner through assisted insemination with donor sperm, and the position of commissioning parents unrelated to the child in surrogacy cases. Janet Finch noted that 'the ways in which kinship is defined and lived in the contemporary world is a subtle blend of . . . the given and the chosen'.[19] At the same time, the scope of choice in family formation is not uncontroversial. As Mackenzie deftly pointed out, 'surrogacy remains contentious in that its potential to disrupt notions of kinship exceeds that of other means of treating infertility'.[20] This is particularly true of traditional surrogacy, in which the surrogate mother becomes pregnant through artificial insemination with the sperm of the intended father,[21] whereas the child is to be raised by the father and his partner – a woman, or indeed a man, who is not genetically related to the child. Moreover, for those who reject the idea of

[19] Janet Finch, 'Kinship as "Family" in Contemporary Britain', in Fatemeh Ebtehaj, Bridget Lindley and Martin Richards (eds.), *Kinship Matters* (London: Hart, 2006) 295–306, at 304.

[20] Mackenzie, 'Beyond Genetic and Gestational Dualities', 189.

[21] See, e.g., Rubin and Phillips, 'Infertility and Assisted Reproduction Technologies', 190: 'In traditional surrogacy, a woman is inseminated with sperm for the purpose of conceiving a child for an intended recipient. . . . The advent of IVF has enabled gestational surrogacy, in which embryos created through IVF by intended parents either with their own, or donor gametes, are transferred into the surrogate's uterus . . . Thus, in gestational surrogacy, the "carrier" has no genetic link to the fetus.'

surrogacy as medical treatment involving organ donation (or organ 'lending'), the debate veers onto the subject of child trafficking. The law of many countries (including the UK) criminalises the private transfer of children for adoption (save for in-family adoptions) and makes it an offence to provide payment for agreeing to an adoption or facilitating adoption arrangements; the analogy with adoption makes surrogacy suspect.[22] Relying on the well-established Strasbourg case law on the recognition of families based on social reality, as opposed to biological links, the chapter discusses the right to the protection of voluntary parenthood in assisted reproduction cases. In particular, it examines the ECtHR's outlook on non-genetic commissioning parents in foreign surrogacy cases (seen against the backdrop of cases concerning foreign adoption and foster care), as well as its approach to social parents raising children born to their life partners through donor insemination.

Chapter 4 defends the ambitious (and, no doubt, controversial) thesis that there is a human right to a healthy child, to the extent that medical technology can detect and prevent disease in future offspring. The chapter considers the relationship between healthcare rights and autonomy rights and proceeds to examine two claims arising in relation to the desire for a healthy child: (a) the right to prenatal diagnosis and therapeutic abortion if the foetus is found to suffer from any congenital illness, and (b) embryo preimplantation diagnosis aimed at disability screening, where the aspiring parents are afflicted by any serious hereditary illness. The chapter examines a series of objections to selection against disability. As Rubin and Phillips noted: 'Among the most deep-seated anxieties concerning ARTs are their "brave-new-world" associations with genetic engineering. PGD, often (albeit somewhat inaccurately) referred to as the "designer-baby" method, is one of the most recent of the [new reproductive technologies] to inspire anxiety about the appropriate limits of human intervention in the arena of reproduction.'[23] The chapter concludes by expanding the analysis to a potential future right to a bespoke child, for example, embryo screening aimed at sex selection for non-medical reasons, or the creation of saviour siblings through tissue typing and embryo selection so that the future child is a cord blood stem cell donor for a seriously ill existing child.

Chapter 5 examines the ways in which gender, civil status and sexual orientation impact access to ARTs or the recognition of de facto family life created through ARTs. Aspiring single parents and same-sex couples are

[22] See Mackenzie, 'Beyond Genetic and Gestational Dualities', 194.

[23] Rubin and Phillips, 'Infertility and Assisted Reproduction Technologies', 185–186.

entirely reliant on gamete donation and, for men, surrogacy in order to have a biologically related child. Consequently, in addition to laws reserving treatment to (heterosexual) couples, neutral prohibitions on certain reproductive techniques can affect singles, male couples or female couples with particular force. The chapter discusses the contribution of ECHR case law to safeguarding the *fait accompli* in donor insemination and surrogacy cases involving single, homosexual and transgender parents (typically following overseas treatment in permissive jurisdictions). Finally, the chapter challenges what it perceives to be a gender-based difference in the Strasbourg treatment of genetic commissioning parents. Even where the surrogate is neither genetically related to the child nor an effective social parent, many jurisdictions remain attached to the link between childbirth and motherhood.[24] The chapter suggests that the ECtHR ought to question domestic rules on the allocation of parenthood for surrogacy-born children that give priority to the surrogate's gestational function over the commissioning mother's genetic/intentional/social parenthood; in fact, the position of genetic commissioning mothers is indistinguishable in respect of all these three facets of parenthood from that of genetic commissioning fathers.

In its concluding remarks, the book reconstructs an emerging catalogue of reproductive rights based on the claims successfully established *de lege lata* in international case law, most notably within the ECHR framework. The final chapter also considers the obstacles to the development of procreative rights to date, from jurisdictional issues (such as the emphasis on the subsidiary nature of international supervision and States' wide margin of appreciation in sensitive moral-driven areas) to substantive assumptions underlying judicial analysis (e.g. the identification of marriage as the foundation of intentional non-genetic parenthood). Finally, the concluding chapter discusses incipient and potential rights, that is, claims that the ECtHR did not have an opportunity to examine, or those in relation to which it has adopted a *non liquet* position, leaving their protection to the discretion of national legislatures. Although it is conceded that many procreative rights are still aspirational in nature, the conclusions suggest that the evolving interpretation of the ECHR, aimed at aligning its requirements with medical advances and social perceptions, will eventually expand the scope of Article 8.

The legal analysis of procreative liberty put forward in this book, informed by modest engagement with bioethical perspectives on the subject, aims to enrich the scholarly debate on private choice and public regulation in

[24] See, e.g., for English law, s. 33 Human Fertilisation and Embryology Act 2008, which always treats the woman who gives birth to a child as the child's legal mother.

reproductive matters as well as to aid the practical assessment of assisted reproduction policies. While ARTs have inspired a vast literature, the conversation has taken place predominantly in the realm of bioethics, medical law, comparative law and socio-legal studies, with a focus on issues such as the moral status and appropriate legal classification of the embryo and the foetus; the costs and risks of assisted reproduction, especially surrogacy; future inequalities and social justice in relation to procreation; and the principles governing reproductive treatment in specific jurisdictions. The place of universal human rights in the regulation of medically assisted procreation tends to feature in case commentaries and writings addressing discrete aspects. This book, therefore, aims to fill a gap in the literature on reproductive technologies by adding an international human rights perspective, based on a comprehensive and systematic analysis of this area of jurisprudence.

1

Parenthood Aspirations and Justiciable Rights

1.1 REPRODUCTIVE TECHNOLOGIES, BIOETHICS AND THE RISE OF NEW HUMAN RIGHTS CLAIMS

The central claim of this book is that the regulation of reproductive technologies ought to promote, to the fullest extent and subject only to the prevention of harm to others, the 'unalienable' right to 'the pursuit of Happiness', robustly affirmed in one of the oldest and most famous statements on human rights.[1] Restrictions on access to reproductive treatment facilitating that pursuit should not be dictated by techno-conservative prejudice or the unease with the triumph of human design over nature. Rather, medically assisted procreation should be governed by the principles of respect for individual self-determination and tolerance of diverse notions of self-fulfilment. For instance, one person's endeavour to conceive a child free from disability should not be undermined by another's perception that laws accommodating preferences for healthy offspring devalue existing disabled people.[2] Similarly, the indifference to genetic ties of those who view parenthood as the experience of raising a child cannot dilute the interest others have in perpetuating their family line and genetic heritage.[3] Individuals unable to have a biological child with their chosen partner without recourse to surrogacy or gamete donation should not face blanket objections from others, unaffected by infertility, based on opaque rhetoric about the dignity of the human body; instead, the focus ought to be

[1] See US Congress, *Declaration of Independence*, 4 July 1776: 'We hold these truths to be self-evident, that all men are created equal, that they are endowed by their Creator with certain unalienable Rights, that among these are Life, Liberty and the pursuit of Happiness.'

[2] The debate on embryo screening and disability rights concerns is considered in detail in Chapter 4, Section 4.3.4.

[3] On the various meanings of 'parenthood', see Chapter 2, Section 2.1.

on regulation capable of excluding exploitative elements and safeguarding the well-being of any resulting children.[4]

Drawing on an ever-growing body of international case law, particularly prolific in the European Court of Human Rights (ECtHR), the book maintains that respect for autonomy and family life should be construed as entitling an individual to, at least, the following set of procreative rights: the right to have a biologically related child through any route permitted by medical advances in reproduction, such as the use of donor gametes for in vivo and in vitro fertilisation, whether as a single aspiring parent or as part of a couple; the right to posthumous procreation, using cryopreserved gametes or embryos, with the prior (express or inferable) consent of both gamete providers; the right to pursue the conception of a healthy child to the greatest extent of medical capabilities, for instance, through recourse to prenatal tests enabling either selective abortion or prenatal therapy and the screening of embryos for genetic illnesses though preimplantation genetic diagnosis; the right to the recognition of parenthood following surrogacy arrangements compliant with the law of the forum, without additional hurdles for the intended parent who is also biologically related to the child; the right to the recognition of intention-based parenthood for the spouse/partner of a genetic parent when they embarked jointly upon a procreative project involving third-party contributions (gamete donation or surrogacy).

The book acknowledges not only the limited progress towards the recognition of such rights in international litigation to date but also the possible objection to the application of the human rights narrative to assisted reproduction policies. In fact, the past few decades have witnessed a substantial proliferation of human rights treaties and the expansive interpretation of rights in international courts and quasi-judicial bodies; at the same time, the idea that human rights hold the answer to any controversy arising in society has been met with scepticism. Hurst Hannum has argued that complex social problems cannot be resolved by a one-dimensional appeal to fundamental rights:

> Human rights were never intended to provide a solution to all of the world's problems, and those who offer human rights as a panacea for such problems do a disservice both to human rights and to the causes they seek to promote. Many of the criticisms in this book are directed at the unrealistic expansion

[4] See the discussion in Chapter 2, Sections 2.2 and 2.4.

or overreach of human rights, which undermines their legitimacy and acceptance.[5]

While not every new claim is amenable to human rights analysis, international human rights law has developed the tools required to achieve principled, legitimate, cross-border minimum standards in the regulation of life sciences, including medically assisted procreation. In fact, ethics, politics and social change are already embedded in the human rights framework. Concerns pertaining to public health, morality and any other competing public and private interests are absorbed by the clawback clauses contained in human rights treaties, which limit the exercise of most rights.[6] Moreover, the protection of non-persons such as the human embryo, the foetus or the child yet to be conceived, albeit apparently left out of the rights discourse (focused on existing individuals) – indeed a criticism sometimes raised by bioethicists[7] – can be achieved through the open-textured references to morals and *ordre public* in those clauses. International human rights courts have accommodated State policies oriented towards the protection of such interests, occasionally at the expense of reproductive autonomy, for instance, by viewing embryos/foetuses as belonging to the human race and entitled to protection in the name of human dignity, even if they are not rights holders (e.g. in cases regarding embryo selection against genetic illness, therapeutic abortion, the donation of embryos for research), or by allowing concerns over the to-be-born child's welfare to compete with, and possibly prevail upon, the rights of aspiring parents (e.g. in posthumous or heterologous conception cases).[8] Consequently, restrictions upon procreative freedom incapable of justification

[5] Hurst Hannum, *Rescuing Human Rights: A Radically Moderate Approach* (Cambridge: Cambridge University Press, 2019) xvii.

[6] See, e.g., the limits to the right to respect for private and family life set by Art. 8(2) ECHR: 'There shall be no interference by a public authority with the exercise of this right except such as is in accordance with the law and is necessary in a democratic society in the interests of national security, public safety or the economic well-being of the country, for the prevention of disorder or crime, for the protection of health or morals, or for the protection of the rights and freedoms of others.' Naturally, absolute rights (e.g. freedom from torture or slavery) do not lend themselves to the application of clawback clauses.

[7] See Richard Ashcroft, 'The Troubled Relationship between Bioethics and Human Rights', in Michael Freeman (ed.), *Law and Bioethics* (Oxford: Oxford University Press, 2008) 31–51, at 39: 'The notion of human rights can provoke a bioethicist's scepticism in part because of the nature of bioethical inquiry. Given that bioethics is partly speculative inquiry into the nature and boundaries of the human, concerned with determining the status of embryos, the brain dead, modification of human genomes, and so on, privileging the category of human *a priori* poses intellectual difficulties.'

[8] See in particular Chapter 2, Sections 2.1.2, 2.1.3, 2.2, 2.3.1 and Chapter 4, Sections 4.2.1 and 4.3.3.

under human rights law are unlikely to be saved by bioethical or other arguments.

Additionally, international human rights law, as a well-established system of values and procedures, has the ability to provide transnational and non-culturally dependent responses to bioethics concerns.[9] As Robert Baker has noted, human rights discourse 'is already the accepted language of international ethics'.[10] It therefore has the potential to achieve shared standards in new and challenging areas of bioethics. The impact of the rights discourse in the medical context to date was usefully described by Daniel Sperling as threefold: empowering patients in the relationship with their physician by conferring control over treatment and ensuring respect for privacy, autonomy and bodily integrity (e.g. informed consent to treatment); providing security from State intervention in accessing medical assistance for health-related goals (e.g. abortion, end-of-life decision-making); and promoting a right to access healthcare services, including services enhancing reproductive freedom (e.g. posthumous insemination).[11] Not only does international human rights law come with a universal moral claim, based on widespread consensus, but it also provides binding norms and an accepted enforcement machinery. Elizabeth Fenton has highlighted the strategic benefits of human rights law as a foundation for bioethics:

> As part of a legal regime, human rights carry significantly more weight than ethical principles that may be ignored without consequence. Bioethics may benefit from yoking itself to a doctrine with significant legal clout on the global stage. … Taking the language of human rights as its foundation could allow bioethics to advance its goals on the wheels of this established political machine.[12]

[9] See Lori Knowles, 'The Lingua Franca of Human Rights and the Rise of a Global Bioethic' (2001) 10 *Cambridge Quarterly of Healthcare Ethics* 253–263; David Thomasma, 'Proposing a New Agenda: Bioethics and International Human Rights' (2001) 10 *Cambridge Quarterly of Healthcare Ethics* 299–310.

[10] Robert Baker, 'Bioethics and Human Rights: A Historical Perspective' (2001) 10 *Cambridge Quarterly of Health & Ethics* 241–252, at 249. Johan Brännmark, 'Respect for Persons in Bioethics: Towards a Human Rights-Based Account' (2017) 18 *Human Rights Review* 171–187, at 171–172, argued that human rights can serve not just to set basic global healthcare standards but also as a framework for considering bioethical questions in public discussions about the regulation of healthcare.

[11] See Daniel Sperling, 'Law and Bioethics: A Right-Based Relationship and Its Troubling Implications', in Michael Freeman (ed.), *Law and Bioethics* (Oxford: Oxford University Press, 2008) 52–78, at 56–57 and 60–61.

[12] Elizabeth Fenton, 'Genetic Enhancement – A Threat to Human Rights?' (2008) 22(1) *Bioethics* 1–7, at 2.

It is also worth recalling that bioethical concerns, such as the prohibition on medical human experimentation, found an early embodiment in human rights and humanitarian law, specifically in the 1949 Geneva Conventions[13] and the International Covenant on Civil and Political Rights (ICCPR).[14] The relationship between human rights and bioethics has also been acknowledged in soft law instruments such as UNESCO's 1997 Universal Declaration on the Human Genome and Human Rights[15] and its 2005 Universal Declaration on Bioethics and Human Rights.[16] In its Explanatory Memorandum on the elaboration of the latter, the Drafting Group mandated by UNESCO, a consultative committee of independent experts, stressed 'the importance of taking international human rights legislation as the essential framework and starting point for the development of bioethical principles'[17] and recognised that 'declarations and documents on bioethics should be in harmony with human rights'.[18] Interestingly, the Drafting Group had been originally entrusted with drafting an instrument entitled 'Universal Declaration on Bioethics', and the 'Human Rights' addition was the product of the experts'

[13] Humanitarian law provides that the wounded, sick and shipwrecked members of the armed forces, the prisoners of war and persons finding themselves in the hands of an occupying power shall not be subjected to biological experiments (Art. 12 Geneva Convention I for the amelioration of the condition of the wounded and sick in armed forces in the field, Geneva, 12 August 1949, in force 21 October 1950, UNTS 75 (p. 31); Art. 12 Geneva Convention II for the amelioration of the condition of the wounded, sick and shipwrecked members of the armed forces at sea, Geneva, 12 August 1949, in force 21 October 1950, UNTS 75 (p. 85); Art. 13 Geneva Convention III relative to the treatment of prisoners of war, 12 August 1949, Geneva, in force 21 October 1950, UNTS 75 (p. 135); Art. 32 Geneva Convention IV relative to the protection of civilian persons in time of war, Geneva, 12 August 1949, in force 21 October 1950, UNTS 75 (p. 287)); conducting experiments on such persons is a grave breach of Geneva law (Art. 50 Geneva Convention I, Art. 51 Geneva Convention II, Art. 130 Geneva Convention III, Art. 147 Geneva Convention IV). See also Arts. 11 and 85 Additional Protocol I to the Geneva Conventions of 12 August 1949 and relating to the protection of victims of international armed conflicts, Geneva, 8 June 1977, 7 December 1978, UNTS 1125 (p. 3) and Art. 5(2)(e) Additional Protocol II to the Geneva Conventions of 12 August 1949 and relating to the protection of victims of non-international armed conflicts, Geneva, 8 June 1977, 7 December 1978, UNTS 1125 (p. 609).

[14] See Art. 7 International Covenant on Civil and Political Rights, New York, 16 December 1966, in force 23 March 1976, UNTS vol. 999 (p. 171): 'No one shall be subjected to torture or to cruel, inhuman or degrading treatment or punishment. In particular, no one shall be subjected without his free consent to medical or scientific experimentation.'

[15] UNESCO General Conference, Universal Declaration on the Human Genome and Human Rights, Paris, 11 November 1997, BR/2001/PI/H/1.

[16] See UNESCO General Conference, Universal Declaration on Bioethics and Human Rights, Paris, 19 October 2005, SHS/EST/BIO/06/1.

[17] UNESCO, *Explanatory Memorandum on the Elaboration of the Preliminary Draft Declaration on Universal Norms on Bioethics*, Paris, 21 February 2005, SHS/EST/05/CONF.203/4 [11].

[18] Ibid., [43].

reflection on the need for bioethical norms to be consistent with human rights principles. The Explanatory Memorandum emphasised this key objective of the Universal Declaration on Bioethics and Human Rights: 'to establish the conformity of bioethics with international human rights law'.[19] The drafters also acknowledged the anchorage of the notions of personal autonomy and human dignity in international human rights law:

> Respect for personal *autonomy* is strongly linked to . . . the notion of human dignity. It is directly derived from binding international human rights law. Individuals cannot be instrumentalized and treated merely as means to a scientific end; they should be granted the authority to make autonomous decisions in all aspects of their lives where their decisions do no harm to others.[20]

Furthermore, the human rights discourse permeates the way in which restrictions on the operation of bioethical norms are worded in UNESCO's Explanatory Memorandum, in a language reminiscent of Article 8 of the European Convention on Human Rights (ECHR) and its case law interpretation:

> Restrictions may be placed on the operation of the principles set out in the declaration only in accordance with international human rights law, and then only if they are prescribed by domestic law and only when such restrictions are necessary in a democratic society in the interest of public safety, for the prevention of crime, for the protection of public health or for the protection of the rights and freedoms of others. In choosing between various possible restrictive measures, *proportionality* has to be respected, because, when a restriction is considered to be necessary in accordance with the foregoing principles, rights derived from principles may then be restricted only in the least restrictive manner and only to an extent proportional to the legitimate end of the restriction.[21]

In addition to these developments at universal (UN/UNESCO) level, international regional instruments tend to align bioethics with human rights, supporting an increased role for human rights law applications in the field of biosciences. Under the aegis of the Council of Europe, the 1997 Oviedo Convention on Human Rights and Biomedicine[22] afforded the ECtHR jurisdiction to interpret its provisions, albeit only in the form of advisory opinions

[19] Ibid., [12].
[20] Ibid., [60] (original emphasis).
[21] Ibid., [123] (original emphasis).
[22] Council of Europe, Convention for the Protection of Human Rights and Dignity of the Human Being with Regard to the Application of Biology and Medicine, Oviedo, 4 April 1997, in force 1 December 1999, ETS No. 164.

on legal questions and at the request of Member States.[23] Moreover, the Oviedo Convention, postulating the 'primacy of the human being', follows the same individualistic, non-utilitarian philosophy typical of human rights instruments: 'The interests and welfare of the human being shall prevail over the sole interest of society or science.'[24] Significantly, this tenet was echoed verbatim in UNESCO's 2005 Universal Declaration on Bioethics and Human Rights.[25] Like the ECHR and its UN/regional counterparts, the Oviedo Convention contemplates restrictions on the rights protected; notably, the language of its Article 26(1), regulating such restrictions, closely emulates the standard phraseology of human rights treaties:

> No restrictions shall be placed on the exercise of the rights and protective provisions contained in this Convention other than such as are prescribed by law and are necessary in a democratic society in the interest of public safety, for the prevention of crime, for the protection of public health or for the protection of the rights and freedoms of others.

The Oviedo Convention also lists several norms not subject to restrictions. According to Article 26(2), the restrictions in Article 26(1) may not be placed on Articles 11, 13, 14, 16, 17, 19, 20 and 21. Several of these exceptions are potentially relevant for the regulation of assisted procreation: non-discrimination on grounds of genetic heritage (Article 11); the admissibility of interventions on the human genome only for preventive, diagnostic or therapeutic purposes (Article 13); non-selection of sex, except to avoid serious sex-related hereditary disease (Article 14); and the prohibition of the use of the human body and its parts for financial gain (Article 21).

The strategy of appealing to the human rights framework in the instruments addressing bioethical issues produced by UNESCO and the Council of Europe can be explained, according to Roberto Andorno, by several factors: the link between biomedical activities and basic human rights (life, physical integrity); the 'universalistic claim of human rights, which facilitates the formulation of transcultural standards'; the fact that the vague notion of human dignity, 'the cornerstone of global bioethical norms', necessitates more concrete notions in order to operate, borrowed from human rights terminology, for example, informed consent, physical and mental integrity,

[23] See ibid., Art. 29.

[24] Ibid., Art. 2.

[25] See UNESCO General Conference, Universal Declaration on Bioethics and Human Rights, Paris, 19 October 2005, SHS/EST/BIO/06/1, Art. 3(2): 'The interests and welfare of the individual should have priority over the sole interest of science or society.'

non-discrimination, privacy, confidentiality, protection of vulnerable persons, access to healthcare; and the practical availability of mechanisms for global normative foundations.[26] Although this strategy has not been without detractors,[27] the human rights system remains unparalleled in its international reach and effectiveness; in fact, no binding mechanism, with the added fast-paced transformative power of international jurisprudence, has emerged for the governance of bioethics as a standalone field.

At the same time, the relationship between human rights and bioethics is a dialogical one. The Strasbourg Court has relied on bioethical instruments to develop the principles of the European Convention.[28] References to the Oviedo Convention on Human Rights and Biomedicine can be found in numerous judgments,[29] and UNESCO's Universal Declaration on Bioethics and Human Rights has also made its way into the case law.[30] Additionally, there are Strasbourg decisions citing other initiatives of the Council of Europe in the area of bioethics, in particular references to the work of its Steering Committee on Bioethics and the expert Council-of-Europe body preceding it.[31] This interpretive method is rather uncontroversial. Bioethical instruments adopted by the Council of Europe's States constitute relevant practice for the interpretation of the ECHR within the meaning of Article 31(3) of the Vienna

[26] See Roberto Andorno, 'Global Bioethics and Human Rights' (2008) 27(1) *Medicine and Law* 1–14, at 9–10, 14. He noted, however, the limits of human rights' ability to deal with some bioethical issues: since rights only belong to individuals already in existence, they do not apply to potential persons or persons who have not been conceived (they could not claim, e.g., a 'right' not to be genetically predetermined), hence the reliance on the broader concept of 'human dignity' to protect future generations (ibid., 10–11).

[27] Ashcroft, 'The Troubled Relationship between Bioethics and Human Rights', 36–38, examined the controversy surrounding UNESCO's 2005 Universal Declaration, with criticisms ranging from its perceived underlying Western view of human rights, to UNESCO's place to adopt such an instrument (as opposed to the World Health Organisation) and to the fact that the UNESCO experts drafting it allegedly lacked the requisite qualifications as bioethicists.

[28] See Francesco Seatzu, 'The Experience of the European Court of Human Rights with the European Convention on Human Rights and Biomedicine' (2015) 31(81) *Utrecht Journal of International and European Law* 5–16.

[29] See *Vo* v. *France* [GC], App. No. 53924/00, 8 July 2004, [35]; *Evans* v. *The United Kingdom* [GC], App. No. 6339/05, 10 April 2007, [50]; *R.R.* v. *Poland*, App. No. 27617/04, 26 May 2011, [83]; *V.C.* v. *Slovakia*, App. No. 18968/07, 8 November 2011, [76]–[77]; *Costa and Pavan* v. *Italy*, [21]–[22]; *M.S.* v. *Croatia (No. 2)*, App. No. 75450/12, 19 February 2015, [51], *Parrillo* v. *Italy* [GC], App. No. 46470/11, 27 August 2015, [54], [181].

[30] See *Evans* v. *The United Kingdom* [GC], [52].

[31] See *Vo* v. *France* [GC], [38]–[39]; *Evans* v. *The United Kingdom* [GC], [51]; *S.H. and Others* v. *Austria* [GC], App. No. 57813/00, 3 November 2011, [35]; *Costa and Pavan* v. *Italy*, App. No. 54270/10, 28 August 2012, [25]; *Paradiso and Campanelli* v. *Italy* [GC], App. No. 25358/12, 24 January 2017, [79].

Convention of the Law of Treaties, either as 'subsequent practice in the application of the treaty which establishes the agreement of the parties regarding its interpretation' or as 'relevant rules of international law applicable in the relations between the parties'.[32]

Consequently, in turn, bioethical standards have assisted the process of updating human rights law, particularly within the ECHR framework, so as to respond to divisive questions in the field of reproductive technologies.[33] Although the rights advocated for in this book are still the subject of vast controversy, ethical diversity finds a limit in the universality of fundamental human rights, which encompass minimum values shared by democratic societies.[34] To that extent, they offer analytical tools comparable to the core principles of biomedical ethics (acceptable to everyone regardless of their ethical stance), as famously theorised by Tom Beauchamps and James Childress: respect for autonomy, non-maleficence, beneficence and justice.[35] A human rights–driven regulation of genetic technology is likely to increase the protection of aspiring parents by adequately probing the aims of restrictions and weighing the impact of societal gains on individual autonomy and self-fulfilment.

While genetic technologies developed after the adoption of general human rights treaties and could not inspire the inclusion of specific guarantees, some of the existing norms had the potential to accommodate a right to assisted reproduction,[36] in particular the 'right to respect for private and family life' in

[32] See Vienna Convention on the Law of Treaties, Vienna, 23 May 1969, in force 27 January 1980, UNTS vol. 1155 (p. 331), Art. 31(3)(b) and (c).

[33] The book is concerned with the desire to have a biological child and the use of assisted reproduction technologies for those purposes; it does not address the other facet of procreative autonomy, namely elective abortion; however, therapeutic abortion is examined in relation to the right to a healthy child. For a discussion of the ECtHR's approach to unwanted parenthood, see Carmen Draghici, *The Legitimacy of Family Rights in Strasbourg Case Law: 'Living Instrument' or Extinguished Sovereignty?* (Oxford: Hart, 2017) 164–175.

[34] Alasdair Maclean, 'Magic, Myths, and Fairy Tales: Consent and the Relationship between Law and Ethics', in Michael Freeman (ed.), *Law and Bioethics* (Oxford: Oxford University Press, 2008) 111–135, at 111, suggested that law and ethics 'both purport to provide guidance in our dealings with other members of our social community', but 'law tends to focus on the minimally acceptable', providing 'a single standard of behaviour', whereas 'different ethical standards ... may coexist'.

[35] See Tom Beauchamps and James Childress, *Principles of Biomedical Ethics* (Oxford: Oxford University Press, 2019, 8th ed.) 99–326.

[36] See Vincent Coussirat-Coustère, 'Famille et Convention Européenne des Droits de l'Homme', in Paul Mahoney et al. (eds.), *Protection des droits de l'homme: la perspective européenne. Mélanges à la mémoire de Rolv Ryssdal* (Köln: Carl Heymanns, 2000) 281–307, at 304.

Article 8 ECHR (and corresponding provisions in the ICCPR[37] and the American Convention on Human Rights (ACHR))[38] and the 'right to found a family' in Article 12 ECHR (and its ICCPR/ACHR equivalents).[39] Although doubts were expressed vis-à-vis a future reinterpretation of the ECHR placing a positive duty on States to provide human fertilisation treatment,[40] the judicial practice has proved bolder than anticipated. The Strasbourg Court has unequivocally established that the notion of private and family life incorporates the right to respect for the decision to become a genetic parent,[41] and that the choice to make use of medically assisted procreation in order to conceive a child is an expression of private and family life protected by Article 8.[42] Mulligan has noted that the location of the legal basis for assisted reproduction claims can be significant: 'If they are protected by the right to respect for private life then they are enjoyed by all people, married, in a relationship or single. If they are based on the right to respect for family life they may not be enjoyed by single people at all.'[43] The Court appears to cite 'private life' when the applicant is a single aspiring parent[44] and 'private and family life' when the applicants are a couple,[45] without discernible consequences. More importantly, the ECtHR has relied on Article 8, rather than Article 12, to develop procreative rights, dissociating them, to some extent, from marriage and coupledom.

At the same time, as an international tribunal, the Strasbourg Court has been slow to establish prescriptive obligations in the area of medically assisted procreation and to interfere with Member States' policy choices. This reflects a more general self-restraint tendency in the Court's bioethical jurisprudence; whenever a claim touches upon the sensitive and contested area of bioethics, and especially when there is no evidence of European consensus on the

37 See Art. 17 ICCPR (protection against arbitrary or unlawful interference with a person's privacy or family).

38 See, analogously, Art. 11 American Convention on Human Rights, San José, 22 November 1969, in force 18 July 1978.

39 See Art. 23(1) ICCPR (protection of the family as the natural and fundamental unit of society), Art. 23(2) ICCPR (right to marry and to found a family), Art. 17(1) ACHR (protection of the family as the natural and fundamental group unit of society) and Art. 17(2) ACHR (right to marry and to raise a family).

40 See David Harris, Michael O'Boyle and Colin Warbrick, *Law of the European Convention on Human Rights* (London: Butterworths, 1995) 441.

41 *Dickson* v. *The United Kingdom* [GC], App. No. 44362/04, 4 December 2007, [66].

42 *S.H. and Others* v. *Austria* [GC], [82].

43 Andrea Mulligan, 'Reproductive Rights under Article 8: The Right to Respect for the Decision to Become or Not to Become a Parent' (2014) 4 *European Human Rights Law Review* 378–387, 385.

44 See *Evans* v. *The United Kingdom* [GC].

45 See *S.H. and Others* v. *Austria* [GC].

matter before it, the Court affords States a wide margin of appreciation. For instance, in *Vo* v. *France*, the absence of European consensus on the scientific and legal definition of when life begins led the Court to conclude that States retained a wide margin of appreciation as to whether the Article 2 'right to life' protection applies to the foetus and, in such an event, if medical errors resulting in involuntary abortion fall under homicide and manslaughter laws.[46] In vitro fertilisation (IVF) treatment has inspired a similar approach:

> Since the use of IVF treatment gives rise to sensitive moral and ethical issues ..., and since the questions raised by the case touch on areas where there is no clear common ground amongst the member States, the Court considers that the margin of appreciation to be afforded to the respondent State must be a wide one.[47]

Nevertheless, the Court's case law has increasingly recognised that Article 8 imposes certain minimum obligations as regards the provision of assisted reproductive treatment (ART), some construed as obligations of abstention and some requiring positive measures calculated to ensure the effective enjoyment of the right. It has been argued that a clear distinction exists between the negative right not to be physically coerced in one's reproductive choices and the positive right to assisted conception, in that the failure to provide fertility treatment would not be an outrage of the same order as forced abortion or sterilisation.[48] However, the ECtHR has interpreted most ART claims as engaging active interferences (i.e. obstacles to using certain reproductive techniques such as sperm or ova donation, IVF treatment, preimplantation genetic diagnosis, posthumous insemination) and, therefore, through the lens of negative obligations. The relevance of this distinction will be discussed in the following section.

1.2 REPRODUCTIVE FREEDOM BETWEEN NEGATIVE AND POSITIVE OBLIGATIONS

1.2.1 *Classic Negative Obligations in Relation to Natural Procreative Capacity*

Any active interference by public authorities with a person's decision or physical ability to procreate engages States' negative obligations to respect

46 *Vo* v. *France*, [82].
47 *Evans* v. *The United Kingdom* [GC], [81].
48 Ruth Deech and Anna Smajdor, *From IVF to Immortality* (Oxford: Oxford University Press, 2007) 138.

private and family life and the right to found a family. International law requires States to refrain from placing constraints on an individual's parenthood plans, such as the timing, number or spacing of children. Article 4 of the Declaration on Social Progress and Development, proclaimed by the UN General Assembly in 1969, established that 'parents have the exclusive right to determine freely and responsibly the number and spacing of their children'.[49] Demographic policies limiting the number of children a family is permitted to have, the practices of forced sterilisation and forced abortion, as well as any coerced family planning methods will place the State in breach of international human rights law.[50] Mariblanca Staff Wilson has observed that the importance of reproductive rights in international law is confirmed by the classification of forced sterilisation or pregnancy as international crimes in the Rome Statute of the International Criminal Court[51] (crime against humanity, war crime, element of genocide).[52] The Chinese 'one-child policy' was tangentially before the UN Human Rights Committee in *X.Q.H.* v. *New Zealand*.[53] The author of the communication indicated that her deportation to China would prejudice her New Zealander son in that, as a second child, he would be considered a 'black child', resulting in the denial both of registration as part of the household and of access to medical care, education or employment, unless the parents paid a substantial fine for breaching family planning regulations.[54] The complaint was dismissed as hypothetical, insofar as the author's marriage to a New Zealand citizen and obtainment of a work visa rendered those concerns moot, and hence she could not claim victim status.[55] Express confirmation of the principle against forced contraception or sterilisation came from several judgments issued by the ECtHR, which clearly establish not only negative obligations (to refrain from interfering with a person's reproductive capacity) but also positive obligations (to protect against third-party interference, including through an adequate legislative and regulatory framework – for example, criminal legislation capable of deterring perpetrators).

49 UN General Assembly, Declaration on Social Progress and Development, Resolution 2542 (XXIV), 11 December 1969.

50 See Susana Sanz Caballero, *La familia en perspectiva internacional y europea* (Valencia: Tirant Lo Blanch, 2006) 53.

51 Rome Statute of the International Criminal Court, Rome, 17 July 1998, in force 1 July 2002, UNTS 2187 (p. 3).

52 See Mariblanca Staff Wilson, *Derechos sexuales y derechos reproductivos: parte esencial de los derechos humanos* (Panamá: Instituto de la Mujer, Universidad de Panamá, 2010) 38–39.

53 See *X.Q.H.* v. *New Zealand*, Communication No. 2197/2012, 29 April 2014.

54 See ibid., [3.2], [6.2].

55 See ibid., [6.3].

The Strasbourg Court held in *V.C.* v. *Slovakia* and *N.B.* v. *Slovakia* that sterilisation without the patient's *full and informed consent*[56] violates both Articles 3 and 8 ECHR. From the viewpoint of Article 3, sterilisation 'constitutes a major interference with a person's reproductive health status', with repercussions on 'manifold aspects of the individual's personal integrity including his or her physical and mental well-being and emotional, spiritual and family life';[57] consequently, its imposition without consent is 'incompatible with the requirement of respect for human freedom and dignity'.[58] In *N.B.*, where the patient was seventeen, 'at an early stage of her reproductive life', the sterilisation 'grossly interfered with her physical integrity, as she was thereby deprived of her reproductive capacity'.[59] Moreover, the conduct of medical staff – in asking the patient to agree to the removal of an important capacity while in labour, with her cognitive abilities impaired by tranquilising medication, and in wrongfully indicating to her that the procedure was indispensable to preserve her life – 'was grossly disrespectful of her human dignity'.[60] In relation to Article 8, the judgments found that the deprivation of reproductive capability interfered with patient autonomy, but also had repercussions on various aspects of private and family life.[61]

I.G. and M.K. v. *Slovakia* condemned *a fortiori* the sterilisation of two Roma women during a caesarean delivery in a public hospital *without their consent or knowledge*; the procedure – not a life-saving intervention and performed without prior informed consent – was deemed incompatible with respect for human freedom and dignity, despite doctors' belief that a further pregnancy would threaten the patient's life and health.[62] Moreover, the length of both civil and criminal proceedings instituted against those responsible for the forced sterilisation breached the procedural aspect of Article 3, which requires a prompt investigation.[63]

56 See *V.C.* v. *Slovakia*, App. No. 18968/07, 8 November 2011, [120], [155] (procedure carried out immediately after a caesarean delivery, based on consent signed while the patient was still in labour, without understanding that the process was irreversible or having the alternatives explained, and after being told that, if she had a third child, either she or the baby would die); *N.B.* v. *Slovakia*, App. No. 29518/10, 12 June 2012, [76].

57 *V.C.* v. *Slovakia*, [106].

58 Ibid., [107].

59 *N.B.* v. *Slovakia*, [79].

60 Ibid., [77].

61 *V.C.* v. *Slovakia*, [143], *N.B.* v. *Slovakia*, [95].

62 See *I.G. and M.K.* v. *Slovakia*, App. No. 15966/04, 13 November 2012, [122], [125].

63 See ibid., [132]–[134].

In all these cases, the Court noted the widespread practice of sterilisation of Roma women without informed consent in Slovakia[64] and emphasised the State's positive obligations under Article 8 to put in place effective safeguards for the protection of the reproductive health of Roma women.[65] It concluded that the respondent had failed to comply with 'its positive obligation to secure to them a sufficient measure of protection enabling them to effectively enjoy their right to respect for their private and family life'.[66]

Regrettably, in forced sterilisation cases, the ECtHR tends to focus almost exclusively on the affront to human dignity, self-determination and bodily integrity, with rather limited acknowledgement of procreative interests. In *V.C.* and *I.G. and M.K.*, having found a violation of Article 8, the Court did not consider it necessary to proceed to a separate examination of the complaints under Article 12.[67] The Court reasoned that 'the exercise of the right to marry and found a family gives rise to personal, social and legal consequences as a result of which there is a close affinity between the rights under Articles 8 and 12 of the Convention'.[68] The complaint that forced sterilisation breached the victims' right to found a family, and that the respondent had failed to take adequate preventative measures,[69] arguably deserved further analysis and the recognition of an additional violation.

Article 3 was also the Court's focus in forced abortion cases. The recent *S.F.K.* v. *Russia* judgment concerned an abortion performed in a public hospital without adequate care by State-employed health professionals to ensure that the patient *freely consented* to the procedure.[70] Considering the patient's young age, her dependency on her parents, who pressurised her into the abortion, and the negligence of medical staff witnessing these circumstances, this was seen as a case of forced abortion 'contrary to the applicant's human dignity' and 'an egregious form of inhuman and degrading treatment'.[71] Although the applicant lamented a violation of Article 8, the Court did not find it necessary to examine it separately, given its findings under

[64] See *V.C.* v. *Slovakia*, [146]–[149] and [152]–[153]. See also *I.G. and M.K.* v. *Slovakia*, [75], on the alleged history of sterilisation of Roma women, apparently originating under the communist regime in Czechoslovakia in the early 1970s.

[65] See *V.C.* v. *Slovakia*, [145].

[66] Ibid., [154]; see also *N.B.* v. *Slovakia*, [98], *I.G. and M.K.* v. *Slovakia*, [144], [150]–[151].

[67] See *V.C.* v. *Slovakia*, [159]–[161]; *I.G. and M.K.* v. *Slovakia*, [150].

[68] *V.C.* v. *Slovakia*, [159].

[69] See ibid., [157], *I.G. and M.K.* v. *Slovakia*, [148].

[70] See *S.F.K.* v. *Russia*, App. No. 5578/12, 11 October 2022, [63]–[68], [80]–[83].

[71] Ibid., [81].

Article 3.[72] In its brief assessment of admissibility of the Article 8 claim, it reaffirmed, nevertheless, that 'the decision of a pregnant woman to continue her pregnancy or not belongs to the sphere of private life and autonomy'.[73] A stronger statement to the effect that forced abortion constitutes a breach of a person's private and family life under Article 8 would have been desirable; the Court's characterisation of the woman's loss of her unborn child as 'a serious immediate damage to her health'[74] does not reflect the free-standing importance of parenthood rights.

The Court chose to concentrate on human dignity issues again in *G.M. and Others* v. *The Republic of Moldova*, where it condemned the authorisation of involuntary abortions and contraceptive measures (implantation of intrauterine devices) in respect of intellectually disabled women with legal capacity institutionalised in a neuropsychiatric residential asylum.[75] The Court found both substantive and procedural obligations under Article 3 breached by the lack of safeguards against, and adequate investigation into, the administration of such invasive medical procedures without the informed consent of patients living in psychiatric institutions, premised on the treatment of intellectual disability as a contraindication for pregnancy.[76] Although the complaint had relied on Article 8, the Court recategorised the case as falling under Article 3, given the gravity of the alleged non-consensual procedures and the applicants' vulnerability resulting from their gender, intellectual disability and institutionalisation.[77] The Court noted that, generally and, in particular, in the respondent State, 'harmful stereotypes exist according to which persons with mental disabilities should not procreate'.[78] It concluded that the Moldovan legal framework lacked safeguards to ensure prior consent to medical interventions for intellectually disabled persons, as well as adequate criminal legislation to dissuade the practice of non-consensual medical interventions on such persons; the respondent had thereby failed to meet its positive obligation to

72 Ibid., [95].

73 Ibid., [92], citing the earlier *R.R.* v. *Poland*, a case concerning the effective exercise of the domestic right to timely access to prenatal diagnostic and information, enabling an expectant woman to decide whether to seek a therapeutic abortion (see Chapter 4, Section 4.2.1).

74 *S.F.K.* v. *Russia*, [81].

75 *G.M. and Others* v. *The Republic of Moldova*, App. No. 44394/15, 22 November 2022.

76 Ibid., [109], [128], [141], [147].

77 See ibid., [67]–[68], [84]–[91]. The Court recalled that the position of inferiority and powerlessness of patients confined in psychiatric hospitals called for increased vigilance in assessing ECHR compliance (ibid., [87]), and that 'forced abortion, sterilisation and birth control are forms of gender-based violence', according to UN and Council of Europe legal instruments (ibid., [88], based on the examination of instruments at [45]–[46], [51], [54], [57]).

78 Ibid., [122].

establish and implement a system providing protection to women living in psychiatric institutions against 'serious breaches of their integrity'.[79]

Interestingly, by placing the case on the terrain of non-derogable Article 3 rights, the Court avoided taking a stand on whether the welfare of future children justifies non-elective contraceptive measures for patients institutionalised on an indefinite basis and incapable of assuming the responsibility of a child. The ruling rejects paternalism and conveys support for nearly absolute rights to bodily self-determination, even where the exercise of reproductive rights is interlinked with the interests of children born to parents who cannot look after them (and those of society as a whole, considering the burden on the public care system). The Court's choice of moving the complaint under Article 3 intimates that non-consensual treatment preventing reproduction is so profoundly incompatible with human dignity and so abhorrent to a civilised society that there is no scope for a balancing of interests. By the same token, if the welfare of the child to be born does not justify compulsory birth control measures for patients institutionalised on account of intellectual disability and unable to rear children, it is exceedingly difficult to justify the refusal to provide ART to functional parents on the grounds of the future child's welfare – for example, the refusal to authorise donor insemination or the posthumous use of frozen gametes on the basis of the future child's right to know and be cared for by his/her birth parents.

Albeit less extensive, the judicial practice under the ACHR echoes Strasbourg principles on protection against forced sterilisation. In *I.V. v. Bolivia*, the Inter-American Court of Human Rights (IACtHR) held that the sterilisation, by tubal ligation, performed on a woman in hospital during an emergency caesarean section without her informed consent breached her rights to health and personal autonomy.[80] The judgment stressed that the absence of legal safeguards for the protection of the patient's reproductive health was a serious violation of the rights to autonomy and *reproductive freedom*, and specifically the right to make autonomous decisions in relation to one's body and *life plans*.[81] In the medical context, informed consent was said to ensure the practical effect of the norm guaranteeing individual autonomy, which in turn is an element of human dignity.[82] The judgment recalled that both the ACHR and the Inter-American Convention on the Prevention,

[79] Ibid., [128].
[80] *I.V. v. Bolivia*, Case No. 329, 30 November 2016 (available only in Spanish). For an analysis, see Martín Hevia and Andrés Constantin, 'Gendered Power Relations and Informed Consent: The *I.V. v. Bolivia* Case' (2018) 20(2) *Health and Human Rights Journal* 197–203.
[81] *I.V. v. Bolivia*, [157].
[82] Ibid., [159].

Punishment, and Eradication of Violence against Women[83] established positive obligations, such as the adoption of preventative measures to secure the right to reproductive health and autonomy against violations, including through the clear regulation of health services and by monitoring the observance of the informed consent requirement in both public and private medical centres.[84]

Article 8 ECHR has further been interpreted as requiring reparation for unlawful sterilisation. In *G.B. and R.B.* v. *The Republic of Moldova*,[85] the non-consensual sterilisation at a State-owned hospital had already been assessed by domestic courts as a 'serious interference with the first applicant's physical and psychological integrity'.[86] The Strasbourg dispute focused on the level of compensation in civil proceedings against the hospital and the obstetrician for medical negligence and on the fact that domestic courts had absolved the obstetrician of criminal liability. It was held that the failure to provide a victim of unlawful sterilisation adequate compensation in civil proceedings against the hospital and the medical professional guilty of negligence violated Article 8. The level of compensation was found considerably below the minimum level of compensation the ECtHR awards for breaches of Article 8, especially considering the extreme nature of the interference with the woman's Convention rights.[87] Remarkably, the patient's husband was a co-applicant and claimed a breach of *his* right to respect for family life. Although the Court chose to address the case through the lens of the woman's right to respect for her physical integrity,[88] it recognised 'the devastating effect on the first applicant from having lost her ability to reproduce'[89] and also 'the particularly serious effect ... on her family life with the second applicant', awarding the spouses compensation *jointly* in respect of non-pecuniary damage.[90]

83 Inter-American Convention on the Prevention, Punishment and Eradication of Violence against Women, Belém do Pará, adopted 6 September 1994, in force 3 May 1995.

84 *I.V.* v. *Bolivia*, [206]–[210].

85 *G.B. and R.B.* v. *The Republic of Moldova*, App. No. 16761/09, 18 December 2012.

86 Ibid., [30] (removal by an obstetrician of a woman's ovaries and fallopian tubes without her permission during a caesarean section). The ECtHR endorsed the domestic courts' assessment (see ibid., [31]).

87 *G.B. and R.B.* v. *The Republic of Moldova*, [31]–[35]. The equivalent of EUR 607 awarded by the domestic courts in respect of non-pecuniary damage was found considerably below the minimum level of compensation awarded by the ECtHR for Article 8 violations; the judgment cites *Codarcea* v. *Romania* (App. No. 31675/04, 2 June 2009), where the Court had awarded the applicant EUR 20,000.

88 See *G.B. and R.B.* v. *The Republic of Moldova*, [24].

89 Ibid., [32].

90 Ibid., [39].

Finally, medical errors causing irreparable damage to a person's reproductive capacity can also trigger a breach of Article 8 ECHR. *Csoma* v. *Romania* condemned the failures in the treatment inducing a non-urgent abortion on foetal abnormality grounds, which compromised the woman's ability to bear children.[91] The applicant's private life was found infringed 'by not being involved in the choice of medical treatment and properly informed of the risks involved in the medical procedure'.[92] The Court's emphasis was on the privacy-related rights to informed consent to treatment, including the foreseeability of risks, and physical integrity.[93] The impact on family life under Article 8 and on the right to found a family under Article 12 may have deserved separate acknowledgement.[94] The ruling also indicated that deficiencies in the investigation into the doctors' liability for medical negligence irreversibly impairing the ability to bear children breached Article 8.[95]

In sum, when Strasbourg claims concern natural procreation, the right to respect for private and family life primarily gives rise to negative obligations (occasionally assessed under Article 3 due to the gravity of the interference with physical integrity and human dignity). However, there are also positive obligations, designed to prevent interferences with a person's reproductive capacity: to ensure that the law requires doctors to inform patients of the risks involved in a medical procedure (e.g. loss of procreative capacity);[96] to afford redress for infringements of private life caused by the lack of informed consent to a procedure involving the risk of losing the ability to reproduce (e.g. through civil/disciplinary proceedings capable of establishing liability for medical negligence and awarding compensation);[97] to establish and effectively apply a system providing protection to intellectually disabled women in psychiatric institutions against serious breaches of their physical integrity,[98] such as forced birth control and forced termination of pregnancy, in light of their special vulnerability;[99] to ensure legal safeguards for the reproductive health of women whose ethnicity places them at risk, in particular protection

91 *Csoma* v. *Romania*, App. No. 8759/05, 15 January 2013.
92 Ibid., [68].
93 Ibid., [42].
94 The Court's award of EUR 6,000 in non-pecuniary damage (ibid., [72]) does not reflect the magnitude of the consequences of the breach on the victim's family-related rights.
95 Ibid., [60]–[68].
96 See ibid., [42].
97 See ibid., [43].
98 *G.M. and Others* v. *The Republic of Moldova*, [112], [124], [128].
99 Ibid., [89]–[90].

against sterilisation without the patient's knowledge[100] or without their full and informed consent.[101]

This stream of case law firmly established an obligation to protect against, and offer redress for, actions impairing an individual's natural capacity to procreate. When the exercise of reproductive autonomy goes beyond natural conception, human rights obligations to permit or facilitate parenthood projects have been slower to crystallise. Only recently has international jurisprudence started to identify such obligations, in the Strasbourg Court and marginally elsewhere. These developments will be considered in the following section.

1.2.2 *Medically Assisted Procreation: Interferences or Lacunae?*

The conceptual boundary between negative and positive obligations is much less clear-cut in relation to assisted procreation claims. As Erin Nelson has argued, 'women's reproductive autonomy and reproductive health are interwoven' and hence respect for reproductive autonomy 'demands an active and engaged State'.[102] The ability to effectively exercise procreative choice may require State regulation and State assistance. Indeed, occasionally the Court has refused to clarify whether the issue in contention concerned a positive or negative obligation. In *Dickson* v. *The United Kingdom*, the parties disagreed on whether the refusal of assisted insemination facilities for prisoners constituted an interference with the 'existing right to beget a child' or a 'failure by the State to grant a right which did not previously exist'; for the Chamber, the complaint regarded a positive obligation.[103] The Grand Chamber did not consider it necessary to decide on the exact classification of the obligation at stake, insofar as the core issue was 'whether a fair balance was struck between the competing public and private interests involved',[104] a question common to both types of obligations:

> Although the object of Article 8 is essentially that of protecting the individual against arbitrary interference by the public authorities, it does not merely compel the State to abstain from such interference. . . . There may be positive obligations inherent in an effective respect for private and family life. These obligations may involve the adoption of measures designed to secure respect

[100] See *I.G. and M.K.* v. *Slovakia*, [144].
[101] See *V.C.* v. *Slovakia*, [154], *N.B.* v. *Slovakia*, [98].
[102] Erin Nelson, *Law, Policy and Reproductive Autonomy* (Oxford: Hart, 2013) 353.
[103] *Dickson* v. *The United Kingdom* [GC], [69].
[104] Ibid., [71].

> for private and family life even in the sphere of the relations of individuals between themselves. The boundaries between the State's positive and negative obligations under Article 8 do not lend themselves to precise definition. The applicable principles are nonetheless similar. In particular, in both instances regard must be had to the fair balance to be struck between the competing interests.[105]

Moreover, the Court sometimes acknowledges that both analytical approaches are equally appropriate in the dispute at hand. In *S.H. and Others* v. *Austria*, the Grand Chamber viewed the prohibition on the use of donated gametes for IVF treatment as potentially concerning either a positive or a negative obligation:

> The legislation in question can be seen as raising an issue as to whether there exists a positive obligation on the State to permit certain forms of artificial procreation using either sperm or ova from a third party. However, the matter can also be seen as an interference by the State with the applicants' rights to respect for their family life as a result of the prohibition ... of certain techniques of artificial procreation that had been developed by medical science but of which they could not avail themselves because of that prohibition. In the present case, the Court will approach the case as one involving an interference with the applicants' right to avail themselves of techniques of artificial procreation ... since they were in fact prevented from doing so by the operation of the law.[106]

The Court's preference for the latter model seems appropriate, as the ban prevented both the use of donor gametes by part-infertile couples and the donation of gametes by individuals who were willing to enable others to reproduce. As Harris et al. suggested, 'where a couple can procreate by whatever means, the state should not impose unreasonable restrictions on their possibility of doing so'.[107] Nor is it obvious that measures promoting social parenthood (already accommodated through adoption and presumptions of fatherhood) should be more exceptional in the assisted reproduction context. Similarly, in *Pejřilová* v. *The Czech Republic*, the Court found that the refusal to allow a widow to use her late husband's frozen gametes to conceive a child through artificial insemination could be seen as concerning either positive or negative obligations; again, it chose the latter approach.[108]

[105] Ibid., [70].
[106] *S.H. and Others* v. *Austria* [GC], [88].
[107] David Harris et al., *Harris, O'Boyle & Warbrick: Law of the European Convention on Human Rights* (Oxford: Oxford University Press, 2014, 3rd ed.) 762.
[108] See *Pejřilová* v. *The Czech Republic*, App. No. 14889/19, 8 December 2022, [47].

In other cases, the Court attached a label to the dispute without clarifying the exact obligation at stake or the basis for its categorisation. In *Evans* v. *The United Kingdom*, the Grand Chamber merely disagreed with the domestic examination of the case as one involving an interference, in circumstances where the law precluded the preservation/implantation by the clinic of embryos created with the applicant's ova after the male gamete provider had withdrawn his consent.[109] Without further justification, the Court 'consider[ed] that it is more appropriate to analyse the case as one concerning positive obligations, the principal issue ... being whether the legislative provisions as applied in the present case struck a fair balance between the competing public and private interests involved'.[110] The absence of elaboration is all the more problematic since several dissenters viewed the case 'as one of interference with the applicant's right to respect for the decision to become a genetically related parent';[111] in fact, an essential feature of the case was the applicant's supervened infertility, making the cryopreserved embryos her last chance at parenthood. For the Chamber, the question was 'whether there exists a positive obligation on the State to ensure that a woman who has embarked on treatment for the specific purpose of giving birth to a genetically related child should be permitted to proceed to implantation of the embryo notwithstanding the withdrawal of consent by her former partner, the male gamete provider'.[112] Since the statute authorised the destruction of embryos upon the unilateral request of one progenitor, regardless of the circumstances of the other, the complaint arguably concerned an obligation to refrain from interfering with the applicant's last surviving genetic material.

The categorisation of the case can be counterintuitive sometimes. In *Callamand* v. *France*, the refusal to grant the applicant contact with the child born to her former cohabitant through donor insemination was viewed through the lens of positive obligations to ensure effective respect for private and family life; for the Court, the adverse impact on the applicant's family life stemmed from the couple's separation, not from an active interference of a public authority, and the judge had not terminated *existing* contact rights (even though the appellate courts had quashed the favourable first-instance decision).[113] Conversely, in *K.K. and Others* v. *Denmark*, the refusal to allow the intended non-genetic mother to adopt her husband's surrogate-born

[109] See *Evans* v. *The United Kingdom* [GC], [76].
[110] Ibid.
[111] Ibid, Joint Dissenting Opinion of Judges Türmen et al., [6].
[112] *Evans* v. *The United Kingdom* [GC], [58].
[113] *Callamand* v. *France*, App. No. 2338/20, 7 April 2022 (available only in French), [32]–[33].

children was assessed as an interference with the parents' and children's private and family life,[114] even though there is no right to adopt an unrelated child under the Convention,[115] and other legal mechanisms were in place to prevent any practical disadvantages for the children.

Unexpectedly perhaps, given the medical support and legal framework required to establish parenthood through recourse to new genetic technologies, reproductive rights emerge from the case law as engaging mostly negative obligations, rather than obligations of assistance. As soon as a particular technology exists in the realm of medical possibility, the failure to grant access is seen as raising an obstacle to procreative autonomy, not as a lacuna. This is evident in the case law concerning the right to a healthy child and the right of access to treatment with donated gametes. Thus, in *Costa and Pavan* v. *Italy*, the ban on IVF and PGD allowing the selection of healthy embryos was analysed as an interference with the prospective parents' private and family life.[116] When access to a particular technology is legally available but hindered by a private party such as a private hospital or a doctor not employed by the State, a negative obligation still arises in relation to the conduct of court proceedings for compensation for medical negligence (e.g. the failure to refer a patient at risk of foetal abnormality for antenatal screening in *A.K.* v. *Latvia*).[117] The retrospective application, to cases pending in court, of a new bar restricting the level of compensation for parents whose children's disabilities had gone undetected before birth, due to inappropriate tests, was also seen as an active interference in *Maurice* v. *France*,[118] specifically with the right to peaceful enjoyment of one's possessions under Article 1 of Protocol 1.[119] In the area of third-party reproduction, the Court has recognised that 'the right of a couple to conceive a child and to make use of

[114] *K.K. and Others* v. *Denmark*, App. No. 25212/21, 6 December 2022, [42].

[115] See Carmen Draghici, 'Adoption and the European Court of Human Rights: From Laissez-faire to Judicial Law-Making', in Lina Panella and Ersiliagrazia Spatafora (eds.), *Scritti in Onore di Claudio Zanghì* (Torino: Giappichelli, 2012) 255–282.

[116] *Costa and Pavan* v. *Italy*, App. No. 54270/10, 28 August 2012, [58].

[117] See A.K. v. *Latvia*, App. No. 33011/08, 24 June 2014, [84]–[85], [80]. The issue for the ECtHR was whether the domestic courts had respected the applicant's Art. 8 rights in proceedings for compensation for medical negligence (the arbitrariness in their examination of the complaint was found to amount to a violation of Art. 8's procedural limb).

[118] See *Maurice* v. *France* [GC], App. No. 11810/03, 6 October 2005, [79]: 'The Law ... entailed interference with the exercise of the right to compensation which could have been asserted under the domestic law applicable until then, and consequently of the applicants' right to peaceful enjoyment of their possessions.' See, analogously, *Draon* v. *France* [GC], App. No. 1513/03, 6 October 2005.

[119] Protocol 1 to the European Convention on Human Rights and Fundamental Freedoms, Paris, 20 March 1952, in force 18 May 1954.

medically assisted procreation for that purpose is also protected by Article 8, as such a choice is an expression of private and family life';[120] consequently, as held in *S.H. and Others* v. *Austria*, the prohibition on the use of donated gametes for IVF 'involves an interference with the applicants' right to avail themselves of techniques of artificial procreation'.[121] Interestingly, so far, the case law has focused on legal bans rather than on access to State-subsidised treatment, which might be seen, by contrast, as a matter of positive obligations. While the idea that policymakers can decide who deserves to procreate is unappealing,[122] future case law might entertain challenges to the allocation of resources and the scope of public assistance for reproductive plans one can legitimately expect.

Cases concerning a couple's ability to use their frozen embryos for reproductive purposes have also been assessed from the perspective of negative obligations vis-à-vis the decision to become a parent and the right to make use of medically assisted procreation.[123] Specifically, in *Knecht* v. *Romania*, the seizure of a couple's embryos during the course of investigations into the fertility clinic's credentials, delaying the applicants' reproductive plans, was recognised as an interference.[124] In fact, 'the joint parental project of the applicants, who wish to have a child by making use of assisted procreation using their own embryos is an intimate aspect of their private life'.[125] While the intention to become a parent is absent in cases regarding the ability to decide the fate of embryos no longer intended for procreation, the Court conceded in *Parrillo* v. *Italy* that 'the ban ... on donating to scientific research embryos obtained from an in vitro fertilisation and not destined for implantation constitutes an interference with the applicant's right to respect for her private life'.[126] Indeed, 'the applicant's ability to exercise a conscious and considered choice regarding the fate of her embryos concerns an intimate

120 *S.H. and Others* v. *Austria* [GC], [82].

121 Ibid., [88].

122 See Emily Jackson, *Regulating Reproduction: Law, Technology and Autonomy* (Oxford: Hart, 2001) 259: 'Wanting to have a child is not equivalent to other desires that we might consider underserving of public subsidy, like an aesthetics preference for a more attractive nose. ... Like other medical treatments, clinical and cost-effectiveness must be relevant to the extent of NHS provision; but doctors, legislators and regulators are indubitably ill equipped to make moral judgments about whether an individual deserves to procreate.'

123 *Knecht* v. *Romania*, App. No. 10048/10, 2 October 2012, [54].

124 Ibid., [57]. See also *Nedescu* v. *Romania*, App. No. 70035/10, 16 January 2018, [72] (a six-year delay in retrieving the embryos seized by the authorities meant that the applicants lost the chance of having another child).

125 Ibid., [70], building on *Knecht* v. *Romania*, [54].

126 *Parrillo* v. *Italy* [GC], App. No. 46470/11, 27 August 2015, [161].

aspect of her personal life and accordingly relates to her right to self-determination'.[127]

In the context of *biological* parenthood achieved through a surrogacy arrangement (first addressed in *Mennesson* v. *France*), the refusal of domestic authorities to legally recognise the family ties created abroad between the intended parents and their surrogate-born children was seen to amount to an interference with their right to respect for their private and family life and, hence, to raise an issue with regard to the State's negative obligations rather than positive obligations.[128] So was the refusal, in *Foulon and Bouvet* v. *France*, to recognise biological single commissioning fathers as the legal fathers of children born through foreign surrogacy.[129] In a similar vein, in *A.L.* v. *France*, the rejection of the biological father's request to establish his paternity vis-à-vis a child born through a failed illegal gestational surrogacy arrangement (after the surrogate mother sold the child to another couple) amounted to an interference with his private life and required justification.[130] In *D.* v. *France*, the refusal to register the full details of a child's foreign birth certificate, in particular not recognising the genetic/intended mother as the legal mother, constituted an interference with the child's right to private life.[131] In a case brought by a surrogate-born child whose birth certificate indicated the genetically unrelated surrogate and her husband as her parents (*H.* v. *The United Kingdom*), the Court indicated that the legal uncertainty flowing from the automatic recognition of the surrogate's husband, rather than the genetic intended father, as her father on her birth certificate constituted an interference with her private life.[132] Finally, in *D. and Others* v. *Belgium*, the refusal to provide a travel document allowing the admission into the country of a child born through surrogacy abroad, leading to its separation from the parents for several months, constituted an interference with the three applicants' right to respect for family life and required justification under Article 8(2).[133]

[127] Ibid., [215].

[128] *Mennesson* v. *France*, App. No. 65192/11, 26 June 2014, [48]–[49]; *Labassee* v. *France*, App. No. 65941/11, 26 June 2014 (available only in French), [49]–[50]; *Laborie and Others* v. *France*, App. No. 44024/13, 19 January 2017 (available only in French), [29]–[31].

[129] *Foulon and Bouvet* v. *France*, App. Nos. 9063/14; 10410/14, 21 July 2016 (available only in French), [55], [57].

[130] *A.L.* v. *France*, App. No. 13344/20, 7 April 2022 (available only in French), [46].

[131] *D.* v. *France*, App. No. 11288/18, 16 July 2004 (available only in French), [40]–[42].

[132] *H.* v. *The United Kingdom*, App. No. 32185/20, 31 May 2022, [48].

[133] *D. and Others* v. *Belgium*, App. No. 29176/13, 8 July 2014, [50].

Even when the applicants seek a legal fiction of parenthood, as opposed to the recognition of genetic ties created through ART, the dispute tends to be framed in terms of a negative obligation. Thus, in *K.K. and Others* v. *Denmark*, the refusal to allow the commissioning mother to adopt the surrogate-born children raised with her husband (the children's genetic and intended father) was treated as an active interference.[134] In *C. and E.* v. *France*, the refusal of the authorities to transcribe the full details of the foreign birth certificates of children born through surrogacy with the intended fathers' sperm and donor ova, in particular not recognising the intended mothers, was equally seen as an interference with the private lives of the children.[135] In the context of male couples and surrogacy (*D.B. and Others* v. *Switzerland*), the refusal to recognise the non-biological intended father based on the foreign birth certificate, without providing an alternative route to recognition (e.g. adoption), was also assessed as an interference with the family life of all those concerned.[136] In *A.M.* v. *Norway*, the failure to recognise the intended mother who was no longer in a relationship with the genetic father, despite her involvement in the child's conception and initial care after birth, was similarly assessed as an interference with her private life.[137] For many scholars, legal affiliation is 'an eminently cultural datum', not reducible to tracing biological reproduction;[138] indeed, often the individuals fulfilling a parental role are not genetically related to the children. However, it is not unremarkable to see the creation of legal ties between a person and a non-biological child in the ART context being described as a negative obligation.

Negative obligations were also found at stake in cases regarding surrogacy arrangements in which neither intended parents had biological links to the child. In *Paradiso and Campanelli* v. *Italy*, the judicial decisions resulting in the removal of a child born through foreign surrogacy from the intended non-genetic parents, his placement in the care of social services with a view to adoption, and the termination of contact with the parents amounted to an

[134] *K.K. and Others* v. *Denmark*, [42]. The parties agreed that their dispute concerned a negative obligation.

[135] *C. and E.* v. *France*, App. Nos. 1462/18; 17348/18, 19 November 2019 (available only in French), [37].

[136] *D.B. and Others* v. *Switzerland*, App. Nos. 58817/15; 58252/15, 22 November 2022, [70].

[137] *A.M.* v. *Norway*, App. No. 30254/18, 24 March 2022, [120].

[138] See Pierre Murat, 'Filiation et vie familiale', in Frédéric Sudre (ed.), *Le droit au respect de la vie familiale au sens de la Convention européenne des droits de l'homme* (Bruxelles: Némésis-Bruylant, 2002) 161–208, at 161.

interference with the latter's private life.[139] The refusal to recognise the intended parents of an unrelated surrogate-born child as his legal parents was examined as an interference with both the child's and the parents' right to family life in circumstances where family life was established de facto over several years under a foster care arrangement (*Valdís Fjölnisdóttir and Others* v. *Iceland*).[140]

The Court, in *Lia* v. *Malta*, also chose to approach a complaint regarding the age limit for receiving IVF treatment as one involving an interference, because 'it concerns the State's decision to deny the applicants' access to IVF procedures which were available to the population and which they sought to pay for themselves'.[141] Where no public funding for ART is available to any category of patients, the refusal to fund treatment might be seen as an omission, in that the effective exercise of reproductive choice by couples afflicted by infertility requires special measures of protection, subject to competing health needs. Some might even view State-funded ART as an economic right, governed by State discretion in the allocation of resources, rather than instrumental to the protection of civil rights and liberties. Indeed, support for publicly funded ART is not unanimous. Nelson has suggested that 'reproductive autonomy, while an important interest, does not justify an entitlement for funding for ARTs, given all of the many healthcare needs that place demands on the finite resources of healthcare systems'.[142] The analysis ultimately depends on where one situates reproductive needs in the hierarchy of medical needs, which involves value judgments. However, the denial of publicly funded treatment for failure to meet eligibility criteria is more likely to constitute an interference (which requires justification), as well as differential treatment, potentially raising issues under Article 14 read in conjunction with Article 8.

139 *Paradiso and Campanelli* v. *Italy* [GC], App. No. 25358/12, 24 January 2017, [166]. The Chamber rendering the initial judgment had found an interference with both private and family life; see *Paradiso and Campanelli* v. *Italy* [Chamber], App. No. 25358/12, 27 January 2015, [69]–[71].

140 See *Valdís Fjölnisdóttir and Others* v. *Iceland*, App. No. 71552/17, 18 May 2021, [63].

141 *Lia* v. *Malta*, App. No. 8709/20, 5 May 2022, [62].

142 Nelson, *Law, Policy and Reproductive Autonomy*, 289. For the opposite conclusion, based on the Dworkian notion of 'redistributive compensation' where individuals have suffered handicaps, and rejecting the 'non-essential treatment' nomenclature used to justify denying funding for ART, see Justine Burley, 'The Price of Eggs: Who Should Bear the Costs of Fertility Treatments?', in John Harris and Søren Holm (eds.), *The Future of Human Reproduction. Ethics, Choice, and Regulation* (Oxford: Clarendon Press, 1998) 127–149, 148 and passim.

Conversely, fewer issues in relation to ART-born children or planned recourse to ART have been examined by the Court as requiring it to pronounce on positive obligations. One such question, arising in the context of intentional parenthood and gamete donation (*C.E. and Others* v. *France*), was whether States are required to permit the creation of legal ties between a child born though donor insemination and her mother's former female companion, who also acted in a parental role (this was viewed as a possible ramification of the obligation to ensure effective respect for private and family life).[143] The same approach was taken in relation to visitation rights: in *Callamand* v. *France*, the refusal to grant post-separation contact with the child born to the former same-sex cohabitant through medically assisted procreation with donor was analysed from the viewpoint of positive obligations to ensure effective respect for a person's private and family life,[144] seen as requiring the authorities to strike a fair balance between competing interests.[145] The Court has also considered whether a positive obligation, inherent in effective respect for family life, mandates the recognition – as the legal father of a child born through donor insemination – of the transgender social father who was not biologically related to her (*X, Y and Z* v. *The United Kingdom*).[146]

As to potential rights at the conception stage, also framed as a matter of positive obligations was the claim in *Evans* v. *The United Kingdom* that the State must permit a woman, under special circumstances (such as intervening infertility), to use the frozen embryos created with a former partner, notwithstanding his withdrawal of consent; for the Court, the question was whether such an obligation fell within the broader obligation to ensure effective respect for a person's decision to become a genetic parent, by striking a fair balance between competing rights (to become/not to become a parent) in the IVF context.[147] At prenatal stage, *R.R.* v. *Poland* considered the existence of a positive obligation to ensure, in practice, expecting women's access to timely foetal diagnosis services (in fact, the State's positive obligation to secure effective respect for physical and psychological integrity may necessitate the

[143] *C.E. and Others* v. *France*, App. Nos. 29775/18; 29693/19, 24 March 2022 (available only in French), [79]–[80].

[144] *Callamand* v. *France*, [32]–[33].

[145] Ibid., [34]. See also *Honner* v. *France*, App. No. 19511/16, 12 November 2020 (available only in French), [52]–[53] (whether a positive obligation existed to secure respect for the family life of the former same-sex partner of the mother of an ART-born child by ordering contact).

[146] See *X, Y and Z* v. *The United Kingdom* [GC], App. No. 21830/93, 22 April 1997, [41], [52].

[147] *Evans* v. *The United Kingdom* [GC], [75]–[76].

adoption of regulations concerning access to information about an individual's health).[148]

The ECtHR has recently had an opportunity to systematise its jurisprudence and to elaborate on the distinction between positive and negative obligations, in general and with specific reference to the regulation of parenthood following ART. In *C.E. and Others* v. *France*, both parties viewed the impossibility of establishing a parent–child relationship between a child born via donor insemination and her mother's former female partner as an interference by a public authority with the exercise of the right to respect for private and family life.[149] The Court rejected this analysis and interpreted the case as concerning lacunae in French law, adversely impacting the applicants' private and family life and hence the scope of positive obligations to guarantee effective respect for Article 8 rights.[150] The Court distinguished the case from previous cases analysed through the lens of negative obligations: in *Mennesson* v. *France*[151] and *Wagner and J.M.W.L.* v. *Luxembourg*,[152] it had examined the refusal to recognise legal ties between surrogate-born/adoptive children and their intended/adoptive parent as engaging negative obligations, to the extent that those ties had already been established under foreign laws.[153]

Nonetheless, the Court recalled that the principles governing positive and negative obligations under the ECHR are similar; in both cases, the Convention requires a fair balance between the general interest and the interests of those concerned, in which the legitimate objectives listed in Article 8(2) play a certain role.[154] It conceded that the notion of 'respect' lacks clarity, especially as far as positive obligations are concerned, given the diversity of Member States' practices; however, relevant elements include (a) the importance of the interest at stake for the applicant and whether the measure affects fundamental values or essential aspects of his/her private life; (b) the impact on the individual of a conflict between social reality and law; (c) the coherence of legal and administrative practices; and (d) the impact on the State, in the event that the Court requires it to accommodate the claim in question.[155]

148 See *R.R.* v. *Poland*, [188].
149 *C.E. and Others* v. *France*, [78]–[79].
150 Ibid., [80], [82].
151 *Mennesson* v. *France*, discussed in Chapter 2, Section 2.4.
152 *Wagner and J.M.W.L.* v. *Luxembourg*, App. No. 76240/01, 28 June 2007 (discussed in Chapter 3, Section 3.3.2).
153 *C.E. and Others* v. *France*, [81].
154 Ibid., [83].
155 Ibid.

In addition, States enjoy a certain margin of appreciation in implementing both positive and negative obligations.[156] The margin is narrow when a particularly important aspect of the individual's existence or identity is at stake; it is, conversely, wider when there is no consensus in Europe on the relative importance of the right at stake or the means for safeguarding it, particularly where the case raises delicate moral or ethical questions; it is also wide when the State must achieve a balance between competing private and public interests or different rights protected by the Convention.[157] Sometimes, there are both elements expanding and restricting the margin. In the case at hand, the Court found that the recognition of a parent–child relationship between a child and an unrelated person raised ethical questions, and no consensus existed in Europe on the establishment of legal affiliation between a child and the former same-sex partner of the child's mother, both of which supported a significant margin of appreciation.[158] At the same time, an essential aspect of the individual's identity was at stake (the parent–child link, especially during a person's minority), which reduced the margin left to the State as regards the child's rights.[159] Moreover, the ruling stressed that, even within this narrow margin, States' choices do not escape the control of the Court, upon which falls the task of ensuring that the child's best interests are treated as the primary consideration.[160]

An examination of Strasbourg decisions in the area of procreative rights suggests that the scrutiny of States' compliance with positive obligations is not less stringent than in cases seen as raising questions of negative obligations. Although the Court has repeatedly maintained that similar principles apply under either theoretical approach,[161] if a case regards the obligation to ensure effective respect for the right, one might expect States to retain greater discretion in striking a fair balance and choosing the appropriate means of protection, whereas, if the case is construed as regarding a negative obligation, the burden is on the State to demonstrate the necessity and proportionality of the interference. Nonetheless, the case law on procreative rights appears to confirm that the categorisation of the obligation potentially breached as positive or negative does not have a decisive impact on the applicants' prospects of

156 Ibid., [84].
157 Ibid., [85].
158 Ibid., [86]–[87].
159 Ibid., [88]–[89].
160 Ibid., [90].
161 See, e.g., *Dickson* v. *The United Kingdom* [GC], [70]; *S.H. and Others* v. *Austria* [GC], [88]; *C.E. and Others* v. *France*, [83].

success; in fact, it is a poor predictor of the outcome of the case.[162] Against this backdrop, the following chapters will explore the factors hampering the development of reproductive rights in international case law, but also its rather extraordinary departure from a narrow view of procreation and parenthood.

[162] When claims are framed as entailing negative obligations, findings of violation (*A.K.* v. *Latvia*; A.L. v. *France*; *Costa and Pavan* v. *Italy*; *D.B. and Others* v. *Switzerland*; *Draon* v. *France*/*Maurice* v. *France*; *Foulon and Bouvet* v. *France*; *K.K. and Others* v. *Denmark*; *Mennesson* v. *France*/*Labassee* v. *France*/*Laborie* v. *France*; *Nedescu* v. *Romania*) are as frequent as findings of non-violation (*A.M.* v. *Norway*; *C. and E.* v. *France*; *D. and Others* v. *France*; *H.* v. *The United Kingdom*; *Knecht* v. *Romania*; *Paradiso and Campanelli* v. *Italy*; *Parrillo* v. *Italy*; *S.H. and Others* v. *Austria*; *Valdís Fjölnisdóttir* v. *Iceland*; *Pejřilová* v. *The Czech Republic*). The distribution of outcomes in relation to claims couched in terms of positive obligations is not significant, with findings of violation in *Callamand* v. *France* and *R.R.* v. *Poland* and findings of non-violation in *C.E. and Others* v. *France*, *Evans* v. *The United Kingdom*, *Honner* v. *France* and *X, Y and Z* v. *The United Kingdom*. In some cases (e.g., *Knecht* v. *Romania*), looking at the outcome of the application is misleading, as the general right asserted by the applicants is upheld, whereas the application is unsuccessful on the facts.

2

A Right to a Genetically Related Child?

2.1 THE RIGHT TO MEDICALLY ASSISTED PROCREATION AND TO CONTROL OVER ONE'S GENETIC MATERIAL

However central to human experience, the right to have a genetically related child is not free from controversy in scholarly debates. For many, procreation is essential for individual self-fulfilment for a whole host of reasons: a primordial sense of ensuring the survival of the species; partaking in the miracle of creating new life; perpetuating the family's lineage and gene pool as a responsibility towards ancestors; giving one's parents the satisfaction of grandchildren that continue their genetic heritage; the ability to recognise oneself and identify traits of family members in one's child; the immutable bond with a child that is an extension of oneself; the sense of gaining immortality by producing offspring; the desire to avoid the genetic lottery of adoption of unrelated children; the fear of rejection by a non-biological child in adulthood, sometimes associated with the search for the birth family. Prominent amongst these motivations is the innate, but also socially fortified, need to seek genetic continuity and permanence. As Maya Sabatello noted, 'procreation is often regarded as a natural desire to "continue the family line" and a desire to leave a piece of oneself behind'.[1]

Others, however, equate procreation with the opportunity to experience parenthood and hence view genetic continuity as immaterial. The desire for parenthood in a social sense is also associated with 'the need for children who will provide economic support for parents in their old age'.[2] This understanding of procreation occasionally leads to unfair criticism of the right to a genetic

[1] Maya Sabatello, 'Posthumously Conceived Children: An International and Human Rights Perspective' (2014) 27 *Journal of Law and Health* 29–67, at 61.

[2] Gillian Douglas, *Law, Fertility and Reproduction* (London: Sweet and Maxwell, 1991) 103.

child as devaluing social parenthood. According to Michael Boucai, promoting the geneticist ideal of procreation 'might demean nonbiological parenthood',[3] and human rights arguments for assisted reproduction treatment (ART) carry the risk of 'glorifying biological reproduction at the expense of adoption'.[4]

Nonetheless, a right cannot be negated due to the fear of offending those who value it less. To deny medical support for biological parenthood on the basis that non-biological parenthood is available is to prevent individuals from making their own judgments on the meaning of procreation. The deferral to personal choice in family formation does not diminish the importance of social parenthood; it merely recognises that individuals have different priorities. The fact that some people derive self-fulfilment from *rearing children* (whether or not biological) cannot justify restrictions on others' desire to *reproduce*. It was reported that women mistakenly implanted with other patients' embryos following in vitro fertilisation (IVF) underwent emergency procedures to have those embryos removed;[5] given the costs of IVF treatment, the low chances of an embryo becoming a foetus and the trauma of a further surgical intervention, the decision to remove unrelated embryos showcases the importance some aspiring parents attach to genetic continuity in reproduction. A pluralist, tolerant and open-minded society ought to safeguard the right to choose genetic parenthood, even if it is not a high-ranking priority for everyone.

The same reductive view of parenthood as rearing children has inspired some commentators to suggest that it is selfish and irresponsible of individuals to wish to bring new biological children into the world when there are many abandoned minors in need of a home.[6] However, those children are not the responsibility of reproductively challenged individuals any more than they are of individuals who can reproduce without medical assistance; by the same token, one could argue that fertile couples should refrain from reproducing as long as there are children needing a family. This would require some individuals to sacrifice their procreative rights in order to repair the damage created

3 Michael Boucai, 'Is Assisted Procreation an LGBT Right?' (2016) *Wisconsin Law Review* 1065–1125, at 1121.

4 Ibid., 1123.

5 See Merle Spriggs, 'IVF Mixup: White Couple Have Black Babies' (2003) *Journal of Medical Ethics* 65.

6 See Elizabeth Bartholet, *Family Bonds: Adoption and the Politics of Parenting* (Boston, MA: Houghton Mifflin, 1993) 35–36, cited in Boucai, 'Is Assisted Procreation an LGBT Right?', 1117: 'A sane and human society should encourage people to provide for existing children rather than bringing more children into the world.'

by others who exercised theirs irresponsibly (by reproducing while unfit or ill-equipped to become parents); the inequity of this position is obvious. Society as a whole has a responsibility for children in care (borne by taxpayers collectively); conversely, every individual is entitled to the same choice between adoption and reproduction (whether natural or assisted). The right to resort to ART in pursuit of a genetic child must be disconnected from social agendas. As Gillian Douglas aptly pointed out:

> It may also be argued that childless couples should seek to adopt the many children waiting in care, or the millions who suffer deprivation in the third world. . . . But there is no reason why infertile couples should be expected to fulfil the needs of such children, rather than anyone else. . . . To expect them to be taken on, for lack of anything else, by infertile couples, is to devalue both the children and the childless.[7]

In addition, the moral interest in procreating does not hinge upon whether or not an individual or a couple requires medical assistance to do so.[8] Nor is the criticism of assisted conception as unnatural a sufficient justification against the provision of treatment to those who depend on it to have a biological child. As Emily Jackson noted, 'in order to restrict other people's reproductive freedom, these critics must do more than establish personal distaste for artificial means of reproduction'.[9]

Medically assisted procreation remains, however, particularly controversial when it involves third-party contributions: the donation of gametes or surrogacy. There are qualitative distinctions between the functions performed by gamete donors and surrogate mothers. The surrogate's role 'involves the nurture of the child for nine months followed by a painful and risky delivery'.[10] However, both techniques presuppose the participation of an individual who does not intend to reproduce but merely to facilitate another's reproductive plans. They raise the question of whether the right to respect for private

[7] Douglas, *Law, Fertility and Reproduction*, 106–107. See also Emily Jackson, *Regulating Reproduction: Law, Technology and Autonomy* (Oxford: Hart, 2001), 174, arguing that, since deliberate procreation among the fertile population is not dismissed as selfish and immoral, there is no reason to assign moral responsibility for neglected children to the infertile.

[8] See John Robertson, 'The Presumptive Primacy of Procreative Liberty', in Tom Beauchamp, LeRoy Walters, Jeffrey Kahn and Anna Mastroiani (eds.), *Contemporary Issues in Bioethics* (Boston, MA: Wadsworth Cengage Learning, 2014, 8th ed.) 245–251, at 248: 'The moral right of the coitally infertile to reproduce is based on the same desire to reproduce . . . They too wish to replicate themselves, transmit genes, gestate and rear children biologically related to them . . . neither the noncoital nature of the means used nor the infertility of their beneficiaries mean that the presumptively protected moral interest in reproduction is not present.'

[9] Jackson, *Regulating Reproduction*, 169.

[10] Douglas, *Law, Fertility and Reproduction*, 150.

and family life requires the State to facilitate genetic or gestational assistance to procreate and to allocate parenthood according to the parties' intentions.

To date, the European Court of Human Rights (ECtHR) has proved cautious when interpreting obligations related to medically assisted reproduction, affording States a wide margin of appreciation in this sensitive area:

> The Court's task is not to substitute itself for the competent national authorities in determining the most appropriate policy for regulating matters of artificial procreation, ... especially since the use of IVF treatment gave rise then and continues to give rise today to sensitive moral and ethical issues against a background of fast-moving medical and scientific developments. ... The margin of appreciation to be afforded to the respondent State is a wide one.[11]

Nevertheless, the Court was prepared to uphold a number of minimal guarantees regarding access to ART and relationships created through recourse to ART. These will be examined in the following sections.

2.1.1 *Respect for the Decision to Become a Parent and Make Use of ART*

It is currently well established that the European Convention on Human Rights (ECHR) protects the right to respect for a person's decision to become a genetic parent. The issue has first arisen in the context of deprivation of liberty, specifically in relation to the claim that the denial of conjugal visits in prison breached the right to found a family under Article 12. In *X* v. *The United Kingdom*, the former European Commission on Human Rights acknowledged the absolute nature of the right to found a family (to which no express restrictions similar to those in Article 8(2) apply), but clarified that Article 12 does not require States to guarantee 'that a person must at all times be given the actual possibility to procreate his descendants'.[12] In *E.L.H. and P.B.H.* v. *The United Kingdom*, the Commission analysed the rule prohibiting 'conjugal visits' in prison as an interference with both Articles 8 and 12, but legitimate (i.e. responding to the need to prevent disorder or crime) and proportionate (in that artificial insemination was allowed).[13] The parties'

[11] *Knecht* v. *Romania*, App. No. 10048/10, 2 October 2012, [59].

[12] *X* v. *The United Kingdom*, App. No. 6564/74, 21 May 1975 (Commission). For a discussion, see Bart van der Sloot, 'Between Fact and Fiction: An Analysis of the Case-Law on Article 12 of the European Convention on Human Rights' (2014) 26(4) *Child and Family Law Quarterly* 397–420, at 408.

[13] *E.L.H. and P.B.H.* v. *The United Kingdom*, App. Nos. 32094/96; 32568/96, 22 October 1997 (Commission), [2].

conscientious objection to artificial insemination did not detract from this conclusion; in fact, Article 9 'does not guarantee the right to be exempted from rules which apply generally and neutrally'.[14] The decision suggests that, as long as a route to conceive is available, States are not required to respect the prisoner's preferred method of conception.

The Grand Chamber in *Evans* v. *The United Kingdom* firmly anchored the right to pursue genetic parenthood in Article 8 as a ramification of 'privacy':

> 'Private life', which is a broad term encompassing, inter alia, aspects of an individual's physical and social identity including the right to personal autonomy, personal development and to establish and develop relationships with other human beings and the outside world . . ., incorporates the right to respect for both the decisions to become and not to become a parent.[15]

While noting that nothing precluded the applicant from becoming a parent in a social sense (through adoption), the Court agreed that the 'right to respect for the decision to become a parent in the genetic sense' also fell within the scope of Article 8.[16] The ruling thus acknowledged that biological parenthood is qualitatively different from parental status and that the interest in becoming a genetic parent is protected by the Convention. The importance of the right to make decisions about procreation was reaffirmed by the finding in *Dickson* v. *The United Kingdom* that this right is not automatically forfeited upon imprisonment; on the contrary, any restrictions upon detainees' right to make procreative decisions require justification.[17] The subsequent *Lukács* v. *Hungary* decision, while dismissing the complaint because the parties had not availed themselves of domestic avenues for pursuing conjugal meetings,[18] did not contest the premise that the couple's ability to procreate remains protected during the course of detention.

Depending on personal circumstances, the effective enjoyment of the right to respect for the decision to become a genetic parent may require medical assistance. In *Dickson* v. *The United Kingdom*, the Grand Chamber held that 'the refusal of artificial insemination facilities concerned [the applicants'] private and family lives, which notions incorporate the right to respect for

[14] Ibid.

[15] *Evans* v. *The United Kingdom* [GC], App. No. 6339/05, 10 April 2007, [71].

[16] Ibid., [72].

[17] See *Dickson* v. *The United Kingdom* [GC], App. No. 44362/04, 4 December 2007, [68] and [75] (reiterating *Hirst* v. *United Kingdom (No. 2)* [GC], App. No. 74025/01, 6 October 2005, [70]).

[18] See *Lukács* v. *Hungary*, App. No. 61924/15, 16 December 2020, [18]–[20].

their decision to become genetic parents'.[19] Furthermore, the availability of ART when it is 'the only realistic hope . . . of having a child together' becomes a matter 'of vital importance' to the couple.[20] This in turn narrows the State's margin of appreciation: 'Where a particularly important facet of an individual's existence or identity is at stake (such as the choice to become a genetic parent), the margin of appreciation accorded to a State will in general be restricted'.[21] *S.H. and Others* v. *Austria* expressly articulated the *right* to resort to ART in order to become a parent; according to the Grand Chamber, 'the right of a couple to conceive a child and to make use of medically assisted procreation for that purpose is also protected by Article 8, as such a choice is an expression of private and family life'.[22] Article 12 should equally apply whenever fertility treatment is sought by a married couple, because restrictions affect their right to 'found a family'; however, ECHR case law on ART has developed exclusively around Article 8. In *Dickson* v. *The United Kingdom*, having ascertained a violation of Article 8, the Court found it unnecessary to consider the complaint under Article 12,[23] and subsequent applications have focused on Article 8. Article 12 was no longer invoked in *S.H. and Others* v. *Austria* by married couples prevented from using gamete donation to found a family.[24] Similarly, in *Nedescu* v. *Romania*, although a married couple's loss of the opportunity to have a second child due to the seizure of their embryos was eminently relevant under Article 12, the complaint only relied on Article 8.[25]

While the right to make use of ART is not absolute, measures precluding access require justification. The *Dickson* v. *The United Kingdom* ruling found that the blanket refusal to provide access to assisted fertilisation facilities to individuals deprived of liberty, and hence incapable of natural procreation for a considerable time, failed to strike a fair balance between the interests at stake. The applicant, a prisoner serving a lengthy sentence for murder, had unsuccessfully sought access to artificial insemination, indicating that his wife would no longer be likely to conceive by the time he was released. The Court

[19] *Dickson* v. *The United Kingdom* [GC], [66].

[20] Ibid., [72]. In *Dickson*, artificial insemination was the only option due to the wife's age and the incarcerated husband's release date, but it is also the only option when medical conditions in either member of the couple preclude natural procreation.

[21] Ibid., [78].

[22] *S.H. and Others* v. *Austria* [GC], App. No. 57813/00, 3 November 2011, [82]. See also *Knecht* v. *Romania*, [54].

[23] *Dickson* v. *The United Kingdom* [GC], [86].

[24] The applicants had invoked Article 12 in the domestic proceedings; see *S.H. and Others* v. *Austria* [GC], [15].

[25] See *Nedescu* v. *Romania*, App. No. 70035/10, 16 January 2018, [54].

agreed that the punitive function of imprisonment and maintaining public confidence in the penal system constituted legitimate aims;[26] the welfare of the child to be born, while playing a role, could not go so far as to prevent couples from attempting to conceive, since the wife could look after the child until her husband's release[27] (a finding potentially important for single aspiring parents). The judgment also confirmed that, although many States had introduced conjugal visits in prison, the Convention could not be interpreted as mandating them;[28] the choice of the method of conception remains, therefore, subject to limitations, as long as the right to procreate is safeguarded (as seen in *E.L.H. and P.B.H.* a decade earlier).

Although the lack of European consensus widened the State's margin of appreciation in *Dickson*, it was held that the absence of an assessment of proportionality in a specific case, on a matter of 'significant importance' to the individual, 'must be seen as falling outside any acceptable margin of appreciation so that a fair balance was not struck between the competing public and private interests involved'.[29] The policy contested in *Dickson* 'effectively excluded any real weighing of the competing individual and public interests, and prevented the required assessment of the proportionality of a restriction, in any individual case', in that it 'placed an inordinately high "exceptionality" burden on the applicants when requesting artificial insemination facilities'.[30] Equally unsatisfactory was the nature of the instrument prohibiting the assistance sought by the applicants, namely a policy issued by the Secretary of State. For the Court, this did not allow for democratic debate, as Parliament had not had an opportunity to weigh the competing interests at stake and consider proportionality issues.[31]

Another weighty contribution of *Dickson* v. *The United Kingdom* to the consolidation of procreative rights was the rejection of 'the possibility of justifying the restriction of the applicants' Convention rights by the minimal number of persons adversely affected'.[32] This principle can also be applied against the denial of other procreative rights benefitting small segments of the population, such as the ban on the use of IVF and embryo screening by prospective parents who are carriers of genetic illnesses.[33]

26 *Dickson* v. *The United Kingdom* [GC], [75].
27 See ibid., [76].
28 See ibid., [81].
29 Ibid., [85].
30 Ibid., [82].
31 Ibid., [83].
32 Ibid., [84].
33 See Chapter 4, Section 4.3.

The right to pursue biological parenthood was indirectly cemented by the ECtHR's support for the right to know one's origins, which acknowledged the importance of genetic ties. In *Odièvre* v. *France*, the Grand Chamber stressed that 'a person's identity as a human being' is relevant to 'personal development', hence 'the vital interest protected by the Convention in obtaining information necessary to discover the truth concerning important aspects of one's personal identity, such as the identity of one's parents'.[34] Consequently, as emphasised in *Jäggi* v. *Switzerland*, cogent justifications are required for restrictions on the right to establish parentage.[35] *Mennesson* v. *France* further upheld 'the importance of biological parentage as a component of identity'[36] even in the context of reproductive methods running counter to public policy (e.g. surrogacy).[37] Andrew Bainham also noted a 'strongly genetic flavour' in the approach to parenthood in the UN Convention on the Rights of the Child (UNCRC), whose Article 7 proclaims 'the right of the child *from birth* "to know and be cared for by his or her parents", that is to say, surely, the mother and the genetic father'.[38] In addition, the value of genetic ties emerges distinctly from the Strasbourg case law on parenthood outside wedlock. As recalled in *Anayo* v. *Germany*, a child and his/her biological father 'are inalterably linked by a natural bond'.[39] Arguably, the right to know one's birth parents and the right to respect for the decision to have a biological child are symmetrical expressions of a broader right; in fact, a person's genetic make-up and linkage to a family are core components of their identity, both as ascendants and as descendants.

An absolute prohibition on IVF treatment, albeit not examined by the ECtHR, was found to violate several provisions of the American Convention on Human Rights (ACHR) in *Artavia Murillo et al.* v. *Costa Rica*: Article 5(1) (right to physical, mental and moral integrity), Article 7 (personal liberty), Article 11(2) (prohibition of arbitrary interference with private life and the family) and Article 17(2) (right to marry and raise a family); additionally, it amounted to indirect discrimination in relation to disability, gender and

34 See *Odièvre* v. *France* [GC], App. No. 42326/98, 13 February 2003, [29].

35 See *Jäggi* v. *Switzerland*, App. No. 58757/00, 13 July 2006, [37]: 'The right to an identity, which includes the right to know one's parentage, is an integral part of the notion of private life. In such cases, particularly rigorous scrutiny is called for when weighing up the competing interests.'

36 *Mennesson* v. *France*, App. No. 65192/11, 26 June 2014, [100].

37 See Section 2.4.

38 Andrew Bainham, 'Whose Sperm Is It Anyway?' (2003) 62(3) *Cambridge Law Journal* 566–570, at 569 (original emphasis).

39 *Anayo* v. *Germany*, App. No. 20578/07, 21 December 2010, [60].

financial situation.[40] Relying on Article 25 of the UN Convention on the Rights of Persons with Disabilities (CRPD), which requires States to take 'all appropriate measures' to ensure the right of such persons to enjoy 'the highest attainable standard of health',[41] the Inter-American Court of Human Rights (IACtHR) inferred a right 'to have access to the necessary techniques to resolve reproductive health problems'.[42]

Considering the wide definition of disability, extending to functional limitations, in the CRPD's Preamble, in Article 18 of the Additional Protocol to the American Convention[43] and in the Inter-American Convention for the Elimination of All Forms of Discrimination against Persons with Disabilities,[44] as well as the definition of infertility by the World Health Organisation as a 'disease of the reproductive system',[45] the IACtHR concluded that 'a disability is not defined exclusively by the presence of a physical, mental, intellectual or sensorial impairment, but ... it is interrelated to the barriers or limitations that exist in society for the individual to be able to exercise his rights effectively'.[46] In particular, 'infertility is a functional limitation recognized as a disease' and requires special measures of protection.[47] Additionally, due to the existence of stereotypes in society (acknowledged but not validated by the IACtHR),[48] whereby the woman's status is often defined by motherhood,[49] and due to the fact that 'the use of assisted reproduction technologies is especially related to the woman's body', the ban on IVF 'has a disproportionately negative impact on women'.[50] Finally, 'the ban on IVF had a disproportionate impact on infertile couples who did not have the financial resources to undergo IVF abroad'.[51]

The respondent's justification for the ban, namely avoiding embryonic loss, gave the IACtHR an opportunity to assess the relative importance of the

40 *Artavia Murillo et al. ('In Vitro Fertilisation')* v. *Costa Rica*, Case No. 12.361, 28 November 2012.
41 Convention on the Rights of People with Disabilities, New York, 13 December 2006, in force 3 May 2008, UNTS vol. 2515 (p. 3).
42 *Artavia Murillo et al.* v. *Costa Rica*, [289].
43 Additional Protocol to the American Convention in the Area of Economic, Social and Cultural Rights, San Salvador, 17 November 1988, in force 16 November 1999.
44 Inter-American Convention for the Elimination of All Forms of Discrimination against Persons with Disabilities, Guatemala City, 8 June 1999, in force 14 September 2001.
45 See *Artavia Murillo et al.* v. *Costa Rica*, [288].
46 Ibid., [291].
47 Ibid., [293].
48 Ibid., [302].
49 Ibid., [294]–[296].
50 Ibid., [302].
51 Ibid., [303].

protection of the embryo when compared to infertile couples' rights. The IACtHR criticised the absolute protection of the embryo in the domestic court's decision, which, by failing to weigh up competing rights, 'involved an arbitrary and excessive interference in private and family life', compounded by 'discriminatory effects'.[52] On the one hand, the impact of IVF treatment on the protection of prenatal life was said to be limited, since the risk of embryonic loss is also present in natural pregnancy, and before implantation embryos do not enjoy the right to life enshrined in Article 4 ACHR;[53] on the other hand, the Court emphasised 'the severity of the limitation of the rights involved in this case as compared to the importance of the protection of the embryo', in particular 'the effects on the rights to personal integrity, personal liberty, private life, intimacy, reproductive autonomy, access to reproductive health services, and to found a family', which 'are annulled for those persons whose only possible treatment for infertility is IVF'.[54] The incompatibility with ACHR provisions of the absolute prohibition on IVF was reiterated by the Inter-American Commission on Human Rights in *Gómez Murillo and Others* v. *Costa Rica*.[55]

The Strasbourg Court has faced more detailed questions on access to IVF as opposed to total bans. For instance, in *Lia v. Malta*, it was called upon to consider the rejection of a couple's request for a self-funded second homologous IVF procedure owing to the woman's age.[56] The ECtHR held that the interference was not 'in accordance with the law', because the judicial and administrative authorities' interpretation and application of the statute lacked consistency and foreseeability. Specifically, the administrative authorities had interpreted the word 'desirable' as 'mandatory' in the statutory guidance on eligibility and applied this version without consideration of individual circumstances, despite the highest courts' contrary interpretation.[57] The least favourable interpretation was thus applied and the one 'most at odds with the clear wording of the law, as supported by its drafters as well as the highest courts'.[58]

[52] Ibid., [316].
[53] Ibid., [315].
[54] Ibid., [314].
[55] *Gómez Murillo and Others* v. *Costa Rica*, Report No. 1/15, Case 12.798 (Merits), 29 January 2015, [39]–[44]. The report was followed by a friendly settlement, noted by the IACtHR in *Gómez Murillo and Others* v. *Costa Rica*, Case No. 12.798, 29 November 2016, [11], [44]–[48].
[56] *Lia* v. *Malta*, App. No. 8709/20, 5 May 2022. Other aspects of IVF regulation challenged in Strasbourg proceedings concerned the use of donated gametes and posthumous treatment; see Sections 2.2 and 2.3.
[57] *Lia* v. *Malta*, [56], [63]–[69].
[58] Ibid., [66].

The Court did not proceed to a substantive analysis of the age limit of forty-three, because the interference failed the first hurdle (legality); nor did the Court find it necessary to examine the discrimination claim separately. However, the Court has addressed a discrimination case based on the prospective mother's age in relation to adoption. In *Schwizgebel* v. *Switzerland*, concerning the refusal to allow a forty-seven-year-old single woman to adopt a second child, the Court accepted that there was no common denominator in Europe as regards the upper age limits for adopters, and hence the respondent had acted within the boundaries of its broad margin of appreciation.[59] Future litigation might establish whether the narrower margin in relation to procreative autonomy yields different results.

2.1.2 *Gamete Providers' Right to Use Their Embryos for Reproductive Purposes*

The legal status of the embryo remains an unsettled issue in international human rights law. Questions of when human life begins and whether the embryo or the foetus have any autonomous rights were deferred to States in cases challenging the authorisation of an abortion without consulting the father of the unborn child and the non-criminalisation of medical errors causing an involuntary abortion.

In *Paton* v. *The United Kingdom*, the former Commission concluded that the use of the term 'everyone' in the Convention (Articles 1, 5, 6, 8–11, 13) 'is such that it can apply only postnatally', although prenatal application in a rare case (e.g. under Article 6 (1)) 'cannot be entirely excluded'.[60] Moreover, the decision noted that the express limitations in Article 2 (death penalty, deprivation of life during law enforcement operations) suggest that it does not address prenatal life, because 'all the above limitations, by their nature, concern persons already born and cannot be applied to the foetus'.[61] Therefore, cumulatively, the general use of the term 'everyone' and the contexts in which it is used in Article 2 'tend to support the view that it does not include the unborn'.[62] The Commission recalled, *a contrario*, the express protection of life 'since the moment of conception' in Article 4(1) ACHR.[63] It also acknowledged 'the wide divergence of thinking on the question of

[59] *Schwizgebel* v. *Switzerland*, App. No. 25762/07, 10 June 2010.
[60] *Paton* v. *The United Kingdom*, App. No. 8416/78, 13 May 1980 (Commission), [7].
[61] Ibid., [8].
[62] Ibid., [9].
[63] Ibid., [11].

where life begins', whether 'with conception' or 'upon the moment of nidation, upon the point that the foetus becomes "viable", or upon live birth'.[64] The Commission noted that construing Article 2 as protecting life since conception in absolute terms could compromise the expectant woman's right to life, in that it would prohibit an abortion even where the continuance of the pregnancy poses serious risks to the woman's life, effectively assigning unborn life higher value than the life of the pregnant woman.[65] The Commission discounted this interpretation insofar as 'contrary to the object and purpose of the Convention', given that, in 1950, all signatories permitted abortion when necessary to save the life of the mother, and abortion laws had since evolved towards further liberalisation.[66] It also held that, even assuming that Article 2 applied to the foetus at the initial stage of pregnancy, there was an implied limitation, designed to protect the life and health of the woman.[67]

As regards the male progenitor's rights under Article 8, the Commission found that the authorisation of the abortion interfered with his family life, but that interference was necessary for the protection of the rights of others, namely his wife, seeking 'to avert the risk of injury to her physical or mental health'.[68] The ancillary claim – that the law denied the father of the foetus a right to be consulted about a proposed abortion – was judged inadmissible *ratione materiae*; in fact, the Convention could not guarantee procedural rights vis-à-vis an abortion the pregnant woman intends to have performed on her, given the latter's right to respect for her private life as 'the person primarily concerned in the pregnancy and its continuation or termination'.[69]

In *Vo* v. *France*,[70] the Grand Chamber recognised that, while 'there is no consensus on the nature and status of the embryo and/or foetus', it is common ground among ECHR States that they 'belong to the human race', and that 'the potentiality of that being and its capacity to become a person . . . require protection in the name of human dignity, without making it a "person" with the "right to life" for the purposes of Article 2'.[71] The Court dismissed the applicant's argument that the unintentional killing of an unborn child as a result of medical negligence ought to be classified as manslaughter, entitling the parent to institute criminal proceedings; instead, it regarded an action for

64 Ibid., [12].
65 Ibid., [19].
66 Ibid., [20].
67 Ibid., [23].
68 Ibid., [26].
69 Ibid., [27].
70 *Vo* v. *France* [GC], App. No. 53924/00, 8 July 2004.
71 Ibid., [84].

damages in the administrative courts as an effective remedy.[72] The Strasbourg assessment of the rights of embryos/foetuses in *Vo* is broadly aligned with the IACtHR's stance in *Artavia Murillo* v. *Costa Rica* on the 'gradual and incremental protection of prenatal life'.[73]

The legal treatment of cryopreserved embryos engages not only their protection in the name of human dignity but also the rights of the progenitors: the right to respect for the decision to become genetic parents, and privacy rights, insofar as their genetic material is linked to their identity. The contribution of Strasbourg case law to placing human rights constraints on the regulation of the use of embryos has been twofold. First, the Court has recognised the applicability of Article 8 to decisions regarding the use of embryos destined to generate a pregnancy. Second, it has confirmed that respect for private life includes, in principle, an individual's right to decide the fate of embryos no longer intended for a pregnancy.

The issue of Article 8 rights in private disputes over frozen embryos intended for procreation arose in *Evans* v. *The United Kingdom*. The case concerned the absolute ban on the use of embryos by one progenitor after the other withdrew consent thereto, even where the former could not produce further gametes and the latter had given consent in contemplation of this precise circumstance. The applicant had resorted to IVF treatment with her partner before receiving cancer treatment, which entailed the removal of her ovaries and the loss of her ability to produce ova. After the creation of the embryos, the relationship had broken down and the man had asked the clinic to destroy the embryos, relying on the right provided by law to withdraw consent any time prior to implantation. Domestic courts had upheld that right. In Strasbourg proceedings, the applicant complained that the destruction of the embryos, depriving her of the only chance of having a genetic child, would breach her Article 8 rights.

For the Court, the dispute engaged two irreconcilable rights: the right to become a parent and the right not to become a parent; to allow either the use or the destruction of the embryos would have led to the interests of one party to the treatment or the other 'being wholly frustrated'.[74] Couching one of the rights at stake as 'the right not to become a parent' distorted the reality of the parties' positions. Coerced parenthood is different from a bar on unilateral retraction from consensual, jointly planned parenthood, when the other party stands to lose everything if retraction is permitted. Mr Jones had voluntarily

72 Ibid., [94].

73 *Artavia Murillo et al.* v. *Costa Rica*, [264].

74 *Evans* v. *The United Kingdom* [GC], [73].

embarked upon fertility treatment with his partner for the purpose of enabling her to have a genetic child after her ovarian cancer treatment. Once a woman becomes (deliberately or accidentally) pregnant, the man cannot assert his right 'not to become a parent' at any cost, for example, by compelling the woman to undergo an abortion. Although the woman's physical self-determination is not at stake when the embryos are outside her body, other aspects of her privacy are involved. While the ECtHR majority interpreted the *Evans* complaint as requiring some positive obligation from the State,[75] authorising the destruction of the applicant's genetic material went beyond a decision not to offer her affirmative assistance to have a genetic child. Rather, it was an active interference with her rights over her own genetic material and her *existing* chances at motherhood. The ruling overlooked the fact that domestic courts had authorised the destruction of the applicant's own genetic material – indeed, her only surviving procreative material. The Dissenting Opinion perceptively emphasised that 'the act of destroying an embryo also involves destroying the applicant's eggs'.[76] Arguably, once the procreative treatment is well underway, the ability of the male progenitor to reject fatherhood should be rather exceptional and subordinated to a judicial determination that weighs competing interests. Allowing the man to destroy joint embryos *at will* undervalues the physical and financial costs of ova extraction, fails to protect the dignity and potentiality for life of the embryos and inflicts greater psychological harm on the woman where the destruction of embryos entails childlessness *tout court*.

Moreover, the analysis in *Evans* is predicated on the equal worth of the rights at stake: purportedly, the Court 'does not consider that the applicant's right to respect for the decision to become a parent in the genetic sense should be accorded greater weight than J.'s right to respect for his decision not to have a genetically related child with her'.[77] However, in practice, the judgment protected the man's right not to have *this child* at the expense of the woman's right to *ever* have *any child* at all. Therefore, it attached *greater* – not *as great* – importance to his right, instead of avoiding 'the unjust preservation of one person's right by negating the rights of the other'.[78] The dissenters' account of the implications of the decision for one party is compelling:

[75] Ibid., [76].
[76] *Evans* v. *The United Kingdom* [GC], Joint Dissenting Opinion of Judges Türmen et al., [8].
[77] *Evans* v. *The United Kingdom* [GC], [90].
[78] Jacco Bomhoff and Lorenzo Zucca, 'The Tragedy of Ms Evans: Conflicts and Incommensurability of Rights, *Evans* v. *The United Kingdom*, Fourth Section Judgment of 7 March 2006, Application No 6339/05' (2006) 2(3) *European Constitutional Law Review* 424–442, at 429.

> The majority's approach resulted not simply in the applicant's decision to have a genetically related child being thwarted but in the effective eradication of any possibility of her having a genetically related child, thus rendering any such decision now or at any later time meaningless.[79]

As expected, the Court afforded the respondent a wide margin of appreciation in regulating IVF treatment, insofar as it 'gives rise to sensitive moral and ethical issues against a background of fast-moving medical and scientific developments' and 'there is no clear common ground amongst the member States'.[80] However, considering the importance of the matters at stake to the individual (a criterion recognised in *Dickson* a few months later), an inflexible rule applying regardless of personal circumstances and with no recourse in case of dispute should have been found outside the scope of State discretion. According to the Grand Chamber, 'the absolute nature of the rule served to promote legal certainty and to avoid the problems of arbitrariness and inconsistency inherent in weighing, on a case-by-case basis, what the Court of Appeal described as "entirely incommensurable" interests'.[81] Yet, only the opportunity for a case-by-case assessment can avoid a disproportionate impact on an individual. In other judgments, bright-line rules preventing tailored decisions were deemed intrinsically disproportionate – for example, irreducible life sentences, the blanket prohibition on prisoners' right to vote, prisoners' lack of access to ART facilities;[82] the *Evans* situation was no different. Additionally, as Nicole Gallus has perceptively noted, the preference for the general and abstract norm over the norm's application to the individual case is incompatible with the principle of effective protection of Article 8 rights.[83]

Regrettably, the Court attached insufficient weight to several case-specific facts when accepting the respondent's balancing exercise as appropriate. First, for the now-infertile woman, authorising the destruction of embryos brought about the complete loss of any chance at parenthood, rather than a one-off interference with the use of her genetic material in a particular instance.[84]

79 *Evans* v. *The United Kingdom* [GC], Joint Dissenting Opinion of Judges Türmen et al., [6].
80 *Evans* v. *The United Kingdom* [GC], [81].
81 Ibid., [89].
82 See Carmen Draghici, *The Legitimacy of Family Rights in Strasbourg Case Law: 'Living Instrument' or Extinguished Sovereignty?* (Oxford: Hart, 2017) 142–143.
83 Nicole Gallus, 'La procréation médicalement assistée et la jurisprudence de la Court européenne des droits de l'homme', in Nicole Gallus (ed.), *Droit des familles, genre et sexualité* (Limal: Anthemis, 2012) 203–225, at 216.
84 See Craig Lind, '*Evans v United Kingdom* – Judgments of Solomon: Power, Gender and Procreation' (2006) 18(4) *Child and Family Law Quarterly* 576–592, at 587: 'I . . . do not wholly approve of the obsession we have with raising our own children, but I understand that we have this desire embedded (socially) within us. . . . If having a child genetically related to a

Second, both gamete providers had embarked upon IVF treatment specifically to preserve the woman's ability to have a biological child following the removal of her ovaries. Third, the male partner had given reassurances that he would not oppose the future use of the embryos, despite the legal opportunity to reconsider, especially since the woman was accommodating *his* desire for future children related to both of them; the woman had relied on her partner's reassurances to her detriment (by fertilising her ova with donor sperm, she would have retained sole control over the embryos), and the law should have made provision for a bar on withdrawal of consent to avoid situations of injustice. Fourth, the impact on the applicant of not having a biological child was unmitigated, whereas the male partner could have acted as a donor, relinquishing parental status.[85] Finally, unlike sperm donation, ova extraction is an invasive surgical procedure, and the substantially unequal contribution of the parties to the creation of the embryo ought to give the female participant protection against the change of mind of the male participant, at least in extreme circumstances such as the case at hand. The disproportionate power given to the male partner – while the process of creating embryos was much more onerous for the female partner – and his lack of accountability for breach of promise, at the expense of the woman's last hope for genetic motherhood, make for an unbalanced scheme.

The absence of any legal recourse against the automatism of the law is all the more problematic in the context of private agreements, potentially vitiated by undue influence or misrepresentation. Effective protection of Article 8 rights extends to protection against third-party conduct. The law challenged in *Evans* gave the man an unqualified right to withdraw consent, compounded by the courts' refusal to treat his self-binding promise as a waiver of his statutory right. This application of the law was particularly rigid against the background of English law's treatment of verbal agreements as enforceable when ignoring them would have unconscionable results (e.g. in case of detrimental reliance on an agreement to share property, in relation to

person remains of considerable importance in this society, we should be slow to terminate a person's final capacity to do so – even if to do so would compel another, who wishes to avoid genetic parenthood, into parenthood.'

85 This is not to downplay the psychological implications of knowing that a genetic child exists and is raised by someone else; domestic courts had noted that 'J.'s clear position in withdrawing his consent was one of fundamental rather than purely financial objection' (*Evans* v. *The United Kingdom* [GC], [24]). However, treating the man as an anonymous donor where *his* change of mind permanently ends the woman's chance at parenthood is a more balanced compromise than affording the man no accountability at the woman's expense.

constructive trusts and proprietary estoppel);[86] the law of nullity also recognises waivers of a statutory right through conduct, barring an application for annulment on grounds of, for example, pregnancy by another man if the husband encouraged the wife to believe that he would not avail himself of the option to have the marriage annulled.[87] Additionally, legal certainty cannot take priority over the need to avoid disproportionate adverse effects on a person's rights. While Ms Evans had made a conscious decision to fertilise her ova with her partner's (as opposed to donor) gametes, the law placed the entire responsibility for the outcome of the reproductive arrangement on the woman, penalising her for trusting her partner's reassurances, rather than holding him accountable for misleading her.

According to Judit Sándor, 'the Court recognized that [in cases of *in vitro* treatment] the father's right not to become a parent should prevail over the woman's interest in becoming a mother'.[88] This may be an unwarranted extrapolation, because the Court conceded that a different legislative scheme, permitting the woman's use of the embryos, would have also been compliant with the Convention.[89] However, the ruling sanctioned as acceptable an unbalanced approach to competing rights. The interest in protecting the embryos from destruction if at least one progenitor wanted them to survive should have further tipped the balance in favour of the woman's position, if the two rights of the former partners were otherwise equally worthy of protection.

The ECtHR's dismissal of the discrimination claim in *Evans* was also unsatisfactory. For the Court, the law did not discriminate against the applicant when compared to women who could conceive naturally 'because the reasons given for finding that there was no violation of Article 8 also afford a reasonable and objective justification under Article 14'.[90] While the balance struck between gamete providers' rights may have been found in principle justified, a different balancing exercise was required in the case of a woman in the applicant's position. The bright-line rule treated dissimilar cases alike: a woman having lost her capacity to produce further oocytes, therefore

86 See Jonathan Herring, *Family Law* (Harlow: Pearson, 2021, 10th ed.) 185–189, 193–196.

87 See s. 13(1) Matrimonial Causes Act 1973.

88 Judit Sándor, 'Bioethics and Basic Rights: Persons, Humans, and Boundaries of Life', in Michel Rosenfeld and András Sajó (eds.), *The Oxford Handbook of Comparative Constitutional Law* (Oxford: Oxford University Press, 2012) 1142–1162, at 1149.

89 *Evans* v. *The United Kingdom* [GC], [91].

90 Ibid., [95].

dependent on existing embryos to achieve genetic parenthood, and a woman who can conceive naturally or undergo fertilisation treatment again. ECHR case law recognises that treating unlike situations alike, to the detriment of the category insufficiently distinguished in its special needs, constitutes reverse discrimination. As held in *Thlimmenos* v. *Greece*:

> The right not to be discriminated against in the enjoyment of the rights guaranteed under the Convention is also violated when States without an objective and reasonable justification fail to treat differently persons whose situations are significantly different.[91]

The rule allowing the man to withdraw consent to the use of the embryos at any stage affected a woman with impaired reproductive capacity differently. She was denied not just the child potentially born through that course of treatment but also any future child. This unnuanced law failed to protect her against the bad faith of a partner prevailing upon her to create joint embryos. The clarity of the rule does not relieve the State from an obligation to ensure that persons whose characteristics or circumstances make them vulnerable in respect of reproduction are adequately safeguarded (the law should recognise the vulnerability of a woman facing cancer, preparing for infertility and having one opportunity to choose joint children with her partner over single motherhood with the use of an anonymous donor). For instance, in similar circumstances, the law could only permit the creation of embryos with a man's sperm if he gives irrevocable consent. This is regardless of any European consensus on the substantive rules of IVF treatment and embryo cryopreservation. To be ECHR-compliant, the domestic scheme cannot be excessively detrimental to one party to ART. The Strasbourg Court ought to have required special measures of protection in cases of impaired procreative capacity, departing from the general rule on withdrawal of consent.

An interesting example of accommodation of exceptional circumstances is offered by the UK Supreme Court's ruling in *Whittington Hospital NHS Trust* v. *XX*, addressing the issue of compensation for the loss of procreative capacity.[92] Several negligent tests had failed to detect the claimant's cervical cancer before it was too advanced for her to retain the ability to bear her own child. The judgment awarded the woman the cost of donor ova and a commercial surrogacy abroad. This solution is highly innovative, inasmuch as it afforded the victim a remedy clashing with the domestic prohibition of

[91] *Thlimmenos* v. *Greece* [GC], App. No. 34369/97, 6 April 2000, [44].
[92] *Whittington Hospital NHS Trust* v. *XX* [2020] UKSC 14.

commercial surrogacy.[93] It thereby acknowledged that exceptions from the rules may be necessary to ensure effective respect for the right to have a child.

The IVF regime sanctioned in *Evans* presented two further discriminatory features. First, as Lind has noted, the mutual continued consent rule merely offered *formal* equality between men and women (both being able to withdraw consent before implantation); sperm storage has the same chances of fertilisation as embryo storage, whereas ova storage is less successful, making women dependent on embryos to increase the likelihood of conception and subjecting them to the male veto.[94] Men can also store sperm unilaterally – with minimal costs and no physical discomfort or risks – for future use in case the woman withdraws consent. In practice, the right to reconsider only benefitted men, whereas the partner's withdrawal of consent only affected women. It was therefore open to the ECtHR to conclude that the rule failed to achieve substantive equality.

Second, this de facto inequality was deepened by the law's failure to acknowledge 'the difference in the burden of physical involvement in the procedure' of creating embryos, that is, the lengthy hormonal treatment for women and the invasive extraction of ova.[95] In fact, the woman is 'the locus of medical treatment' in IVF procedures, including when infertility arises from a male factor: she receives injections to stimulate her ovaries, and she is put under general anaesthesia for her oocytes to be aspirated.[96] The oocyte retrieval procedure is very different from sperm donation; oocytes 'are obtained through an ultrasound-guided needle inserted into the ovaries through the vaginal wall'.[97]

Douglas has suggested that 'the woman's interest in the fate of the in vivo embryo is much greater, since she must carry it and bear the risks, while the stored embryo presents no such problem and its genitors are in an equal position'.[98] However, the woman's interest in stored embryos is also superior to the man's, given the financial costs, the physical and psychological burden and the health risks involved in obtaining ova to create other embryos. Her

93 See s. 2(1) Surrogacy Arrangements Act 1985. For Lord Carnwarth, dissenting, it would go against the principle of legal coherence for civil courts to award damages based on conduct which, in the UK, would conflict with criminal law.

94 See Lind, '*Evans v United Kingdom*', 587–588. See further ibid., 588: 'The *de facto* privileging of one gender is as unacceptable in law as is (unlawful) direct discrimination.'

95 See Sándor, 'Bioethics and Basic Rights', 1149.

96 Lisa Rubin and Aliza Phillips, 'Infertility and Assisted Reproduction Technologies: Matters of Reproductive Justice', in Joan Chrisler (ed.), *Reproductive Justice: A Global Concern* (Santa Barbara: Praeger, 2012) 173–199, at 177–178.

97 Ibid., 192 (note 10).

98 Douglas, *Law, Fertility and Reproduction*, 127.

investment in in vitro embryos is higher, and her ability to replace destroyed embryos lower. For genuine equality to be achieved, the man's consent to the provision of sperm for the creation of embryos should arguably be irrevocable, with possible mitigations, such as an option for him to convert his initial agreement into sperm donation and be released from parental obligations.[99] This solution would reconcile, rather than choose between, incompatible rights.

Even making allowance for the light-touch nature of international supervision in the sensitive area of assisted reproduction, the Grand Chamber in *Evans* v. *The United Kingdom* failed to address the crux of the case: whether States are required to protect the right to have a biological child against the blunt application of indiscriminate laws, which only secure formal equality between the parties to the assisted reproduction process and do not cater for exceptional circumstances.

Where there is no conflict between private interests in reproduction, a person's rights in relation to their genetic material acquire even greater force. The ECtHR recognised in *Knecht* v. *Romania* that Article 8 may be breached whenever State authorities prevent a person from using embryos containing their genetic material and obstruct their reproductive plans. The applicant in this case had her frozen embryos stored at a private fertility clinic. Further to a criminal investigation into that clinic's accreditation, the applicant's embryos had been seized by the authorities and deposited elsewhere. Her request to have the embryos retrieved and transferred to a specialised clinic of her choice, licensed to carry out IVF procedures, was initially refused. The applicant complained about the difficulties in securing the transfer of the embryos to a licensed clinic, which had prevented her from progressing with her planned IVF treatment.

The *Knecht* judgment reaffirmed the right to respect for the decision to become a parent and 'to make use of medically assisted procreation'.[100] The ECtHR agreed that the applicant's private life had been affected, since the Romanian authorities had temporarily prevented her from using her embryos. It was not disputed that the interference arising from the placement of the embryos in custody during the investigation pursued legitimate aims: the prevention of crime, the protection of health or morals and the protection of

99 If the woman reconsiders, there are no compelling reasons to allow the man to use the embryos to become a father with another woman or through gestational surrogacy, unless he is unable to produce new sperm. Naturally, the female gamete provider may consent to repurposing the embryos and her treatment as a donor.

100 *Knecht* v. *Romania*, [54].

the rights and freedom of others.[101] The parties' arguments focused on the necessity of the measure. The ECtHR reasoned that domestic courts had ultimately ordered the transfer of the embryos to an authorised specialist clinic, acknowledged that the authorities' refusal to allow the transfer breached the applicant's Article 8 rights, and offered redress, and the judgment had been enforced within a relatively short period of time. The respondent had therefore complied with its obligations to secure respect for the applicant's private life.[102] This suggested, *a contrario*, that significant delays in gaining access to stored embryos for the purpose of IVF treatment would constitute a disproportionate interference.

Indeed, *Nedescu* v. *Romania* presented the Court with a case concerning protracted obstacles to the use of frozen embryos. A married couple had undergone successful IVF treatment at a private clinic and had the remaining embryos cryogenised and deposited with the clinic for a second pregnancy. Following a criminal investigation into its authorisation, the clinic was closed, and the prosecuting authorities seized all genetic material stored there; the applicants' embryos were transferred between different public bodies, and the bureaucratic requirements for their retrieval changed repeatedly.[103] Although, as in *Knecht*, the couple obtained a High Court order permitting them to retrieve the embryos, they were unable to enforce it. During the attempts to retrieve the embryos, it was ascertained that Ms Nedescu's state of health did not allow her to undergo another ovarian stimulation, which made the couple entirely reliant on using the existing embryos before they became non-viable or got damaged. In Strasbourg proceedings, the applicants claimed that, overall, the various public authorities' conduct amounted to a disproportionate interference with their private and family life; for over six years, they had not been allowed to use their embryos for a new insemination procedure, thereby irreversibly losing the chance of having another child.

[101] Ibid., [57].
[102] Ibid., [61].
[103] The embryos were initially placed in the custody of the Institute of Forensic Medicine (IFM); the applicants were advised that, to retrieve them, they had to be accompanied by an embryologist and provide a special container with liquid nitrogen for the transfer to a different clinic. Having done so, they were instead told that they had to obtain the approval of the National Transplant Agency (NTA) for the transfer; this was denied due to the prosecutorial authorities' irregular transfer of embryos to the IFM, which was not accredited as a bank of genetic material. The investigating authorities appointed a public hospital as the new custodian, which raised unreasonably high bureaucratic hurdles for the retrieval (to be accompanied by an NTA representative, an embryologist from the closed clinic and a representative of the prosecutorial authorities). The applicants unsuccessfully asked the public prosecutor's office to appoint them as custodians of the embryos.

The *Nedescu* judgment relied on the Court's earlier jurisprudence, developed in the context of surrogacy, on the relevance of 'a genuine intention' to become parents 'both for their right to respect for their decision to become parents, and for their personal development through the role of parents that they wished to assume vis-à-vis the child'.[104] The Court held that 'the joint parental project of the applicants ... is an intimate aspect of their private life'.[105] It distinguished the case from *Knecht*, in that the refusal by various administrative authorities to comply with judicial orders to return the embryos had deprived the couple from the possibility of having another child.[106] The Court found that the interference was not 'in accordance with the law', as required by Article 8(2):[107] by preventing the applicants from retrieving their embryos, despite a court order, the authorities had interfered with their right to respect for their private life in a manner not provided for by law. This allowed the Court to conclude that Article 8 had been breached without having to examine the aim and proportionality of the interference.[108]

2.1.3 *The Right to Decide the Fate of Embryos No Longer Intended for a Pregnancy*

Reproductive autonomy claims are also indirectly advanced by the recognition in Strasbourg case law of a qualified right for gamete providers to decide the fate of embryos no longer intended for a pregnancy. The Court's approach to the issue of 'custody' of such embryos expands self-determination rights from the ability to make decisions over one's own body[109] to decisions about one's genetic material. In *Parrillo* v. *Italy*,[110] the Grand Chamber was called upon to rule on the right to decide the fate of one's embryos, specifically the right to donate them to scientific research. The applicant had started IVF treatment with her partner and no longer wished to proceed with the embryo implantation after his death. She complained that the clinic refused to release the embryos to her, so that she could donate them to scientific research,

[104] *Nedescu* v. *Romania*, [67], citing *Paradiso and Campanelli* v. *Italy* [GC], App. No. 25358/12, 24 January 2017, [163]–[164].

[105] *Nedescu* v. *Romania*, [70], citing *Knecht* v. *Romania*, [54].

[106] *Nedescu* v. *Romania*, [72].

[107] See ibid., [84]: 'The manner in which the judicial and administrative authorities involved implemented and interpreted the relevant legal provisions concerning the seizure, the storage following such a seizure and the return of the applicants' embryos was incoherent and thus lacked the required foreseeability.'

[108] Ibid., [86]–[87].

[109] See *Pretty* v. *The United Kingdom*, App. No. 2346/02, 29 April 2002.

[110] *Parrillo* v. *Italy* [GC], App. No. 46470/11, 27 August 2015.

compelling her to keep them in cryopreservation until natural death. The complaint relied on both Article 8 (respect for private life) and Article 1 of Protocol No. 1 (protection of property).

Importantly, the Court recognised 'the link existing between the person who has undergone *in vitro* fertilisation and the embryos thus conceived', because 'the embryos contain the genetic material of the person in question and accordingly represent a constituent part of that person's genetic material and biological identity'.[111] Consequently, Article 8 applied to a person's ability to dispose of their embryos. Indeed, 'the applicant's ability to exercise a conscious and considered choice regarding the fate of her embryos concerns an intimate aspect of her personal life and accordingly relates to her right to self-determination'.[112] Conversely, the complaint under Article 1 of Protocol No. 1 was dismissed as incompatible *ratione materiae*: 'Human embryos cannot be reduced to "possessions", given the "economic and pecuniary scope" of that provision.'[113]

Under Article 8, the ban on donating embryos no longer intended for implantation to scientific research was found to interfere with privacy rights.[114] The ECtHR accepted that the 'protection of the embryo's potential for life', invoked by the respondent, 'may be linked to the aim of protecting morals and the rights and freedoms of others'.[115] It stressed, however, confirming the view in *Vo* v. *France*, that it was not thereby taking a position on whether the word 'others' in Article 8(2) extends to human embryos.[116] As regards the 'morals' justification for the restriction, the applicant challenged the consistency of Italian legislation (an argument previously successful in *Costa and Pavan* v. *Italy*),[117] because researchers could lawfully use cell lines obtained from embryos destroyed abroad. For the Court, this was not a circumstance directly affecting the applicant and therefore it was irrelevant.[118] This assessment arguably misreads the applicant's observation, which did not concern proportionality (to which impact is relevant), but the credibility of the moral ground invoked.[119] Arguably, even conceding that the State's interest in

[111] Ibid., [158].
[112] Ibid., [159]; reiterated in *Nedescu* v. *Romania*, [68].
[113] *Parrillo* v. *Italy* [GC], [215].
[114] See ibid., [161].
[115] Ibid., [167].
[116] Ibid.
[117] *Costa and Pavan* v. *Italy*, App. No. 54270/10, 28 August 2012, [71]. See further Chapter 4, Section 4.3.1.
[118] See *Parrillo* v. *Italy* [GC], [189]–[192].
[119] Admittedly, 'the deliberate and active destruction of a human embryo cannot be compared with the use of cell lines obtained from human embryos destroyed at an earlier stage' (ibid.,

protecting embryos trumped self-determination rights, that interest was not served by their preservation until natural disintegration. The second legitimate aim identified in *Parrillo* as a basis for the ban was the right to self-determination of the deceased partner whose gametes had contributed to the embryos; in fact, there was no evidence that he would have wished to donate them to medical research.[120] Additionally, the Court afforded the State a wide margin of appreciation on delicate moral and ethical questions in the absence of European consensus. It further attached weight to the extensive parliamentary debates leading to the enactment of the relevant legislation, during which all the rights and interests at stake had been considered. The Court concluded that Italy had not overstepped its margin of appreciation.

Significantly, the decision was influenced by the consideration that donating embryos to scientific research was not one of the core rights under Article 8, by contrast with the use of embryos for procreative purposes. This indicates that the Court is prepared to engage in closer scrutiny of measures interfering with the use of one's embryos when it affects the right to become a parent:

> The instant case does not concern prospective parenthood. Accordingly, while it is of course important, the right ... to donate embryos to scientific research is not one of the core rights attracting the protection of Article 8 of the Convention, as it does not concern a particularly important aspect of the applicant's existence and identity.[121]

For some commentators, the *Parrillo* judgment 'is a strong foundation for the pro-life movement', in that 'the Court moved away from allowing a parent to have complete control over the fate of an embryo'.[122] This may be an overstatement. Firstly, the ban on donation to research did not ensure the survival of the embryos, but merely their cryopreservation until natural death (unlike the donation of the embryos for a third-party pregnancy). Secondly, an important rationale underlying the Court's decision was the equal self-determination right of the deceased progenitor, whose intentions could not be ascertained; it is not obvious if, in case of embryos conceived with donor sperm, the public interest would trump the woman's rights, or if the same outcome would be reached when both progenitors support donation to

[194]). However, complicity in a practice seen as morally repugnant (and encouraging it by offering an outlet) casts doubt on the justification for interfering with privacy rights.

120 Ibid., [196].

121 Ibid., [174].

122 Palmer Hurst and Christina Hurst, 'Baby Steps: The European Court of Human Rights Moves Closer to Protecting the Unborn in *Parrillo v. Italy*' (2015) (2) *Journal of Global Justice and Public Policy* 155–163, at 156.

research. Indeed, the judicial recognition of the progenitors' decisional autonomy in relation to embryos no longer intended for procreation is not unremarkable, as this is an area of ethical controversy. Some question the priority of parental consent over the interests of the embryos (e.g. to be used by another patient), of the scientific community or of society at large.[123]

The *Parrillo* case left several questions unanswered. First, should the parties contributing genetic material to the embryo be seen as 'joint tenants', leaving the use of the embryos to the survivor in case one of them dies? Arguably, the surviving partner's rights, especially prospective parenthood, are more immediate and compelling and should prevail over the unascertainable wishes and more remote interests of the deceased. A parallel with joint custody of children/shared parental responsibility may be informative. If one parent dies, it is incumbent on the other to make all the decisions about the child's upbringing, even going against the wishes of the deceased parent (as evinced by past decisions or court proceedings regarding the choice of religion, education or medical treatment); for example, the deceased parent may have formerly objected to the change of surname or relocation abroad, but no legal dispute arises once there is only one holder of parental authority.

Moreover, since the deceased intended the embryos for joint parenthood, once that purpose is frustrated by death, the legislator is ill-placed to infer the deceased's wishes (donation for a pregnancy/donation to research/destruction/cryopreservation until natural death). The next of kin is often permitted to make decisions such as the authorisation to harvest the deceased's organs for donation and transplant; this is predicated on the closer link between the deceased and their immediate family. A global survey, reviewing the practice of fifty-four States (75 per cent of States with an organ donation programme, according to the World Health Organisation), has concluded that the next of kin are involved in the organ procurement process in most nations, regardless of whether the wishes of the deceased to be a donor were expressed or unknown.[124] For most of the jurisdictions requiring explicit consent to organ donation, the next of kin's consent is necessary even if the deceased's wishes are documented;[125] in many cases, the next of kin can veto donation notwithstanding the deceased's express advance consent, as the law takes into account

[123] See Ruth Deech and Anna Smajdor, *From IVF to Immortality: Controversy in the Era of Reproductive Technology* (Oxford and New York: Oxford University Press, 2007) 42.

[124] Amanda Rosenblum, Lucy Horvat, Laura Siminoff, Versha Prakash, Janice Beitel and Amit Garg, 'The Authority of Next-of-Kin in Explicit and Presumed Consent Systems for Deceased Organ Donation: An Analysis of 54 Nations' (2012) 27(6) *Nephrology Dialysis Transplantation* 2533–2546, at 2541.

[125] Ibid., 2543.

the impact on the family.[126] If the next of kin can make decisions about the deceased's organs, and the law deems it compatible with the deceased's autonomy rights and human dignity,[127] they should also be entitled to decide the fate of embryos conceived with the deceased's gametes, especially joint embryos, containing their own genetic material.

Even assuming that a presumption of intention is preferable to granting sole decision-making powers to the surviving gamete provider, why should the law presume that the deceased would have wished for the embryos to be preserved until their natural death? Further assuming that indefinite preservation is viewed by default as the likely wish of the deceased, why should it prevail over the survivor's express wish? If a pregnancy is no longer pursued due to a supervening event, but the parties agree on donating the embryos to infertile couples or to research, self-determination rights presumably require State authorities to yield to that joint decision (indeed, the *Parrillo* ruling hinged on the self-determination rights of the deceased; the State's interests were not decisive on their own). If the supervening event is the death of one of the partners, the survivor has a greater right to decide the fate of their genetic material, because he/she is immediately impacted.

The alternatives to donation to scientific research deserve further consideration. As Judge Sajò, dissenting, explained: 'The choices open to [Mrs Parrillo] were to use the embryos herself, or allow another couple to use them, or to let her biological material languish indefinitely.'[128] Both outright destruction and indefinite cryopreservation result in the death of the embryos, just like their utilisation for research, except they will have served no useful purpose. Jessica Giles and Simon Lee noted the life-affirming aspect of donation to research when compared to indefinite preservation: 'The human embryos were then not going to be given the opportunity to grow in a womb. ... The best she thought she could do to give meaning to the creation of life in these embryonic forms was to offer them for medical research.'[129] The option of donating to infertile couples clashed with the right not to become a biological parent (and live in perpetual anxiety about the fate of a child raised by others in unknown conditions). As eloquently captured by Ruth Deech and Anna Smajdor, for couples whose fertility treatment led to the creation of surplus embryos, 'leaving their embryos unclaimed in clinics

[126] Ibid., 2542.

[127] The discussion could be extended to the next of kin's life-and-death decision-making power for comatose patients.

[128] *Parrillo* v. *Italy* [GC], Dissenting Opinion of Judge Sajò, [14].

[129] Jessica Giles and Simon Lee, '*Parrillo v Italy*: Is There Life in the European Court of Human Rights?' (2016) 5(1) *Oxford Journal of Law and Religion* 162–167, at 166.

may be preferable to the idea that "their" child would go into the world in circumstances beyond their control on being donated to another couple'.[130] A law requiring the donation of unused embryos for the treatment of others would be as extreme an interference with the rights of gamete providers as non-consensual adoption, except children's rights would not be in the balance to justify it.

The flaw in the *Parrillo* approach to self-determination is that, by not authorising the surviving spouse to make decisions about joint frozen embryos, the State does not necessarily respect the wishes of the deceased (the purported justification for the interference). The deceased's wishes (use of embryos for procreation) become unattainable as a result of death, and the decision to store the embryos indefinitely is not more 'neutral' than the decision to repurpose them; it is just another deviation from the deceased's original plans, benefitting no one. Critically, it affects the surviving spouse's right 'to act as a free and autonomous individual with regard to her genetic footprint'.[131]

2.2 GAMETE DONATION: RECONCILING GENETIC PARENTHOOD AND FREE CHOICE OF PARTNER

While Article 8 protects 'the right of a couple to conceive a child and to make use of medically assisted procreation for that purpose',[132] it does not entitle them to the choice of *any* reproductive method. A highly contentious technique is heterologous fertilisation, involving the use of donated gametes, as opposed to homologous artificial insemination or IVF procedure, involving the use of only gametes from the aspiring parents. According to Douglas, the idea of assisted insemination with donor is resisted on two related grounds: first, 'traditional sexual morality', in that 'the use of donor semen introduces a third party into the marital relationship', and second, the fact that it 'introduces a stranger's genes into the blood line of the man's family, thus spoiling the line of succession'.[133] Some authors support an absolute prohibition or narrow eligibility for heterologous fertilisation (limited to certain forms of infertility or genetically transmissible diseases), because the attribution of parenthood to the non-biological intended parent (the mother in case of ova

[130] Deech and Smajdor, *From IVF to Immortality*, 41.
[131] *Parrillo* v. *Italy* [GC], Dissenting Opinion of Judge Sajò, [1].
[132] *S.H. and Others* v. *Austria* [GC], [82], reiterated in *Knecht* v. *Romania*, [54].
[133] Douglas, *Law, Fertility and Reproduction*, 109.

donation, or the father in case of sperm donation) affects the certainty of affiliation and the child's identity.[134]

Arguments based on the certainty of affiliation and the child's identity appear weak to the extent that the law makes no effort to ensure the accuracy of birth records, that is, it allows registration by the alleged parents without the submission of genetic proof, and it presumes the husband of the woman who gives birth to be the father. The emphasis on the certainty of affiliation is also at odds with the availability of paternity challenges, while the existence of bars on such proceedings calls into question the prevalence of the child's right to know the biological truth. Additionally, the law views neither the certainty of affiliation nor identity rights as impaired by adoption, even though the new birth certificate reallocates parenthood and does not reflect the child's parentage. In *Odièvre* v. *France*, the ECtHR accepted that the adopted child's right to know is not an absolute one and can be limited by the birth mother's right to confidential birthing.[135] The adoptive parents' rights also prevail over the child's right to know, since the law grants them discretion whether to reveal the circumstances of the child's arrival into the family. If the attribution of legal parenthood to individuals who are not the genetic parents is not seen as detrimental to the child's sense of identity, it cannot be an insurmountable objection to heterologous fertilisation. Furthermore, the right to knowledge of one's origins could be promoted through access to information about the donor; a complete ban on the practice of gamete donation, going beyond the objective of safeguarding identity rights, is arguably a disproportionate interference with prospective parents' rights. In fact, for some individuals, the use of donor gametes is the only way to reconcile their choice of partner with the desire to have a biological child. A person whose spouse is infertile should not have to choose between ending the marriage and renouncing biological parenthood. The law could, for instance, allow the woman to be treated with donor sperm alone (rather than as part of a couple) and permit her husband to adopt the child; however, it is doubtful whether the child's welfare is better protected by step-parent adoption than parenthood *ab initio*, as the latter facilitates the full integration into the family since birth.

The ECtHR examined the issue of heterologous fertilisation in *S.H. and Others* v. *Austria*, a case challenging the ban on the use of donated gametes for IVF treatment and the absolute prohibition of ovum donation. The impugned legislation permitted the unification of ovum and sperm in vitro only if they

134 See Paolo Morozzo Della Rocca, 'Riflessioni sul rapporto tra adozione e procreazione medicalmente assistita' (2005) 1 *Il diritto di famiglia e delle persone* 211–226, at 217.

135 See *Odièvre* v. *France* [GC], [49].

both proceeded from the intended parents, whereas it allowed sperm donation for in vivo fertilisation.[136] The applicants were two married couples wishing to conceive through IVF: one couple needed a sperm donor, while the other needed donated ova. They complained in Strasbourg that the impossibility of conceiving a child genetically related to one parent – due to the law permitting only homologous IVF, using both male and female gametes from the spouses – breached their Convention rights.

The initial Chamber judgment held that the right of couples to procreate by availing themselves of ART fell within the ambit of Article 8, the decision to embark upon such treatment being an expression of the right to private and family life.[137] The Chamber rejected the idea that the unease of certain sections of the population with the new techniques can justify the interference with other individuals' rights; in fact, 'concerns based on moral considerations or on social acceptability are not in themselves sufficient reasons for a complete ban on a specific artificial procreation technique'.[138] While accepting as legitimate the aim of avoiding the risks of exploitation of women from poor backgrounds or the abuse of the technique for genetic selection, the Chamber found that the prohibition of ova and sperm donation for IVF is not 'the only or the least intrusive means of achieving the aim pursued'.[139] A regulatory framework, as opposed to a total ban, would have been a proportionate response (the decision cites the existing prohibition on the remuneration of gamete donation).[140] As regards the concerns over the division of motherhood between biological/gestational/social aspects and legal certainty, the Court noted that the family law framework already accommodated 'unusual family relations', 'which do not follow the typical parent–child relationship based on a direct biological link' (the institution of adoption).[141] The conflict between the interests of donors requesting anonymity and the children's right to know their genetic origin, which is not an absolute one,[142] was similarly rejected as an insufficient justification.[143] The Chamber concluded that the prohibition violated Article 14 taken in conjunction with Article 8, because the different treatment of couples who needed ova/sperm donation for IVF and those who

[136] *S.H. and Others* v. *Austria* [GC], [28]–[31].
[137] *S.H. and Others* v. *Austria* [Chamber], App. No. 57813/00, 1 April 2010, [60].
[138] Ibid., [74].
[139] Ibid., [76].
[140] Ibid., [77].
[141] Ibid., [81].
[142] The Court recalled *Odièvre* v. *France* [GC], [49].
[143] *S.H. and Others* v. *Austria* [Chamber], [82]–[84].

could use sperm donation for in vivo fertilisation had no objective and reasonable justification and was disproportionate.[144]

Regrettably, the Grand Chamber reversed the Chamber decision, finding that Austria had not exceeded its margin of appreciation as regards the regulation of gamete donation. It accepted the precautionary principle as a justification for the prohibition, namely the unforeseeable consequences of allowing a dissociation between genetic and legal parenthood. It reasoned that, given the fast development of artificial procreation and the difficulties in anticipating the effects of a regulatory measure, it was 'understandable that the States find it necessary to act with particular caution'.[145] The Court accepted further unconvincing justifications for the ban on ovum donation, such as avoiding the possibility that two women could claim to be the biological mother of a child.[146] The very practice of gamete donation is premised on the fact that donors are not treated as legal parents and hence on the distinction between donation for the treatment of others and self-reproduction. Moreover, the law already allowed a person to acquire parental status without being the child's genetic parent, through adoption and artificial insemination with donor sperm in cases of male infertility.[147] According to the respondent, the use of donor sperm for in vivo fertilisation was lawful because that technique was already in practice and, since it did not require a medical professional, any prohibition would have been unenforceable. Justifications based on practice or tradition alone have been rejected elsewhere in ECHR case law as inadequate.[148]

Rosamund Scott has argued that 'in *SH* the Grand Chamber diminished the function of donated gametes as *treatment* and portrayed their use as aligned with *choice*, thereby disregarding the applicants' underlying treatment *needs*'.[149] While treatment and choice are not mutually exclusive, the Court failed to acknowledge that, for some couples, the choice to procreate is intrinsically related to the availability of treatment enabling them to overcome infertility issues. The Chamber's focus on the different needs of couples

144 Ibid., [70]–[85], [94].

145 *S.H. and Others* v. *Austria* [GC], [103].

146 Ibid., [104].

147 On this inconsistency, see also Jens Scherpe, 'Medically Assisted Procreation: This Margin Needs to Be Appreciated' (2012) 71(2) *Cambridge Law Journal* 276–279.

148 See *Burghartz* v. *Switzerland*, App. No. 16213/90, 22 February 1994, [28] (even in the presence of a tradition, the ECHR 'must be interpreted in the light of present-day conditions, especially the importance of the principle of non-discrimination').

149 Rosamund Scott, 'Reproductive Health: Morals, Margin and Rights' (2018) 81(3) *Modern Law Review* 422–451, 444 (original emphasis).

disadvantaged by the ban on gamete donation for IVF was closer to the Inter-American Court's position in *Artavia Murillo* v. *Costa Rica*, which viewed infertility in the context of reproductive health, as a disability requiring measures of protection. Another lacuna in the Grand Chamber's judgment, also overlooked in the Chamber proceedings and the literature, is the insufficient consideration of the fertile person's right to become a genetic parent, the enjoyment of which is disproportionately affected if it requires divorce and repartnering.

Additionally, the Grand Chamber placed excessive emphasis on the lack of a common European approach to gamete donation and the wide margin of appreciation retained by States.[150] Although it acknowledged a 'clear trend in the legislation of Contracting States towards allowing gamete donation' and hence 'an emerging European consensus', it unduly raised the bar for evolutive interpretation, adducing that said consensus was not 'based on settled and long-standing principles' and hence it did not 'decisively narrow the margin of appreciation'.[151] The 'settled and long-standing' qualification appears inconsistent with the Court's case law. While the practice in a small number of jurisdictions was considered insufficient to establish consensus (e.g. in *Schalk and Kopf* v. *Austria* on same-sex marriage),[152] an enduring tradition was not required. On the contrary, in *Marckx* v. *Belgium* the Court relied on legislative reforms still in progress, noting that 'the domestic law of the great majority of the member States of the Council of Europe has evolved and is continuing to evolve'.[153] In *Goodwin* v. *The United Kingdom*, the Court 'attache[d] less importance to the lack of evidence of a common European approach . . . than to the clear and uncontested evidence of a continuing international trend'.[154] Against this background, 'a clear trend' across the ECHR membership in favour of gamete donation for IVF should have satisfied the test for consensus. The superimposition of an additional criterion attracted justified criticism from the dissenters, for whom a high threshold for consensus is 'potentially extending the States' margin of appreciation beyond limits'.[155] Moreover, requiring long-term practice to establish European consensus delays the

[150] *S.H. and Others* v. *Austria* [GC], [94]–[116].

[151] Ibid., [96].

[152] See *Schalk and Kopf* v. *Austria*, App. No. 30141/04, 24 June 2010, [58] (same-sex marriage was permitted in only six out of forty-seven States).

[153] See *Marckx* v. *Belgium*, App. No. 6833/74, 13 June 1979, [41]. On the consensus doctrine, see Carmen Draghici, 'The Strasbourg Court between European and Local Consensus: Anti-democratic or Guardian of Democratic Process?' (2017) *Public Law* 11–29, at 13–20.

[154] *Christine Goodwin* v. *The United Kingdom* [GC], App. No. 28957/95, 11 July 2002, [85].

[155] See *S.H. and Others* v. *Austria* [GC], Dissenting Opinion of Judges Tulkens et al., [8].

development of human rights standards in an era of fast advances in medical technology.

Equally problematic is the Court's reasoning that the restriction was mitigated by the option left to couples needing gamete donation to travel abroad and receive this type of treatment in jurisdictions where it was legally available. On the one hand, the respondent's reliance on 'procreative tourism' to defend the proportionality of the ban undermines its claim that the restriction was rendered necessary by the community's core ethical values.[156] Couples seeking ova donation, to allow a man to become a genetic father and his wife to experience gestational motherhood, are a very small section of the population. As any exiguous minorities with an unpopular cause (much like prisoners in *Dickson v. The United Kingdom*), they run the risk of unempathetic majorities being dismissive of procedures on which they themselves do not depend. The ECtHR can correct the imbalance of a situation in which individuals who are not affected by an issue make decisions impacting those who are. On the other hand, as the IACtHR recognised in *Artavia Murillo*, treating overseas IVF as a solution discriminates against couples based on their financial status.

Albeit disappointing in its deference to national regulation, the Grand Chamber's ruling in *S.H.* v. *Austria* had the merit of consolidating the principle that Article 8 protects the right to make use of medical advances for procreation. This contribution is highlighted by the contrast with the ultra-conservative Separate Opinion of Judge De Gaetano, for whom all assisted reproduction techniques (ARTs) are contrary to human dignity and 'the "desire" for a child cannot ... become an absolute goal which overrides the dignity of every human life'.[157] More moderate objections to ART in the literature do not view human dignity as incompatible with all non-natural procreation, but only with commercial or eugenic abuses of ARTs.[158] Judge De Gaetano's opinion also overlooks the fact that the reproductive function of the human body is not less worthy of medical assistance than any other function; therefore, ART cannot be condemned any more than other medical treatment – for example, organ transplant – which seeks to offer a better quality of life.

The Court's preference for categorising the ban on gamete donation for IVF as an interference is also significant,[159] especially since it stressed the

[156] See Gallus, 'La procréation médicalement assistée', 222.
[157] *S.H. and Others* v. *Austria* [GC], Separate Opinion of Judge De Gaetano, [2].
[158] See Gallus, 'La procréation médicalement assistée', 223.
[159] See *S.H. and Others* v. *Austria* [GC], [88].

importance of keeping under review the law's response to fast-moving scientific developments in the field of artificial procreation. As with previous judgments containing future-oriented *obiter dicta* (e.g. on transgender rights in *Rees* v. *The United Kingdom* and *Cossey* v. *The United Kingdom*),[160] the Court noted that this is an area in which ECHR standards may change subject to further domestic developments: 'Even if it finds no breach of Article 8 in the present case, the Court considers that this area, in which the law appears to be continuously evolving and which is subject to a particularly dynamic development in science and law, needs to be kept under review by the Contracting States.'[161] This suggests that a different conclusion on heterologous fertilisation may be reached in the future. Indeed, *Christine Goodwin* v. *The United Kingdom* has demonstrated the Court's willingness to revisit its position and condemn a State persisting in its restrictive approach to evolving rights.[162]

Significantly, the Grand Chamber passed judgment in *S.H. and Others* v. *Austria* well over a decade after the applicants' complaint before the Austrian Constitutional Court, and it expressly confined its findings to the prevailing circumstances at the time of the domestic proceedings. In particular, it emphasised that the judgment was not reflective of ECHR standards at the time of the ruling:

> It is not for the Court to consider whether the prohibition of sperm and ovum donation at issue would or would not be justified today under the Convention. The issue for the Court to decide is whether these prohibitions were justified at the time they were considered by the Austrian Constitutional Court. ... Since the Constitutional Court's decision in the present case many developments in medical science have taken place to which a number of Contracting States have responded in their legislation.[163]

[160] See *Rees* v. *The United Kingdom*, App. No. 9532/81, 17 October 1986, [47]: 'The need for appropriate legal measures should therefore be kept under review having regard particularly to scientific and societal developments.' See, analogously, *Cossey* v. *The United Kingdom*, App. No. 10843/84, 27 September 1990, [42].

[161] *S.H. and Others* v. *Austria* [GC], [118]. See also Andrea Mulligan, 'Reproductive Rights under Article 8: The Right to Respect for the Decision to Become or Not to Become a Parent' (2014) 4 *European Human Rights Law Review* 378–387, at 383: 'The Court did take the time to warn the Austrian government that it was under a duty to ensure that its laws keep up to date with developments in this dynamic and evolving area of science.'

[162] See *Christine Goodwin* v. *The United Kingdom*, [92]–[93]: 'The respondent Government can no longer claim that the matter falls within their margin of appreciation, save as regards the appropriate means of achieving recognition of the right protected under the Convention.'

[163] *S.H. and Others* v. *Austria* [GC], [84].

This caveat suggests that Convention standards at the time of the *S.H. and Others* decision may have already evolved so as to require States to permit gamete donation for IVF treatment.

2.3 POSTHUMOUS PARENTHOOD: DEFERRED PROCREATION AND RESPECT FOR PRIVACY BEYOND DEATH

2.3.1 *Posthumous Conception and Reproductive Testaments*

Assisted reproduction technologies allow conception after death through (a) the use of a deceased man's frozen sperm for artificial insemination or IVF, enabling a woman to have children biologically related to her late partner; (b) the use of frozen eggs proceeding from a deceased woman for IVF followed by the implantation of the resulting embryos into a surrogate mother, enabling the surviving male partner to become a father; or (c) the use of frozen embryos after the death of one or both members of the couple (in the latter case, allowing their parents to have biologically related grandchildren). Couples may have a legitimate interest in the use of these techniques – for example, due to a sudden illness of one spouse and the other spouse's desire to have a child biologically related to both; to give an existing child a sibling of the full blood; or because existing embryos created with both parties' gametes are the only route to conceiving a biological child due to intervening reproductive health issues.

In principle, deferred procreation is protected by the ECHR to the extent that Article 8 entitles everyone to respect for the decision to conceive a child, to make use of medical assistance to that end and to decide on the timing of a pregnancy (*Dickson* v. *The United Kingdom, S.H.* v. *Austria*). Consequently, the couple's right to conceive after the death of one partner cannot be denied without adequate justification. The to-be-born child's welfare could be invoked, although single parenthood is a widespread social phenomenon, and the law of many countries accepts single adopters and provides donor insemination treatment to single women. Moreover, the availability of only one parent for the effective care of the child was not seen as a sufficient justification for restrictions on the right to procreate in *Dickson* v. *The United Kingdom*. Part of the scholarship has advocated for the right to a family life that the spouses have consciously decided to postpone and that the woman wishes to prolong.[164] This view finds support in Strasbourg case law on the

[164] See Vincent Coussirat-Coustère, 'Famille et Convention Européenne des Droits de l'Homme', in Paul Mahoney et al. (eds.), *Protection des droits de l'homme: la perspective*

protection of the 'intended family life' of natural fathers with their children (despite the absence of effective ties after birth),[165] usually linked to a planned pregnancy.[166] Naturally, the widow's desire to use her deceased husband's frozen sperm without his advance (express or implied) consent to the posthumous use of his genetic material might be problematic. Her claim is stronger for the use of frozen embryos, created for reproductive purposes with both parties' genetic material, but superseded by the intervening death of her husband. Symmetrically, the husband might have a legitimate claim to the use of the embryos through a surrogacy arrangement to continue the parenthood project interrupted by the wife's death. Additionally, a person's right to exercise control over their genetic material (*Parrillo* v. *Italy*) should arguably extend to their ability to decide the fate of frozen gametes/embryos in the event of their death, including their use for a pregnancy (within the family or to assist third parties afflicted by infertility), as opposed to their destruction or donation to medical research.

The question of whether a person's decision-making rights in relation to their stored gametes/embryos end after death, or whether their next of kin can substitute them, was addressed in *Petithory Lanzmann* v. *France*.[167] The Court viewed with scepticism the applicant's request for access to her deceased son's frozen gametes for the purposes of donation to an infertile couple or gestational surrogacy, enabling the applicant to become a grandparent. Firstly, the Court dismissed the claim that the refusal to allow the applicant to use her deceased son's sperm, so as to become a grandparent, prevented her from continuing the family line. Article 8 was said not to encompass the right to found a family and have grandchildren.[168]

Secondly, the complaint brought as an indirect victim on behalf of her son was declared inadmissible; the Court held that the right to become a parent was a non-transferable right.[169] This assessment is disappointing, because the son himself, upon being diagnosed with a fatal illness, had taken steps to

européenne. Mélanges à la mémoire de Rolv Ryssdl (Köln: Carl Heymanns, 2000) 281–307, at 306.

[165] *Tóth* v. *Hungary*, App. No. 48494/06, 12 February 2013, [27].

[166] See *Keegan* v. *Ireland*, App. No. 16969/90, 26 May 1994, [45]; *M.B.* v. *The United Kingdom*, App. No. 22920/93, 6 April 1994 (Commission), [2]; *Ahrens* v. *Germany*, App. No. 45071/09, 22 March 2012, [58]–[59]. For an analysis, see Carmen Draghici, 'Unplanned Fatherhood Is Not Sperm Donation: An Unduly Moralistic Approach to Natural Fathers in ECHR Case Law' (2022) 2 *Child and Family Law Quarterly* 123–147.

[167] *Petithory Lanzmann* v. *France*, App. No. 23038/19, 12 November 2019 (available only in French).

[168] See ibid., [20]. See further Subsection 2.3.2.

[169] *Petithory Lanzmann* v. *France*, [16].

ensure he would be able to have offspring in the event of his death, by banking sperm with a French hospital and contacting a healthcare establishment abroad for artificial insemination services. The refusal of the French medical authorities to allow the deceased's mother to have the gametes transferred to a country permitting their post-mortem use for medically assisted reproduction or gestational surrogacy, therefore, ran contrary to the express wishes of the deceased.

Although the evidence did not include a formal authorisation by the deceased to his mother to continue his reproduction plans,[170] he had clearly embarked upon that enterprise in contemplation of his own death, and his mother, as next of kin, should have been found entitled to act on his behalf to ensure respect for his wishes. In denying the mother legal standing, the Court referred to its previous case law on the notion of indirect victim, summarised in *Centre for Legal Resources on Behalf of Valentin Câmpeanu* v. *Romania*: the next of kin may pursue the application, provided that he/she has sufficient interest in the case,[171] for example, in the event of death or disappearance allegedly engaging the State's responsibility,[172] where they have a moral interest in having the late victim exonerated of guilt or in protecting the reputation of their family, or where they have a material interest owing to the effect of the alleged violation on their pecuniary rights.[173] Nothing in this jurisprudence would have been inconsistent with allowing the applicant in *Petithory* to challenge the domestic authorities' interference with her son's posthumous parenthood plans. There was, in fact, a sufficient link between the alleged violation and the mother's moral interest in protecting the survival of the family line and her late child's decisional autonomy. While the right to control over one's genetic material is non-transferable, so is the right to life or to protection against torture or slavery, or the right to personal liberty, and yet parents have been found to have *locus standi* to bring a claim on behalf of deceased children. In forced disappearance, torture, human trafficking and unlawful killing cases, the Court has accepted applications under Articles 2, 3, 4 and 5 brought on behalf of the victims by their next of kin.[174] Although what

[170] See ibid., [19].

[171] *Centre for Legal Resources on Behalf of Valentin Câmpeanu* v. *Romania*, App. No. 47848/08, 17 July 2014, [97].

[172] Ibid., [98].

[173] Ibid., [100].

[174] See *McCann and Others* v. *The United Kingdom* [GC], App. No. 18984/91, 27 September 1995 (death during law enforcement operations); *Timurtaş* v. *Turkey*, App. No. 23531/94, 13 June 2000 (disappearance while in State custody); *Kurt* v. *Turkey*, App. No. 24276/94, 25 May 1998 (failure to account for the fate of a person taken into custody);

these cases had in common was the family member's death in circumstances engaging the responsibility of the State, it is not obvious that an alleged breach of Article 2 is necessary to activate the next of kin's legal standing in relation to breaches of other provisions. Indeed, in decided cases, the Article 2 claim failed, but the claim in relation to another provision was upheld.[175]

By raising a questionable admissibility hurdle, the Court missed the opportunity to examine a possible right to leave advance directions on the use of one's genetic material, the implementation of which can be legitimately overseen by the next of kin. There was, in fact, no ambiguity over the deceased's wishes for his sperm to be used either for the treatment of infertile couples seeking a donor or for a gestational surrogacy arrangement. The case was incorrectly framed as regarding the *mother's* right to decide on the use of the late son's genetic material. Rather, it regarded the son's self-determination rights, including the ability to decide the fate of his genetic material after his death; the mother was instrumental in enforcing *his* rights. The Court may have decided that public authorities were under no obligation to respect a person's reproductive testament rather than deny the next of kin's indirect victim status. In cases concerning frozen embryos (as opposed to frozen gametes), it would arguably be more difficult to defend that position, since it also involves the death of the embryos.

The *Petithory* decision left further questions unresolved. Would the Court have treated the case differently had the complaint been brought by the deceased's wife seeking posthumous insemination for herself? Does the welfare of the child resulting from the use of the frozen gametes, growing up without a father, play any role if the law already allows *donor* insemination? Where does the balance lie between the adults' rights and the interests of the children born to satisfy the aspirations of adults? The case of *Pejřilová* v. *The Czech Republic* required the Court to consider some of these questions.[176] The application concerned the dismissal of a widow's request to have her ova fertilised with her deceased husband's frozen sperm, in circumstances where they had started IVF treatment together, interrupted by the husband's death. Domestic law only permitted fertilisation treatment for couples and *inter vivos*,

Salman v. *Turkey* [GC], App. No. 21986/93, 27 June 2000 (death and torture while in custody); *Keenan* v. *The United Kingdom*, App. No. 27229/95, 3 April 2001 (failure to protect against suicide in the course of detention); *Budayeva and Others* v. *Russia*, App. No. 15339/02, 20 March 2008 (failure to protect life against foreseeable mudslides); *Rantsev* v. *Cyprus and Russia*, App. No. 25965/04, 7 January 2010 (inadequate protection against human trafficking).

175 See *Kurt* v. *Turkey*, finding the Article 2 and Article 3 claims unsubstantiated, but upholding the Article 5 complaint.

176 *Pejřilová* v. *The Czech Republic*, App. No. 14889/19, 8 December 2022.

and the consent of both parties before each occasion on which sperm was thawed for IVF had to be less than six months old.

The Court reiterated in this context that Article 8 protected the right to conceive a child and to make use of medically assisted procreation for that purpose.[177] It recognised the State's wide margin of appreciation in the regulation of IVF treatment, the use of which gives rise to sensitive moral and ethical issues,[178] especially against the background of a lack of common ground among Member States in this area.[179] As in previous cases, the Court approached the complaint as involving an interference with the widow's right to avail herself of ARTs.[180] However, it concluded that her right to respect for the decision to have a child genetically related to her late husband did not outweigh the legitimate general interests protected by the legislation: the right of to-be-born children to know their parents and the respect for the free will of gamete providers, whose further consent to treatment could not be prejudged or replaced by a court decision after death.[181]

The judgment failed to take notice of the lacuna in domestic law whereby a person was unable to leave a reproductive testament, enabling their spouse to continue a joint parental project. The Czech government successfully relied on the indication, in the informed consent form signed by the deceased, that the storage of sperm would be discontinued in the event of death;[182] however, the pro forma did not permit the individual undergoing treatment the choice of authorising the use of his gametes post mortem. It could further be argued that, even where advance directives have not been given, the law should allow sufficient flexibility to assess continuing consent. A court decision ascertaining the deceased's wishes on procreation after death, based on written evidence and testimonies, would not be more ill-suited to protect free will than existing procedures relating to comatose patients' views on withdrawal of life support or the retrospective assessment of liability in cases of assisted dying.[183]

Two applications currently pending before the ECtHR are expected to cast light on these issues. They concern the prohibition of the transfer abroad, for posthumous assisted reproduction, of a deceased spouse's frozen gametes or of embryos created with the deceased spouse's gametes, notwithstanding the

[177] Ibid., [42].
[178] Ibid., [46].
[179] Ibid., [45], [55].
[180] Ibid., [47].
[181] Ibid., [51]–[52], [59]–[62].
[182] See ibid., [61].
[183] See Carmen Draghici, 'Assisted Dying', in Ian Loveland (ed.), *Canadian and British Public Law in Comparative Perspective* (Oxford: Hart, 2021) 25–74, at 28, 49.

man's advance consent to the procedure. The claimant in *Dalleau v. France*[184] is a woman whose civil partner had asked the clinic where he had deposited a sperm specimen to transfer it to a hospital for artificial insemination shortly before he died of cancer. After his death, the applicant had requested the clinic to transfer the specimen to a medical centre in Spain, where medical assistance is provided based on advance directives by the deceased to initiate a pregnancy in his wife/partner, and legal fatherhood is recognised if treatment is provided within twelve months of the death. In the absence of a reply from the clinic, the applicant unsuccessfully sought relief in the courts. Her application and appeals were dismissed on the grounds that the prohibition of exportation of gametes for uses banned in France was intended to prevent any circumvention of French law. Two factors were emphasised in the domestic decisions: first, the deceased partner had been informed that the storage of spermatozoa was strictly personal and would be terminated in the event of death; second, the absence of any link between the surviving civil partner and Spain.

Key features of this case are the existence of advance directives and hence the denial of posthumous insemination notwithstanding the deceased's express prior consent; the surviving civil partner's standing to apply both for herself and on behalf of her late partner; and the prohibition on the transfer of the deceased's frozen gametes to an overseas clinic for the purposes of ART. The case thus requires the respondent to demonstrate not only why posthumous insemination with consent from both parties is not permitted but also why preventing the surviving member of the couple from receiving treatment abroad is a proportionate interference with the right to respect for the couple's decision to become parents through the use of ART. In fact, the *Pejřilová* ruling invoked the protection of the deceased's free will, noting that in jurisdictions permitting posthumous ART procedures, those were 'surrounded by guarantees related to the deceased man's prior informed consent'.[185] As part of the proportionality assessment, it also relied on the absence of prohibition on the transfer of frozen gametes abroad for post-mortem treatment in countries permitting it, subject to the deceased's advance consent.[186] By contrast, the legislation impugned in *Dalleau* prevents overseas treatment notwithstanding the deceased's express prior consent, a restriction which ought to be found unnecessary in a democratic society.

184 *Dalleau* v. *France*, App. No. 57307/18.
185 See *Pejřilová* v. *The Czech Republic*, [59]–[60].
186 Ibid., [60].

The second pending case, *Caballero* v. *France*,[187] differs from *Dalleau* in that the measure affected the applicant's right to use embryos created with her own genetic material (in addition to her deceased husband's gametes). Consequently, the French courts' refusal to allow the transfer of the embryos abroad for posthumous implantation ran counter to both the deceased's advance directives and the woman's privacy rights; the Court's jurisprudence has already acknowledged that Article 8 protects the woman's right to make decisions in relation to embryos created with her ova, especially for procreative purposes (*Knecht* v. *Romania*, *Nedescu* v. *Romania*),[188] albeit potentially also for scientific research (*Parrillo* v. *Italy*).[189] The respondent's case hinges on the State's prerogative to prevent individuals from circumventing the French prohibition on posthumous reproduction. While the Court might find that the Convention does not require States to permit posthumous embryo implantation domestically, even with adequate safeguards, it should decide that measures preventing individuals from using embryos created with their genetic material for treatment abroad to which the deceased gamete provider consented in advance is a disproportionate interference with the right to respect for private and family life.

A further factor, recalled in the Court's information note, is a 2019 Opinion of the French Conseil d'État highlighting the inconsistency between the prohibition of embryo implantation/use of the husband's gametes if one partner is deceased, and the option for the widow to use insemination with donor sperm. Indeed, concerns over the right of the to-be-born child to know his/her father in one case but not the other are illogical; if anything, in the former case, the child would have adequate information about the birth father and a connection with the paternal family. The Opinion recommended legal reform to authorise posthumous artificial insemination or embryo transfer, subject to the deceased spouse/partner's prior consent and a specified time-frame for the procedure. Relying on *Costa and Pavan* v. *Italy* (internal inconsistency of reproductive laws discrediting bioethical justifications)[190] and *Oliari* v. *Italy* (popular and judicial support for change ignored by the legislative),[191] the Court could well reach a conclusion, at least limited to

[187] *Caballero* v. *France*, App. No. 37138/20.
[188] See Section 2.1.2.
[189] See Section 2.1.3.
[190] See *Costa and Pavan* v. *Italy*, [71].
[191] See *Oliari* v. *Italy*, Apps. No. 18766/11 and 36030/11, 21 July 2015, [179]–[185]. For a discussion, see Carmen Draghici, 'The Strasbourg Court between European and Local Consensus', 25–28.

France, that an obligation to permit posthumous embryo implantation with the consent of both spouses can be derived from Article 8 ECHR.

2.3.2 *Use of a Deceased Child's Cryopreserved Gametes to Become a Grandparent*

While Strasbourg case law has established that the relationship between grandparents and grandchildren amounts to 'family life' and is entitled to protection under Article 8,[192] the *Petithory Lanzmann* v. *France* decision indicated that the Convention does not guarantee a right to *become* a grandparent. The applicant had unsuccessfully attempted to have her deceased son's sperm transferred to an overseas establishment (in Israel or the United States) for the purposes of medically assisted reproduction or gestational surrogacy – procedures permitted in those jurisdictions. In addition to bringing a complaint on behalf of her deceased son,[193] she also claimed to be a direct victim of a violation of Article 8, insofar as she had been deprived of the possibility of becoming a grandparent. The decision suggested, however, that the desire to become a grandparent does not benefit from the Court's approach to parenthood aspirations; Article 8 only protects the interest in becoming a genetic parent.

Arguably, the Court ought to have acknowledged at least the special position of individuals whose child is deceased and who have an opportunity of second-generation procreation through ART. The argument made in relation to *Evans* v. *The United Kingdom* applies here as well: the ECHR minimum standards should require States to cater for exceptional circumstances, so as to mitigate personal tragedies. A person having lost a child and wishing to extend that child's life through the posthumous use of their gametes should be seen as having at least an arguable case, worthy of further examination. This is especially so when the applicant's wishes coincide with the child's genetic testamentary disposition. On the facts, the advanced age or economic capacity of the prospective grandparent might raise child welfare concerns. The adult-centric idea of bringing into the world an orphan to satisfy the grandparent's emotional needs may also inspire opposition on moral grounds. Additionally, the recognition of the grandmother as a parent, if she wishes to carry the child herself, might be said to lead to confusion for the

[192] See *Marckx* v. *Belgium*, [45]: '"Family life", within the meaning of Article 8 (art. 8), includes at least the ties between near relatives, for instance those between grandparents and grandchildren, since such relatives may play a considerable part in family life.'

[193] See Section 2.3.1.

child. However, the deprivation of the last opportunity of family life with a biologically related grandchild should be analysed as an interference with Article 8 rights and should require the demonstration of a pressing need.

2.4 RECOGNITION OF LEGAL TIES FOLLOWING OVERSEAS SURROGACY ARRANGEMENTS: RESPECT FOR BIOLOGICAL PARENTAGE

One of the most controversial aspects of the right to become a genetic parent is the recourse to surrogacy arrangements. The literature is highly divided on the subject. Some scholars see surrogacy as a legitimate alternative for aspiring parents afflicted by infertility, an exercise of procreative choice and an expression of bodily autonomy for the surrogate; conversely, others condemn surrogacy for the alleged commodification of the woman's body; the exploitation of vulnerable, underprivileged women; the commercialisation of babies (especially in the case of remunerated surrogacy services); the psychological trauma of the surrogate relinquishing the baby; and the endangerment of the welfare of the children born as a result of such agreements (inter alia the emotional impact of being abandoned by the 'mother' at birth).[194]

Although, in principle, such objections can form the basis of an interference with aspiring parents' rights, they do not fare well under close scrutiny. The moral objection that 'the surrogate is seen as no more than an incubator for the child'[195] loses strength if a comparison is drawn with organ (e.g. kidney) or bone marrow donation, which are not seen as exploitative or morally reprehensible, and in which the donor is not treated as a means to an end (their status as donor does not mean that their worth is reduced to a

[194] As noted by Robin Mackenzie, 'Beyond Genetic and Gestational Dualities: Surrogacy Agreements, Legal Parenthood and Choice in Family Formation', in Kirsty Horsey and Hazel Biggs (eds.), *Human Fertilisation and Embryology: Reproducing Regulation* (London: Routledge-Cavendish, 2007) 181–203, at 189, 'surrogacy arrangements have been equated with baby-selling, prostitution and slavery'. According to Claire Achmad, 'Children's Rights to the Fore in the European Court of Human Rights' First International Commercial Surrogacy Judgments' (2014) 6 *European Human Rights Law Review* 638–646, at 638–639, international commercial surrogacy jeopardises the human rights of women, especially from less developed countries, whose reproductive function is used as a result of their economic marginalisation. Against the legalisation of surrogacy, citing the exploitation of underprivileged women, given their financial pressures, reduced bargaining power and lack of informed consent, see Sonia Allan, 'The Surrogate in Commercial Surrogacy: Legal and Ethical Considerations', in Paula Gerber and Katie O'Byrne (eds.), *Surrogacy, Law and Human Rights* (London: Routledge, 2015) 113–143, at 122–128, 142–143. For a survey of arguments for and against surrogacy and further references, see Douglas, *Law, Fertility and Reproduction*, 145–151.

[195] Douglas, *Law, Fertility and Reproduction*, 147.

source of transplant organs); nor are human organs seen as commodified by that process. The same medical risks are associated with organ donation, and the same incentive is created for less-well-off members of society to act as donors. If surrogacy is appropriately regulated, surrogates are assessed for (physical and psychological) risk and rejected if the risks are too high, in the same way as living donors of organs are; indeed, other services involving physical labour that poses risks are deemed ethically permissible (e.g. nursing).[196] Allowing individuals to help the medical treatment of others is not more debasing in case of reproductive, as opposed to other, health issues. Leslie Francis has warned against the hasty assumption that kidney or liver donation is acceptable insofar as it is a life-saving measure, whereas carrying a child for another person is not: 'To defend this distinction … is to rely on contested judgments about whether assisted reproduction is a sufficiently weighty purpose to override the risks it might impose.'[197] While most critics of surrogacy emphasise the risks of harm to the surrogate, Emily Jackson has aptly drawn attention to the vulnerability of the commissioning parents, especially where the law creates an opportunity for extortion (e.g. where it gives the surrogate absolute freedom to withdraw from the contract) or offers no remedy if the arrangement breaks down.[198]

Objections based on the transactional nature of paid surrogacy, often likened to the sale of children and prostitution, overlook the economic motivation underlying adoption. Deech and Smajdor have pointed out that 'financial considerations are frequently a primary factor in motivating mothers to give their children up for adoption',[199] namely 'their future lives are relieved of the financial burden that the child would have represented'.[200] Additionally, studies have shown that, although financial gain is an important incentive for surrogates, the factors underlying that decision are complex, including sympathy with childless couples, the desire to re-experience pregnancy and childbirth without the responsibility of rearing the child, the desire for enhanced self-worth, and 'attempts to resolve feelings associated with previous reproductive losses'.[201]

[196] See Leslie Francis, 'Is Surrogacy Ethically Problematic?', in Leslie Francis (ed.), *The Oxford Handbook of Reproductive Ethics* (Oxford: Oxford University Press, 2017) 388–406, at 392.
[197] Ibid.
[198] See Jackson, *Regulating Reproduction*, 314.
[199] Deech and Smajdor, *From IVF to Immortality*, 162.
[200] Ibid., 162–163.
[201] Rachel Cook, 'Donating Parenthood: Perspectives on Parenthood from Surrogacy and Gamete Donation', in Andrew Bainham, Shelley Day Sclater and Martin Richards (eds.), *What Is a Parent? A Socio-Legal Analysis* (Oxford: Hart, 1999) 121–136, at 135.

Nonetheless, some authors have gone so far as to consider that commercial surrogacy may fall under Article 2 of the 2000 Optional Protocol to the UNCRC on the sale of children, child prostitution and child pornography.[202] This provision prohibits the sale of children, defined as 'any act or transaction whereby a child is transferred by any person or group of persons to another for remuneration'. Nevertheless, the interpretation of this provision 'in its context' (as required by Article 32 of the Vienna Convention on the Law of Treaties)[203] must take into account Article 3(a)(i), which lists the purposes of transfers of children deemed unlawful: 'sexual exploitation', 'transfer of organs of the child for profit', 'forced labour'. The purpose of surrogacy – enabling infertile couples to become parents through third-party gestation – is too remote from the text and spirit of Article 3(a)(i) for the situation to fall within the purview of the Protocol. Furthermore, Katherine Wade has aptly noted that the purpose of surrogacy is non-exploitative, that the child is born to parents capable of providing adequate care and that the intended parents do not acquire ownership over the children.[204] Supporting a similar conclusion, Paula Gerber and Katie O'Byrne have pointed out that compensated surrogacy arrangements are not premised on a transfer of any entitlement over the child, but rather on 'an allocation of responsibility between the parties to the arrangement as to the care of the child at different points in time, with the aim of bringing the child into its intended family'.[205] It is also worth recalling that the 2018 Report of the Special Rapporteur on the sale and sexual exploitation of children – mandated by the UN Human Rights Council to investigate these issues – while expressing concerns over the dangers of improper regulation of

202 Optional Protocol to the Convention on the Rights of the Child on the Sale of Children, Child Prostitution and Child Pornography, New York, 25 May 2000, in force 18 January 2002, UNTS vol. 2171 (p. 227). See John Tobin, 'To Prohibit or Permit: What Is the (Human) Rights Response to the Practice of International Commercial Surrogacy?' (2014) 63(2) *International & Comparative Law Quarterly* 317–352, at 335–338, arguing that Article 2 does apply to surrogacy arrangements because Article 3 of the Protocol only specifies a minimal, non-exhaustive list of acts that States must prohibit and because any transfer of the child in exchange for remuneration, not necessarily for exploitative purposes, falls within the definition of sale.

203 Vienna Convention on the Law of Treaties, Vienna, 23 May 1969, in force 27 January 1980, UNTS vol. 1155 (p. 331).

204 Katherine Wade, 'The Regulation of Surrogacy: A Children's Rights Perspective' (2017) 29(2) *Child and Family Law Quarterly* 113–131, at 120–121.

205 Paula Gerber and Katie O'Byrne, 'Souls in the House of Tomorrow: The Rights of Children Born via Surrogacy', in Paula Gerber and Katie O'Byrne (eds.), *Surrogacy, Law and Human Rights* (London: Routledge, 2015) 81–112, at 98.

surrogacy does not suggest that either altruistic or commercial surrogacy are incompatible with the Optional Protocol to the UNCRC.[206]

Furthermore, the object of the transaction in commercial surrogacy is not the child but the services necessary to complete the process of bringing the child into the world: hosting the embryo/allowing the development of the foetus and delivering the child. Gamete donors lend remunerated support in the early stage of the reproductive process without being seen as prostituting themselves or 'selling a baby'; similarly, the surrogate participates in the later stages, by allowing the use of her uterus. According to Robin Mackenzie, the social acceptability of gamete donation 'has hinged upon analogies made with praiseworthy altruistic and socially valued activities such as blood or organ donation and medico-surgical procedures'.[207] Lisa Rubin and Aliza Phillips perceptively noted the duplicity of the language distinguishing between gamete 'donation', which actually involves a costly transaction, and surrogacy:

> The common use of the term *donation*, which suggests generosity and gift giving, illustrates the ways in which language regarding *third-party* reproduction is euphemized to avoid discomfort with a marketplace model of reproduction, despite the fact that the majority of gamete transfers involve monetary exchanges.[208]

In gestational surrogacy, where genetic reality and the parties' intentions overlap, the autonomy rights of the surrogate and the intended parents should require State authorities to recognise the arrangement and register the birth accordingly. Indeed, 'the activities involved in surrogacy arrangements, impregnation, child-birth and the formation of a family, might be regarded as quintessentially private decision-making protected by human rights'.[209] Empirical studies conducted in jurisdictions permitting commercial surrogacy have shown the parties involved in surrogacy arrangements 'as capable of protecting their own interests and making responsible and realistic judgments', so that 'fears of exploitation and commodification' are not borne out by the evidence.[210] It has also been noted that the liberalisation of surrogacy, albeit viewed as anti-feminist by those concerned by 'the commodification and

[206] Report of the Special Rapporteur on the sale and sexual exploitation of children, including child prostitution, child pornography and other child sexual abuse material, A/HRC/37/60, 15 January 2018.
[207] Mackenzie, 'Beyond Genetic and Gestational Dualities', 189.
[208] Rubin and Phillips, 'Infertility and Assisted Reproduction Technologies', 189 (original emphasis).
[209] Mackenzie, 'Beyond Genetic and Gestational Dualities', 189.
[210] Ibid., 196.

control of women's bodies', is for others eminently feminist; in fact, 'any attempt to restrict surrogacy is paternalistic and represents a threat to reproductive autonomy'.[211]

Speculative objections to surrogacy include the concern that, upon learning of the circumstances of their conception, children may experience 'emotional insecurity' knowing that they were 'given away by the carrying mother – or sold'.[212] On the contrary, for surrogacy-born children, the knowledge that they were very much wanted, and that their parents went to great lengths to conceive them, is more likely to reinforce the security of a loving family environment. The aforementioned objection also assumes that children perceive the surrogates as their 'mothers', hence the idea of abandonment, which is certainly mistaken in cases of gestational surrogacy. Even in traditional surrogacy cases, it is improper to speak about abandonment when, from the outset, the woman carrying the child did not intend to procreate.

To date, surrogacy-related Strasbourg litigation has focused on *existing* children born as a result of (usually overseas) surrogacy arrangements, rather than on *access* to surrogacy. The first case, however, concerned the treatment of private organisations facilitating surrogacy arrangements. In *Lavisse* v. *France* ('Les Cigognes' case),[213] the authorities had declared illegal an association assisting infertile couples in contacting women willing to act as gestational mothers. Although the case revolved around Article 11 ECHR (the interference with the applicant's right to freedom of association), the analysis touched upon Article 8 issues. The Commission held that the interference pursued the legitimate aim of preventing the offence of inciting the abandonment of babies at birth. States were found to enjoy wide discretion in an under-regulated and divisive area such as surrogacy, and given the need to strike a fair balance between the collective and individual rights concerned, the interference was 'necessary in a democratic society'.

The Strasbourg response is more nuanced when at stake is not the advertisement of surrogacy services but actual parent–child relationships arising from such agreements. Most applications have revolved around the recognition, in jurisdictions prohibiting surrogacy, of legal effects flowing from surrogacy agreements lawfully concluded abroad. In *Mennesson* v. *France* and *Labassee* v. *France*,[214] the applicants were two married heterosexual couples who had resorted to gestational surrogacy in the United States (the

[211] Rubin and Phillips, 'Infertility and Assisted Reproduction Technologies', 191.
[212] Douglas, *Law, Fertility and Reproduction*, 149.
[213] *Lavisse* v. *France*, App. No. 14223/88, 5 June 1991 (Commission).
[214] *Labassee* v. *France*, App. No. 65941/11, 26 June 2014 (available only in French).

Mennessons in California and the Labassees in Minnesota) and their respective children. In both cases, the procedure had involved embryos created through IVF using the husband's gametes and donor ova. The California and Minnesota courts had ordered prenatally that the applicants were to be considered parents once the children were born, and the birth certificates were issued accordingly. The French authorities had refused to register the births in accordance with the children's US birth certificates, on the basis that recording the commissioning parents as the children's parents would give effect to agreements that were null and void in France insofar as contrary to public policy.[215]

Significantly, Article 8 was found applicable under both its 'private life' and 'family life' limbs. 'Family life', a notion depending on the reality of the relationships between the parties, was found engaged, insofar as the commissioning parents had raised the children since birth and they lived together in a manner indistinguishable from the usual understanding of family life; 'private life' was said to encompass social identity and affiliation, hence the direct link between the surrogate-born children's private life and the legal determination of their affiliation.[216] The Court agreed that the refusal to recognise the parent–child relationship interfered with both the children's and the adults' rights.[217] However, the Court accepted that the measure pursued the legitimate aim of protecting public health and the rights of others (children, surrogate mothers) by deterring nationals from engaging abroad in practices contravening domestic public policy.[218] The Court also considered the State's wide margin of appreciation as regards the lawfulness of surrogacy and the recognition of such arrangements when lawfully concluded abroad, given the absence of European consensus on the matter.[219] While recognising the daily difficulties that could arise from the lack of registration (e.g. having to present the US documents accompanied by an official translation to demonstrate the relationship), the Court noted that the applicants were not prevented from leading a family life together in France.[220] There was no discussion of the obligation to allow those concerned – at least the biological fathers and their children – to 'lead a normal family life', as required in *Marckx* v. *Belgium* in relation to a biological mother and her child.[221] For the Court, the interference with the

[215] See *Mennesson* v. *France*, [60].
[216] Ibid., [45]–[46]. See, analogously, *Labassee* v. *France*, [38]–[39].
[217] *Mennesson* v. *France*, [48]; *Labassee* v. *France*, [49].
[218] *Mennesson* v. *France*, [62]; *Labassee* v. *France*, [54].
[219] *Mennesson* v. *France*, [77]–[79]; *Labassee* v. *France*, [56]–[57].
[220] *Mennesson* v. *France*, [92],[94]; see also *Labassee* v. *France*, [71], [73].
[221] See *Marckx* v. *Belgium*, [31].

parents' family life was not disproportionate; in fact, the practical difficulties they faced as a result of the refusal of recognition were not so egregious as to outweigh the public interests at stake.[222]

Conversely, the Court found that the respondent State's discretion as regards the children's Article 8 rights was narrowed by several factors. First, 'an essential aspect of the identity of individuals is at stake where the legal parent–child relationship is concerned' and hence 'the margin of appreciation … needs to be reduced'.[223] The refusal to register the foreign birth certificates deprived the children of the recognition of parentage in respect of the biological parent (the father); given 'the importance of biological parentage as a component of identity', this was not in the children's best interests.[224] Second, for the children, the consequences of the non-recognition were far-reaching, adversely impacting their identity rights, the acquisition of French nationality (despite the fact that their biological fathers were French) and inheritance rights. The Court noted the misalignment between the acceptance that the children were related to the applicants under US law and the denial of that status under French law, which both deprived them of the opportunity to become French citizens and undermined their identity as full members of French society.[225] The French authorities had not safeguarded the children's best interests, which should be the primary consideration whenever decisions concerning children are made.[226] Moreover, while the parents were aware of the consequences of their actions when they embarked upon surrogacy abroad, the law greatly affected the children as well.[227] The Court thus applied a stricter proportionality test to the interference with the children's rights, insofar as the latter were not responsible for the parents' choices, and found that the respondent had overstepped its margin of appreciation when regulating the consequences of foreign surrogacy. The judgment, therefore, unanimously found a violation of the children's Article 8 rights:[228] the refusal to recognise the parent–child relationships lawfully

[222] *Mennesson* v. *France*, [94], [102]; see also *Labassee* v. *France*, [73], [81].
[223] *Mennesson* v. *France*, [80]. See also ibid., [81], on the Court's continued supervisory role even when a wide margin is left to the State: 'The solutions reached by the legislature – even within the limits of this margin – are not beyond the scrutiny of the Court. It falls to the Court to examine carefully the arguments taken into consideration and leading to the solution reached and to determine whether a fair balance has been struck between the competing interests of the State and those directly affected by that solution.'
[224] See ibid., [100]; see also *Labassee* v. *France*, [79].
[225] *Mennesson* v. *France*, [97]; see also *Labassee* v. *France*, [75].
[226] *Mennesson* v. *France*, [84], [99]–[101]; see also *Labassee* v. *France*, [78]–[80].
[227] *Mennesson* v. *France*, [99]; see also *Labassee* v. *France*, [78].
[228] *Mennesson* v. *France*, [102]; see also *Labassee* v. *France*, [81].

established overseas between children born through surrogacy and their commissioning parents breached the children's right to respect for their private life.

The judgment is particularly emphatic about 'the need to strike a fair balance between the interest of the community ... and the interest of the applicants – *the children's best interests being paramount* – in fully enjoying their rights'.[229] A parallel can be drawn between the Court's case law on children born through overseas surrogacy, in circumstances where the commissioning parents' national law prohibits it, and its case law on children's rights in unlawful immigration cases. As held in *Jeunesse* v. *The Netherlands*, in immigration decisions, the children's best interests must be afforded significant weight;[230] general immigration policy considerations are not sufficient to justify a measure resulting in hardship for the children (if the primary carer is returned to the country of origin or if the entire family must relocate abroad).[231] While parents crossing borders illegally cannot face the destination States with a *fait accompli* and expect the authorities to uphold the family life established after an illegal settlement in the country, children at risk of deportation cannot be held responsible for the parents' illegal conduct.[232] Similarly, in *Mennesson*, the Court accepted that the respondent 'may wish to deter its nationals from going abroad to take advantage of methods of assisted reproduction that are prohibited on its own territory';[233] however, the law was also penalising the children:

> The effects of non-recognition in French law of the legal parent–child relationship between children thus conceived and the intended parents are not limited to the parents alone, who have chosen a particular method of assisted reproduction prohibited by the French authorities. They also affect the children themselves, whose right to respect for their private life – which implies that everyone must be able to establish the substance of his or her identity, including the legal parent–child relationship – is substantially affected. Accordingly, a serious question arises as to the compatibility of that

[229] *Mennesson* v. *France*, [84] (emphasis added); see also *Labassee* v. *France*, [78]. Although the Court's conclusion is driven by the paramountcy of the children's interests, the requirement to respect biological reality in the treatment of overseas surrogacy arrangements is an important principle, which may in future consolidate the biological intended parent's free-standing right to recognition.

[230] *Jeunesse* v. *The Netherlands* [GC], App. No. 12738/10, 3 October 2014, [118].

[231] Ibid., [119]–[121].

[232] See Draghici, *The Legitimacy of Family Rights*, 356–357.

[233] *Mennesson* v. *France*, [99]; see also *Labassee* v. *France*, [78].

situation with the children's best interests, respect for which must guide any decision in their regard.[234]

Lydia Bracken also remarked that laws penalising surrogate-born children fall foul of the international obligation, enshrined in Article 2(2) of the UNCRC,[235] to protect children against 'all forms of discrimination or punishment' based on their parents' 'activities'.[236]

The case of *Laborie* v. *France*[237] gave the Court an opportunity to consolidate its jurisprudence in *Mennesson* v. *France* and *Labassee* v. *France* (which had been followed in *Foulon and Bouvet* v. *France* in relation to single commissioning fathers).[238] The applicants were a French married couple who had entered into a lawful surrogacy agreement in Ukraine, the children being genetically related only to the father. The registration of the birth certificate had been refused on the ground of incompatibility with public policy, insofar as the surrogacy arrangement was null and the birth certificate was inaccurate as regards maternal affiliation. The Court concluded again that the non-recognition of the parent–child relationship did not breach the family life of the commissioning parents or the children but breached the children's privacy rights. The Court limited its analysis to a referral to its previous rulings, indicating that the factual matrix was similar and there was no reason to depart from the principles already established.[239] This line of jurisprudence marks a modest ideological triumph, but an important practical victory, for families formed through overseas surrogacy arrangements. ECHR States can no longer deny legal recognition to the relationship between a biological parent and the surrogate-born child; this would violate children's right to the protection of not only their social identity as members of the community where they reside but also their genetic identity, defined by the link with biological parents.

The importance of genetic ties also pervades the 2019 Advisory Opinion No. P16-2018-001 on the recognition of the intended mother of a surrogate-born child,[240] in principle confined to a situation where the child was

[234] *Mennesson* v. *France*, [99]; see also *Labassee* v. *France*, [78].

[235] See Art. 2(2) Convention on the Rights of the Child, New York, 20 November 1989, in force 2 September 1990, UNTS vol. 1577 (p. 3).

[236] See Lydia Bracken, *Same-Sex Parenting and Best Interests* (Cambridge: Cambridge University Press, 2020) 209.

[237] *Laborie and Others* v. *France*, App. No. 44024/13, 19 January 2017 (available only in French).

[238] *Foulon and Bouvet* v. *France*, App. Nos. 9063/14; 10410/14, 21 July 2016. See Chapter 5, Section 5.4.

[239] See *Laborie* v. *France*, [29]–[32].

[240] Advisory Opinion concerning the recognition in domestic law of a legal parent–child relationship between a child born through a gestational surrogacy arrangement abroad and the intended mother, Request No. P16-2018-001, 10 April 2019. See Chapter 3, Section 3.3.1.

conceived using the intended father's sperm and donated ova. In addition to requiring the recognition of the non-biological commissioning mother's relationship with the child through an expedited procedure (not necessarily the transcription of the foreign birth certificate), the Court suggested in an *obiter dictum* that, where the embryo was created with the intended mother's ova and donor sperm, 'the need to provide *a possibility of recognition* of the legal relationship between the child and the intended mother *applies with even greater force*'.[241] Problematically, the Court's wording left States a spectrum of options, rather than mandating registration as the legal mother and hence parental status *ab initio*.

A subsequent ruling confirmed that States meet their Article 8 obligations where legal affiliation with the commissioning genetic mother is established through step-parent adoption. *D.* v. *France*[242] concerned the refusal to record in the French civil register the full details of the Ukrainian birth certificate of a child born through gestational surrogacy, designating the intended genetic mother as the legal mother and her husband as the legal father. Under French law, a presumption of accuracy and direct effect applied to foreign birth certificates as regards the legal father (save for situations of demonstrable fraud),[243] and therefore the husband's paternity was not queried (while the applicants claimed that they were both genetic parents,[244] this did not appear tested). Conversely, the authorities refused to register the mother's details, insofar as she had not given birth to the child. In Strasbourg, the applicants complained that the authorities had breached the child's Article 8 right to respect for her private life and had discriminated against her on the grounds of birth.[245]

The parties and the Court agreed that the refusal to register the intended mother as the legal mother constituted an interference with the child's right to private life, carried out in accordance with the law.[246] For the Court, the protection of the interests of the child and the surrogate mother and the policy of discouraging surrogacy (a practice which was unlawful in France) fell

[241] Advisory Opinion P16-2018-001, [47] (emphasis added). As Alice Margaria noted, the Court 'ends up partially ignoring its own disclaimer . . . by providing some guidance . . . on a situation that is different from the one pending before the national court'; see Alice Margaria, 'Parenthood and Cross-Border Surrogacy: What Is "New"? The ECtHR's First Advisory Opinion' (2020) 28(2) *Medical Law Review* 412–425, at 419.

[242] *D.* v. *France*, App. No. 11288/18, 16 July 2004 (available only in French).

[243] See ibid., [10], [13].

[244] See ibid., [38].

[245] See ibid., [29], [73].

[246] See ibid., [40]–[43].

within the legitimate aims in Article 8(2).[247] The application did not appear to substantiate the claim that the measure failed to protect the child or the surrogate;[248] however, the surrogate's disinterest in acting as a parent and the child's interest in preserving the relationship with the genetic mother should have been discussed. As to the necessity of the interference, the Court recalled that the failure to recognise the legal relationship between a child and the intended biological father violated Article 8, but sought to reinterpret the authorities.[249] It maintained that *Mennesson/Labassee* did not require the State to establish legal ties between the child and the father through the transcription of the foreign birth certificate; rather, respect for the child's private life had to be ensured through an effective and speedy mechanism for establishing legal affiliation, but not necessarily through the transcription of the birth certificate. Adoption, a procedure with an average duration of 4.1 months according to the government, was deemed equally satisfactory. The Court further noted that, as indicated in its Advisory Opinion No. P16-2018-001, adoption produced similar effects to registration of the foreign birth details and adequately recognised the legal relationship between the child and the intended (non-genetic) mother.[250] In attempting to rationalise its decision that no violation of Article 8 had occurred, because the impugned decision was within the respondent's margin of appreciation, the Court took a regrettable step back from the advances made in *Mennesson* and *Labassee*. Its restatement of the previous jurisprudence unhelpfully downplays genetic affiliation, requiring States to ensure *some avenue* for establishing legal ties between the child and the commissioning genetic parent.[251]

D. v. France further found no violation of Article 8 read in conjunction with Article 14 in relation to the different treatment of French children born abroad through surrogacy, when compared to other French children born abroad, as regards the means of recognition of legal ties with the genetic mother. For the Court, adoption achieved the same result as the registration of the foreign birth details, and judicial scrutiny of the circumstances was necessary to protect the interests of the child.[252] To some extent, the *D. v. France* anomaly (and the step backwards from *Mennesson*) can be explained by the Court's unease with split motherhood and its deference to States' order of priority between gestational and genetic motherhood. However, where the

[247] See ibid., [44].
[248] See ibid., [35].
[249] See ibid., [45]–[49].
[250] See ibid., [51]–[54].
[251] See ibid., [51].
[252] See ibid., [85]–[88].

surrogate is not biologically related to the child, accepted to carry the foetus for the intended parents and consented to the latter's treatment as the legal parents, there is no compelling reason to depart from the general principle that the child's identity rights require the recognition in law of the genetic links with the commissioning mother. This would not compel States to revisit the domestic meaning of 'mother'; it would merely require them to accommodate an agreement lawfully entered into abroad with the consent of all relevant parties, lest they disadvantage the surrogate-born child. The recognition of maternal affiliation also finds support in the effectiveness of social ties and in the legal ties in the jurisdiction where the child was born.

The procedural discretion enjoyed by ECHR States vis-à-vis the recognition of parent–child relationships established through a foreign surrogacy was confirmed in *D. and Others* v. *Belgium*.[253] The application regarded the temporary separation (almost four months) of a child born through surrogacy in Ukraine from his Belgian parents. This separation arose from the refusal by Belgian authorities to issue the child a Belgian passport or other travel documents permitting entry into the country, based on the Ukrainian birth certificate, which identified the applicants – a Belgian married couple – as his parents. The Court reasoned that the applicants wished to look after the child since his birth and had taken action to establish an effective family life; it recalled that, despite the separation, 'intended family life' is also covered by Article 8.[254] The Court drew on its jurisprudence regarding adoptive parents who are not yet living with their adopted children; spouses who have not yet set up home together after the marriage ceremony; and the potential family life that natural fathers may expect to develop with children born out of wedlock after a relationship breakdown. The application of these principles to foreign surrogacy cases is particularly useful where the parents have not had a chance to establish an effective family life with the child. The protection of intended family life allowed the Court to analyse the separation in *D. and Others* as an interference with the applicants' right to respect for their family life.[255]

The Court conceded, however, that the interference pursued the legitimate aim of preventing crime, specifically the traffic in human beings, by verifying compliance with Belgian and Ukrainian legislation.[256] There was also a brief reference to the protection of the 'rights of others' – the surrogate and the

[253] *D. and Others* v. *Belgium*, App. No. 29176/13, 8 July 2014.
[254] Ibid., [49].
[255] Ibid., [50].
[256] Ibid., [52].

child.[257] It further held that 'the Convention cannot require States Parties to authorise the entry into their territory of children born to a surrogate mother without prior legal verifications on the part of the national authorities'[258] and found that the length of the proceedings had not been 'unreasonably long'.[259] The Court stressed the foreseeability of the procedure required for the recognition of the family relationship and the child's ability to enter the country[260] as well as the applicants' partial contribution to the delay.[261] Nor was the government responsible for the applicants' difficulties in remaining in Ukraine with the child while proceedings were pending before the Belgian authorities.[262] The application was dismissed as manifestly ill-founded, a conclusion perhaps unwarranted since the separation stemmed from the non-recognition of a valid foreign document.

All the surrogacy cases considered by the Court until 2022 focused on the effects of *lawful overseas* surrogacy arrangements. The recent *A.L.* v. *France* judgment confirmed that, even when created through an *unlawful domestic* surrogacy agreement, the biological link between the intended parent and the child remains protected by Article 8.[263] The domestic case at the origin of the Strasbourg complaint was a triangular paternity dispute after a failed surrogacy arrangement. The applicant (and his male companion) had been deceived by the surrogate mother, who had claimed that the child had died, whereas she had entrusted him to another couple in exchange for payment; that couple had recognised and raised the child since birth. Unlike *Mennesson* and similar applications, the *A.L.* complaint was introduced exclusively on behalf of the genetic intended father.[264] To that extent, it is the first judgment upholding the parent's, rather than the child's, right to private life in the context of surrogacy.

The Court found a breach of Article 8 due to the unreasonable delays in the conduct of paternity proceedings, which irreversibly affected the relationship between the child and his biological father; in fact, due to the passage of time, the recognition of affiliation and the transfer of care from the social parents to the biological father were no longer in the child's best interests. There is an

[257] Ibid., [53].
[258] Ibid., [59].
[259] Ibid., [58].
[260] Ibid., [60].
[261] Ibid., [62].
[262] Ibid., [61]. Due to the imminent expiry of their Ukrainian residence permit, the applicants had to return to Belgium, leaving the child behind with a nanny (see ibid., [14]).
[263] *A.L.* v. *France*, App. No. 13344/20, 7 April 2022 (available only in French).
[264] Ibid., [1].

evident parallel with *Keegan* v. *Ireland*,[265] although in that case the planned conception by a betrothed couple also engaged 'family life'. With that distinction, the principle upheld in *A.L.* is reminiscent of *Keegan*. Although surrogacy was illegal in France, and the father had been found guilty of incitement to abandon a child,[266] the Court held that the time elapsed since the introduction of the paternity action did not meet the special diligence standard required under Article 8; in fact, in paternity cases, such delays are likely to predetermine the outcome of the case (the child was four months old when paternity proceedings were instituted and was six years old by the time the case was decided).[267]

The ECtHR was satisfied that the domestic courts' decision was primarily motivated by the child's best interests, which included a right to a stable home with the family that had raised him since birth, especially in light of the passage of time.[268] Commendably, it rejected the respondent's contentions that the delays were caused by the complexities of the case and that the burden was on the individual litigant to use the tools available to expedite proceedings.[269] There are, however, important arguments in the applicant's submissions that deserved greater attention. One of the reasons for the father's lack of success in domestic proceedings was the authorities' reliance on the nullity of surrogacy contracts. The applicant appropriately denounced the inconsistency of this approach with (a) the recognition of natural affiliation in foreign surrogacy cases, (b) the determination in criminal proceedings that he was the father and (c) the courts' treatment of the social parents' conduct (purchasing a baby for EUR 15,000) as less objectionable than his entering a surrogacy agreement to have a biological child.[270] For future cases, it would have been desirable for the Court to address these submissions and unequivocally clarify that the biological link between the commissioning father and the child must be protected in all surrogacy cases, whether foreign or domestic, lawful or unlawful. Indeed, if the domestic surrogacy contract is null, the law should allocate paternity according to biology, recognising the commissioning

265 See *Keegan* v. *Ireland*, [55]: 'Where a child is placed with alternative carers he or she may in the course of time establish with them new bonds which it might not be in his or her interests to disturb or interrupt by reversing a previous decision as to care. Such a state of affairs not only jeopardised the proper development of the [father's] ties with the child but also set in motion a process which was likely to prove to be irreversible, thereby putting the [father] at a significant disadvantage in his contest with the prospective adopters for the custody of the child.'
266 *A.L.* v. *France*, [13].
267 Ibid., [68]–[69], [73].
268 Ibid., [58]–[60].
269 Ibid., [68]–[69].
270 Ibid., [38]–[39].

father as a legal parent not by virtue of the contract but based on genetic reality.[271] By focusing on the procedural breach of Article 8 (excessive length of proceedings), the Court missed the opportunity to advance the understanding of substantive obligations. In cases where the surrogate sells the baby to another couple, there is no public policy rationale for allowing an unmitigated illegal situation to prevail over biological ties, corroborated by intended family life; Article 8 should require the swift return of the child to the biological parent.

Different considerations may apply when the surrogate is the genetic mother and wishes to raise the baby herself. Although *A.L.* v. *France* was a case of traditional surrogacy, the mother did not intend to act as a social parent and there was no conflict of rights between two genetic parents. Even where the surrogate reconsiders and wishes to keep the child, regardless of whether or not she is requested to surrender the baby (based on contract, estoppel or other doctrines), the biological father's rights should encompass at least the recognition of affiliation and contact with the child. In fact, but for the surrogacy agreement, the father would not have impregnated the surrogate; moreover, he never agreed to act as a sperm donor for her and her husband. Arguably, the residence dispute should also be resolved in favour of the father; having to choose between two genetic parents with equal rights, the private agreement should tip the balance to the father's advantage. There should be, *a fortiori*, little hesitation as to the recognition of the genetic father when the surrogate reneguing on the agreement is not a genetic parent herself.

This was the factual matrix before the Court in *H.* v. *The United Kingdom*,[272] a case regarding a failed gestational surrogacy arrangement in a jurisdiction permitting surrogacy. The application was brought by a surrogate-born child whose birth certificate indicated as parents the genetically unrelated surrogate and her husband. Following the breakdown of the surrogacy

[271] The applicant relied on *Mandet* v. *France*, App. No. 30955/12, 14 January 2016 and *Ostace* v. *Romania*, App. No. 12547/06, 25 February 2014 to assert the right to biological truth in disputed paternity cases, but these precedents do not establish an absolute priority thereof. *Mandet* viewed as within the domestic courts' discretion the decision that the child's best interests were better served by establishing his real paternity than preserving the legal relationship with the mother's husband (*Mandet* v. *France*, [59]), in circumstances where parental responsibility remained with the mother and the family unit constituted by the mother, her husband and the son continued its life undisturbed (ibid., [58]). In *Ostace*, a bar on the disavowal of paternity failed to strike a fair balance in circumstances where all the parties (the man, his now adult son and his mother) supported establishing biological truth, but was otherwise accepted as safeguarding the stability of family relations and the child's interests (*Ostace* v. *Romania*, [42]–[45]).

[272] *H.* v. *The United Kingdom*, App. No. 32185/20, 31 May 2022.

arrangement, and given the veto right of the surrogate and her husband under domestic law as regards the issuing of parental orders to the intended parents, a court had placed the child with the commissioning couple, who also received shared parental responsibility; the surrogate and her husband continued to be the legal parents and could exercise limited parental responsibility and contact.[273] The case was essentially an identity case: the applicant complained that the registration of the surrogate's husband as the father on her birth certificate (instead of her genetic father), not open to legal challenge, breached her right to respect for her private life.[274]

Disappointingly, the Court was satisfied that the child 'ha[d] not been wholly deprived of a legal relationship with' the genetic father, in that she resided with him, had taken his surname and he was able to make parenting decisions.[275] The low threshold for the right to establish one's identity is astounding: 'After all, there is nothing preventing A and B from telling her about the circumstances of her birth and her national and cultural heritage.'[276] The Court seemingly equated knowledge of biological truth and the ability to oppose it to the world. In parentage cases (e.g. *Kroon* v. *The Netherlands*),[277] the parties' knowledge of the biological truth does not exonerate the State of its responsibility to permit them to align legal status with biological and social reality.[278] The Court also placed weight on the absence of 'practical or material disadvantages' for the child,[279] an approach emphatically abandoned in *K.K.* v. *Denmark* a few months later insofar as inconsistent with identity rights.[280] In particular, it accepted that any inheritance difficulties could be overridden by way of testamentary disposition,[281] a remedy which *K.K.* deemed unsatisfactory because other children were automatic

[273] See ibid., [4]–[9].
[274] See ibid., [32].
[275] Ibid., [46].
[276] Ibid., [47].
[277] *Kroon* v. *The Netherlands*, App. No. 18535/91, 27 October 1994.
[278] The Court's considerations in *Kroon* v. *The Netherlands*, [40], apply, *mutatis mutandis*, to private life: '"Respect" for "family life" requires that *biological and social reality prevail over a legal presumption* which . . . flies in the face of both established fact and the wishes of those concerned without actually benefiting anyone' (emphasis added). The English rule in *H.* did not benefit the child or the parents, and very marginally benefitted the surrogate and her husband, insofar as their parental status was largely notional.
[279] *H.* v. *The United Kingdom*, [47].
[280] *K.K. and Others* v. *Denmark*, App. No. 25212/21, 6 December 2022. See Chapter 3, Section 3.3.1.
[281] *H.* v. *The United Kingdom*, [47].

beneficiaries on intestacy.[282] In *H.*, the Court also minimised the possible interference arising 'from whatever degree of legal uncertainty might flow from the automatic recognition of [the surrogate's husband]' and considered it 'very limited indeed'.[283] Moreover, the observation that 'to date the Court has not held that the intended parents must immediately and automatically be recognised as such in law'[284] does not justify the lack of *any* legal avenue for the father or the child to establish their parentage if the gestational surrogate and/or her husband opposed it. This decision suggests that the Court remains deferential in the face of anomalies affecting surrogate-born children in purely domestic situations, possibly to avoid interfering with the domestic regulation of surrogacy, a contested field.

A key factual difference between *Mennesson* v. *France*/*K.K.* v. *Denmark* and *H.* v. *The United Kingdom* was the lack of competing parent figures in the former two.[285] In the latter, the gestational surrogate's husband was by default the legal father, a status he could only lose voluntarily, although he had no genetic ties to the child and the indirect legal (marital) bond to the surrogate was too remote to offset the father's genetic and intentional parenthood. Even accepting the initial presumption of paternity in favour of the husband of the woman who gives birth to the child, a statutory rule treating that presumption as irrebuttable – whereas even the fatherhood of the *genetic* mother's husband can be contested in paternity proceedings[286] – is a disproportionate interference with the child's and the genetic father's rights as well as amounting to discrimination against the child on grounds of conception.

Although the claim was not brought on behalf of the father, it is difficult to reconcile the Court's stance in *H.* v. *The United Kingdom* with the finding in *A.L.* v. *France*, decided only a month earlier, that the natural father's rights in a failed *illegal* surrogacy arrangement are entitled to protection in the form of expeditious paternity proceedings. *A fortiori* a genetic father who complied with the law should receive protection. The inflexible application of a legal

282 Although in *K.K.* v. *Denmark* there is no express analysis of the discriminatory nature of the law, there is an implied reference to the different (less advantageous) treatment received on account of the circumstances of conception, departing from the normalcy of family relationships.

283 *H.* v. *The United Kingdom*, [48].

284 Ibid., [56].

285 See ibid., [53], distinguishing *H.* from *Mennesson*: 'By the time the children arrived in France, it was clear that their intended parents (one of whom was the biological father) were the only persons who had, and who wished to exercise, parental responsibility.'

286 Section 55A Family Law Act 1986 allows the putative father to petition the court for a declaration of parentage displacing the *pater est* presumption operating in favour of the husband of the woman who gives birth to the child.

regime running counter to both genetic and social reality, in that it offers no avenue to establish affiliation between the child and the genetic and moral author of conception, fails to strike a fair balance between competing rights. By contrast with foreign lawful surrogacy and illegal domestic surrogacy cases, where the commissioning father's rights may be outweighed by his conduct contrary to domestic law, the full force of Article 8 rights should be upheld when surrogacy was a legal reproductive route under domestic law. Indeed, ECHR case law on natural fathers' rights shows that they are entitled to the protection of their private and family life with the child when conception was planned and the father played an active role in raising the child.[287] There is no reason to treat the natural father who procreates through lawful recourse to surrogacy differently, only to benefit a man who did not intend to become a father and does not have biological links with the child.

H. v. *The United Kingdom* also sits uncomfortably with the *Mennesson/Labassee/Foulon and Bouvet/Laborie* line of jurisprudence, namely with the principle that the surrogate-born child's identity rights require the establishment of legal affiliation with the genetic commissioning father. It is equally at odds with *K.K.* v. *Denmark*, where the child's identity rights were also found to require the recognition of legal affiliation, and no lesser measures, between the child and the *non-genetic* intended parent; this was so even if the practical impact of non-recognition was minimal, given the legal mechanisms safeguarding the stability of the family unit.

Furthermore, the adverse consequences for the child would have deserved a less cavalier approach in *H.* v. *The United Kingdom*. One cannot underestimate the confusion for the child of being brought up by a couple she views as her parents (one of them indeed a biological parent), while the law treats as parents another couple with whom she has infrequent contact and who are not biologically related to her. This situation could not be said to serve the child's best interests. The certainty and clarity of who the law treats as a parent, invoked by the respondent as a legitimate aim,[288] in practice is negated by the unnecessary complexity of different layers of parenthood and the confusing dissociation between genetic/social fatherhood and legal fatherhood. The aim of 'ensuring that donors of gametes used in the process of assisted procreation were not treated as legal parents'[289] is certainly irrelevant, insofar as commissioning parents embarking upon surrogacy are not acting as donors. The third aim invoked, 'ensuring that surrogacy arrangements, while lawful, were not

[287] See Draghici, 'Unplanned Fatherhood Is Not Sperm Donation', 127–132.
[288] See *H.* v. *The United Kingdom*, [49].
[289] See ibid.

enforceable in domestic law',[290] is in itself questionable, because it fails to protect both the individuals who enter such arrangements in good faith and the resulting children. If surrogacy is lawful, that is, not viewed as morally objectionable, the uncertainty of the fate of one's genetic material and parenthood plans, left at the will of third parties, is problematic. Particularly iniquitous is the veto right given to the surrogate's husband, a party who does not have any contribution to either conception or gestation.

Since 'there remains no consensus among the Contracting States when it comes to the acceptance of surrogacy arrangements', the Court endorsed the objectives presented by the respondent as pursuing the legitimate aim of protecting the rights and freedoms of others.[291] As regards the necessity and proportionality of the interference, the Court recited its general principles on the lack of consensus on delicate ethical matters and the conflict between rights widening the margin of appreciation, and on identity issues restricting it.[292] The Court's conclusion misses the crux of the complaint, which did not question the lack of automatic recognition of the child's relationship with the genetic father or the rule attributing fatherhood to the surrogate's husband at birth, but challenged the absolute impossibility of recognition of the father's parenthood if the surrogate or her husband oppose it:

> In light of the potential for considerable uncertainty regarding the parentage of a child born by way of assisted reproduction, borne out by the facts of the case at hand, in the Court's view the decision of the respondent State to create a clear rule governing parenthood in cases of assisted reproduction from the moment of the child's birth fell within the wide margin of appreciation enjoyed by the State when deciding such matters.[293]

As in *D. v. France*, the Court read down *Mennesson* to accommodate its conclusion that the UK's surrogacy regime was ECHR-complaint:

> To date the Court has not held that the intended parents must immediately and automatically be recognised as such in law ... where a child is born through a surrogacy arrangement and the intended father is also the

[290] Ibid.
[291] Ibid.
[292] Ibid., [51]–[52].
[293] Ibid., [54]. The Court refers to the fact that both commissioning fathers' gametes had been used to impregnate the surrogate and consequently paternity could not have been known with certainty at the time of birth. Given the widespread use of DNA tests, and the numerous cases of natural intercourse where paternity is uncertain before birth, the overmagnification of this detail gives the impression that the Court is grasping at straws in an attempt to rule in favour of the respondent.

> biological father, Article 8 of the Convention only requires that domestic law provide a possibility of recognition of the legal relationship between him and the child. … In *Mennesson*, for example, the Court recognised that other formal means of recognition of parentage may satisfy Article 8 of the Convention.[294]

Even applying the Court's reasoning, no 'possibility of recognition', through any 'formal means of recognition of parentage', was available to the genetic father, as the surrogate and/or her husband's lack of consent was an insurmountable bar. This rigid regime reserved to surrogacy cases stands in contrast with natural conception cases, in which fatherhood can be reallocated by a court based on DNA or other evidence. The Court's reading appears in part influenced by the applicant's submission that there should be 'a "normative presumption" in favour of recognising the biological father on the birth certificate',[295] which was interpreted by the Court as a presumption at birth (i.e. automatic registration), instead of a presumption that the birth certificate ought to reflect – possibly at the end of a court process, not necessarily *ab initio* – genetic fatherhood.

The *H.* v. *The United Kingdom* ruling, albeit excessively deferential in its acceptance of indirect means of securing family ties instead of legal affiliation, does not detract from the pivotal role of genetic links between the child and (one of) the intended parent(s) in activating ECHR protection. This is further demonstrated, *a contrario*, by the different treatment of surrogacy agreements in which neither member of the couple was genetically related to the child. In *Paradiso and Campanelli* v. *Italy*, where neither parent had biological ties with the child (due to the foreign clinic's error or fraud), the Grand Chamber found that 'family life' did not exist, the intended parents had no standing to apply on behalf of the child, and the interference with the adults' 'private life' was justified.[296] This suggests that intentional parenthood, even where corroborated by (incipient) effective social parenthood, does not entitle the couple to legal recognition as parents, notwithstanding the legal affiliation established abroad.

In *Valdís Fjölnisdóttir and Others* v. *Iceland*, the Court accepted that a married same-sex female couple and the child conceived through surrogacy in the United States, unrelated to either but placed in their foster care in Iceland (where the prohibition on surrogacy meant that the couple could not be registered as his legal parents), had developed bonds amounting to 'family

294 Ibid, [56].
295 Ibid., [57].
296 *Paradiso and Campanelli* v. *Italy* [GC], discussed in Chapter 3, Section 3.3.2.

life' during the course of long-term effective care (four years at the time of the final domestic judgment).[297] The Court distinguished that situation from *Paradiso and Campanelli* v. *Italy*, where, despite the existence of a 'parental project' and 'the quality of emotional bonds', the brevity of the relationship between the intended parents and the child (eight months) and the uncertainty of legal ties meant that the criteria for 'family life' had not been met.[298] However, by contrast with cases where a genetic link existed between one commissioning parent and the child born through foreign surrogacy (e.g. *Mennesson*), *Valdís Fjölnisdóttir* indicated that respect for family life can be ensured through routes other than legal affiliation when the child is not biologically related to the couple, such as a foster care arrangement. This reinforces, by contrast, the notion that biological parenthood, which is central to a person's identity, requires special measures of protection, in particular the prompt legal recognition of the parent–child relationship.

It could be thought that the raison d'être of surrogacy is to allow a person to have a biologically related child in circumstances where their partner's infertility (or the absence of a partner) threatens their procreative future. Where neither of the commissioning parents is related to the child, conception via double gamete donation and surrogacy has less to do with the aspiration to reproduce and more to do with the desire to fulfil a parental role. The extent to which Article 8 protects the position of non-biological intended parents is discussed in Chapter 3.

2.5 CONCLUDING REMARKS

Albeit reined in by the margin of appreciation doctrine, the judicial reinterpretation of the rights enshrined in the ECHR in light of scientific advances has progressively expanded reproductive freedom. Case law developments have propelled a new cluster of reproductive rights centred around geneticism: first, the right to respect for the decision to become a genetic parent, even when a person can acquire the status of legal parent to an unrelated (e.g. adoptive) child (*Evans* v. *The United Kingdom*), and the right to make use of the available ARTs in order to conceive a child, such choice being an expression of private and family life (*Dickson* v. *The United Kingdom*, *S.H.* v. *Austria*, *Knecht* v. *Romania*, *Nedescu* v. *Romania*, *Pejřilová* v. *The Czech Republic*, *Lia* v. *Malta*); second, the right to use embryos created with one's

[297] *Valdís Fjölnisdóttir and Others* v. *Iceland*, App. No. 71552/17, 18 May 2021, [59], discussed in Chapter 3, Section 3.3.2.

[298] *Valdís Fjölnisdóttir and Others* v. *Iceland*, [59].

gametes for the purposes of reproduction, subject to the equal rights of the other gamete provider and public policy interests (e.g. ensuring that clinics only operate with appropriate credentials); third, the gamete providers' right to decide the fate of embryos no longer intended for a pregnancy, subject to competing interests, such as the protection of embryos or deceased partners' self-determination rights (albeit not parenthood-oriented, it reinforces the right to exercise control over one's genetic material); fourth, the right of surrogacy-born children to the recognition of legal ties with the genetic intended parent. Thus, the indiscriminate refusal of assisted insemination facilities for prisoners and unreasonable delays in gaining access to one's frozen embryos for treatment amount to breaches of Article 8. In inter-American jurisprudence, the right to make use of ART (specifically IVF) is also linked to the acceptance of infertility as disability, requiring special measures of protection (*Artavia Murillo* v. *Costa Rica*). The right to make use of ART in order to become a genetic parent has been cemented by the relative success of other geneticism-based claims, such as the right to exercise control over one's own genetic material, inter alia over embryos created with one's gametes, albeit limited by the free will of the other gamete provider or the State's interest in protecting human embryos (*Parrillo* v. *Italy*).

Alice Margaria has noted the incremental shift from the recognition of the right to respect for the decision to become a parent as subsumed under 'private life' in *Evans* to its protection under both the 'family' and 'private life' limbs of Article 8 in *Dickson* and *S.H.*[299] One might conjecture that what attracted the application of the 'family life' limb was the presence of married couples; indeed, reiterations of the principle can be found in *Knecht*, *Pejřilová* and *Lia*, all cases involving married couples. Although the right to 'found a family' under Article 12 has fallen in desuetude in Strasbourg practice after *E.L.H. and P.B.H.* v. *The United Kingdom*, apparently the historical association in this provision between marriage and procreation has transferred to the analysis of (planned) 'family life' under Article 8.

Despite these achievements, the ECtHR's emphasis on State discretion in the sensitive field of bioethics continues to inhibit the further development of procreative rights. The Court has been reluctant to require States to permit certain medically assisted procreation techniques in pursuit of parenthood aspirations: techniques involving third-party contributions, in particular ova donation and heterologous IVF (*S.H.* v. *Austria*) and posthumous reproduction, for example, fertilisation with the deceased husband's frozen gametes

299 See Alice Margaria, *The Construction of Fatherhood. The Jurisprudence of the European Court of Human Rights* (Cambridge: Cambridge University Press, 2019) 52.

(*Pejřilová* v. *The Czech Republic*). While a claim to the legalisation of surrogacy has not been entertained, the case law on the recognition of legal effects to overseas treatment indicates that ECHR States are entitled to view it as contrary to public policy (*Mennesson* v. *France*). Although the refusal to allow access to certain assisted reproduction methods has been qualified as an active interference with Article 8 rights, it was nevertheless found within the States' margin of appreciation.

This deferral to State regulation of ART does not recognise that the effective enjoyment of the right to exercise the choice of becoming a genetic parent may require access to third-party–assisted reproduction, for example, where the use of donor gametes and/or surrogacy is the only means to conceive a child genetically related to (at least a member of) the couple. To that extent, gamete donation should be permitted in order to reconcile genetic parenthood and the free choice of partner; the refusal to treat aspiring parents with donated ova/sperm places them in an unenviable position of having to sacrifice either their family life with an infertile partner or the pursuit of biological parenthood. There is limited acknowledgement of infertility as a disability rights issue in ECHR case law, and Article 14 should play a more prominent role. The refusal to permit access to certain forms of ART, albeit evenly applied, affects reproductively challenged couples significantly more. Scott recommended that the ECtHR should 'develop its understanding of reproductive interests under Article 8 with reference to the concept of reproductive health' and recognise that 'those with fertility problems cannot choose to reproduce without some form of medical assistance'.[300] It would be desirable for the ECtHR to borrow from the jurisprudence of its inter-American counterpart, who established an unequivocal link between reproductive health and autonomous choice and the discriminatory nature of bars on ART, which fail to acknowledge infertility as a disability (*Artavia Murillo* v. *Costa Rica*).[301]

Surrogacy remains the most disputed route to securing a biologically related child. By contrast with access to gamete donation (initially upheld by the Chamber judgment in *S.H. and Others* v. *Austria*), there is no indication that Article 8 might be interpreted as requiring States to allow individuals/couples to resort to surrogacy. However, notable advances have been made towards the protection of family life built on overseas surrogacy arrangements. The surrogate-born child's right to respect for private life requires the recognition of parentage, which is an important facet of a person's identity. Although this

[300] Scott, 'Reproductive Health', 443.

[301] Albeit established in relation to homologous IVF in *Artavia Murillo* v. *Costa Rica*, these considerations are also relevant in the context of third-party reproduction.

indirectly benefits the genetic commissioning parent, on a principled level, it is not unproblematic that the Court has only upheld the child's rights in foreign surrogacy cases.

The ECtHR's position is rather questionable in its ambiguous treatment of genetic intended mothers. It did not require the immediate recognition of maternal affiliation through the transcription of the foreign birth certificate, viewing step-parent adoption as equally appropriate (*D.* v. *France*), by contrast with the (at least initial) approach to genetic intended fathers (*Mennesson/Labassee/Foulon*), later read down to merely require some possibility of recognition (*D.* v. *France*) and not even necessarily through the rectification of the birth certificate (*H.* v. *The United Kingdom*). The failure to recognise a genetic parent *ab initio* runs counter to well-established Article 8 principles: (1) the law must allow the reality of biological ties corroborated by de facto ties to prevail over rigid presumptions of parenthood (*Kroon* v. *The Netherlands*); (2) hurdles to the recognition of affiliation, such as the requirement that a biological mother adopt her own child to create legal ties, leave the child temporarily in a legal limbo and prevent the development of normal family life (*Marckx* v. *Belgium*); (3) the 'right to know one's parentage' is an integral part of the notion of 'private life'.[302] Even making allowance for the concerns raised by commercial surrogacy, human rights law should promote respect for biological parenthood (with the sole exception of parents uninterested in fulfilling a parental role). Mulligan has argued that

> for the Court to extend its analysis [in *Mennesson*] to genetic mothers would require the Court to stray into the complex territory of defining whether a genetic or gestational mother has a greater right to be recognised as a child's mother, a question that it might understandably not wish to address, and one which certainly engages sensitive ethical issues which generally tend towards a wide margin of appreciation.[303]

However, the rights of the genetic and the gestational mother are not in conflict in overseas surrogacy cases, in that the surrogate is not interested in asserting parenthood and that the legal transfer of parenthood has been completed under the relevant law. Upholding the genetic mother's parental status would not require States to choose between competing private rights, nor to revisit their legal definition of motherhood.

[302] See *Mikulić* v. *Croatia*, App. No. 53176/99, 7 February 2002, [54]; *Jäggi* v. *Switzerland*, [37].
[303] Andrea Mulligan, 'Identity Rights and Sensitive Ethical Questions: The European Convention on Human Rights and the Regulation of Surrogacy Arrangements' (2018) 26(3) *Medical Law Review* 449–475, at 469–470.

The regulation of fatherhood following domestic *lawful* surrogacy agreements has also attracted unwarranted deference (*H. v. The United Kingdom*). While the objective of ensuring legal certainty as to a person's maternal and paternal affiliation is laudable, a rigid scheme, always identifying the surrogate mother and her husband as the legal parents if they are unwilling to surrender the child, ought to have been found disproportionate and outside the margin of appreciation, insofar as it does not allow courts to make the decision that promotes the best interests of the child. Whenever a child's identity is at stake, the margin is narrower and calls for a closer scrutiny, even in the absence of European consensus. When the surrogate and her husband are not genetically related to the child and a court has determined that the child's welfare is promoted by being raised by the intended parents, that court should also have the authority to transfer legal fatherhood to the genetic commissioning father, in the way it is already able to do in disputed paternity proceedings involving children born through natural intercourse. The aim of clear allocation of parenthood is not seen by the legislator as frustrated by declarations of parentage or adoption orders; the rigidity of the law in connection with surrogacy-born children is therefore inconsistent. The disproportionate veto power given to the surrogate's husband in relation to the genetic father's parental status, despite the former's lack of genetic or other ties with the child, and considering the child's identity rights, does not strike a fair balance between competing interests. Moreover, a child born via surrogacy in a country such as the UK is arguably discriminated against on the ground of conception when compared to children born via natural intercourse; the latter's identity rights are protected by legal avenues for establishing their true parentage and enjoying the rights flowing from legal affiliation with the genetic parent.

The ECtHR's apparent concern to preserve States' prerogative to regulate ART has led to the endorsement of further questionable domestic balancing acts. A notable example was the UK's IVF scheme, which gave absolute protection to male gamete providers' right not to become a parent, at the expense of the woman's right to become a parent, even in circumstances where the joint frozen embryos were the woman's last surviving procreative material and she had relied on the man's reassurances of continued consent when choosing to fertilise her oocytes with his sperm. The Court ought to recognise a positive duty for States to protect a person's ability to become a genetic parent against third-party interference (including misrepresentations and breach of promise). It should also voice the need to acknowledge the different reproductive burdens of men and women when striking a balance, in that ova extraction is much more invasive and requires medical facilities, and ova cryopreservation has much lower chances of success when compared to embryo or sperm cryopreservation, hence the different impact on women of belated withdrawal of consent to the preservation and use of shared embryos.

The Court will soon have an opportunity to revisit its approach to posthumous reproduction, specifically the widow's right to make use of her late spouse's stored gametes or joint embryos for the purposes of ART. The new cases pending before the Court (*Dalleau* v. *France*; *Caballero* v. *France*) feature clear evidence of the deceased's anticipatory decision to become a parent. Subject to child welfare considerations, the ECtHR ought to require States to accommodate the deceased's advance directives and the surviving spouse's decision to continue the reproductive project. The judgments issued to date, while invoking the free will of the deceased, could have requested States to prioritise the rights of the surviving spouse – at least by affording an opportunity to demonstrate the deceased's support for posthumous insemination in a court – through a process analogous to existing ones for inferring the wishes of patients in permanent vegetative state or for the retrospective assessment of a request for assistance in dying. Even in the absence of incontrovertible evidence as to the wishes of the deceased, a law preventing a woman from using embryos created with her own genetic material when her spouse dies unexpectedly should be viewed as an excessive interference. The position of the parent of the deceased (*Petithory Lanzmann* v. *France*) should also be revisited: in particular, the legal standing as next of kin to defend the deceased child's reproductive wishes and their own right either to become a biological grandparent by using the deceased child's frozen embryos or to donate them to an infertile couple – especially when this coincides with the deceased's wishes and the alternative is the destruction of the embryos. Naturally, this should remain subject to a case-by-case determination.

In the future, the Court may also hear economic claims related to ART. Although the Court has preferred to examine the refusal to allow ART as an interference (affecting a negative obligation), the issue of provision of treatment free of charge may require the demonstration of a positive obligation. Concerns have been expressed in the literature over the cost to supply fertility treatment services if States were found to have any such obligation as a matter of human rights. It was suggested that the provision of food, housing and healthcare needs can be seen as a more legitimate imposition on the public.[304] This concern over the burden on public finances, if a right to subsidised ART in the furtherance of parenthood aspirations were to be

[304] Deech and Smajdor, *From IVF to Immortality*, 139.

recognised, overlooks the burden already imposed on taxpayers by the duty to provide financial support for any number of children a person chooses to have naturally, as well as the costs associated with children in State care, which stem in part from irresponsible natural reproduction (i.e. reproduction regardless of the couple's interest or ability to support their children). Although the focus of public assistance to low-income and unemployed parents is on the well-being of *existing* children, many children would not be brought into existence but for welfare policies providing the wrong incentive to procreate. Indeed, the stimulus effects of welfare generosity on reproductive behaviour are well documented.[305] Indirect discrimination can arise if the State respects the wish to procreate – at the public's expense – of people who can procreate naturally (regardless of whether they have ever contributed to the public purse), while the wish of those who need State support to *conceive*, but are capable and willing to bring up their children without State assistance (and are possibly long-term tax payers), is not respected. Filtering the desire to be a parent based on the amount of public funding required to become pregnant, but not the amount required to raise a child (which is greater), creates an unethical double standard. Moreover, if, in countries offering taxpayer-supported healthcare, the public cost of antenatal care for mothers during pregnancies is not invoked to limit the number of children a person can have if they can procreate naturally, the costs for the national healthcare system to assist reproductively challenged couples to procreate should not prevent the development of the right.

If the practice of surrogacy becomes more widespread, further questions will be facing Strasbourg judges as regards the appropriate regulation of competing rights, notably the conflict between the surrogate mother's rights and those of the commissioning parents. From that perspective, the single most contentious issue, resolved differently by different jurisdictions, is whether or not the surrogate should be permitted to renege on the arrangement and refuse to surrender the child.[306] Arguably, at least in gestational surrogacy cases in which the commissioning mother's ova were used to create

305 See, e.g., Robert Moffitt, 'The Effect of Welfare on Marriage and Fertility', in Robert Moffitt (ed.), *Welfare, the Family, and Reproductive Behaviour: Research Perspectives* (Washington, DC: The National Academies Press, 1998), 50-97; Alma Cohen, Rajeev Dehejia and Dmitri Romanov, 'Financial Incentives and Fertility' (2013) 95(1) *Review of Economics and Statistics* 1–20. A law removing children from parents who do not work to support them might generate a different incentive structure.

306 For examples of English cases where the surrogate wished to keep the baby, see A v. C [1985] FLR 445, *Re P (Minors) (Wardship: Surrogacy)* [1987] 2 FLR 421, recalled in Douglas, *Law, Fertility and Reproduction*, 154.

the embryo implanted in the surrogate, genetic and intentional parenthood and good-faith private agreements should trump the surrogate's rights. The latter merely rely on the assumption of pregnancy risks; the provision of the environment for the development of the foetus; giving birth; and historical attachment to viewing the woman who gave birth as the mother. Indeed, the commissioning mother never agreed to act as an egg donor for the surrogate, and her private and family life would be disproportionately curtailed by the opposite solution. In traditional surrogacy cases, the father's Article 8 rights should prevail on the surrogate's rights when deciding the child's residence; they both have an equal biological link, but the child would not have been born but for the agreement that the child would be a part of the father's family. A law permitting a radical change in the commissioning couple's circumstances (from a joint child to the father co-parenting with the surrogate and the commissioning mother assuming a step-parent role), only to accommodate the surrogate's refusal to honour freely agreed arrangements, should be seen as disproportionate. Indeed, it also breaches the commissioning father's right *not* to procreate with a person he has not chosen for those purposes. In a distant future, the Strasbourg Court may have to address similar dilemmas, left for now to domestic legislatures.

3

A Right to the Recognition of Intentional Parenthood?

3.1 PARENTHOOD CLAIMS IN THIRD-PARTY REPRODUCTION

The development of regional human rights law could not remain oblivious to the increasing recognition of family formation built around de facto social ties in the law and practice of European countries. As Janet Finch has noted, 'in the contemporary world, it is now more explicitly recognised that family relationships may be based on social rather than biological definitions', a trend illustrated by the 'greater prevalence of step-families following divorce and re-partnering' whereby 'children live in complex kin groups'.[1] In addition, sociological studies have shown that the parent–child bond and the quality of parenting in adoptive families and families formed through gamete or embryo donation are no less positive when compared to families where the parents are genetically related to their children.[2] In particular, children born through assisted reproduction with donor are said to be equally well adjusted and enjoy positive relationships with their parents, which suggests that the genetic link is not indispensable for the children's well-being.[3] Many scholars have thus reached the conclusion that 'a genetic relationship is not essential for good social parenting or the satisfactory social and emotional development of children'.[4] This chapter will inquire whether this widespread social

[1] Janet Finch, 'Kinship as "Family" in Contemporary Britain', in Fatemeh Ebtehaj, Bridget Lindley and Martin Richards (eds.), *Kinship Matters* (London: Hart, 2006) 295–306, at 303.

[2] Fiona MacCallum, 'Parenting Genetically Unrelated Children: A Comparison of Embryo Donation and Adoption', in Kirsty Horsey and Hazel Biggs (eds.), *Human Fertilisation and Embryology* (Abingdon: Routledge, 2007) 135–154, at 144–145.

[3] Katherine Wade, 'The Regulation of Surrogacy: A Children's Rights Perspective' (2017) 29(2) *Child and Family Law Quarterly* 113–131, at 118–119.

[4] Rachel Cook, 'Donating Parenthood: Perspectives on Parenthood from Surrogacy and Gamete Donation', in Andrew Bainham, Shelley Day Sclater and Martin Richards (eds.), *What Is a Parent? A Socio-Legal Analysis* (Oxford: Hart, 1999) 121–141, at 129.

acceptance of a broader notion of parenthood, not confined to biological descent, has also given rise to new procreative rights under the European Convention on Human Rights (ECHR). Indeed, the recognition of social parenthood in relation to *existing* children (e.g. a step-parent replacing an absentee parent through adoption) does not necessarily translate into a person's right to cause *new* unrelated children to be born with the expectation to be treated as their legal parent.

The chapter will consider three key assisted reproduction techniques (ARTs) involving third-party contribution (genetic and/or gestational) and a legal fiction of parenthood: (a) gamete donation (sperm or ova) for the purposes of IVF treatment or in vivo heterologous insemination (a woman's direct artificial insemination with the sperm of a man who is not her partner and the intended father); (b) embryo donation for another couple's IVF treatment; and (c) surrogacy arrangements, whether traditional (in which the surrogate is impregnated with the commissioning father's sperm and hence is also the genetic mother) or gestational (in which the embryo transferred into the surrogate's uterus is created with the commissioning mother's ova or donated ova). All these scenarios presuppose the deliberate dissociation between aspects of parenthood traditionally cumulated in the same two persons: genetic (for mothers also gestational), social and legal. Third-party reproduction – reproduction with the assistance of a person outside the couple – revolves around the notions of intentional parenthood (i.e. purposefully creating a new life albeit without one's genetic material) and non-parenthood-oriented reproductive activity (producing gametes/embryos for the purposes of donation to others, using the uterus to allow the development of another couple's foetus).

It is the decision to embark upon a reproductive project and to bring about new life that distinguishes intentional parenthood from step-parenthood and adoptive parenthood, in which an individual assumes the care of, and responsibility for, an existing child. Moreover, unlike adoption, the recourse to ARTs remains an adult-centric method of creating legal ties between children and unrelated adults. As detailed in Chapter 2, the rationale for third-party reproduction is usually found in the desire of a fertile partner for a biological child. Intentional parenthood thus tends to arise in conjunction with a stable intimate relationship with a partner whose gametes will contribute to the genetic make-up of the future child. This legal association between the two adults legitimises the claim to parenthood on the basis of an existing family unit, of which the assisted procreative act is a natural extension.

That said, intentional parenthood does not always presuppose the existence of a couple, nor does it exist solely to further the genetic parenthood aspirations of the fertile member of a couple. For instance, a donated embryo – possibly from the so-called surplus embryos of a couple having undertaken assisted reproduction treatment (ART) and completed their family – may be transferred into a single woman's body. She may also resort to the use of donated ova and donated sperm to create an embryo in vitro for implantation into her womb. This way, albeit not genetically related to the child, she can experience pregnancy and birth, as well as forge prenatal bonds with the child. On the other hand, a single man or a couple can use both male- and female-donated gametes and a surrogate to have a child in jurisdictions permitting this type of arrangement. Intention can therefore sometimes form the sole basis for non-genetic parenthood. If the right-to-a-biological-child rationale for third-party reproduction in part-infertile couples lapses, and one or two people decide to have a child using exclusively donated gametes/embryos and surrogacy services, one may query the basis on which they are entitled to bring into the world a made-to-order baby and to demand the recognition of parental status. Is the fact that the future child will not be hurt, and no harm will be caused to the general public, sufficient to conclude that the individual's/couple's family aspirations ought to be accommodated through ART? The question could be, however, articulated in reverse: on what grounds, and in what circumstances, can the State prohibit the attainment of non-biological parenthood with the support of ART? This might be the more appropriate question in a liberal analytical framework, which places the burden of proof on those who wish to restrict choices otherwise available and benefitting someone's pursuit of self-fulfilment.

The concept of intentional parenthood was prominently asserted in a failed surrogacy arrangement case opposing the commissioning genetic mother to the gestational mother. In its *Johnson* v. *Calvert* ruling, having to assign motherhood to either the genetic or gestational mother after the latter refused to surrender the child to the commissioning couple, the Supreme Court of California reasoned that, faced with two equally valid claims to motherhood, both women having presented acceptable proof of maternity (blood tests/fact of giving birth), the decisive factor had to be *intention*:

> Mark and Crispina are a couple who desired to have a child of their own genes but are physically unable to do so without the help of reproductive technology. They affirmatively intended the birth of the child, and took the steps necessary to effect in vitro fertilization. But for their acted-on intention, the child would not exist. Anna agreed to facilitate the procreation of Mark's and Crispina's child. The parties' aim was to bring Mark's and Crispina's child into the world, not for Mark and Crispina to donate a zygote to Anna. Crispina from the outset intended to be the child's mother. Although the

> gestative function Anna performed was necessary to bring about the child's birth, it is safe to say that Anna would not have been given the opportunity to gestate or deliver the child had she, prior to implantation of the zygote, manifested her own intent to be the child's mother.[5]

Gillian Douglas noted the peculiar basis for decision in this case: rather than relying on 'a preference for the blood tie', the court 'regarded the *intellectual* conception of the child as being the fundamental cause of his creation'.[6] Naturally, unless the law recognises the possibility of two legal mothers, the 'intellectual conception' test does not help allocate motherhood in a case of 'reciprocal IVF' in lesbian couples, whereby one woman provides the oocytes and the other carries the pregnancy;[7] in fact, both the genetic and the gestational mother are intended mothers. Douglas further suggested that, even though, in *Johnson* v. *Calvert*, intention served to break the tie between two maternity claims, if intention to create the child is the decisive factor in allocating parenthood, 'those who set out to use assisted reproduction . . . to give them a child with whom they have no genetic *or* gestational tie, deserve equal recognition'.[8] This may be a leap too far: intention to be a parent can be a substantial factor corroborating genetic ties for the purposes of legal recognition, but can it independently create legal ties, especially when neither commissioning parent is related to the child?

The legal relevance of intention *alone* may be less persuasive, especially for scholars attached to the idea of genetic parenthood as the quintessential form of parenthood. That said, the scholarly debate on whether the law should prioritise social parenthood or genetic parenthood mainly focuses on the allocation of legal parenthood when there are two competing candidates, typically a biological father and a social father (e.g. in relation to the law's approach to presumptions of paternity and legal standing to bring a paternity challenge).[9] It is worth bearing in mind that, in most ART cases, there is no

5 *Johnson* v. *Calvert*, 5 Cal. 4th 84 (1993), 93, examined in Stuart Bridge, 'Assisted Reproduction and the Legal Definition of Parentage', in Andrew Bainham, Shelley Day Sclater and Martin Richards (eds.), *What Is a Parent? A Socio-Legal Analysis* (Oxford: Hart, 1999) 73–88, at 77–78.

6 Gillian Douglas, 'The Intention To Be a Parent and the Making of Mothers' (1994) 57 *Modern Law Review* 636–641, at 637 (original emphasis).

7 See Dorothy Greenfeld and Emre Seli, 'Assisted Reproduction in Same Sex Couples', in Mark Sauer (ed.), *Principles of Oocyte and Embryo Donation* (London: Springer-Verlag, 2013) 289–301, reprinted in Helga Kuhse, Udo Schüklenk and Peter Singers (eds.), *Bioethics: An Anthology* (Chichester: John Wiley and Sons, 2016, 3rd ed.) 74–85, at 79.

8 Douglas, 'The Intention To Be a Parent', 639 (original emphasis).

9 See Andrew Bainham, 'Whose Sperm Is It Anyway?' (2003) 62(3) *Cambridge Law Journal* 566–570; Carmen Draghici, 'Unplanned Fatherhood Is Not Sperm Donation: An Unduly

other candidate competing for the status of legal parent for the child. In principle, donors and surrogates do not intend to procreate and become parents (save for a change of heart in the case of surrogate mothers). The issue, therefore, is not whom the law should treat as the legal parent out of the two potential candidates (the centuries-old dilemma arising from infidelity or relationship breakdown and repartnering); rather, it is whether the law should permit individuals to bring into the world – with the assistance of other willing individuals – children to whom they are not genetically related but whom they plan to rear as their own. This chapter sets out to explore the possible human rights foundations for the claims of aspiring non-genetic parents.

Outside the ART sphere, the ECHR case law on the notion of 'family' has contributed to reshaping the answer to the fundamental question in human reproduction: what makes a parent? As indicated in *L. v. The Netherlands*, 'the existence or non-existence of "family life" for the purposes of Article 8 is essentially a question of fact depending upon the real existence in practice of close personal ties'.[10] Genetic affiliation, not corroborated by effective ties or legal bonds, is not in itself sufficient to give rise to 'family life', whereas social units not based on biological ties may qualify as such.[11] 'Family life' claims brought by natural fathers relying exclusively on genetic ties, where they had no opportunity for contact with the children through no fault of their own, tend to fail unless the child was the product of a committed relationship with the mother and planned conception.[12] Conversely, the biological father's family aspirations are treated as a mere privacy interest if the birth resulted from an extramarital or fleeting relationship, and the Court readily accepts justifications for interferences based on the child's welfare and the relationship with the social father (the mother's husband or new partner).[13] However, this approach, whereby the protection of social parenthood displaces a willing and capable biological parent, can be rationalised by the desire to safeguard the new family unit formed by the child, the mother and her new husband, rather than as devaluing genetic parenthood. This line of jurisprudence further

Moralistic Approach to Natural Fathers in ECHR Case Law' (2022) 2 *Child and Family Law Quarterly* 123–147.

[10] *L.* v. *The Netherlands*, App. No. 45582/99, 1 June 2004, [36].

[11] See, e.g., *X, Y and Z* v. *The United Kingdom* [GC], App. No. 21830/93, 22 April 1997; *Moretti and Benedetti* v. *Italy*, App. No. 16318/07, 27 April 2010.

[12] See *M.B.* v. *The United Kingdom*, App. No. 22920/93, 6 April 1994 (Commission), [2]; *Ahrens* v. *Germany*, App. No. 45071/09, 22 March 2012, [58]–[59]; *Schneider* v. *Germany*, App. No. 17080/07, 15 September 2011, [82].

[13] See Draghici, 'Unplanned Fatherhood Is Not Sperm Donation', 131–133 and 136–143; Brian Sloan, 'Unmarried Fathers and the Frustration of Family Life' (2011) 70(2) *Cambridge Law Journal* 314–317.

indicates that biological ties are not absolutely necessary to establish parenthood. If this is true in the case of children who are born through natural procreation (and hence have two parents at birth, one of whom is replaced by a social parent), a consistent approach to parenthood requires the same flexibility for ART-born children, especially since, without the recognition of intentional parenthood, they would have only one parent (in fact, the donor is, by definition, not interested in acting as a parent).

Strasbourg case law further suggests that intention to act as a parent plays some role in both creating and negating parenthood. In fact, the former European Commission on Human Rights indicated in *J.R.M.* v. *The Netherlands* that gamete donation in the context of assisted reproduction does not attract the protection of Article 8 ECHR: 'The situation in which a person donates sperm only to enable a woman to become pregnant through artificial insemination does not of itself give the donor a right to respect for family life with the child.'[14] The negative outcome of the application was explained by several cumulative factors, rather than by intention alone, but significant weight was attached to the initial agreement between the parties, whereby the applicant would act as a sperm donor for a lesbian couple and the women would have exclusive custody of the child. In addition, the applicant had had very limited contact with the baby during the first few months of his life and did not contribute financially to his upbringing. The Commission thus concluded that, absent other elements (such as effective ties/contribution to raising the child), the relationship between the sperm donor and the child resulting from ART did not qualify as 'family life' within the meaning of Article 8. The *J.R.M.* decision distinguished between natural fatherhood and sperm donation; it found that the two situations are not comparable, and therefore the different treatment of a sperm donor does not amount to discrimination.[15] The scholarship has also recognised that a sperm donor and a cohabiting father are not similarly situated, and hence the recognition of legal ties between the former and the ART-born child may be legitimately subjected to restrictions aimed at protecting the child's interests.[16]

The relevance of intention in establishing parenthood can also be seen in the case law regarding the claims of natural fathers who never had an opportunity to establish de facto links with their children, due to the

[14] *J.R.M.* v. *The Netherlands*, App. No. 16944/90, 8 February 1993 (Commission), [1].
[15] Ibid.
[16] See Vincent Coussirat-Coustère, 'Famille et Convention Européenne des Droits de l'Homme', in Paul Mahoney et al. (eds.), *Protection des droits de l'homme: la perspective européenne. Mélanges à la mémoire de Rolv Ryssdl* (Köln: Carl Heymanns Verlag, 2000) 281–307, at 305.

breakdown of the relationship with the child's mother before the child's birth, followed by the mother's opposition to contact between the father and the child. According to Strasbourg case law, while genetic ties are insufficient to create 'family life' in the absence of effective ties, depending on the circumstances surrounding conception, Article 8 extends to the *potential/intended* family life that could develop in the future between a father and a planned child. In particular, the Court has accepted that Article 8 protects 'potential' family life if the parents were in a committed relationship and conception was planned.[17] This stands in contrast with the position of the man who acts as a sperm donor, with no intention to start a family or play a part in the child's life. *J.R.M.* suggests that the donor will not benefit from the protection of Article 8 unless the parties' conduct modifies their original agreement – for example, the donor and the child develop an actual relationship. Of course, as indicated earlier, unplanned conception can still generate family life if it takes place within wedlock or if the unmarried father has demonstrated commitment towards the child and effective bonds have developed between them.

Intention acquires particular importance in the area of assisted reproduction, especially for aspiring parents who are unable to contribute their genetic material to the future child. Claims to the recognition of parenthood following gamete donation and/or surrogacy are based on the psychological and practical commitment to the future child. For some commentators, 'it is the *intention* to fulfil the social role of parent which is the crucial element in any right to reproduce'.[18] It is on this basis – the moral authorship of conception – that, in some jurisdictions, the commissioning parents are the default legal parents of the surrogate-born child,[19] and indeed they are regarded as the legal parents even before the child's birth.[20] In fact, the child would not be born but for the decision of the commissioning couple to procreate.

However, intention to act as a parent also defines adoption (with the difference that the intention forms after the child's conception and, usually,

[17] See *Keegan* v. *Ireland*, App. No. 16969/90, 26 May 1994, [44]; *Anayo* v. *Germany*, App. No. 20578/07, 21 December 2010, [62].

[18] Gillian Douglas, *Law, Fertility and Reproduction* (London: Sweet and Maxwell, 1991) 146 (original emphasis). See also ibid., 206: 'The intention to act as a parent is the key to any right to reproduce, and is what deserves protection.'

[19] This is the approach of various US States. See Ruth Deech and Anna Smajdor, *From IVF to Immortality: Controversy in the Era of Reproductive Technology* (Oxford and New York: Oxford University Press, 2007) 160.

[20] Ukraine is such an example. See Andrea Mulligan, 'Identity Rights and Sensitive Ethical Questions: The European Convention on Human Rights and the Regulation of Surrogacy Arrangements' (2018) 26(3) *Medical Law Review* 449–475, at 450.

birth), and yet there is no *right* to adopt a child under the ECHR.[21] The case law merely requires that the regulation of the institution of adoption, where available (i.e. eligibility criteria, procedures, recognition of foreign adoptions), be ECHR-compliant.[22] What then is different about intentional parenthood in relation to ART? The chief argument made in this chapter is that an infertile person's right to resort to ART, with donated gametes or the use of a surrogate, and obtain recognition of parenthood in relation to the resulting child is parasitic on their fertile partner's right to reproduce and have a genetically related child. Third-party ART is the only means to ensure effective respect for the procreative decision of fertile persons who find themselves in a committed relationship with a reproductively challenged partner.

That said, other arguments can be credibly advanced to support the right to become a legal parent through ART. For instance, a woman who can carry a child, albeit incapable of producing oocytes, may have a claim under Article 8 that she ought to be permitted to experience gestational motherhood and form a unique bond with the child through the use of donated ova/embryos, rather than adopt an abandoned child. The justification for the claim that couples should be permitted to conceive a child unrelated to either of them, rather than adopt an existing unrelated child, is more tenuous. Arguably, adoption is unsatisfactory because procreation escapes the intended parents' control, given the uncertainties surrounding the availability of adoptable newborn babies; the existence of competing (birth) mothers/fathers and the desire of the aspiring parents to be solely identified as parents; concerns over the child's genetic background or behavioural problems, since their adoptable status is often rooted in the biological parents' drug or alcohol addiction/mental health issues or the result of being brought up in an abusive environment. In addition, the State should have weighty grounds for prohibiting private agreements whereby some individuals, in the exercise of their physical self-determination, use their gametes or uterus in pursuit of procreative choices that benefit others. Concerns over the welfare of the child may be adduced, in particular the risk of abandonment if the commissioning parents change their mind before or shortly after the child's birth due to, for example,

[21] See X v. *Belgium and The Netherlands*, App. No. 6482/74, 10 July 1975 (Commission): 'The right to adopt is not, as such, included among the rights guaranteed by the Convention. Nor does it appear in the International Covenant on Civil and Political Rights.'

[22] See Carmen Draghici, 'Adoption and the European Court of Human Rights: From Laissez-Faire to Judicial Law-Making', in Lina Panella and Ersiliagrazia Spatafora (eds.), *Studi in onore di Claudio Zanghì* (Torino: Giappichelli, 2011) 255–282; Carmen Draghici, *The Legitimacy of Family Rights in Strasbourg Case Law: 'Living Instrument' or Extinguished Sovereignty?* (Oxford: Hart, 2017) 149–158.

an intervening relationship breakdown and the couple's reluctance to remain attached through a shared parenting arrangement for an unrelated child, or because the child is born with disabilities and the intended parents are not prepared to look after an unrelated disabled child.

The ECHR case law on intentional parenthood appears to disclose a reluctance to support new forms of parenthood, especially as regards female gamete donation and surrogacy. In respect of male gamete donation, the Court has shown readiness to accept that a stable relationship with the biological parent and a joint parenthood project followed by de facto care attract the protection of Article 8. However, the leap from a right to enjoy 'family life' with the partner's child to an entitlement to legal parenthood is still uncertain. Significantly, in *Gas and Dubois* v. *France*, the Court found that family life existed between a child born through medically assisted procreation with an anonymous donor and her mother's same-sex civil partner (and long-term life partner). [23] This finding was largely based on the couple's stable relationship, formalised through a civil partnership, akin to marriage; this reinforced what appears to be an attachment in Strasbourg case law to the spousal paradigm in the construction of family life.[24] A second important element was the fact that the two women had planned a family together. Moreover, the child had lived all her life in the home her biological and legal mother shared with the same-sex partner, who also acted in a parental role. Consequently, Article 8 applied in its 'family life' limb. However, the judgment is deferential on the scope of protection to be afforded to such families; the Court readily accepts that adoption was not practicable, because adoption by a woman necessarily terminated the biological mother's motherhood status.[25] There is no reflection on whether, in a jurisdiction recognising same-sex civil partnerships, the law could have been amended so as to avoid

[23] *Gas and Dubois* v. *France*, App. No. 25951/07, 15 March 2012.

[24] The Court's case law on cohabitants' Article 8 rights is largely predicated on the analogy between stable cohabitation and marriage. See Draghici, *The Legitimacy of Family Rights*, 83–89. The definition provided by the Grand Chamber in *Van der Heijden* v. *The Netherlands* [GC], App. No. 42857/05, 3 April 2012, [50], consolidating earlier jurisprudence, is particularly informative: 'The Court reiterates that the notion of "family life" in Article 8 is not confined solely to families based on marriage and may encompass other de facto relationships .... When deciding whether a relationship can be said to amount to "family life", a number of factors may be relevant, including *whether the couple live together, the length of their relationship and whether they have demonstrated their commitment to each other* by having children together or by any other means' (emphasis added).

[25] The case further raises issues of sexual orientation discrimination. See the discussion in Chapter 5, Section 5.2.1.

the automatic loss of parental status by the mother if her female partner and de facto parent also became an adoptive parent.

The relevance of social parenthood returned before the Court recently in *Callamand* v. *France*.[26] The case regarded the rejection of an application for contact between a woman and the child born to her former same-sex cohabitant (and later spouse) through donor insemination in Spain.[27] The child had not been conceived through a joint enterprise of the cohabiting couple; rather, the biological mother wished to have a child and was the sole moral author of conception, although the applicant had accompanied her to the clinic during her treatment.[28] Nevertheless, the Court found that Article 8 was engaged in relation to both private and family life, owing to the existence of 'genuine personal links' between the applicant and the child, forged over a period exceeding two years.[29] For the Court, the legal issue was whether France had met its positive obligation to ensure effective respect for the applicant's Article 8 rights, in particular whether it had struck a fair balance between the various interests at stake (including those of the child and the biological mother).[30] The Court criticised the disproportionate importance attached by the domestic appellate court, which quashed the contact order initially obtained, to the absence of a joint parental project, in circumstances where the applicant had not sought the establishment of legal kinship or shared parental authority, but merely contact.[31] This suggested that the Court's analysis was likely to be different in a joint parental project case, although it was not clear whether Article 8 would entitle the non-biological carer to parental status as opposed to mere parental authority.[32] On the facts, the position of the applicant in this case appears only marginally distinguishable from that of a step-parent, foster carer or relative/family friend having accommodated the child for a substantial period of time; therefore, the case does not cast light on whether intention to become a parent can supplant

26 *Callamand* v. *France*, App. No. 2338/20, 7 April 2022 (available only in French).
27 See ibid., [4]–[5].
28 See ibid., [12]–[13].
29 Ibid., [19]–[22].
30 Ibid., [32]–[35].
31 See ibid., [41].
32 Parental status, rather than parental responsibility, was found to be required for the intended non-biological parent in foreign surrogacy cases in *K.K. and Others* v. *Denmark*, App. No. 25212/21, 6 December 2022; there seems to be no reason to treat intended parents in assisted reproduction with donor cases differently. In fact, the legal parenthood abroad in surrogacy cases is only one of the factors justifying the Court's position; if the child's identity requires legal ties to both moral authors of conception/de facto parents, that ought to apply to all ART cases.

kinship in ART arrangements for the purposes of establishing parenthood. An important factor in *Callamand*, leading to the conclusion that there had been a violation of the applicant's Article 8 rights, was the lack of careful assessment, based on the child's best interests, in the domestic judgments;[33] in particular, the domestic courts had focused on the civil code provisions, without expressly acknowledging the applicant's Article 8 rights, and the reasons given in the appellate decision did not show that a fair balance had been struck.[34]

The *Gas and Dubois* and *Callamand* decisions both seemed to indicate that intention to act as a parent is only one factor in establishing 'family life', indeed secondary to de facto parenting and emotional ties. The Court has been much more conservative in cases where parent–child bonds did not exist at the time of the hearing, and the issue before it was the applicants' alleged right to found a family through medically assisted procreation. As stated in *Moretti and Benedetti* v. *Italy*, Article 8 entitles individuals to respect for family life already in existence, rather than protecting the mere desire to found a family.[35] This explains perhaps the difficulty of accommodating claims regarding access to certain reproductive techniques in order to fulfil the desire to become a parent (often a parent to a child genetically related to one's spouse). References in ECHR jurisprudence to intentional parenthood, in the context of gamete/embryo donation and surrogacy arrangements, will be explored in the following sections.

3.2 PROTECTING INTENTION-BASED (NON-BIOLOGICAL) PARENTHOOD IN DONOR CASES

3.2.1 *Issues Raised by Gamete Donation*

Gamete donation, regardless of its type, is still facing considerable scepticism. Erin Nelson noted that, although sperm donation and assisted insemination have been practised for well over 100 years, with the first case reported in 1884, many legal questions associated with this practice remain unresolved, most notably the legal status of human gametes.[36] Additionally, some studies have suggested that donor-conceived children often report a need to know

[33] See *Callamand* v. *France*, [44].

[34] Ibid., [39], [45].

[35] See *Moretti and Benedetti* v. *Italy*, App. No. 16318/07, 27 April 2010, [47] (available only in French).

[36] Erin Nelson, *Law, Policy and Reproductive Autonomy* (Oxford: Hart, 2013) 291–292.

their genetic origins, and that the refusal to disclose genetic information can cause psychological damage (low self-esteem, trust issues).[37] Nonetheless, such risks can be managed through the regulation of access to information, counselling and parenting education and do not support a call for banning gamete donation altogether. A more nuanced evaluation is necessary, taking into account all the stakeholders' rights and interests. That said, the contribution of the European Court of Human Rights (ECtHR) to promoting the human rights perspective in this debate has been rather hesitant.

The Strasbourg case law indicates that the objection to the recognition of a right to intention-based parenthood under the ECHR does not stem from hostility to social (non-biological) parenthood; rather, it is inspired by concerns over the implications of third-party reproduction on the understanding of kinship. In *S.H. and Others* v. *Austria*,[38] the Grand Chamber, overturning the Chamber ruling (which had supported the applicants' pleas), held that Article 8 did not require States to permit ova donation for the treatment of infertile couples who depended on it to procreate. Criticising the Court's focus on the 'splitting of motherhood' and 'unusual family relations', Rosamund Scott pointed out that 'extensive empirical literature shows that there is no reason to have particular concern for the welfare of children born from donated gametes'.[39] Indeed, the Court might have been expected to require the respondent to provide empirical evidence of any welfare concerns. More generally, human rights courts ought to be wary of accepting restrictions that are highly detrimental for some individuals based on speculative grounds. Admittedly, the precautionary principle can be invoked when there are very serious concerns, albeit accompanied by a paucity of evidence to confirm or allay them. However, if no serious concerns arise in relation to the psychological welfare of adopted children, they are even less likely to apply to ART-conceived children, who have been gestated and birthed by the (social, possibly also genetic) mother and immediately born into the rearing family, rather than following a transfer of legal parenthood in early life. Importantly, the issue of abandonment (which is at the root of potential distress for adopted children) does not arise; indeed, the child is very much wanted, and the parents will have gone to great lengths to conceive them, whereas the

[37] Wade, *The Regulation of Surrogacy*, 124.

[38] *S.H. and Others* v. *Austria* [GC], App. No. 57813/00, 3 November 2011, overturning *S.H. and Others* v. *Austria* [Chamber], App. No. 57813/00, 1 April 2010.

[39] Rosamund Scott, 'Reproductive Health: Morals, Margin and Rights' (2018) 81(3) *Modern Law Review* 422–451, 440.

biological progenitors never intended to play a social role from the outset, their position being almost indistinguishable from that of organ donors.

The 'split motherhood' concern also does not explain the greater distrust of ova donation when compared to sperm donation. Once legal fictions of parenthood are accepted, and the law accommodates the dissociation between genetic and social/legal parenthood, the same approach should apply to both donors and to both intended parents, regardless of their gender. If the intended mother is impregnated with donor sperm and the intended father, not the genetic father, is treated as the legal father, there should be no greater difficulty in treating as a parent the intended mother into whose body an embryo created with donated ova is transferred, rather than the genetic mother. If anything, the woman who carries and gives birth to the child following ova donation and IVF has a greater connection to the child than the man who, albeit unrelated to the child, is treated as the legal father as a result of sperm donation.[40]

At the same time, the registration of a non-biological parent as the legal parent was said to be inconsistent with the child's right to know his/her genetic origins,[41] an objection acknowledged, but not treated as decisive, in the 2019 Advisory Opinion.[42] In fact, it does not sit well with the acceptance in Europe of non-biological legal parenthood by virtue of adoption and presumptions of paternity. The understanding of parenthood in Europe has evolved towards accepting social parenthood as an alternative means of family formation, even if parental status obscures genetic reality. Naturally, the ECtHR will have to grapple with claims regarding the regulation of access to identifying and non-identifying information about the gamete donors and possibly siblings born as a result of the use of gametes from the same donor. Indeed, two challenges brought by donor-conceived children against the prohibition on access to information about the donors are pending before the Court.[43]

40 It could also be argued that, where the embryo is transferred into a surrogate, as long as one of the intended parents is a genetic parent, the mere fact of third-party gestation is insufficient to explain a deviation from the accepted legal fiction of parenthood.

41 See, e.g., Ekaterina Mouliarova, 'The Legal Recognition of Surrogacy in Russia' (2019) 11(1) *Italian Journal of Public Law* 393–433, at 430, 433.

42 See Advisory Opinion concerning the recognition in domestic law of a legal parent–child relationship between a child born through a gestational surrogacy arrangement abroad and the intended mother, Request No. P16-2018-001, 10 April 2019, [41], citing as an argument against recognition of the legal relationship with the intended mother the possibility of knowing one's origins, per *Mikulic* v. *Croatia*, App. No. 53176/99, 7 February 2002.

43 See *Gauvin-Fournis* v. *France*, App. No. 21424/16; *Silliau* v. *France*, App. No. 45728/17. Interestingly, the complaints raise both questions of knowledge about one's origins and of practical medical concerns about access to one's family health history, in relation to which it is

If (or, perhaps, when) the right to use gamete donation becomes a part of the right to respect for private and family life, in the way the *S.H. and Others v. Austria* Chamber decision had anticipated, the Strasbourg Court will have to reckon with further questions. One issue before domestic legislators has been the eligibility for such treatment. Arguably, reproductively challenged individuals ought to benefit from the same freedom to reproduce enjoyed by those who can reproduce naturally without medical assistance, that is to say, the freedom to reproduce without being subject to public scrutiny and having to satisfy prescribed criteria for access to parenthood. Gillian Douglas has convincingly suggested that 'the "adoption" model of legal regulation of assisted reproduction ... is undesirable, and the law should consistently apply the "sexual intercourse" model'.[44] In fact, in adoption proceedings, the specific needs of existing children and the suitability of the match between prospective adopters and children waiting for a family need to be taken into account. Conversely, these considerations do not apply to future children. Moreover, just because it would be logistically impossible for the State to vet plans for natural reproduction, whereas a sifting process can be put in place for assisted reproduction, a double standard is not justified, that is, additional controls over the procreative plans of individuals afflicted by some form of infertility. For those capable of procreating without medical assistance, the right to become a parent can be exercised freely without any hurdles, for example, without a licence to procreate, without any requirements in terms of the number and spacing of children or without economic/social preconditions in terms of family environment for the future child. When, for a person, the effective exercise of this right requires medical treatment, the freedom to make choices about parenthood must not be restricted in ways that natural procreation is not. Admittedly, the welfare of the future children and the ability to take responsibility for them ought to govern human reproduction in general. However, these principles should operate across both natural and assisted reproduction. It is also worth recalling that, while international human rights law does not guarantee a right to adopt an abandoned child, the right to become a parent is undisputed (as detailed in Chapter 2). It follows that an attempt to regulate access to reproduction for individuals with a physical or social impairment to natural reproduction needs to be more stringently justified than access to adoption.

alleged that donor-conceived children are discriminated when compared to children conceived naturally.

[44] Douglas, *Law, Fertility and Reproduction*, 206.

While the right to resort to assisted fertilisation with donor was rejected in *S.H. and Others* v. *Austria*, a more ambivalent attitude was shown a few years later in *D. and B.* v. *Austria*, a claim that a law allowing heterosexual – but not same-sex – couples to make use of donor insemination and to exercise joint custody of the child so conceived is discriminatory.[45] The case was struck out insofar as legislative reform, intervened shortly after the introduction of the complaint, granted the rights sought by the applicants (when the ART-born child raised by the female couple was approximately two-and-a-half-years old). The Court remarked in this regard the discretion States retain as to the timing of reform in relation to incipient rights: 'The matter in question must still be regarded as one of *evolving rights* with no European consensus established as yet, where States consequently enjoy a *certain* margin of appreciation *in the timing* of the introduction of legislative changes.'[46] Naturally, in the absence of prima facie discrimination in access to ART (e.g. in a jurisdiction prohibiting donor insemination for couples regardless of their sexual orientation), both the parties' submissions and the Court's analysis are likely to be different. A test case is needed to show if *S.H.* v. *Austria* has lost its relevance.

It is also worth noting that, although – in the absence of a clear authority – the conditions for granting access to donor insemination are still left to State discretion, decisions on complaints brought by same-sex couples in relation to *existing* children born through (usually overseas) donor insemination upheld the notion that effective legal mechanisms must exist for the protection of the de facto family life enjoyed by the child with the social parent (*C.E. and Others* v. *France*,[47] *Callamand* v. *France*). A qualitative distinction must be drawn between the Court's readiness to protect social bonds by requiring an avenue to maintain contact and support for the recognition of legal parenthood in the case of female couples using donor insemination. In *Aspisi* v. *Italy*, the Court was satisfied that Italian law contemplated the possibility for a person who had developed de facto family ties with a child to obtain measures aimed at the preservation of those ties.[48] Conversely, it did not agree that the respondent had failed to meet its positive obligation to guarantee effective respect for the applicant's family life by precluding her from legally recognising the child.[49] The Court also attached importance to the mode of conception, the applicant and her same-sex partner having resorted to a

[45] *D. and B.* v. *Austria*, App. No. 40597/12, 31 October 2017.
[46] Ibid., [24] (emphasis added).
[47] *C.E. and Others* v. *France*, App. Nos. 29775/18; 29693/19, 24 March 2022. See Chapter 5, Section 5.2.1.
[48] *Aspisi* v. *Italy*, App. No. 44453/19, 14 February 2023, [19], [21].
[49] Ibid., [22]–[23].

private agreement with a man who had accepted to father a child without recognising it and exercising parental rights; since conception had taken place through natural intercourse, the Italian law on the recognition of parenthood for children conceived through medically assisted procreation did not apply.[50] It is not clear if, had the female couple used DIY artificial insemination, the Court might have found that they were in the same situation as heterosexual couples and that the difference in treatment vis-à-vis the recognition of intended parenthood met Article 14 criteria. An argument can be made that, where access to assisted insemination with donor in medical facilities is denied, same-sex couples only have the option of DIY insemination (foreign treatment being discounted because it requires economic resources), and, therefore, couples resorting to it could be seen as being in a comparable situation to heterosexual couples who use medically assisted insemination.

3.2.2 *Issues Raised by Embryo Donation*

Another unconventional route to parenthood is embryo donation, whereby neither prospective parent is biologically related to the future child, although the intended mother has a gestational bond with the child. More often than not, this circumstance is likely to arise from the availability of excess embryos created during the IVF treatment of other couples; having completed their families, those couples are faced with the choice of either destroying the spare embryos, preserving them indefinitely, donating them to scientific research or donating them to infertile couples.[51] The process differs from adoption in several ways: the child is born only owing to the aspiring parents' intention to procreate; the parents experience the pregnancy and the birth; and the mother forms a bond with the child through gestation.

There is no direct Strasbourg precedent on whether or not this technique ought to be permitted as a matter of human rights law. However, the ECtHR has had an opportunity to discuss the scope of decisional autonomy in relation to embryos created with a person's own genetic material or that of a deceased close family member. The *Parrillo* v. *Italy* judgment, by removing the absolute decision-making power from a progenitor of the embryo, at least when the other progenitor is deceased and their wishes cannot be ascertained,[52] raised issues as to the status of the embryo and intimated that the State is entitled and potentially under a duty to protect it. Thus, *Parrillo* may lend support to the

50 Ibid., [22].
51 See MacCallum, 'Parenting Genetically Unrelated Children', 136.
52 *Parrillo* v. *Italy* [GC], App. No. 46470/11, 27 August 2015; see Chapter 2, Section 2.1.3.

proposition that, if the couple of progenitors are willing to 'adopt out' the surplus embryos to an infertile couple, the State should not force them to destroy, indefinitely preserve (until natural death) or donate the embryos to research; in fact, all these alternatives are less protective of the embryo, as well as disrespecting the autonomy of both sets of couples.

If, however, the progenitors are unwilling to donate their unused embryos to others, it would seem far-fetched to contend that those embryos are entitled to being treated as abandoned embryos and thus to 'adoption', whereby the State would compulsorily make them available for the treatment of others. Firstly, this would result in unintentional biological parenthood for the birth parents and go against the right not to procreate, upheld in *Evans* v. *The United Kingdom* even in the absence of allocation of legal parenthood;[53] forcing individuals to act as donors would constitute a severe interference with their self-determination rights. Secondly, there are practical complexities: after what period of preservation without being used are the embryos deemed abandoned? The couple may wish to defer the extension of the family or at least maintain that option. Is it then after both progenitors' death? If couples must 'use or lose' their embryos by law, should the progenitors have a say in the selection of the 'adoptive' parents, by analogy with the voluntary relinquishment of parental rights in consensual adoption processes? Should the infertile couple chosen by the progenitors of the embryos as future parents be vetted by the State? As Fiona MacCallum has pointed out, 'embryo donation is a medical solution to a medical problem, whereas adoption is a social response to a social problem'.[54] Children born out of embryo donation are integrated into the family before birth and do not have the same needs arising from being abandoned by their parents and from the adjustment to a new family environment (the rationale for a probationary period before adoption); this suggests that State involvement with donors/'adopters' is less justified in the case of embryo donation.

As regards the welfare of any children born through embryo donation, it cannot be simplistically maintained that they would be harmed, if brought into existence, merely by the lack of genetic ties to their parents or by the lack of knowledge of genetic parents/siblings. Naturally, the regulation of access to information for children born through embryo donation is not uncontroversial. Although such children 'do have a gestational link to their rearing parents' and 'do not have the same gap in their life stories' as adopted children, they

[53] *Evans* v. *The United Kingdom* [GC], App. No. 6339/05, 10 April 2007; see Chapter 2, Section 2.1.2.

[54] MacCallum, 'Parenting Genetically Unrelated Children', 136.

may benefit from access to information for their sense of identity.[55] Additionally, assuming that they are aware of the circumstances of their conception, children born from donated embryos have knowledge that they likely have full siblings (children born to the donor couple), which may give rise to a further interest in gaining genetic information. This remains, however, subject to the welfare of the donor couple and their children, as well as to their rights to privacy. Moreover, the rights of children born from donated embryos need to be balanced against the rights of their legal parents, who may wish to preserve the confidentiality of the donation to the outside world and the child. Finally, the removal of donor anonymity may adversely affect the rights of other infertile couples, to the extent that it deters donation, so there may be legitimate policy objections to it.

A comparison with the points raised in *Odièvre* v. *France* in relation to secretive births and adopted children's rights to identifying information might be useful.[56] According to the Grand Chamber in that case, a person's right to know their origins can be trumped by competing interests, such as the natural mother's right to confidentiality and the general interest in discouraging illegal abortions, unsafe births, and children being abandoned in improper ways (the possible consequences of non-consensual disclosure of information); these public policy objections are subsumed under the aim to ensure respect for life, which ranks highly in the Convention scheme.[57] Eva Steiner has commented that 'the concept of "origins", which was at the core of the application to the court and a central issue, is neither fully nor clearly defined'.[58] In particular, for Steiner the ruling was unhelpful in determining whether, applied to medically assisted procreation, the notion may give rise to the same right – as for adopted children – to identifying information about gamete donors.[59] Admittedly, there is some ambiguity in the *Odièvre* judgment as regards the application of the right to know one's origins outside the sphere of children born through intercourse. However, it seems reasonably clear that 'the right to know' is not confined to lineage but is much broader: 'In the Court's opinion, people "have a vital interest, protected by the Convention, in receiving the information necessary to know and to

[55] Ibid., 148.
[56] *Odièvre* v. *France* [GC], App. No. 42326/98, 13 February 2003.
[57] Ibid., [40]–[49].
[58] Eva Steiner, '*Odièvre* v *France* – Desperately Seeking Mother – Anonymous Births in the European Court of Human Rights' (2003) 15(4) *Child and Family Law Quarterly* 425–448, at 446.
[59] Ibid., 446–447.

understand their childhood and early development".'[60] The reliance, for this proposition, on *Gaskin* v. *The United Kingdom*,[61] which concerned not genealogy but the circumstances of one's early upbringing in foster care, further supports this conclusion. The *Odièvre* judgment also recalled 'the vital interest of a person in receiving the information necessary to uncover the truth about an important aspect of his or her personal identity', as established in *Mikulić* v. *Croatia*.[62] It is not obvious that the circumstances surrounding conception are part of early development, but there is a strong case for it; they are certainly an important aspect of identity. This is not to suggest that, when in conflict with other rights (social parents' rights, donors' rights, the donors' families' rights, the general interest not to deter donors), the right to information of embryo donation children would necessarily prevail. Children born through embryo donation do not experience the personal history gap seen as problematic in *Gaskin*, nor the complete lack of paternal affiliation underlying the *Mikulić* decision; as such, a different balancing exercise might be appropriate, including differing to the donors' or parents' choice.

3.3 NON-BIOLOGICAL COMMISSIONING PARENTS IN SURROGACY ARRANGEMENTS

3.3.1 *The Non-biological Parent Married to the Biological Parent: Parasitic Rights*

To date, the interpretation of the ECHR has not established any obligation for States to recognise the legal parenthood of non-biological intended parents of

60 *Odièvre* v. *France*, [42].

61 *Gaskin* v. *The United Kingdom*, App. No. 10454/83, 7 July 1989 (referenced in *Odièvre* v. *France*, [42]); see especially [49] in relation to persons who grew up in State care: 'In the Court's opinion, persons in the situation of the applicant have a vital interest, protected by the Convention, in receiving the information necessary to know and to understand their childhood and early development.'

62 *Odièvre* v. *France*, [42]. The reference is to *Mikulić* v. *Croatia*, [54] (recalling *Gaskin* v. *The United Kingdom*): 'Respect for private life requires that everyone should be able to establish details of their identity as individual human beings and … an individual's entitlement to such information is of importance because of its formative implications for his or her personality.' In paternity proceedings, aimed at 'the establishment of the biological truth' (*Mikulić* v. *Croatia*, [55]), 'the courts are required to have regard to the basic principle of the child's interests' and to 'strike a fair balance between the right of the applicant to have her uncertainty as to her personal identity eliminated without unnecessary delay and that of her supposed father not to undergo DNA tests' (ibid., [65]); see also the reference to the 'state of prolonged uncertainty as to her personal identity' (ibid., [66]).

children born through (foreign) surrogacy,[63] with one important exception. If the child is biologically related to one member of the couple, who has been recognised as a legal parent, the other intended parent, if married to the genetic parent, must be able to avail himself or herself of an efficient, expedited mechanism for the acquisition of parenthood, for example, fast-track adoption proceedings. This principle was first established by the ECtHR in the exercise of its advisory jurisdiction and then confirmed in contentious proceedings.

In 2019, an opinion requested by the French Court of Cassation presented the Grand Chamber with an opportunity to pronounce on ECHR requirements vis-à-vis the recognition of the non-genetic intended parent in foreign surrogacy arrangements. The background to the request was a change in French law in the aftermath of the *Mennesson* judgment,[64] whereby the intended and genetic father of a child born through surrogacy abroad was registered as the legal father, while the intended non-genetic mother had the option to adopt the child, subject to statutory criteria and a child welfare assessment.[65] According to the Advisory Opinion concerning the recognition in domestic law of a legal parent–child relationship between a child born through a gestational surrogacy arrangement abroad and the intended mother, where a child was conceived using the intended father's gametes and donor eggs and born abroad through a gestational surrogacy arrangement, and where the legal parent–child relationship with the intended father has been recognised in domestic law, the child's right to respect for private life requires that domestic law provide *a possibility of recognition* of a legal parent–child relationship with the intended mother, designated in the birth certificate and legally established abroad as the legal mother.[66]

This conclusion was primarily based on two factors. First, the paramountcy of the child's best interests, and most notably the practical disadvantages facing the child in case of non-recognition: the uncertainty surrounding his/her identity within society; obstacles in accessing the intended mother's nationality and the right to stay in her country of residence; problems regarding

[63] On the recognition of the biological parent as a legal parent following overseas surrogacy births, see Chapter 2, Section 2.4. This obligation is now well established under the Convention, albeit not as a right of the parent but exclusively as a right of the child.

[64] As discussed in Chapter 2, Section 2.4, in *Mennesson* v. *France* (App. No. 65941/11, 26 June 2014), the Court found that the lack of recognition of the legal parent–child relationship between a child born through overseas surrogacy and the intended and genetic father breached the child's privacy rights.

[65] See Advisory Opinion P16-2018-001, [10]–[14].

[66] Ibid., [46].

inheritance rights and the continuity of the relationship with the intended mother in the event of her separation from the child's father or of the father's death.[67] Second, the narrow margin of appreciation retained by States, notwithstanding the absence of European consensus, in respect of measures affecting important facets of an individual's identity: in this case, not only the legal child–parent relationship but also the environment in which children live and develop as well as the persons responsible for their care and ensuring their welfare.[68]

This analysis suggests that ECHR Member States are expected to safeguard the relationship between a child born through foreign gestational surrogacy using an egg donor and the intended/social mother. Even though the Opinion appears to require merely an obligation of conduct, rather than one of result (i.e. only to provide an avenue for the acquisition of parenthood, without guarantees of success), restrictive eligibility conditions and an arbitrary 'best interests' assessment leading to the denial of an adoption application may amount to a violation of Article 8. Indeed, the Court's emphasis both on the disadvantages that the child would suffer as a result of non-recognition and on the multidimensional identity issue at stake, which limits domestic discretion, is likely to require rather exceptional grounds for the denial of recognition.

At the same time, the Opinion clarified that there is no obligation to register the intended mother on the birth certificate and recognise the legal affiliation domestically *ab initio*, even though she was designated as the legal mother on the foreign birth certificate and notwithstanding the fact that the surrogacy arrangement entered into abroad had the effect of conferring legal parenthood in that jurisdiction. While underlining that the period of legal uncertainty should be as short-lived as possible,[69] the ECtHR accepted that the child's right to respect for private life does not require the recognition of the parent–child relationship to take the form of entry of the details of the foreign birth certificate into the register of births; a different means, such as the adoption of the child by the intended mother, was equally acceptable for those purposes.[70] The Court viewed the *choice of means* for the recognition as less directly connected to individual identity than the establishment of the *principle* of recognition; coupled with the lack of European consensus on the matter, this left the exact route to recognition within the States' margin of appreciation.[71]

67 Ibid., [37]–[42].
68 Ibid., [43]–[45].
69 Ibid., [49].
70 Ibid., [50], [53]–[55].
71 Ibid., [51].

Importantly, however, an avenue must be available to formalise the relationship as soon as de facto family life has been established: 'What the child's best interests . . . require is for recognition of that relationship, legally established abroad, to be possible *at the latest when it has become a practical reality*.'[72]

The Opinion is thus moderately progressive, in that it creates an obligation to ensure an opportunity to promptly establish affiliation between the surrogate-born child and the intended mother, the details of which are left to the discretion of each State. It is worth noting that, like the recognition of affiliation between the child and the genetic intended father, this obligation is based on the child's right to respect for his or her private life, and not on the intended mother's rights. Moreover, the issue before the Court was limited to the recognition of effects of foreign surrogacy arrangements and does not advance an infertile person's right to use surrogacy domestically together with a fertile spouse and be recognised as a legal parent. The Opinion, therefore, only safeguards family ties already created by lawful foreign surrogacy arrangements. The ability to reproduce through recourse to surrogacy remains the privilege of wealthy couples who can travel abroad for the requisite period of time.

Another interesting aspect of the Advisory Opinion, eloquently noted by Alice Margaria, is the reversal of roles within the married couple as regards the legitimisation of the relationship with the child when contrasted with the *pater est* presumption, namely the construction of motherhood 'as a derivative of fatherhood':

> Traditionally, it has been fatherhood to be understood as a mediated relationship, rather than as an autonomous, direct connection between the father and his child. The 'marital presumption' is emblematic of the crucial function that marriage has long played in connecting men to their children. Here, by way of contrast, legal fatherhood is assigned by virtue of biology, and the (marital) connection between the intended parents emerges as one of the factors that make the relationship between the intended mother and her daughters worthy of legal recognition.[73]

While the Advisory Opinion is technically non-binding, it expresses the Court's authoritative interpretation of Convention obligations. As cogently put across in a Separate Opinion in the case of *D.B. and Others* v. *Switzerland*, the Court's interpretation of Convention law does not vary depending on the form

[72] Ibid., [52] (emphasis added).

[73] Alice Margaria, 'Parenthood and Cross-Border Surrogacy: What Is "New"? The ECtHR's First Advisory Opinion' (2020) 28(2) *Medical Law Review* 412–425, at 424.

in which it is expressed (judgment/opinion), and indeed the interpretation of the Grand Chamber (the only Court formation enabled to render opinions) is particularly authoritative.[74] It was further observed that, in the same way that judgments against a particular State only bind that State, but the interpretation on points of law have *erga omnes* value, the interpretation returned in advisory opinions is opposable to all ECHR States, including those that did not ratify Protocol 16, which is why Article 3 of the Protocol allows third-party intervention by non-ratifying States.[75] The jurisprudence of the Court thus spreads fluidly across judgments and opinions. This was explicitly anticipated in the Explanatory Report on Protocol No. 16:

> Advisory opinions under this Protocol would have no direct effect on other later applications. They would, however, form part of the case-law of the Court, alongside its judgments and decisions. The interpretation of the Convention and the Protocols thereto contained in such advisory opinions would be analogous in its effect to the interpretative elements set out by the Court in judgments and decisions.'[76]

The tenets put forward in Advisory Opinion P16-2018-001 were, unsurprisingly,[77] confirmed and applied in subsequent contentious proceedings.

The first such occasion was the joint admissibility decision in *C. and E. v. France*, issued a few months after the 2019 opinion.[78] The two applications challenged the authorities' refusal to record in the national register of births the full details of the foreign birth certificates of surrogacy-born children (one child born to the first couple in the USA, triplets born to the second couple in Ghana), in particular the designation of the intended mothers as the legal mothers. As the Court noted, the two cases conformed to the matrix examined in the Advisory Opinion: the children had been born through a foreign surrogacy arrangement; conception had been brought about with the gametes of the intended fathers and third-party donor ova; and the affiliation between

74 See *D.B. and Others* v. *Switzerland*, App. Nos. 58817/15; 58252/15, 22 November 2022, Concurring Opinion of Judge Krenc, [15]–[17].

75 See ibid., [20]–[22].

76 See Council of Europe, *Explanatory Report to Protocol No. 16 to the Convention for the Protection of Human Rights and Fundamental Freedoms*, Strasbourg, 2 October 2013, CETS No. 214, Point 27.

77 Lydia Bracken, 'The ECtHR's First Advisory Opinion: Implications for Cross-Border Surrogacy Involving Male Intended Parents' (2021) 21(1) *Medical Law International* 3–18, at 18, noted that the opinion 'signifies the mindset of the Court in relation to cross-border surrogacy that would likely be applied in future cases'.

78 *C. and E.* v. *France*, App. Nos. 1462/18; 17348/18, 19 November 2019 (available only in French).

the intended fathers and the children had been recognised in domestic law.[79] Since, in line with the Advisory Opinion, the route of adoption of their spouses' children was opened to the intended mothers, the applications were declared manifestly ill-founded.[80]

Although it was accepted in *C. and E.* v. *France* that the refusal to fully transcribe the foreign birth certificates amounted to an interference with the children's private lives,[81] that interference was not deemed disproportionate.[82] The Court conceded that an effective mechanism for establishing legal ties had become available with certainty only in July 2017, when the children were seven and three years old, respectively, that is, a considerable time after the relationship between the children and their intended mothers had become a practical reality.[83] However, it reasoned that requiring the applicant children to wait for the adoption procedure to be completed henceforth was not an excessive burden, taking into account the relatively short period of time involved (the average waiting time for a decision was only 4.1 months for a full adoption and 4.7 months for a simple adoption).[84]

There is a certain paradox in the Court's conclusion that the refusal to transcribe the certificates of birth was not disproportionate because an alternative mechanism secured the same result,[85] when that mechanism was unavailable at the material time (in 2014). The Court also departs from the principle, set out in *Marckx* v. *Belgium*, that leaving the child motherless in the eyes of the law even for a short period of time (thirteen days in that case) goes against the child's interests and breaches his/her right to respect for family life.[86]

79 Ibid., [39]–[40].

80 Ibid., [41]–[45].

81 See ibid., [37].

82 See ibid., [44].

83 Ibid., [42].

84 Ibid., [43]. Full adoption (*adoption plénière*) severs the legal ties between the adoptee and his/her family of origin (typically when a couple adopts an orphaned or abandoned child), whereas simple adoption adds (rather than substituting) a descendance tie to the existing legal relationship between the adoptee and his/her family of origin (typically when a step-parent adopts an adult step-child to transmit their inheritance to him/her). See Jean-François Mignot, '"Simple" Adoption in France: Revival of an Old Institution (1804–2007)' (translation by Peter Hamilton) (2015) 56(3) *Revue française de sociologie* 365–394, at 365.

85 *C. and E.* v. *France*, [44].

86 See *Marckx* v. *Belgium*, App. No. 6833/74, 13 June 1979, [37] (with reference to the procedure for a declaration of status whereby the mother could recognise the illegitimate child): 'There is thus a risk that the establishment of affiliation will be time-consuming and that, in the interim, the child will remain separated in law from his mother. This system resulted in a lack of respect for the family life of Alexandra Marckx who, in the eyes of the law, was motherless from 16 to 29 October 1973. Despite the brevity of this period, there was thus also a violation of Article 8 (art. 8) with respect to the second applicant.'

It would seem that, in surrogacy cases, the Court is prepared to stretch legal argumentation in such a way as to avoid penalising States that are at the vanguard of the protection of new and still rather controversial rights. Moreover, the much wider discretion afforded to States as to the manner of establishing maternal affiliation in surrogacy cases where donor ova were used, including concessions to relatively time-consuming procedures found unacceptable in illegitimate children's cases, clearly discloses an understanding of parenthood as primarily biological parenthood.

Similar assumptions guide the Court's analysis of the claim, under Article 14 read in conjunction with Article 8, that the respondent discriminated against children born through foreign surrogacy arrangements when compared to other children born overseas, whose foreign birth certificates are transcribed in their entirety. Relying on its Article 14 jurisprudence, as articulated by the Grand Chamber in *Biao* v. *Denmark*,[87] the Court redefined the difference in treatment more narrowly, that is, consisting of a *different route* to obtaining recognition of the maternal affiliation indicated on the foreign birth certificate (adoption/full transcription of the birth certificate);[88] it thus found that the different means to establish maternal ties in the case of surrogate-born children were objectively and reasonably justified, in that they permitted judicial checks over the circumstances of each case and whether recognition was in the child's best interests.[89] The discrimination claim on behalf of the children was, therefore, also rejected as manifestly ill-founded.[90] Naturally, to couch the issue in the terms chosen by the Court, one needs to gloss over the fact that the adoption route was not guaranteed at the material time. While the decision, therefore, provides an up-to-date assessment of the ECHR compatibility of that particular legislative solution, there is merit in the proposition that it does not do justice to the parties.

The practical relevance of the 2019 Advisory Opinion became more prominent in 2022, in a case where not only was the intended parent not recognised as such *ab initio*, but there was also a bar on step-parent adoption as a

[87] *C. and E.* v. *France*, [51]. The Court references *Biao* v. *Denmark* [GC], App. No. 38590/10, 24 May 2016, [88]–[93], recalling that, for an Article 14 issue to arise, there must be a difference in treatment of persons similarly situated, which amounts to discrimination if the difference does not have an objective and reasonable justification, that is, it does not pursue a legitimate aim or there is no proportionality between the means employed and the aim pursued; moreover, ECHR States enjoy a certain margin of appreciation in determining whether and to what extent differences between otherwise analogous situations justify a difference in treatment.

[88] *C. and E.* v. *France*, [52].

[89] Ibid., [53]–[54].

[90] Ibid., [55].

route to filiation where the woman who had carried the children and whose consent to adoption was required had received remuneration. In *K.K. and Others* v. *Denmark*, applying the principles in the Advisory Opinion, the Court held that the children's right to respect for their private lives had been breached by the complete impossibility of establishing legal ties with the intended mother.[91] It was concluded that the Danish authorities had failed to strike a balance between the children's interests and the public interest in controlling commercial surrogacy.[92]

Conversely, in *K.K. and Others* v. *Denmark*, the societal interest at stake was found sufficient to justify the interference with the intended mother's right to private life;[93] it was also found sufficient, taking into account the State's margin of appreciation, as regards the interference with the family life of those concerned: in fact, the parties did not face any practical difficulties in enjoying family life together; the children had acquired Dutch nationality through their father; and the commissioning mother had obtained shared custody.[94]

Interestingly, while in *C.E. and Others* v. *France* the Court had accepted that legal instruments existed to enable the relationship between the ART-born child and the mother's (former) same-sex partner, including a court order for joint parental responsibility, which permitted the exercise of certain rights and duties associated with parenthood and hence a degree of legal recognition of the relationship,[95] in *K.K.* v. *Denmark*, the shared custody order (albeit not subject to termination by divorce or the death of the father) was not deemed satisfactory.[96] The case thus allowed the Court to consider which alternative to registration as a legal parent *ab initio* and step-parent adoption met the requirements set in the Advisory Opinion for the prompt and effective establishment of a legal relationship between the surrogate-born child and the non-genetic commissioning mother. It would seem that mechanisms falling short of establishing a parent–child relationship do not meet that standard, due to the impact of lesser measures on the child's identity:

> The fact remains, though, that besides adoption, domestic law does not provide for other possibilities of recognition of a legal parent–child relationship with the intended mother. Accordingly, as pointed out by the applicants,

91 *K.K. and Others* v. *Denmark*, [71]–[77].

92 Ibid., [76]. The Court accepted that the impugned law sought 'to avoid commercial exploitation of surrogate mothers and the risk of children being turned into a commodity' (ibid., [60]).

93 Ibid., [55].

94 Ibid., [49]–[50].

95 See *C.E. and Others* v. *France*, [107].

96 *K.K. and Others* v. *Denmark*, [71]–[73].

> when they were refused adoption, they were de facto refused being recognised as having a legal parent–child relationship. Such lack of recognition per se had a negative impact on the children's right to respect for their private life, in particular because it placed them in a position of legal uncertainty regarding their identity within society.[97]

What is also remarkable about the *K.K.* v. *Denmark* judgment is the shift towards a more pragmatic approach to the balancing exercise between competing interests in the case at hand: the Court moves away from the accommodation of speculative interests, such as the surrogate mother's parental rights (evidently not pursued), and associates the notion of the child's best interests with the recognition of the long-term social mother as a legal parent, regardless of any mitigations in the law for the bar on adoption[98] and the absence of practical difficulties:

> The children had thus for a significant time considered them both to be their parents, and it was clearly in their best interest to obtain the same legal relationship with the first applicant as they had with their father. Furthermore, there were no opposing parental interests between the first applicant and the biological father of the children, which may be the case, when intended parents in surrogacy arrangements break up and new partners come into the picture. Nor were there any other persons claiming parentage, which may be the case in assisted reproduction, when a number of different individuals may have been involved in the child's conception.[99]

The approach to inheritance rights is particularly significant. The analysis is brief; it acknowledges the equivalent practical effect of a will by the social mother, but also the departure from the situation of other children under Danish law; in fact, 'the children would not be her heirs by virtue of a legal parent–child relationship, unlike the situation for other children in Denmark'.[100] There is no examination of whether the different treatment of surrogate-born children amounts to discrimination on the grounds of the circumstances of conception. Rather, the underlying concern is reminiscent of the quest for the normalcy of family life in *Marckx* v. *Belgium*, which

[97] Ibid., [72]. See also ibid., [75]: 'The Court is therefore not convinced that . . . the cumulative solutions provided for by Danish law had such an impact on the private life of the children that they could make up for the refusal to let them be adopted by the first applicant.'

[98] In addition to the shared custody order, the Court also mentions the possibility of securing inheritance rights through a will (ibid., [73]).

[99] Ibid., [74]. See also ibid., [76], 'recalling the essential principle according to which, whenever the situation of a child is in issue, the best interests of that child are paramount'.

[100] Ibid., [73].

includes automatic inheritance rights. This is a welcome departure from the treatment of parental status as a largely inconsequential symbolic perk, which may be successfully replaced by other mechanisms conferring some stability and rights associated with parenthood. However, the judgment would have benefitted from a less superficial discussion of this point; in fact, it is precisely on the effective protection of family life through existing mechanisms that the joint dissenting opinion diverges from the majority.[101] A major lacuna in the analysis concerns the social mother's intentional parenthood, without which the observation that the children perceived her as a parent figure blurred the line between step-parents and intended parents. It is arguably the initial parental project, corroborated by social parenthood, that justifies the Court's emphasis on the need to create a parent–child relationship, rather than a package of legal safeguards of equivalent effect. Nor can a long-term step-parent/carer claim central relevance to a person's identity outside the context of surrogacy: what distinguishes the position of the intended mother is that her design led to conception.

The *C. and E.* v. *France* and *K.K.* v. *Denmark* rulings, giving full legal force to the principles put forward in the Advisory Opinion, have withdrawn from ECHR States the ability to deny the recognition of filial ties between the intended mother and the surrogate-born child. At the same time, these cases have cemented the distinction between biological parenthood materialised through a surrogacy agreement and intentional parenthood with no biological link to the surrogate-born child. It is now well established that the ECHR allows States a choice of means in relation to the legal recognition of the unrelated commissioning mother, rather than mandating the transcription of the foreign birth certificate and recognition of maternal affiliation from the outset (by contrast with paternal affiliation); however, the absence of an effective mechanism for establishing legal ties will breach Article 8 ECHR. Even more remarkably, in *D.B. and Others* v. *Switzerland*, the Court has reached a similar conclusion in the case of foreign surrogacy involving same-sex intended fathers.[102]

Notwithstanding these favourable developments, applications by intended parents may still fail, depending on the couple's circumstances. In *A.M.*

[101] See *K.K. and Others* v. *Denmark*, Joint Dissenting Opinion of Judges Kjølbro, Koskelo and Yüksel, [102]: 'Given the fact that parental responsibility for the children on the part of both intended parents was legally established, we find it difficult to accept that the rights provided under Danish law should be considered incapable of satisfying the requirements of "other means" of establishing a "legal parent–child relationship" as contemplated in the Court's Advisory opinion [no. P16-2018-001].'

[102] See Chapter 5, Section 5.2.2.

v. *Norway*, a couple had continued in the USA their endeavours to have a child via surrogacy (which was illegal in Norway) after the breakdown of their relationship, and the US authorities had recognised both parties as parents, although an anonymous donor egg had been used for the IVF procedure, and therefore only the man was genetically related to the child; the child initially lived with the intended mother after birth, while the father visited daily, and subsequently an alternate residence arrangement was put into place.[103] After the recognition by Norwegian authorities of the father (but not of the mother) as a legal parent, a series of disagreements between the parties on contact and parenting arrangements, and the involvement of child welfare services (concerned that daily moves between the parties were not in the child's best interests), the child remained with the father, who discontinued all contact with the mother.[104] All attempts by the latter to adopt the child and secure access to the child remained fruitless. Step-parent adoption was not possible as long as the child had two parents (and the US surrogate was regarded as the child's mother), nor did the former partner, the child's father, consent to adoption;[105] contact rights required a formal legal basis, whereas the intended mother lacked legal ties with the child under Norwegian law, and her American motherhood was treated as irrelevant.[106] Before the Strasbourg Court, the applicant complained that the Norwegian authorities' refusal to grant her contact rights in respect of the child or to recognise her as the child's mother, either by acknowledging the US-issued birth certificate or by approving her requests for parenthood, had violated her right to respect for her private and family life.[107]

The claim in relation to contact was declared inadmissible for non-exhaustion of domestic remedies, and therefore the case does not illuminate the alleged right to contact between the child and the intended mother.[108] As regards the recognition of legal motherhood, the Court found Article 8 applicable in its 'private life' limb, which extends to 'emotional bonds created and developed between an adult and a child in situations other than the classic situations of kinship'.[109] It did not consider it necessary to examine whether family life also applied, refusing therefore to take a definitive view on the

[103] See A.M. v. *Norway*, App. No. 30254/18, 24 March 2022, [5]–[12].
[104] Ibid., [13]–[24].
[105] Ibid., [25]–[39], [64]–[65].
[106] See ibid., [57], [86]–[88].
[107] See ibid., [101].
[108] See ibid., [102]–[105].
[109] Ibid., [110].

matter.[110] The Dissenting Opinion of Judge Jelić aptly criticised the majority's decision not to examine the family life aspect of the case, noting that 'the applicant's involvement in the first 17 months of X's life means that she played a crucial role in shaping his development as a young child'.[111]

As to the aim of the interference, the Court accepted that the proceedings pursued the protection of the 'rights of others' (the child) and the prevention of 'disorder or crime', in that 'the lack of recognition of parenthood on the basis of the surrogacy agreement was linked to the prohibition against surrogacy in Norway'.[112] The Court also recalled that 'it regards as legitimate under Article 8 § 2 the domestic authorities' wish to reaffirm the State's exclusive competence to recognise a legal parent–child relationship with a view to protecting children'.[113]

In terms of proportionality, the Court noted the applicant's awareness at the time of the surrogacy agreement that the only means for the transfer of parenthood following overseas surrogacy was step-parent adoption with the consent of the parent with parental responsibility, even though she could not anticipate his decision to cut her off from the child's life.[114] It also recalled the sensitive issues involved by the regulation of surrogacy and the lack of consensus in Europe[115] and found that the consent requirement for step-parent adoption as a general rule was not objectionable.[116] Additionally, there is a reference to the diligent judicial exercise of balancing conflict interests and the margin of appreciation enjoyed by domestic courts for those purposes.[117]

Where the Court probably errs is in finding that the applicant's predicament was not the result of any intervention by the authorities, whereas the fact that step-parent adoption made no allowance for situations where the child had been planned jointly and was a legal child in another jurisdiction arguably was a lacuna in domestic law:

> The fact remains that the actual situation for the applicant in the instant case was particularly harsh since E.B. had prevented her from maintaining her relationship with X and essentially put an end to the applicant's parental project in respect of the child after first having been a party to the surrogacy agreement forming the basis for that project together with her; the Court

110 Ibid., [111].
111 A.M. v. *Norway*, Dissenting Opinion of Judge Jelić, [31].
112 A.M. v. *Norway*, [124].
113 Ibid.
114 Ibid., [129].
115 Ibid., [131].
116 Ibid., [132].
117 Ibid., [134].

> finds it however difficult to attribute this consequence to the authorities. It was not an intervention by the respondent State that had brought to an end the applicant's relationship with X.[118]

It is arguably the responsibility of public authorities to protect individuals against the detrimental action of third parties affecting their private and family life (see, *mutatis mutandis*, the discussion of *Evans* v. *The United Kingdom* in Chapter 2, in which the law afforded one party a veto right on the other party's parenthood). The Court ought to have considered (a) whether the State had to treat the applicant's situation differently from step-parent adoption, that is, adoption of a child who was the product of another couple's parenthood plans, and (b) whether measures should have been put in place to reduce the excessive decision-making power held by the genetic parent, capable of nullifying the prospects of continued family life (after seventeen months of de facto care). The emphasis, in Judge O'Leary's Concurring Opinion, on the need for parental consent to adoption[119] overlooks the inadequacy of adoption principles (regulating the creation of legal ties between a child and an unrelated adult) when applied to parenthood following ART (i.e. the creation of legal ties between the child and one of the moral authors of conception as well as a legal parent in the jurisdiction where treatment was received). However, Judge O'Leary also notes that the facts of the case reflect the concern expressed by the Court in the 2019 Advisory Opinion over the precariousness of the relationship between the intended mother and the child (if the relationship is not recognised) in case of separation from, or death of, the genetic father and thus may disclose a gap in legislation.[120]

It is worth recalling that, in donor insemination cases, such as *C.E. and Others* v. *France*, the existence of legal avenues for the allocation of parenthood and contact post separation, independent from the consent of the biological parent, was deemed important in assessing compliance with positive obligations under Article 8 (admittedly, after a lengthier period of cohabitation).[121] By contrast, Judge Jelić's Dissenting Opinion in *A.M.* v. *Norway* highlighted the imbalance of power between the two intended parents, 'one person being able to make life-changing decisions over another person',[122] in

[118] Ibid., [133].

[119] See *A.M.* v. *Norway*, Concurring Opinion of Judge O'Leary, [16]: 'For the Court to endorse the existence of such a unilateral right to adopt under Article 8 would fly in the face of well-established case-law protecting parents and children from non-consensual or unilateral adoption procedures which break de facto and de jure child–parent bonds.'

[120] Ibid., [20].

[121] See *C.E. and Others* v. *France*, [107].

[122] *A.M.* v. *Norway*, Dissenting Opinion of Judge Jelić, [45].

particular the biological parent having the authority to exclude the other from the child's life and to consent to adoption by his new partner.[123] The dissenter also aptly suggested that 'awarding such large powers to one person is not only discriminatory against the parent who was biologically unable to procreate, it also acts contrary to the intended purpose of surrogacy and the interest of the child'.[124] In fact, the child's right to identity is understood as encompassing the right to know one's parents, 'broadened to include intended parents who were supposed to be the mother or father of the child right from the beginning of the surrogacy proceedings'.[125]

This case solidifies the notion that the social parent in surrogacy arrangements has a claim to the transfer of parenthood only to the extent that he/she is in a relationship with the biological parent. The distinction between the applicant in *A.M.* v. *Norway* and the cases considered earlier is that her position was only based on intentional parenthood and de facto care, without being bolstered by her relationship with the other – genetic – intended parent.[126] Naturally, this is unsatisfactory in several respects. The first is the best interests of the child, which are not served by a legal system effectively leaving the child motherless; the notional motherhood of the overseas surrogate, uninterested in parenting, is of no benefit to the child and adds to confusion as to their identity, even more so in gestational surrogacy cases, where the record of the surrogate's name does not provide the child with knowledge of their genetic heritage. Although, procedurally, the applicant in *A.M.* did not have standing to bring a complaint on the child's behalf,[127] the primacy of the child's interests, upheld as a general ECHR principle, should govern the balancing exercise in deciding the allocation of parenthood. The second criticism that the approach in *A.M.* inevitably inspires is that parenthood is anchored in coupledom to such an extent that it sacrifices the

[123] See ibid., [44]–[46].
[124] See ibid., [46].
[125] Ibid., [36].
[126] As noted in *A.M.* v. *Norway*, Concurring Opinion of Judge O'Leary, [16], in the previous cases (the Mennessons' case at the origin of Advisory Opinion No. P16-2018-001, *C. and E.* v. *France*), 'the "family" or parental units involved remained stable units, such that the intended parent seeking legal recognition of the child–parent relationship was supported by the legally recognised biological parent and could be accommodated somehow within the possibilities for legal recognition provided in existing domestic legal frameworks, not least adoption procedures'.
[127] This was emphasised by the Court (*A.M.* v. *Norway*, [127]): 'In contrast to what was the topic of the advisory opinion [no. P16-2018-001], the application in the instant case does not relate to any rights of the child, X, under Article 8 of the Convention: the Court is called upon to examine solely the complaints raised by the applicant on her own behalf.'

legitimate individual expectations of the social parent, left to depend entirely on their partner, despite their participation in the parental project, the effective care given to the child, as well as their formal recognition as a legal parent in the State where the surrogacy arrangement took place. Arguably, the parenthood of the social parent should be irrevocably crystallised when the couple undergoes treatment resulting in conception; save for the event in which the person refuses to act as a parent after the child's birth, their parental status should not be subject to subsequent events in the couple's romantic life. Thirdly, allowing parenthood ties to vary according to the fluctuations of the couple's relationship after conception and birth creates a considerable amount of legal uncertainty over the child's identity, which benefits neither the child[128] nor, indeed, the social parent (deprived of their relationship with the child after substantial emotional and financial investment) or the surrogate (burdened with responsibilities she had not signed up to). It may marginally benefit the genetic parent, although a second parent is also a resource, and the genetic parent's interests should be in alignment with those of the child, including the enjoyment of the support and affection of two parents, where available.

The acknowledgement of parasitic Article 8 rights for the non-genetic commissioning parent in surrogacy arrangements in the Advisory Opinion and subsequent case law mirrors the Court's approach to intentional parenthood in cross-border assisted fertilisation cases, as seen in *Gas and Dubois v. France*. Intention alone does not create parenthood under the Convention case law; it needs to be corroborated by an indirect tie to the child, through the child's genetic parent. The dependency of any successful claim in Strasbourg upon the legal relationship (typically marriage) between the intended social parent and the child's genetic parent is further confirmed by the outcome of applications in which neither commissioning parent is genetically related to the child. This situation will be examined in greater detail in the following section.

3.3.2 *Intentional Parenthood Where Neither Commissioning Parent Is Genetically Related to the Child*

Perhaps more than any other reproductive technique, surrogacy arrangements in which both intended parents are biological strangers to the child conjure

[128] See *A.M. v. Norway*, Dissenting Opinion of Judge Jelić, [37]: 'I cannot see the benefits, inter alia in terms of protecting the best interests of the child, of recognising the non-existent relationship between the surrogate mother and X, rather than the relationship between the latter and the applicant.'

up 'baby selling' scenarios, although the objection that surrogacy commodifies children is wider.[129] In some jurisdictions, in order for the intended parents to be treated in law as the parents of the surrogate-born child, at least one of them must have a genetic link with the child (i.e. the gametes of at least one of them must have been used to bring about the creation of the embryo placed in the surrogate or for her artificial insemination).[130] Similarly, in the case of proceedings brought by a sole applicant, a parental order can be awarded only if the latter is genetically related to the child.[131] Katherine Wade has pointed out that, although the rationale invoked for the need for a genetic link is 'to protect against parents "commissioning" children for adoption', this justification is called into question by the fact that 'no such requirement exists in the case of non-surrogate birth following double gamete donation'.[132] Admittedly, to some extent, this inconsistency may appear problematic; however, in the case of non-surrogate births with no genetic ties to the woman who carries the child (or to her partner), the gestational link between the intended mother and the child may be seen as establishing a connection that the law could legitimately endorse as a form of affiliation. In Strasbourg jurisprudence, the absence of a genetic link has proven fatal to Article 8 applications, but for very different reasons: one substantive and one procedural.

First, from a substantive viewpoint, for the ECtHR it is the surrogate-born child's right to the preservation of his/her identity that triggers the obligation to recognise affiliation with the genetic parent and his spouse, not the 'intellectual' responsibility for the child's birth. Second, from a procedural perspective, commissioning couples without any genetic link to the child were deemed to lack *locus standi* to bring an application on behalf of the child in Strasbourg proceedings. These two hurdles to establishing ECHR entitlements in relation to surrogacy-born children were highlighted by *Paradiso and Campanelli* v. *Italy* and *Valdís Fjölnisdóttir and Others* v. *Iceland*, both of which indicate that, for the ECtHR, intention to become a parent alone does not attract the application of 'family life' guarantees in the assisted reproduction context.[133] If the surrogacy arrangement fails and, due to error or fraud, neither member of the couple is genetically related to the child (the *Paradiso and Campanelli* scenario), or if the parental plan did not include genetic ties from the outset

[129] See Chapter 2, Section 2.4.
[130] This is the case in the UK; see s. 54(1) Human Fertilisation and Embryology Act 2008.
[131] See, for the UK, s. 54A(1) Human Fertilisation and Embryology Act 2008.
[132] Wade, 'The Regulation of Surrogacy', 118.
[133] *Paradiso and Campanelli* v. *Italy* [GC], App. No. 25358/12, 24 January 2017, overturning *Paradiso and Campanelli* v. *Italy* [Chamber], App. No. 25358/12, 27 January 2015; *Valdís Fjölnisdóttir and Others* v. *Iceland*, App. No. 71552/17, 18 May 2021.

(the *Valdís Fjölnisdóttir* scenario), the notion of 'family life' does not apply to the relationship between the commissioning parents and the children, except where the passage of time (four years in *Valdís Fjölnisdóttir*) creates a de facto family-like situation.

As discussed in Chapter 2, even the biological father's Article 8 claim has been unsuccessful in foreign surrogacy cases, and his right to be recognised as a legal parent is a mere consequence of the child's privacy rights, which include the protection of genetic affiliation. The previous section (Section 3.3.1) has shown that the non-genetic intended parent's right to recognition as a parent (e.g. through adoption) is also a parasitic right, depending not only on the child's right to a stable family environment but also on the marital ties with the child's biological parent. *Valdís Fjölnisdóttir*, a case where neither party was a genetic parent by design, established that foster care arrangements in relation to the surrogate child are suitable to protect existing long-term family-like arrangements; the recognition of legal parenthood is not required. In addition, but for the long-term care situation tolerated by the domestic authorities, despite the non-recognition of the foreign birth certificate (by contrast with *Paradiso*, where the child was swiftly removed from the commissioning parents), in all likelihood, the Court would not have found 'family life' engaged at all.

The *Paradiso and Campanelli* v. *Italy* case reveals a particularly unfavourable approach to intentional parenthood in foreign surrogacy cases where no genetic ties exist, the territorial State does not permit surrogacy, and the cohabitation has not been extensive. The case concerned the removal by the Italian authorities of a child born in Russia through a gestational surrogacy contract between an Italian couple and a Russian company (entirely licit according to the law of the forum) once it was ascertained that the child did not have biological links with the father. The complaint lamented the placement of the child in a children's home at the age of nine months and his ultimate adoption by strangers, following an adoption procedure which excluded the intended parents and de facto carers since birth.

The facts of the case are somewhat peculiar, in that the parenthood project, based on genetic fatherhood, had been thwarted by the fertility clinic, unbeknownst to the commissioning parents. The in vitro fertilisation procedure the couple had undergone in Russia had purportedly used the commissioning father's sperm, and the child had been registered in Russia as the applicant's son with the surrogate mother's consent. Following the request for registration in Italy of the Russian birth certificate, which contained no reference to the gestational surrogacy, the Italian authorities had placed the applicants under investigation for the alteration of civil status. A DNA test carried out at a court's request after the public prosecutor had opened proceedings to release the child for adoption (on the basis that he was to be considered abandoned) showed that there was no genetic link between the commissioning father and the child. The child was removed from the applicants; all contact was terminated; he was given a new name and adopted by another family; in the adoption proceedings, the domestic court held that the applicants did not have legal standing to intervene.

Relying on Article 8 ECHR, the applicants alleged that the refusal to recognise the legal parent–child relationship, the removal of the child from their home and his placement in State care infringed the right to respect for their private and family life. The Court determined that the couple did not have legal standing to apply on behalf of the child, and therefore, unlike *Mennesson*, the case revolved exclusively around the commissioning parents' rights. This decision is questionable: the applicants, albeit the legal parents of the child in one of the jurisdictions participating in the ECHR system,[134] were treated as strangers in relation to the child, according to an interpretation adhering to the respondent State's legal system, to which the Court owed no allegiance or preference. Parental status according to the law of one State (the child's birth country) should arguably give rise to standing and permit international judicial oversight. Since the nationality of a Member State is not a prerequisite for filing a complaint before the ECtHR,[135] the individuals and families applying in Strasbourg bring with them their own personal law (including potentially the law of a non-ECHR State), and the Court accepts their status as defined by that law. In diversely regulated cross-border situations, such as international surrogacy arrangements, and given the importance of the children's best interests, one relevant legal connection between the child and the carers (albeit not recognisable in all ECHR States) should be sufficient to allow the Court to consider whether the impugned measure was respectful of the child's welfare. Otherwise, treating as relevant only the legal ties recognised by the respondent State leads to paradoxical gaps in the protection of foreign family units, such as the failure to recognise as related same-sex spouses – where the State of residence does not recognise gay marriage – or heterosexual spouses, if one of them was

[134] As it then was; Russia ceased being a party to the ECHR on 16 September 2022, following its expulsion from the Council of Europe in accordance with Resolution CM/Res(2022)3 adopted by the Committee of Ministers on 23 March 2022.

[135] See Art. 34 ECHR, allowing applications from any person claiming to be a victim of a violation by one of the ECHR parties of the rights set forth in the ECHR.

seventeen at the time of the marriage ceremony and the respondent State sets the minimum marriageable age at eighteen.[136]

The radical contrast between the Chamber's and the Grand Chamber's evaluation of the same set of facts demonstrates the potential for wide-ranging legal arguments in assisted reproduction cases, leading to opposite conclusions. Although, notwithstanding the commissioning parents' intention, neither had a biological link with the child (owing to fraud or error in the Russian IVF procedure), the Chamber that initially examined the case found that the parent–child relationship established abroad (the child having lived with, and being cared for by, the applicants for the first few months of his life) engaged both the 'private life' and 'family life' facets of Article 8. In fact, the Chamber reiterated that 'the existence or non-existence of family life is essentially a question of fact depending upon the real existence in practice of close personal ties';[137] it thus found that 'the applicants had acted as parents towards the child ... [and] there existed a *de facto* family life between the applicants and the child'.[138] Importantly, the ruling required the interference with Article 8 rights to be proportionate, according to Convention standards, even in an area of wide State discretion and characterised by a lack of European consensus. Critical for the development of human rights standards in the field of ART, the Chamber decision confirmed that the Strasbourg Court can perform an assessment of proportionality without having to proceed to a consensus analysis. Thus, it was held that, irrespective of the level of convergence among domestic laws on surrogacy, the Italian courts had acted disproportionately by removing the child from his carers and placing him with adopters; the applicants, who had previously been assessed as fit to adopt by the relevant domestic authorities, 'were found to be incapable of bringing up and loving the child on the sole ground that they had circumvented the adoption legislation, without any expert report having been ordered by the courts'.[139]

Moreover, from the child's perspective, the consequence of the authorities' actions was that 'he had had no official existence for more than two years'.[140]

[136] In England and Wales, the Marriage and Civil Partnership (Minimum Age) Act 2022 increased the minimum marriageable age to eighteen and removed the ability of parents to consent to the marriage of their sixteen-/seventeen-year-old children; however, where such marriages were entered into abroad, the couple ought to be able to rely on their marital status in proceedings against the UK.

[137] *Paradiso and Campanelli* v. *Italy* [Chamber], [67].

[138] Ibid., [69].

[139] Ibid., [84].

[140] Ibid., [85].

Following the *Mennesson* precedent, the Chamber stressed the State's duty to ensure that the child is not penalised for being born to a surrogate mother in respect of citizenship or identity rights. The lack of proportionality of the measure was arguably compounded by the fact that insufficient consideration had been given to the irreversibility of the measure. Indeed, the Chamber's decision in *Paradiso and Campanelli* noted that, since the child had developed emotional ties with the adopters, its finding of a breach of Article 8 was not to be read as requiring the return of the child to the applicants.[141] The standard of diligence required of the authorities in failed surrogacy cases should be the one developed in the area of non-consensual adoption; the child is, in fact, irrevocably separated from the only parents he has known all his life, who are also his legal parents according to the foreign jurisdiction where the birth took place.

The Grand Chamber's revisitation of *Paradiso and Campanelli*, as with *S.H. and Others* v. *Austria*, reversed the Chamber's decision in a way that expands State discretion. According to the Grand Chamber, the applicants had disregarded international adoption procedures by bringing into the country a child with whom neither of them had a biological tie, and had acted illegally by entering into an assisted reproduction agreement that was unlawful in Italy.[142] The judgment thus failed to acknowledge the deception to which the applicants fell victims in Russia and the legality of the surrogacy contract under Russian law. It only made a minimal concession to intentional parenthood followed by actual emotional bonds:

> Having regard to the above factors, namely the absence of any biological tie between the child and the intended parents, the short duration of the relationship with the child and the uncertainty of the ties from a legal perspective, and *in spite of the existence of a parental project and the quality of the emotional bonds*, the Court considers that the conditions enabling it to conclude that there existed a de facto family life have not been met.[143]

The analysis of the relationship between the intended parents and the surrogate-born child under Article 8 appears unduly influenced by the alleged

[141] Ibid., [88].

[142] *Paradiso and Campanelli* v. *Italy* [GC], [147]: 'There had been illegality, firstly in that they had brought to Italy a foreign child who had no biological ties with either parent, in breach of the rules laid down on international adoption, and, secondly, in that they had entered into an agreement providing for the handing over of the second applicant's seminal fluid in order to fertilise ovocytes from another woman, which was in breach of the prohibition in Italian law on heterologous assisted reproduction.'

[143] Ibid., [157] (emphasis added).

illegality of the commissioning couple's conduct. By contrast with the Chamber's decision and despite the existence of a parental project, effective care and emotional bonds, the Grand Chamber's ruling concluded that there was no de facto family life, citing the absence of biological ties, the short period during which the applicants had acted as parents (eight months) and the uncertainty of legal ties from the outset. This seems to be a punitive finding. It is, indeed, a regrettable departure from *Moretti and Benedetti* v. *Italy*,[144] *Kopf and Liberda* v. *Austria*[145] and *Wagner and J.M.W.L.* v. *Luxembourg*,[146] where Article 8 was found to apply to the relationship between young children and the persons who had acted as long-term carers despite the absence of biological ties (whether foster parents or adoptive parents under non-recognised foreign adoption decrees), and it seems intended to chastise the couple's attempt to circumvent Italian law on parenthood.

From a 'private life' perspective, considering the commissioning couple's intention to become parents and the exploration of various options to that end, the Grand Chamber accepted that Article 8 was applicable. In fact, what was at stake was the right to respect for the applicants' decision to become parents and their personal development through the parental role they wished to assume; it is in this context that the Grand Chamber dwells more on intentional parenthood, linking it to personal development rather than family life:

> The Court notes that the applicants had a genuine intention to become parents, initially by attempts to conceive via *in vitro* fertilisation, then by applying for and obtaining formal approval to adopt, and, lastly, by turning to ova donation and the use of a surrogate mother. A major part of their lives was focused on realising their plan to become parents, in order to love and bring

[144] See *Moretti and Benedetti* v. *Italy*, [48] (the existence of de facto family life depends on the amount of time spent together, the quality of the relationships and the role assumed by the adult towards the child). The applicants had had a baby in their care for nineteen months from the age of one month; she was well integrated into the family and attached to the applicants and their children; they had contributed to her social development (by enrolling her in a crèche, taking her on holidays, etc.); a close interpersonal bond amounting to de facto family ties thus existed between the child and the foster carers, who had acted as her parents in every respect – a bond further evidenced by their application to adopt her (see ibid., [49]–[52]). The adoption procedure, whereby the child had been adopted by a different family, had not respected the foster carers' interests (their request for adoption had not been considered before the child was declared adoptable and was subsequently rejected without any justification being given), in violation of Art. 8 (ibid., [65]–[71]).

[145] See *Kopf and Liberda* v. *Austria*, App. No. 1598/06, 17 January 2012, [37], relying on *Moretti and Benedetti* to find Art. 8 applicable to the relationship between a child and the persons who had raised him from the age of two for forty-six months and tried to adopt him.

[146] See *Wagner and J.M.W.L.* v. *Luxembourg*, App. No. 76240/01, 28 June 2007, [117].

> up a child. Accordingly, what is at issue is the right to respect for the applicants' decision to become parents . . ., and the applicants' personal development through the role of parents that they wished to assume *vis-à-vis* the child.[147]

In addition, the domestic proceedings seeking to verify the child's biological ties with one of the intended parents and the establishment of genetic facts impacted the child's identity and the relationship between the child and the alleged father. It was further accepted that the removal of the child had amounted to an interference with the applicants' private life, which can extend to 'the emotional bonds created and developed between an adult and a child in situations other than the classic situations of kinship', as 'this type of bond also pertains to individuals' life and social identity'.[148]

This modest finding in relation to the 'private life' limb of Article 8 has nevertheless had its critics. According to Beaumont and Trimmings, 'if the "close personal ties" between an adult and a child are not enough to constitute de facto "family life" then the removal of the child from the care of an adult should not be treated as an interference with their "private life"'.[149] This objection does not take into account the significantly broader interpretation of private life when compared to family life. The relationship between same-sex partners, while not crossing the 'family law' threshold until 2010,[150] was already accepted as engaging private life in the 1980s.[151] An extramarital affair, even when it produced children, was not analysed as 'family life' in the absence of stable cohabitation, but was found to constitute an aspect of private life.[152] The relationship between putative fathers and children with whom they never had an opportunity to develop effective ties, and hence family life, also falls within the notion of 'private life'.[153]

Genetic ties appear central to the assessment of the parenthood project under Article 8, that is, to determining whether the intention to become a parent, acted upon, engages 'family life'. In *S.H. and Others* v. *Austria*, the mere decision to use ART in order to conceive a child was also seen as an

147 *Paradiso and Campanelli* v. *Italy* [GC], [163].
148 Ibid., [161].
149 Paul Beaumont and Katarina Trimmings, 'Surrogacy before the European Court of Human Rights', in Jens Scherpe, Claire Fenton-Glynn and Terry Kaan (eds.), *Eastern and Western Perspectives on Surrogacy* (Cambridge, Antwerp and Chicago: Intersentia, 2019) 331–354, at 343.
150 See *Schalk and Kopf* v. *Austria*, App. No. 30141/04, 24 June 2010, [94].
151 See Draghici, *The Legitimacy of Family Rights*, 189–194.
152 See ibid., 85–87.
153 See Draghici, 'Unplanned Fatherhood Is Not Sperm Donation', 127–132.

expression of family life; the Grand Chamber held that 'the right of a couple to conceive a child and to make use of medically assisted procreation for that purpose is also protected by Article 8, as such a choice is an expression of private and family life'.[154] The distinction between *S.H.* and *Paradiso* is the absence, in the latter, of a genetic link. The Article 8 analysis was muddied in *Paradiso* by the discrepancy between the applicants' initial plans (genetic parenthood for one of them) and the outcome (de facto care of a child unrelated to the couple, akin to adoption).

Even so, Strasbourg case law has indicated that, although the ECHR does not guarantee a right to become a parent through adoption, and no genetic link exists between adopter and adoptee, adoptive families are covered by the notion of 'family life' by virtue of the 'adoption contract':

> The fact that the applicant cannot claim 'the right to found a family' does not mean, however, that the relationship between an adoptive parent and an adoptive child is not of the same nature as the family relations protected by Article 8 of the Convention. . . . A State cannot separate two persons united by an adoption contract, or forbid them to meet, without engaging its responsibility under Article 8 of the Convention.[155]

It could be argued that the surrogacy arrangement – an agreement of quasi-contractual nature to transfer parenthood which produces legal effects in the jurisdiction where it is concluded, followed by birth registration or order vesting parenthood in the commissioning parents – creates legal ties analogous to adoption orders. Naturally, foreign adoption orders are more readily recognised, insofar as the institution of adoption is accepted in virtually all European States. However, this is not always the case, in particular where the eligibility criteria differ greatly (e.g. single applicants are able to adopt abroad, whereas the adopter's country of residence only permits adoption by couples).[156] This leads to difficulties similar to those encountered by the holders of foreign parental orders following surrogacy. In both cases, the foreign decisions create legal status, consolidated by de facto care. The fact that parental orders are more diversely regulated in Europe and elsewhere (and hence more controversial from a public policy perspective) should not

[154] *S.H. and Others* v. *Austria* [GC], [82].

[155] X v. *Belgium and The Netherlands*, reiterated in X v. *France*, App. No. 9993/82, 5 October 1982 (Commission), *Pini and Bertani & Manera and Atripaldi* v. *Romania*, App. Nos. 78028/01; 78030/01, 22 June 2004, [140].

[156] See *Wagner and J.M.W.L.* v. *Luxembourg*, discussed later, illustrating the importance of the distinction between conflict of laws and domestic illegality in the context of adoption; the same distinction should be recognised in foreign surrogacy cases.

detract from this analogy. By the same token, the fact that the Convention does not guarantee a right to reproduce through surrogacy should not mean that surrogacy-based families are not entitled to protection. The length of cohabitation should also not be decisive. In *Pini and Bertani* v. *Romania*, the relationship created by a lawful adoption order was sufficient to create 'family life' even in the absence of close personal ties, which suggests that the potential family life expected in accordance with the order creating parenthood ought to be protected.[157]

Despite finding that private life was engaged in *Paradiso*, the Grand Chamber viewed the interference with Article 8 rights as having a basis in the law and pursuing the legitimate aims of preventing disorder and protecting the rights of others (both the child at stake and future children). The domestic courts' decisions were found to be appropriately based on the absence of genetic ties between the applicants and the child and on the applicants' breach of domestic laws on international adoption and medically assisted reproduction. The well-foundedness of this assessment is questionable. The reference to international adoption rules ought to be seen as irrelevant, because the applicants had not pursued the adoption of an abandoned unrelated child from a foreign jurisdiction.[158] Nor were domestic laws on medically assisted procreation breached: the assisted fertilisation treatment in question had been received abroad, in accordance with the laws governing it in that jurisdiction. It is submitted that the real crux of the case was whether the general policy objections against recognition of foreign civil status acts should prevail over the individual interests at stake. By focusing on the perceived culpability of the applicants, the Court failed to engage with the more difficult question before it.

The Grand Chamber ruling found that domestic courts were justified in attaching considerable weight to the illegality of the applicants' conduct (undertaking abroad conduct contrary to Italian law) and to the need to take urgent measures to safeguard the welfare of the child, whom the authorities treated as abandoned, and to put an end to the illegal situation. It is far from

[157] The reference to 'potential family life' features in the case law on the rights of natural fathers who have not had an opportunity to establish de facto ties with their children due to the mother's opposition and repartnering. For a discussion, see Draghici, 'Unplanned Fatherhood Is Not Sperm Donation', 126–136 and 146–147.

[158] The judgment noted that, having been approved for inter-country adoption, the applicants had circumvented the Adoption Act by bringing the child into the country without the approval of the Commission for Inter-Country Adoption. This ignores the fact that, although they had looked into international adoption, the applicants had opted for surrogacy abroad, not inter-country adoption; therefore, a different framework for analysis had to be applied.

obvious why the child was to be considered at risk with the applicants, since no flaws had been found in the care given to him. If the child did not have legal parents in the eyes of Italian law, or there was a public policy objection to the recognition of its parents under Russian law, the existing carers' status could have been formalised in a manner consistent with public policy, for example, fostering or adoption rather than transcription of the Russian birth certificate. At the very least, the intended parents and, indeed, the parents according to Russian law should have been considered by the domestic courts as a placement option and allowed to apply for adoption.

Admittedly, the ECtHR was entitled to uphold the State's prerogative to establish affiliation through adoption rather than the transcription of the foreign birth certificate, due to the public policy objection to surrogacy. It was also entitled to recognise that the case touched upon ethically sensitive issues (adoption, care proceedings, medically assisted reproduction, surrogate motherhood), in relation to which States enjoyed a wide margin of appreciation. However, the Court failed to consider whether the conflict of laws had been resolved through a necessary and proportionate interference with the applicants' and the child's rights. The decision appears dominated by the concern expressed by the dissenters at the Chamber stage over the State's legislative freedom, rather than any genuine balancing of rights:

> If it suffices to create, illegally, a link with the child abroad in order for the national authorities to be obliged to recognise the existence of 'family life', then it is clear that the States' freedom not to give legal effect to gestational surrogacy, a freedom that has nonetheless been acknowledged by the Court's case-law ..., is reduced to nought.[159]

The Grand Chamber's attempt to rationalise the pro-State decision arguably distorted the legal qualification of the dispute. Although the applicants bore partial responsibility for a foreseeably difficult legal situation, the Court's readiness to endorse the excessive focus in domestic proceedings on the illegality of their conduct is open to criticism.[160] In fact, the couple had acted in accordance with the laws of the jurisdiction where the surrogacy arrangement and birth registration took place; consequently, the case did not concern the applicants' moral turpitude – such that they would not be fit to parent the child – but a technical conflict-of-law issue. In its previous *Thlimmenos v. Greece* ruling, the Grand Chamber had recognised that the law excluding

[159] *Paradiso and Campanelli* v. *Italy* (Chamber), Joint Partly Dissenting Opinion of Judges Raimondi and Spano, [15].
[160] *Paradiso and Campanelli* v. *Italy* [GC], [149].

a conscientious objector from the profession of chartered account due to his criminal conviction for refusing to comply with draft obligations unjustifiably treated him as a person having committed morally reprehensible acts and being unfit for certain occupations.[161] Analogously, in *Paradiso and Campanelli*, the Court ought to have found that nothing in the applicants' conduct, albeit illegal under domestic law, denoted moral infirmity rendering them unfit parents. The dispute hinged, rather, on the balance between Italy's interest in enforcing its private international law rules (including non-recognition of foreign surrogate births in relation to Italian residents) and the interests of the applicants and the child. The Court could have found the non-recognition of affiliation within the Article 8(2) parameters, but the removal of the child – instead of an alternative solution allowing the child to remain in a stable, loving family environment – should have been found disproportionate to the aim of discouraging Italian residents from entering into surrogacy arrangements abroad.

In addition, the case law on the recognition of adoption-based relationships lawfully created abroad, albeit in a manner inconsistent with domestic rules on the eligibility for adoption, suggests that the children's best interests may require an exceptional departure from domestic law and the accommodation of otherwise incompatible foreign adoption decrees.[162] In fact, notwithstanding the State's legitimate policy objections against recognition, the failure to offer legal protection to existing family life may be a disproportionate interference with the parties' Article 8 rights. For instance, in *Wagner and J.M.W.L. v. Luxembourg*, a single woman had adopted a three-year-old girl in Peru and sought to have the Peruvian adoption decision declared enforceable in Luxembourg, so as to secure her daughter's acquisition of Luxembourg nationality. However, her application had been dismissed insofar as, under domestic law, only married couples were eligible to adopt. The Strasbourg Court agreed that there had been an interference with the applicant's and her daughter's right to respect for family life,[163] which pursued the legitimate aim of protecting 'health or morals' and the 'rights and freedoms' of the child.[164] Conversely, the Court did not find that the measure was 'necessary in a democratic society'. It noted the broad European consensus in favour of single adoption by unmarried persons,[165] but also reasoned that the refusal to

[161] See *Thlimmenos v. Greece* [GC], App. No. 34369/97, 6 April 2000, [47].
[162] On the recognition of foreign adoptions in Strasbourg case law, see Draghici, *The Legitimacy of Family Rights*, 158–160.
[163] *Wagner and JMWL v. Luxembourg*, [118]–[23].
[164] Ibid., [125]–[126].
[165] Ibid., [129].

recognise the applicants as a family did not take into account social reality and the significant difficulties they encountered in their everyday lives, such as the need to regularly apply for a resident permit and a visa to travel to certain destinations.[166] Importantly, the ruling concluded that the impugned measure did not promote the best interests of the child,[167] as well as amounting to discrimination; in fact, the child had been penalised on account of her status as the adoptive child of an unmarried mother whose family ties were based on a foreign adoption order.[168]

The recognition of foreign surrogacy exhibits the same tension – seen in the treatment of foreign adoption – between the aim of discouraging residents from circumventing domestic rules and the need to protect the welfare of minors, and it should arguably be similarly resolved by giving precedence to the latter. The argument that social parents should not be allowed to face the State with a *fait accompli* is appealing;[169] however, notice must be taken of the fact that they acted legally abroad, according to the law of the State where surrogacy arrangements and the administrative or judicial procedure allocating legal parenthood took place. Allowing them to benefit from a foreign law incompatible with their national law should not be confused with allowing a person to profit from their wrongdoing. This distinction regrettably appears to escape part of the scholarship; criticising the dissenters' observation in *Paradiso* (the Grand Chamber's judgment) that 'family life' did exist, Beaumont and Trimmings suggested that the 'illegality of the formation of family life' should contribute to 'determining the "factual" question as to whether there is de facto family life'.[170] Family life in this case was formed in Russia, where the aspiring parents had acted lawfully when using services provided in accordance with Russian regulations and proceeding with the birth registration procedure available under municipal law. Non-recognition of the family ties under Italian rules of private international law is not

[166] Ibid., [132].
[167] Ibid., [133].
[168] Ibid., [155]–[159].
[169] According to Beaumont and Trimmings, 'Surrogacy before the European Court of Human Rights', 338, not removing the child from the care of the commissioning parents 'will encourage commissioning parents to circumvent national legislation prohibiting surrogacy'.
[170] Ibid., 341. By contrast, a foreigner starting to cohabit with a citizen after an exclusion order or the expiry of their visa ought to have known that family life built on an irregular immigration status was going to be precarious (this is the prevailing Strasbourg approach; see Draghici, *The Legitimacy of Family Rights*, 353–357). Even in those cases, rather than finding that family life did not exist, the Court merely finds that it is not decisive, that is, the wrongdoer cannot rely on it to compel the State to authorise their stay (see *Baghli* v. *France*, App. No. 34374/97, 30 November 1999, [48]; *Dalia* v. *France*, App. No. 26102/95, 19 February 1998, [54]).

tantamount to the illegal formation of the family. The family life in *Paradiso* would have been based on illegality if, for example, the applicants had kidnapped a baby from the hospital and then bonded with him – in such a case, the very formation of de facto family life would have been tarnished by the initial illegal conduct (child abduction is illegal in every jurisdiction and can legitimately influence the Article 8 assessment). But there is yet a further problem with the suggestion that the parents of surrogate-born children should not benefit from the 'family life' qualification: should *Russian* commissioning parents with a valid Italian visa (or dual Russian-Italian nationals) relocating to Italy with their surrogate-born child not be recognised as a family unit? Clearly, when the distinction between illegality and conflict of laws is blurred, the consequences can be illogical.

Moreover, the analysis of 'family life' made no concession to the father's decision to become a biological parent (subverted by the negligence or fraud of the fertility clinic) and to his emotional investment during six months in which he believed he was raising his biological child. Marianna Iliadou noted that, according to the decision in *Nazarenko* v. *Russia*,[171] 'the belief of genetic parenthood supports a finding of *de facto* family ties where the duration of shared life is long'.[172] Although *Paradiso* can be distinguished on the basis of the relatively short duration of shared life, the judgment was too dismissive of the father's belief that he was the genetic father, which speaks to the quality of the bond and may compensate for the brief cohabitation.

As to the applicants' interest in continuing their relationship with the child, the domestic court in *Paradiso* had expressed concern that the child might be an instrument to fulfil a narcissistic desire of the applicants. The ECtHR regrettably accepted an argument that degrades the human aspiration to become a parent altogether, whether through natural procreation or adoption. Problematically, it failed to address the intolerant, pejorative approach of the domestic courts to surrogacy arrangements lawfully entered into abroad:

[171] *Nazarenko* v. *Russia*, App. No. 39438/13, 16 July 2015. In this case, the man was revealed not to be the genetic father of the eight-year-old he had raised with his former wife, and the termination of paternity had led to the automatic exclusion from the child's life. The failure of the authorities to allow the preservation of family ties between the father and child was analysed as a breach of Art. 8 ECHR. On the signficance of this case, see Olga Khazova, 'Some Reflections on a European Court Case. *Nazarenko v. Russia*', in Jens Scherpe and Stephen Gilmore (eds.), *Family Matters. Essays in Honour of John Eekelaar* (Cambridge: Intersentia, 2022) 612–621.

[172] Marianna Iliadou, 'Surrogacy and the ECtHR: Reflections on *Paradiso and Campanelli v Italy*' (2018) 27(1) *Medical Law Review* 144–154, 148.

> The Minors Court expressed concern that the child might be an instrument to *fulfil a narcissistic desire of the applicants* or to exorcise an individual or joint problem. Furthermore, it considered that the applicants' conduct threw a 'consistent shadow on their possession of genuine affective and educational abilities' and doubted whether they displayed the 'instinct of human solidarity which must be present in any person wishing to bring the children of others into their lives as their own children'.[173]

The ECtHR ought to have questioned the logical link in the domestic ruling between the recourse to reproductive techniques abroad as permitted by the relevant law and a couple's inability to love and educate a biologically unrelated child.

Moreover, the Court acknowledged that 'the Italian courts attached little weight to the applicants' interest in continuing to develop their relationship with a child whose parents they wished to be' and 'did not explicitly address the impact which the immediate and irreversible separation from the child would have on their private life'; however, this was deemed justified in light of 'the illegality of the applicants' conduct and the fact that their relationship with the child was precarious from the very moment that they decided to take up residence with him in Italy'.[174] This is no different from suggesting that a man entering a gay marriage and wishing to be joined by his spouse in his country of residence, which only permits heterosexual marriage, should be treated as a criminal and cannot expect the protection of Article 8. A person's family life should not be seen as unrecognisable under Article 8 ECHR merely because it was not recognised in his State of nationality or because he had foreknowledge of obstacles to recognition.

Additionally, the same finding of discrimination under Article 14 read in conjunction with Article 8 noted in foreign adoption cases is also warranted in foreign surrogacy cases. In fact, in the absence of some form of recognition of legal ties with the social parents, the surrogate-born child is penalised, that is, deprived of legal protections, merely on the basis of the circumstances of his/her conception and place of birth. Whether or not the application is also brought on behalf of the child, the impact of the measure on the child needs to be included in the proportionality assessment. Moreover, albeit stressing that the child was not an applicant, nor a member of the applicants' family within the meaning of Article 8, the Court acknowledged that the domestic courts' treatment of the child's best interests was not irrelevant and recalled

[173] *Paradiso and Campanelli* v. *Italy* [GC], [207] (emphasis added).
[174] Ibid., [211].

that Article 3 of the UN Convention on the Rights of the Child (UNCRC)[175] required the child's best interests to be treated as the primary consideration in any actions concerning children.[176] However, the judgment only paid lip service to this principle. The test it set for the removal of the child by the authorities – whether it caused 'irreparable damage' or not – belies that approach. It is equally obvious that the first consideration was the preservation of the State's prerogative to refuse to recognise overseas surrogacy.

The departure, in foreign surrogacy cases, from the pre-eminence of the child's best interests, upheld in the case law on foreign adoption, might be explained by the added element of discomfort with ARTs. This seems to widen the margin of appreciation and lead the Court to endorse far-fetched domestic assessments of necessity and proportionality. In *Paradiso*, the procedure releasing the child for adoption – without giving those who had cared for him in the first eight months of his life an opportunity to apply to adopt and make representations to the social workers/the court overseeing the case – ran contrary to everyone's interest. Nonetheless, the Grand Chamber readily accepted that any measure other than the immediate removal of the child and termination of all contact carried the risk that the passage of time would have determined the outcome of the case; placing the child in a legal limbo for two years was seen as preferable to allowing the intended parents to be successful in their enterprise. Arguably, the harm of having the case determined by long-term care (inability to send a deterring message to prospective commissioning parents) was not greater than the harm caused to the child by the change in care arrangements and the separation from the only parents he had known. Excessive emphasis seems to be placed in *Paradiso and Campanelli* on the need to avoid sanctioning a *fait accompli*, at the expense of the child's welfare and the applicants' Article 8 rights.

While the State's wish to reaffirm its exclusive competence to define legal parent–child relationships was understandably treated as a legitimate aim, the proportionality analysis was unduly skewed in favour of the State. The Court 'accept[ed] that the Italian courts, having assessed that *the child would not suffer grave or irreparable harm* from the separation, struck a fair balance between the different interests at stake'.[177] It is highly uncharacteristic of ECHR jurisprudence to find a fair balance achieved when the trauma suffered by a child is 'not irreparable'. The State-appeasing judicial agenda

[175] Convention on the Rights of the Child, New York, 20 November 1989, in force 2 September 1990, UNTS vol. 1577 (p. 3).
[176] See *Paradiso and Campanelli* v. *Italy* [GC], [208].
[177] Ibid., [215] (emphasis added).

underlying the distortion of the proportionality and best interests analysis transpires from the conclusion to the judgment: 'Agreeing to let the child stay with the applicants, possibly with a view to becoming his adoptive parents, would have been tantamount to legalising the situation created by them in breach of important rules of Italian law.'[178] The judgment thus upheld the respondent's abstract interest in reaffirming its law-making authority at the expense of individual rights, including the child's best interests. This is especially unsatisfactory since a more sympathetic solution would neither have harmed others nor compromised the State's legislative autonomy; indeed, Italian infertile couples interested in, and able to go through, foreign surrogacy arrangements constitute too narrow a category to raise 'floodgates' concerns.[179]

Both in its outcome and analysis, the Grand Chamber's decision in *Paradiso and Campanelli* is a disappointing moment in ECHR jurisprudence. In an *obiter*, the judgment also took an unfortunate step back on parenthood under Article 8: 'While the Convention *does not recognise a right to become a parent*, the Court cannot ignore the emotional hardship suffered by those whose desire to become parents has not been or cannot be fulfilled.'[180] In fact, previously *Evans* v. *The United Kingdom* upheld 'the right to respect for both the decisions to become and not to become a parent'.[181] Instead of an unnuanced statement on the absence of a right to become a parent, the Court ought to have merely conceded that States do not have to respect *the specific means* chosen by a person/couple to have a child. However, the judgment does not hinder the future expansion of reproductive rights, to the extent that the issue before the Court was limited to the treatment of de facto caregivers unrelated to the child.

The judicial attitude towards intended parents appeared less critical in the subsequent *Valdís Fjölnisdóttir* v. *Iceland*, in which, again, neither applicant was genetically related to the child, this time by design. The applicants, a married couple, had become legal parents in the United States following the use of paid gestational surrogacy and IVF treatment with donated gametes.[182]

178 Ibid.

179 Polygamy runs counter to public policy in all ECHR States, and ECHR case law has given priority to State sovereignty over the families' interest in reunification; see Draghici, *The Legitimacy of Family Rights*, 55–62. However, whereas the presence of polygamous relationships may be disruptive for the community, non-biological parenthood is already common and would not affect the *ordre public*.

180 *Paradiso and Campanelli* v. *Italy* [GC], [215] (emphasis added).

181 See *Evans* v. *The United Kingdom* [GC], [71].

182 See *Valdís Fjölnisdóttir* v. *Iceland*, [5].

One can only speculate that the less condemnatory approach in Strasbourg was due to the respondent's own acceptance of the de facto family ties. Indeed, even though surrogacy was unlawful and gave rise to criminal liability if it occurred in Iceland, the relationship between the intended parents and the child had not been severed; on the contrary, it was protected under foster care arrangements.[183] The Court was therefore prepared to find that family life existed in this case, due to the long-term uninterrupted care of the child (four years), but also because the respondent did not contest the existence of family ties.[184]

The more limited issue before the ECtHR was whether Article 8 entitled the applicants to the recognition of parental status. According to the Court, the refusal to recognise the parent–child relationship in Finland, notwithstanding the Californian birth certificate, amounted to an interference with the intended parents' rights; however, that interference had sufficient basis in law (a Supreme Court judgment ascertaining that the woman who gave birth is the child's legal mother – a decision neither arbitrary nor manifestly unreasonable), and the enjoyment of family life had not been hindered by the State's intervention. Quite the opposite, the State had taken steps to secure the bonds between the social parents and the child: a permanent foster placement was granted, followed by alternate residence and equal access arrangements after the couple's divorce; the child had received Icelandic citizenship; and the option of adoption was available. Consequently, the non-recognition of a formal parental link based on Californian law struck a fair balance between the parties' private interests and the general interests the surrogacy ban sought to protect,[185] such as the interests of women who might be pressured into acting as surrogates and the right of children to know their natural parents.[186]

Despite the finding of family life, the *Valdís Fjölnisdóttir* decision adopted a very different test for the legitimacy of the interference when compared to cases where one of the parents had a biological link (the *Mennesson* matrix).[187] It cemented the finding in *Mennesson* that the recognition of a parental link in foreign surrogacy cases is rendered necessary by the child's right to protection of identity rights by the alignment of legal parenthood with biological parenthood.

183 See ibid., [60].
184 See ibid., [62].
185 See ibid., [75].
186 See ibid., [65].
187 See Chapter 2, Section 2.4.

3.4 CONCLUDING REMARKS

Although Strasbourg references to intentional parenthood are sparse, the concept has started to permeate Article 8 jurisprudence. Rather than attempting to redefine the notion of 'parent', the ECtHR has relied on the more elastic notion of 'family life' to extend its protection to the social ties between children and those who fulfil a parental role without being biologically related to them. Nevertheless, it is apparent from the case law on donor insemination and surrogacy arrangements that the intention to become a parent alone does not entitle a person to either access to treatment with donor gametes or the recognition of a parental link in relation to non-biological children. The applicability of Article 8 rights to a case and their priority over other interests depend on social reality, in particular the intentional parent's marriage to the child's genetic parent and/or a lengthy period of shared family life with the child. On the one hand, the emphasis on social reality is consistent with the judicial treatment of applications concerning children born through natural intercourse (*L.* v. *The Netherlands*). In the case of biological fathers, although 'private life' applies by virtue of genetic ties, 'family life' is established after the father has assumed a parental role, or if he was married to, or cohabited with, the child's mother.[188] On the other hand, this approach requires the passage of time for an ART-based family unit to start enjoying Article 8 rights.

This is largely due to the discretion left to States vis-à-vis the legalisation of certain ARTs and the recognition of legal effects flowing from their use abroad. The comparison with adoption – another legal route to non-genetic affiliation – is informative. When applicants relied on foreign adoption orders inconsistent with domestic eligibility to adopt – and hence unrecognisable due to public policy objections – what brought the case within the scope of Article 8 was the length of effective care and the need to protect adopted children's rights (*Wagner* v. *Luxembourg*). Similarly, lengthy cohabitation and the 'child's best interests' principle can activate Article 8 rights in the case of ART-born children and their social parents (*Valdís Fjölnisdóttir* v. *Iceland*). Moreover, since the case law has recognised that, in certain circumstances, adoption by a step-parent can take place without the consent of the other biological parent,[189] the acquisition of parenthood for a child born to one's

[188] See Carmen Draghici, 'Putative Fathers in English Law: A Human Rights Perspective', in Stephen Gilmore and Jens Sherpe (eds.), *Family Matters. Essays in Honour of John Eekelaar* (Cambridge: Intersentia, 2022) 595–609.

[189] See *Söderbäck* v. *Sweden*, App. No. 24484/94, 28 October 1998.

spouse or partner through donor insemination abroad should be less contentious, since no other parent figure is excluded from the child's life as a result of the transfer of parenthood. This is also the case where domestic law permits single-person access to donor insemination, and the parenthood of the genetic parent's spouse or partner would fill a legal void.

The opposition to intention-based parenthood rights may be motivated by the subordination of technology-assisted reproduction to the adults' desire for a family, rather than the need of abandoned children for a home. Nevertheless, Chapter 2 has argued that the refusal to allow a fertile individual to use ART to found a family with an infertile spouse is an excessive interference with their private and family life. The ECtHR has recognised that the interest in becoming a genetic parent is protected by Article 8, and so is the aspiring parent's family life with a spouse who is unable to procreate. Therefore, legislation respectful of human rights should not require a person to choose between preserving their marriage and the fulfilment of parenthood aspirations. Symmetrically, an infertile person should not be exposed to divorce on account of their incapacity to procreate; in fact, a correlation was shown to exist between infertility and divorce rates, and infertility constitutes a ground for divorce in some jurisdictions.[190] Prohibitions on gamete donation and surrogacy pose a threat to the reproductively uneven family unit, in which one partner can reproduce and the other cannot. The foundation of legal parenthood for the non-biological parent in ART cases can be located in the couple's common intention to become parents to a child biologically related to one of them (planned family life),[191] supported by the need to protect the survival of the couple's marriage (existing family life).

Joint treatment and registration as parents *ab initio* is arguably more beneficial to the child than step-parent adoption, as it avoids leaving the child in a legal vacuum if the biological parent dies before the adoption procedure is completed. Nevertheless, the ECtHR's requirement for States to facilitate the recognition of legal affiliation with non-genetic commissioning parents

[190] See Glenn Weisfeld and Carol Weisfeld, 'Marriage: An Evolutionary Perspective' (2003) 23 *Neuro Endocrinology Letters* (Suppl 4) 47–54, at 50: 'Cross-cultural surveys have identified these factors as important in divorce: infertility, refusing sex, sexual infidelity . . ., cruelty . . ., and economic failure . . .. Infertility is an acceptable grounds [sic] for divorce in many cultures, and around the world the likelihood of divorce declines with increasing fecundity.'

[191] The idea of a common intention underlying legal fictions of parenthood is borrowed, *mutatis mutandis*, from Bainham, 'Whose Sperm Is It Anyway?', 568 (discussing cases where medical mistake/relationship breakdown subverted the couples' initial intention).

through any prompt legal avenues (whether registration or adoption)[192] legitimately takes into account the Convention's role in establishing only a minimum common denominator, accommodating ethical and legislative diversity in Europe. Naturally, adoption of a partner's child from a previous relationship is different from contributing to a parental team that purposefully brings into the world a child to raise together; indeed, the foreign surrogacy arrangements already confer legal parenthood abroad. However, the 2019 Advisory Opinion and subsequent case law (*C. and E.* v. *France*, *K.K.* v. *Denmark*, *D.B. v. Switzerland*) took a balanced approach to individual and State interests in a controversial area. While accepting adoption as a satisfactory route to the acquisition of parenthood, the Court unequivocally indicated that the Convention requires an effective route to recognition. *K.K.* v. *Denmark* made a further important contribution to the crystallisation of obligations in respect of foreign surrogacy and non-genetic commissioning parents, by rejecting cumulative measures for securing the stability of the family unit as an inadequate alternative to legal affiliation. Although it continues to view the interference with the intended parent's rights as justified, this ruling firmly links the child's right to identity to the establishment of parent–child legal ties. *D.B. v. Switzerland* importantly expands the right to recognition of the non-genetic intended parent to a parent of the same sex as the genetic parent and promotes the full integration of the child into the family unit.

Another striking feature of Strasbourg jurisprudence is that intentional parenthood is successfully asserted only if corroborated by marriage to the child's biological parent.[193] This is evident in two foreign surrogacy

[192] In *S.C.* v. *Switzerland*, App. No. 26848/18 (communicated case), the Court is called upon to establish if the 'prompt' recognition requirement in the Advisory Opinion was met by proceedings for the adoption of a child born through overseas surrogacy by the non-genetic intended father lasting until the child was approximately three-and-a-half years. An interesting feature of the case is the fact that the genetic intended father was French and therefore the child was not entitled to Swiss citizenship and the benefits depending on it (e.g. healthcare) before adoption by the father's registered partner, a Swiss national. Applying *Mennesson* v. *France*, *mutatis mutandis*, the Court ought to find that the child's right to nationality and full integration into the community was also affected by the delays in establishing legal ties with the intended father.

[193] Marriage occupies a privileged place in the understanding of family life under the Convention; as noted in *Abdulaziz, Cabales and Balkandali* v. *The United Kingdom*, App. Nos. 9214/80; 9473/81; 9474/81, 28 May 1985, [62]: 'Whatever else the word "family" may mean, it must at any rate include the relationship that arises from a lawful and genuine marriage.'

scenarios.[194] First, if the parties co-parent the child without being married or operating as a family unit, there is no free-standing protection for the link between the surrogate-born child and the non-biological intended parent, with dramatic consequences if the genetic parent decides to terminate the other's involvement in the child's life (*A.M.* v. *Norway*). Second, where neither commissioning parent has genetic ties to the child, 'family life' is not found applicable, unless the residential State permitted long-term de facto care, as seen, contrastingly, in *Paradiso and Campanelli* v. *Italy* and *Valdís Fjölnisdóttir* v. *Iceland*. Therefore, the social parent's marriage to the child's genetic parent triggers 'family life'[195] and makes affiliation with the social parent relevant for the child's identity (*K.K.* v. *Denmark*). The genetic intended father of the surrogate-born child must be recognised as a parent from the outset – and his spouse *as soon as* she starts acting in a parental capacity (Advisory Opinion); conversely, if there is no biological link between the couple and the child, family life arises after a longer period of cohabitation.

Understandably, the ECtHR refused to 'define a minimal duration of shared life' for the purposes of establishing de facto family life, to allow for a composite assessment, including 'the "quality" of the bond and the circumstances of each case'.[196] In *Paradiso*, the Court found eight months insufficient against the background of no genetic ties; in fact, it distinguished the case from *D. and Others* v. *Belgium*, where 'family life' had been found to exist after two months, based on the fact that, in that case, 'there was a biological tie with at least one of the parents and cohabitation had subsequently resumed'.[197] In *Valdís Fjölnisdóttir*, four years attracted the application of 'family life'. In cross-country adoption cases, the applications were heard after many years of de facto parenthood (ten in *Wagner*). Nonetheless, it was shrewdly pointed out that, while in *Paradiso* the duration of cohabitation was 'made a key element for *de facto* family ties' (and a short period was held against the unrelated commissioning parents), the duration of cohabitation had not been a subject of scrutiny in previous cases, and indeed in *Moretti and Benedetti* v. *Italy* nineteen months created family life between *foster carers* and

[194] The application of Art. 8 to a transgender male and the child born to his partner via sperm donation (*X, Y and Z* v. *The United Kingdom* [GC]) also suggests that intention to act as a parent and de facto care generate 'family life' when coupled with the social appearance of conjugality. See Chapter 5, Section 5.5.

[195] This reinforces the conclusion in Chapter 2 that the genetic parent's family life with the child should be also safeguarded on its own.

[196] *Paradiso and Campanelli* v. *Italy* [GC], [153].

[197] Ibid., [154].

the child.[198] The emphasis on duration in *Paradiso* may well be reverse-engineered to support the Court's conclusion.

Third-party reproduction is an area awaiting a more modern approach to intentional parenthood and identity: (a) recognising independent rights for the moral author of conception who is also a de facto carer since birth and a legal parent in the jurisdiction where the child was born; and (b) expanding the notion of 'identity' to include surrogate-born children's right to know, develop and have memorialised in the law the relationship with both intended parents. ECHR case law is currently wedded to the association between genetic descent and 'best interests' analysis, based on a narrow understanding of identity. Andrea Mulligan has convincingly argued that 'in the surrogacy context the concept of identity must be given a richer interpretation which encompasses not just genetic identity but also the child's relationship to gestational and intended parents'.[199] This interpretation is supported by judgments on identity rights suggesting that knowledge of genetic origins is not promoted for practical reasons (medical concerns, inheritance rights) but for abstract reasons pertaining to 'self-formation' and 'self-development'; this would justify expanding the notion so as to include a right to knowledge of the commissioning parents.[200] Knowledge of the moral authors of a person's conception should be seen as part of his or her 'personal history', which goes beyond genetic heritage. The acknowledgement of the pivotal role of genetic ties in defining identity is welcome and strengthens the right to respect for the decision to have a biological child, in future potentially also requiring States to secure biological parent–child affiliation following (illegal) domestic surrogacy; however, moral and legal parenthood abroad should not be discounted.

One particularly problematic aspect of ECHR surrogacy case law is that it depicts commissioning parents as tainted with criminality when they used a fertility service lawfully available in the country where the child was born through surrogacy, and validly registered the birth in accordance with the law of the forum. Portraying commissioning couples as lawbreakers conflates illegality (the inaccurate claim that the parents breached domestic law) and conflict of laws (the incompatibility between different sovereign States' laws, which may be resolved through recognition, or non-recognition, of foreign birth certificates). The problem of family life created in illegal circumstances, with no legitimate expectations to receive protection, has arisen in the context

[198] See Iliadou, 'Surrogacy and the ECtHR', 147.
[199] Mulligan, 'Identity Rights and Sensitive Ethical Questions', 450.
[200] Ibid., 471–472.

of immigration: despite the intervening marriage to a resident or birth of a child, an alien who overstayed a visa, entered the country illegally or stayed after a deportation order cannot require the territorial State to accept their family life as a *fait accompli* and to permit them to stay in the country, thereby profiting from their illegal conduct, unless the spouse/children cannot follow the alien elsewhere due to administrative obstacles or foreseeable great hardship abroad.[201] By contrast, there is nothing illegal in the commissioning couple's conduct abroad or their request for the transcription of foreign acts in their country of habitual residence. In fact, since 2015, the Permanent Bureau of the Hague Conference on Private International Law (HCCH) has been studying the private international law issues encountered in relation to surrogacy arrangements and the legal parentage of surrogate-born children. The Council on General Affairs and Policy (CGAP) of the HCCH convened an Experts' Group to explore the feasibility of a general private international law instrument on legal parentage, with a protocol on legal parentage established following international surrogacy arrangements.[202] This demonstrates international awareness of the fact that recourse to surrogacy abroad is an issue not of transnational crime but of families caught by incompatible national regulatory frameworks and unfavourable rules of recognition of foreign acts.

The case law on inter-country adoption developed under Article 8 also suggests that the ECHR can accommodate legitimate expectations stemming from *sole legal parenthood*, in the absence of genetic and social ties, based on the potential family life that legal parents can expect to enjoy with their children (*Pini and Bertani* v. *Romania*). Legal parenthood in the country where the child was lawfully conceived, born and registered should be treated as relevant when the family returns to their home country or relocates elsewhere. The parent–child relationship should not be denied altogether merely because the parental order/birth certificate, legal in the jurisdiction where they were issued, is non-recognisable domestically; nor should the application of domestic rules take priority over the child's best interests. Robin Mackenzie has argued that surrogacy should be framed neither as a 'type of adoption' nor as 'infertility treatment', but as 'a method of family

[201] See Draghici, *The Legitimacy of Family Rights*, 353–357.

[202] The Experts' Group submitted its final report to CGAP in November 2022, in which it agreed on the general feasibility of rules on recognition of legal parentage as a result of an international surrogacy agreement and on the urgent need for further work. In March 2023, CGAP mandated the establishment of a Working Group. See www.hcch.net/en/projects/legislative-projects/parentage-surrogacy (accessed 1 October 2023).

formation'.[203] However, the analogy with adoption and medical treatment allows for the application of existing human rights principles to this novel and unregulated field. At the same time, the fact that *Paradiso and Campanelli* attached no value to the lawfulness of the surrogacy agreement and the legal acquisition of parenthood in another jurisdiction might benefit parent–child relationships arising from illegal domestic surrogacy. The Court essentially acknowledged that genuine intention to become a parent, coupled with effective bonds, can – subject to a substantial period of cohabitation between the child and the intended parents – generate 'family life' entitled to respect, despite the illegality of its formation.

Non-genetic surrogacy cases also disclose a superficial assessment of the 'best interests' principle, designed to accommodate State sovereignty. Regardless of the circumstances surrounding their conception, children are not responsible for the choices of the adults who caused them to be born; the pre-eminence of children's best interests should thus prevent States from dismantling de facto family units in the name of legislative autonomy. However, the ECtHR – especially when Grand Chamber judgments overrule progressive Chamber judgments – appears wary of antagonising States on matters affecting fundamental beliefs and values. As John Stack perceptively remarked: 'If judges on the European Court do make law, it is made with an eye as to what is politically palatable and what is not.'[204] Extrajudicial considerations arguably influence judicial decisions in the area of ART, in the same way that immigration policies are protected at the expense of the child's best interests in cases concerning expulsion/deportation/admission decisions.[205] The Court has appeared reluctant to interfere with measures regarding border protection/membership of the territorial community, as these are intimately connected with sovereign prerogatives. So is the definition of civil status, and

[203] Robin Mackenzie, 'Beyond Genetic and Gestational Dualities: Surrogacy Agreements, Legal Parenthood and Choice in Family Formation', in Kirsty Horsey and Hazel Biggs (eds.), *Human Fertilisation and Embryology: Reproducing Regulation* (London: Routledge-Cavendish, 2007) 181–203, at 200.

[204] John Stack Jr, 'Judicial Policy-Making and the Evolving Protection of Human Rights: The European Court of Human Rights in Comparative Perspective' (1992) 15(3) *West European Politics* 137–155, at 151.

[205] On the treatment of children's best interests in immigration cases, see Draghici, *The Legitimacy of Family Rights*, 368–379, 392. See, in particular, 392: 'Even where the parents do not pose a threat to the community and removing them would uproot the children from an environment in which they are psychologically and educationally settled, the Court finds that the entire family needs to relocate back to the country of origin in deference to the discretion of States in regulating entry and stay, although an independent analysis of the children's welfare would certainly suggest otherwise.'

wider State practice may be required to inspire greater assertiveness in Strasbourg.

Nonetheless, minimal obligations should already be recognised. The protection of families built on foreign *genetic* surrogacy rests on two pillars: the child's identity rights (including a right to establish legal links with genetic parents) and concerns over the child's statelessness and other practical disadvantages (*Mennesson*). The second pillar applies equally to *non-genetic* surrogacy. Indeed, the child's right to acquire a nationality, enshrined in Article 7 UNCRC, may entitle the surrogate-born child to the recognition of legal affiliation. As Wade has pointed out, 'nationality is linked to a range of entitlements, such as the acquisition of a passport, the right to vote, as well as access to education and medical care', thereby also affecting children's rights to education (Article 28 UNCRC) and healthcare services (Article 24 UNCRC).[206] Significantly, the UN Special Rapporteur on the sale and sexual exploitation of children has recommended that States 'protect the rights of all surrogate-born children, regardless of the legal status of the surrogacy arrangement under national or international law, including by protecting the best interests of the child, protecting rights to identity and to access to origins, and cooperating internationally to avoid statelessness'.[207]

Against the background of the highly divisive nature of third-party reproduction, the interpretation of the ECHR as requiring a possibility of recognition of a legal parent–child relationship with the non-genetic intended parent in foreign surrogacy cases (Advisory Opinion P16-2018-001, *K.K.* v. *Denmark*, *D.B.* v. *Switzerland*) and the protection of family life in donor insemination cases (*C.E. and Others v. France*) is nothing short of remarkable. Nonetheless, the recognition of affiliation between the ART-born child and the social parent (*ex tunc* or through adoption) remains exclusively a right of the child, whose best interests prevail over the abstract assertion of public policy, and it is a response to a *fait accompli*. This is far from establishing an obligation for States to allow aspiring parents afflicted by infertility access to gamete donation or surrogacy arrangements and to grant legal parenthood according to intentions. Having to use ART services abroad restricts access to heterologous fertilisation and surrogacy to wealthy couples, drawing de facto distinctions based on economic status in the enjoyment of procreative rights.

[206] Wade, 'The Regulation of Surrogacy', 128–129.

[207] Report of the Special Rapporteur on the sale and sexual exploitation of children, including child prostitution, child pornography and other child sexual abuse material, A/HRC/37/60, 15 January 2018, [77] (j).

4

A Right to a Healthy Child?

From Medical Therapy to Eugenic Selection

4.1 FROM HEALTHCARE TO AUTONOMY RIGHTS

Conceiving a healthy child is an undoubtedly legitimate aspiration of any prospective parents, underpinned by multiple concerns: the child's welfare, especially if their medical condition hinders their independence in adulthood; the interests of other children of the family, likely to be affected by the financial and time resources required by a critically ill sibling; and the emotional and practical impact of looking after a sick or disabled child on the parents themselves. This chapter will argue that a person's endeavour to avoid a serious illness in their child, with its severe consequences on the child's and the family's quality of life, is equally worthy of respect at the time of conception as it is after birth. Moreover, the chapter sets out to demonstrate that the desire to have a healthy child has become an enforceable right under the European Convention on Human Rights (ECHR). In fact, Strasbourg case law supports a right to informed procreative choice, benefitting from advances in medical genetics, which includes the ability to influence procreative outcomes. This entitles the aspiring parent to rely on embryo pre-implantation genetic diagnosis (PGD) and prenatal testing in order to secure, to the extent possible, a child free from severe illness or disability.

PGD is typically used for fertile couples at a high risk of having a child with a severe genetic disease (and often having terminated earlier pregnancies after prenatal diagnosis) and for infertile individuals treated with in vitro fertilisation (IVF), so as to increase their chances of an ongoing pregnancy; the technique involves the testing of embryos cultured in vitro using the couple's gametes (and possibly donor gametes) for specific genetic defects. One or more cells are removed for analysis from the embryos after they are allowed to develop for two to three days; then only embryos free of defects are transferred to the uterus.[1] One or two of the viable embryos unaffected by the genetic condition(s) running in the family are implanted and, as with any IVF procedure, the chances of a successful pregnancy are 25 per cent or less.[2] Prenatal testing allows for the detection of a foetal abnormality (through ultrasound investigations and amniocentesis), in particular chromosome aneuploidies causing disorders such as Down's syndrome and major congenital malformations.[3]

The availability of PGD and prenatal testing raises issues of both healthcare and self-determination rights. Medically assisted procreation is, in fact, located at the crossroads between the right to health (in that it involves medical treatment aimed at curing infertility and preventing illness in the future child) and the right to respect for private and family life (because treatment permits the effective exercise of the right to become a parent in adverse circumstances, such as genetic illness, low fertility or deprivation of liberty). Thus, 'PGD can enhance reproductive autonomy insofar as it allows people to exercise a greater degree of reproductive control', understood as 'the ability to positively act in ways that conform to one's own reproductive desires or goals and not to be prevented from acting in this way'.[4] Similarly, prenatal testing can be seen as part of medical care rights, but also as a premise for the exercise of informed procreative choice (and hence as a matter of private and family life).

Article 12(1) of the International Covenant on Economic, Social and Cultural Rights (ICESCR) recognises 'the right of everyone to the enjoyment of the highest attainable standard of physical and mental health'.[5] Rebecca Cook et al. have pointed out that access to IVF and PGD engages the right of the future child to the highest attainable standard of health, as well as the right to health of the parents, in particular their 'mental and social wellbeing'.[6]

1 See Karen Sermon, André Van Steirteghem and Inge Liebaers, 'Preimplantation Genetic Diagnosis' (2004 May 15) 363(9421) *Lancet* 1633–1641, at 1633; Peter Braude et al., 'Preimplantation Genetic Diagnosis' (2002) 3(12) *Nature Reviews: Genetics* 941–953, at 941; Søren Holm, 'Ethical Issues in Pre-implantation Diagnosis', in John Harris and Søren Holm (eds.), *The Future of Human Reproduction: Ethics, Choice, and Regulation* (Oxford: Clarendon Press, 1998) 176–190, at 176–177.

2 See Martin Richards, 'Which Children Can We Choose? Boundaries of Reproductive Autonomy', in Shelley Day-Sclater et al. (eds.), *Regulating Autonomy: Sex, Reproduction and Family* (Oxford: Hart, 2009) 197–221, at 200.

3 See Antina de Jong et al., 'Non-invasive Prenatal Testing: Ethical Issues Explored' (2010) 18 *European Journal of Human Genetics* 272–277, at 273.

4 Timothy Krahn and Sophia Wong, 'Preimplantation Genetic Diagnosis and Reproductive Autonomy' (2009) 19 *Reproductive Biomedicine Online* 34–42, at 35.

5 International Covenant on Economic, Social and Cultural Rights, New York, 16 December 1966, in force 3 January 1976, UNTS vol. 993 (p. 3).

6 Rebecca Cook, Bernard Dickens and Mahmoud Fathalla, *Reproductive Health and Human Rights: Integrating Medicine, Ethics, and Law* (Oxford: Oxford University Press, 2003) 359.

Moreover, the steps required of States to achieve the full realisation of the right to health include, pursuant to Article 12(2)(a) ICESCR, 'provision for the reduction of the stillbirth-rate and of infant mortality and for the healthy development of the child'. Although the latter appears to refer primarily to in utero and postnatal measures, in its interpretation of Article 12, the UN Committee on Economic, Social and Cultural Rights has clarified that an adequate standard of care includes the provision of assisted reproduction treatment (ART):

> The failure or refusal to incorporate technological advances and innovations in the provision of sexual and reproductive health services, such as medication for abortion, assisted reproductive technologies and advances in the treatment of HIV and AIDS, jeopardizes the quality of care.[7]

The World Health Organisation (WHO) has also expressly indicated that 'men and women should have access to appropriate health care services that will ... provide couples with *the best chance of having healthy infants*'.[8] This authoritative view lends support to an arguable claim to antenatal assistance, aimed at preventing genetic illnesses in the child. This claim is particularly robust when read in conjunction with Article 15(1)(b) ICESCR, which safeguards everyone's right to 'enjoy the benefits of scientific progress and its applications'.

The link between healthcare and fundamental rights, including self-determination and respect for family life, was affirmed in various international fora. The UN Conference on Population and Development held in Cairo in 1994 and the Fourth UN World Conference on Women held in Beijing in 1995 recognised that the protection of reproductive health is a matter of social justice and can be addressed through the improved application of existing national, regional and international human rights instruments.[9] In its General Comment No. 22 (2016), the Committee on Economic, Social and Cultural Rights noted:

> The right to sexual and reproductive health is also indivisible from and interdependent with other human rights. It is intimately linked to civil and political rights underpinning the physical and mental integrity of individuals and their autonomy, such as the rights to life; liberty and security of person;

[7] Committee on Economic, Social and Cultural Rights, 'General Comment No. 22 (2016) on the Right to Sexual and Reproductive Health (Article 12 of the International Covenant on Economic, Social and Cultural Rights)', E/C.12/GC/22, 2 May 2016, [21].

[8] See WHO, 'Sexual and Reproductive Health', available at www.who.int/europe/health-topics/sexual-health#tab=tab_1 (emphasis added) (accessed 2 October 2023).

[9] See Cook et al., *Reproductive Health and Human Rights*, 148–149.

freedom from torture and other cruel, inhuman or degrading treatment; privacy and respect for family life; and non-discrimination and equality.[10]

It might be adduced, nevertheless, that, under international human rights law, the scope of positive obligations to provide medical services is limited. In fact, the right to health belongs to the category of rights of progressive realisation, contingent upon State resources.[11] It would be likely far-fetched to construe the ICESCR right to health provisions as requiring States to ensure free access to embryo screening and IVF treatment. Cook et al. noted that the right to reproductive health, while falling within the right to health, 'currently exists more as a negative than a positive right, so that reproductive technologies do not compel public funding'.[12] Daniel Brudney has gone so far as to question whether healthcare is truly a human right, since a right would impose correlative obligations on State authorities, whereas those remain doubtful: 'Rights usually correspond to duties, and duties obtain only if some duty-bearer has the power to do some particular thing. But can there be a duty-bearer who has the power to make everyone healthy?'[13]

However, Strasbourg rulings on reproductive health and the pursuit of a healthy child have tended to frame access to ART as a matter of negative obligations.[14] Indeed, the ECHR has demonstrated its capacity to accommodate new, health-related claims traditionally associated with social and economic rights. In fact, Strasbourg case law has read certain aspects of the right to health into Article 2 (the right of cancer patients to medication free of charge as ordered by domestic courts, as seen in *Panaitescu* v. *Romania*)[15] and Article 3 (the right of AIDS sufferers to protection against deportation to a country where no medical services were available, upheld in *D.* v. *The United Kingdom*).[16] As detailed in the following sections, the case law developed under Article 8 ECHR has further confirmed the potential of norms concerning autonomy and family life to bring health-related guarantees within the scope of civil and political rights.

10 'General Comment No. 22' (2016), [10].

11 See Art. 2(1) ICESCR: 'Each State Party to the present Covenant undertakes to take steps, ... to the maximum of its available resources, with a view to achieving progressively the full realization of the rights recognized in the present Covenant.'

12 Cook et al., *Reproductive Health and Human Rights*, 360.

13 Daniel Brudney, 'Is Health Care a Human Right?' (2016) 37 *Theoretical Medicine and Bioethics* 249–257, at 249.

14 See Chapter 1, Section 1.2.2 and references therein.

15 *Panaitescu* v. *Romania*, App. No. 30909/06, 10 April 2012.

16 *D.* v. *The United Kingdom*, App. No. 30240/96, 2 May 1997.

This chapter acknowledges the limits to a parent's right to seek assistance in their endeavour to have a healthy child, to the extent that such assistance is contingent upon finite resources and allocation-related challenges. Rather, it argues that, where technology is available to prevent certain genetic pathologies in the offspring and the only obstacle barring access to it is public policy allegedly based on ethical concerns, the prospective parents' rights are infringed. Interestingly, in Strasbourg case law to date, the cost of treatment has not featured in either the applicants' submissions, which tend to lament legal bars or administrative hindrances, or the governments' justifications for the refusal to permit a certain technique, which usually revolve around public morals and the rights of others.

In the bioethical literature, arguments against choosing children through PGD and prenatal testing invoke the expectation of 'unconditional love and acceptance' from parents and decry the fact that 'the method to achieve the desired child with specific characteristics involves choosing between existing human entities (whether it is the fertilised egg, an embryo or a foetus)', that is, 'selecting a particular human entity and discarding the others'.[17] The claim that parents are expected to show unconditional love and acceptance to any children born to them (including children born with undetected disabilities) is uncontroversial; by contrast, it does not support the conclusion that attempting to influence reproductive outcomes is tantamount to rejecting a child. The expectation of unconditional love for any *existing* children (the term 'child' only applying after birth) is not incompatible with the protection of planned children at the conception stage. Indeed, one may argue that acting to limit avoidable disease in the future child is a responsible parental decision – not only for the child to be born but also for any other existing and future children of the family, in that the expense and attention required by a disabled sibling deprive the former of opportunities (e.g. educational) and have an emotional impact on them. Stephen Wilkinson has pointed out that the principle of unconditional parental love, as an objection to selective reproduction, fails to acknowledge that 'the moral position of prospective parents is different from that of actual parents'.[18] Moreover, Jonathan Glover has rightly criticised the 'morally alarming' claim that individuals with a genetic make-up chosen by the parents are 'artefacts' rather than human

[17] Roy Gilbar, 'Between Unconditional Acceptance and Responsibility: Should Family Ethics Limit the Scope of Reproductive Autonomy?' (2009) 21(3) *Child and Family Law Quarterly* 309–335, at 311.

[18] Stephen Wilkinson, *Choosing Tomorrow's Children: The Ethics of Selective Reproduction* (Oxford: Oxford University Press, 2010) 55.

beings, pointing out that many characteristics are the result of parental choices about upbringing and education.[19] In ultimate analysis, family planning inevitably involves selection from among possible lives, inter alia, discarding gametes during intercourse not aimed at procreation and choosing the timing of conception; indeed, the pursuit of desired characteristics in the future child starts with the choice of partner, an indirect form of genetic selection.

There is also an unproven assumption of conditionality in the anti-PGD discourse; the attempt to influence the future child's characteristics does not mean that the parents will not love a child born with different characteristics. It cannot be presumed that parents wishing for a son, for cultural or pragmatic reasons or for variety, will not love their child if it is a girl; similarly, parents hoping for a healthy child cannot be suspected of not loving a sick child. Choosing between potential lives is different from choosing between existing children (e.g. deciding to entrust a child with disability to adoptive parents). It is worth recalling that aspiring adoptive parents can choose much more detailed attributes in their future children (such as the colour of the eyes or the height) and are entitled to a detailed medical report on the children identified as potential matches; they literally choose from, and discard many, children in need of a family. Parenthood entails significant responsibilities, and prospective adopters are permitted to gain sufficient information to consent to embarking upon it. If adoptive parents can choose, as opposed to accepting the lottery of State allocation, and this is not seen as morally problematic, biological parents should not be denied the much more limited choice of avoiding critical illnesses in their children. Pre-conception choice is also preferable to child abandonment, a potential consequence of the parents' inability to cope with the child's needs.

Offspring selection is also powerfully connected with the right *not* to reproduce, that is, not to reproduce other than in circumstances that the individuals deem satisfactory for themselves. As Rosamund Scott deftly argued, pre-implantation/prenatal selection is underpinned by the value of reproductive choice: 'People are entitled to choose whether to reproduce. They should also be able to avoid reproduction under certain conditions, for instance because of what caring for a severely disabled child may entail.'[20] In *Evans v. The United Kingdom*, the Grand Chamber upheld a person's right 'not to

[19] Jonathan Glover, *Choosing Children: Genes, Disability, and Design* (Oxford: Oxford University Press, 2006) 82, referencing Clive Staples Lewis, *The Abolition of Man* (London: Collins, 1978) 39–40, on the treatment of children as 'artefacts' if genetic choice is permitted.

[20] Rosamund Scott, 'Choosing between Possible Lives: Legal and Ethical Issues in Preimplantation Genetic Diagnosis' (2006) 26(1) *Oxford Journal of Legal Studies* 153–178, at 163–164.

become a parent' even in circumstances where it irreparably compromised another person's ability to reproduce.[21] The right not to become a parent in unwanted circumstances should be all the more safeguarded when there are no other comparable rights in competition. Embryos, while entitled to protection, subsumed under the 'morals' justification permitted by Article 8(2) ECHR, do not benefit from the 'rights' associated with personhood. Even in the inter-American system, where life is protected 'from the moment of conception' under Article 4 of the American Convention on Human Rights,[22] the Inter-American Court of Human Rights (IACtHR) has established that the embryo acquires protection under this provision only after it is implanted in the womb, and that the degree of protection varies with the stage of development of human life:

> The embryo cannot be understood to be a person for the purposes of Article 4 (1) of the American Convention. . . . 'Conception' in the sense of Article 4(1) occurs at the moment when the embryo becomes implanted in the uterus, which explains why, before this event, Article 4 of the Convention would not be applicable. Moreover, . . . the protection of the right to life under this provision is not absolute, but rather *gradual and incremental according to its development*, since it is not an absolute and unconditional obligation, but entails understanding that exceptions to the general rule are admissible.[23]

Strasbourg case law addressing the denial of access to prenatal testing and pre-implantation diagnostic techniques has expanded in recent years. As detailed later, two streams of jurisprudence can be distinguished in the practice of the ECHR. The first regards existing pregnancies and the availability of prenatal testing for the detection of fatal abnormality. The Court has condemned the lack of effective access to prenatal testing provided for under domestic law, in particular delays and errors in testing, which deprived the expectant women of the opportunity to choose whether or not to continue the pregnancy; the absence of domestic remedies in cases of delay and misdiagnosis was similarly found inconsistent with Article 8. The second stream of case law concerns planned pregnancies and the ability of aspiring parents with hereditary diseases to test embryos and select healthy ones for transfer into the womb. Article 8 was also found breached by the refusal to allow PGD and IVF for high-risk couples

[21] See *Evans* v. *The United Kingdom* [GC], App. No. 6339/05, 10 April 2007 (the destruction of embryos produced with both parties' gametes removed all prospects of parenthood for the woman, no longer able to produce ova at that stage). For further discussion, see Chapter 2.

[22] See Art. 4(1) of the American Convention on Human Rights.

[23] *Artavia Murillo et al. ('In Vitro Fertilisation')* v. *Costa Rica*, Case No. 12.361, 28 November 2012, [264] (emphasis added).

in terms of genetic illnesses, who are then left with the traumatic option of therapeutic abortion. The effective enjoyment of procreative autonomy may also require positive action from States, such as the provision of certain health-care services free of charge, but the contentious proceedings under the ECHR have not presented the Court with a test case to date.

4.2 PRENATAL DIAGNOSIS AND THERAPEUTIC ABORTION

4.2.1 *Substantive Rights: Effective Access to Prenatal Testing*

This section does not propose to explore the vast and well-trodden debate on women's right to abortion in international law.[24] Rather, it considers whether, in jurisdictions permitting abortion (which includes nearly all ECHR States),[25] expectant parents have a right to request prenatal testing, so as to be able to terminate a pregnancy in the event of foetal abnormality. In addition to the tension between maternal and foetal interests inherent in the general abortion debate, this narrower issue raises a specific bioethical dilemma: whether procreative freedom includes the right to screen for disability, and whether that right can be curtailed to accommodate superior values connected with public morals or the interests of others.

Access to prenatal tests enabling the choice of therapeutic abortion is arguably grounded in the value of autonomy in the most intimate sphere of a person's life. In fact, autonomy often encompasses 'affirmative demands' for measures 'fostering autonomous decision making'.[26] Perhaps counter-

[24] On this topic, see, e.g., Christina Zampas and Jaime Gher, 'Abortion as a Human Right – International and Regional Standards' (2008) 8(2) *Human Rights Law Review* 249–294; Charles Ngwena, 'Inscribing Abortion as a Human Right: Significance of the Protocol on the Rights of Women in Africa' (2010) 32(4) *Human Rights Quarterly* 783–864; Joanna Erdman, 'Abortion in International Human Rights Law', in Sam Rowlands (ed.), *Abortion Care* (Cambridge: Cambridge University Press, 2014) 244–250.

[25] With the exception of one country (Andorra), all European States currently permit abortion, whether on demand or on specified grounds. See *European Abortion Laws: A Comparative Overview* (New York: Center for Reproductive Rights, 2023), available at https://reproductiverights.org/wp-content/uploads/2023/09/European-Abortion-Laws-A-Comparative-Overview-new-9-13-23.pdf (accessed 2 October 2023). According to this report, in forty-one countries, abortion is legal without the need for a medical professional to certify a particular reason for the request, and one country (the UK) permits abortion on broad social grounds. Five countries have highly restrictive laws: in Andorra, abortion is banned; Malta allows it in case of grave jeopardy to the expectant woman's life or health; Liechtenstein and Poland allow abortion only when a woman's life or health is at risk or where the pregnancy resulted from sexual assault; Monaco allows abortion only when a woman's life or health is at risk, in case of pregnancy resulting from a sexual assault or where a severe foetal anomaly has been detected.

[26] Merle Spriggs, *Autonomy and Patients' Decisions* (Boulder: Lexington Books, 2005), 82.

intuitively, testing for foetal abnormality may also be seen as having a strong negative liberty component. Emily Jackson thus noted: 'Forcing a woman to carry, deliver and bear responsibility for a child that she does not want could be characterised as a potentially harmful interference with her interest in making significant decisions about her life according to her own values.'[27] A right to prenatal diagnosis, as a precondition for procreative choice, is arguably covered by the notion of self-determination. Moreover, justifications for interferences with this right based on 'the rights of others' are doubtful. The foetus is unlikely to be a beneficiary of the right to life; indeed, such a stance is not supported by ECHR case law.[28] John Robertson has pointed out that 'a previable fetus has not yet reached a stage of development at which it has interests in itself', insofar as 'it lacks the neurological capability for sentience'.[29] A foetus is, nevertheless, an entity which deserves legal protection.[30] However, its interests are not capable of justifying coerced pregnancy and the denial of the right not to be a parent. The woman's right to autonomy (bodily self-determination but also procreative choice) prevails over foetal interests, at least when her physical or psychological health is affected by the continuation of the pregnancy. Even accepting the existence of limited rights for pre-sentient human tissue, the dependence of the foetus upon the pregnant woman to acquire life means that any conflicts of rights must be resolved in favour of the latter. Elizabeth Wicks has convincingly argued that a viable foetus is entitled to the 'special protection accorded to the human species', regardless of consciousness, but that that protection does not guarantee 'the right to the use of another's body'.[31] While the Strasbourg Court has refused to take a stance on the legalisation of abortion, this was based on the State's wide margin of appreciation rather than on the Court's own assessment of the comparative weight of foetal rights and expectant women's self-determination

[27] Emily Jackson, 'Abortion, Autonomy and Prenatal Diagnosis' (2000) 9(4) *Social and Legal Studies* 467–494, at 476.

[28] See *Paton* v. *The United Kingdom*, App. No. 8416/78, 13 May 1980 (Commission); *Boso* v. *Italy*, App. No. 50490/99, 5 September 2002, [1]; *Vo* v. *France*, App. No. 53924/00, 8 July 2004, [75]–[85]. For a discussion, see Aurora Plomer, 'A Foetal Right to Life? The Case of *Vo* v. *France*' (2005) 5(2) *Human Rights Law Review* 311–338. English law on child protective measures also rejects the conflation between foetuses and children; see *Re F (In Utero)* [1988] Fam 122.

[29] John Robertson, *Children of Choice: Freedom and the New Reproductive Technologies* (Princeton: Princeton University Press, 1994) 158.

[30] Strasbourg case law has recognised the public interest in regulating abortion; see *Brüggemann and Scheuten* v. *Federal Republic of Germany*, App. No. 6959/75, 12 July 1977 (Commission), [59]–[60].

[31] Elizabeth Wicks, *The State and the Body: Legal Regulation of Bodily Autonomy* (Oxford: Hart, 2016) 52–53.

rights.[32] Rulings concerning the rights of fathers of unborn children have further established that the expectant woman cannot be compelled to carry the pregnancy to term, even when the abortion did not respond to a medical necessity, because the woman is 'the person primarily concerned by the pregnancy and its continuation or termination'.[33]

Another 'rights of others' argument put forward by the opponents of therapeutic abortion is the impact of negative selection on existing children of the family affected by the medical condition the parents seek to avoid. Roy Gilbar wrote: 'a question arises as to how a child with deafness, albinism or dwarfism might feel if his/her mother decides to terminate a pregnancy when the risk of having another child with one of these medical conditions is high.'[34] This argument does not have the weight required for a cogent justification under Article 8(2) ECHR. Firstly, there is no reason for parents to inform their children about adult reproductive decisions, or for insensitive disclosure in later life. Secondly, counselling can help a child distinguish the parents' desire to facilitate the life of future children from the love towards existing disabled children. Thirdly, children are often the product of an unwanted pregnancy, and this does not diminish their parents' love for them; it only means that the circumstances surrounding the birth were inconsistent with the parents' family life plans. In any event, the distress potentially suffered by an existing child with the avoided disability cannot outweigh the individual right not to reproduce, if reproduction entails foreseeable harm for the future child and significant burden for the parents.

It can be conceded that society at large may have an interest in upholding certain core values pertaining to the treatment of human genetic material. However, the 'protection of morals' in Article 8(2) cannot extend to the view that all eugenic practices are impermissible, as this would lead to overbroad restrictions. State-led policies seeking to alter the composition of the human gene pool through coercive measures, such as forced sterilisation, are morally objectionable. By contrast, individual decisions about future offspring, motivated by the desire to promote the welfare of the child and of the family, only reduce the incidence of genetic disorders in the population indirectly, rather than by design, and by a small margin.[35] Furthermore, one needs to be

[32] See *A, B and C* v. *Ireland* [GC], App. No. 25579/05, 16 December 2010, [236]–[237].

[33] See *R.H.* v. *Norway*, App. No. 17004/90, 19 May 1992 (Commission), [4]; *Boso* v. *Italy*, [2].

[34] Gilbar, 'Between Unconditional Acceptance and Responsibility', 335.

[35] On different understandings of eugenics and a rejection of the conflation between historical eugenic practices and the ethos of modern human genetics, see John Gillott, 'Screening for Disability: A Eugenic Pursuit?' (2001) 27 (suppl. 2) *Journal of Medical Ethics* ii21–ii23, at ii21–ii22. See also Jess Buxton, 'Unforeseen Uses of Preimplantation Genetic Diagnosis:

particularly suspicious of arguments based on 'public morals' when a measure severely affects the private sphere of an individual's life. 'Morals' are forged by majority opinion rather than objective criteria, and that opinion is often not informed by first-hand experience; indeed, many issues decided by the majority only affect a minority of the population. In addition, the values of tolerance and broadmindedness underlying the ECHR command respect for private opinion.

The community's widespread belief in the moral status of the foetus could be more credibly adduced under 'public morals'. Even so, the mere existence of a legitimate aim for restricting access to prenatal diagnosis does not suffice; the proportionality of an interference with parental choice with life-long implications remains critical to its legitimacy. As Robertson has pointed out, the 'symbolic cost of ending a fetus's life' (which may, admittedly, be seen as 'devaluation of human life') is justified by the woman's freedom 'to avoid the special burdens of having a handicapped child'.[36] Prenatal tests allow a woman to decide if continuing the pregnancy will offer the meaningful experience that makes procreation a human right. Denial of access to information enabling that decision has a disproportionate impact on the potential mother, for whom the stakes are different when compared to the public at large.

The jurisprudence developed under Article 8 ECHR has recognised – in the context of claims for compensation for medical negligence in prenatal care leading to the failure to detect foetal malformations – that this provision protects 'the parents' desire to conceive a child unaffected by a genetic disease, this choice being a form of expression of their private and family life'.[37] Ambiguities remain as to the exact scope of obligations in this respect. While the relevant judgments tend to address discrete and often country-

Ethical and Legal Issues', in Kirsty Horsey and Hazel Biggs (eds.), *Human Fertilisation and Embryology: Reproducing Regulation* (London: Routledge-Cavendish, 2007) 109–134, at 120: 'there is evidently a world of difference between a State-controlled effort to eliminate certain types of living people and personal reproductive decisions aimed at having a healthy child'. See also Wilkinson, *Choosing Tomorrow's Children*, 155: 'when it comes to an assessment of eugenics' moral status we must be careful not to assume that it will be authoritarian'. Moreover, 'it is vitally important to separate out questions about the morality of pursuing eugenic ends from those about whether this or that *means* of achieving them is acceptable' (151, original emphasis); compulsory sterilisation and killing of the unfit might be examples of unacceptable means.

[36] Robertson, *Children of Choice*, 158–159.

[37] *M.P. and Others* v. *Romania*, App. No. 39974/10, 15 April 2014, [50] (building on *Costa and Pavan* v. *Italy*, App. No. 54270/10, 28 August 2012, [57], discussed in Section 4.3.1). The case was dismissed for lack of victim status, insofar as domestic courts had already acknowledged the breach of Article 8 and awarded non-pecuniary damage (see *M.P. and Others* v. *Romania*, [53]–[55]).

specific aspects of the regulation of prenatal diagnosis and therapeutic abortion, several important principles have emerged.

In a landmark decision on reproductive rights in the case of *R.R.* v. *Poland*,[38] the Strasbourg Court established States' positive obligation to effectively implement domestic laws affording access to timely diagnostic services, so as to detect foetus abnormalities and allow individuals to make an informed decision on therapeutic abortion. According to the judgment, Article 3 and Article 8 rights are breached when practical obstacles prevent expectant parents' access to the diagnostic services available, impacting their ability to decide on the continuation of the pregnancy within the timeframe for legal abortion, with grave consequences for their private life. The tragic facts of the case invite a reconsideration of any sceptical rebuff of antenatal diagnostic techniques or of suggestions that they allow parents to exert whimsical choice. An expectant mother of two, carrying a foetus suspected of suffering from a severe genetic abnormality, was intentionally denied access to prenatal genetic tests (to which the law entitled her) by doctors and hospitals opposing abortion. The results of the amniocentesis were released to the applicant six weeks after the ultrasound scan indicating that the foetus might be deformed, at which stage the legal time limit to request an abortion had passed, depriving her of the right to an informed decision on whether or not to carry the foetus to term. Her third child was thus born with abnormal chromosomes (Turner syndrome); raising and educating a severely ill child had been extremely damaging to herself and her older children. Her husband had also abandoned the family following the birth of their disabled daughter.

The judgment showcases the interplay between access to health-related information, bodily self-determination and parenthood rights. First, the Court reiterated that 'the notion of private live applies to decisions both to have or not to have a child or to become parents'.[39] More specifically:

> The decision of a pregnant woman to continue her pregnancy or not belongs to the sphere of private life and autonomy. Consequently, also legislation regulating the interruption of pregnancy touches upon the sphere of private life, since whenever a woman is pregnant her private life becomes closely connected with the developing foetus.[40]

38 *R.R.* v. *Poland*, App. No. 27617/04, 26 May 2011.

39 Ibid., [180], citing *Evans* v. *The United Kingdom*, [71].

40 *R.R.* v. *Poland*, [181], citing *Bruggeman and Scheuten* v. *Germany*, App. No. 6959/75, 12 July 1977; *Boso* v. *Italy*, App. No. 50490/99, 5 September 2002; *Vo* v. *France* [GC], App. No. 53924/00, 8 July 2004, [76]; *Tysiąc* v. *Poland*, App. No. 5410/03, 20 March 2007, [106]–[107]; *A, B and C* v. *Ireland* [GC], [212].

As a result, the prohibition on termination of pregnancies for reasons of health and/or well-being interferes with the expectant mothers' right to respect for their private lives.[41] The Court limited the dispute before it to the issue of access to prenatal diagnostic, without having to decide on access to abortion in general; in fact, abortion was allowed by Polish law in case of genetic illness in the foetus, but the diagnosis was a prerequisite in order to qualify for a legal abortion: 'It was not access to abortion as such which was primarily in issue, but essentially *timely access to a medical diagnostic service that would, in turn, make it possible to determine whether the conditions for lawful abortion obtained* in the applicant's situation or not.'[42] Although this is not an abortion rights case, the judgment recognises the link between diagnosis (i.e. access to health-related information) and abortion: the denial of prenatal testing breaches Convention rights because it divests the woman of her ability to make an informed reproductive choice:

> The 1993 Act allows for an abortion to be carried out before the foetus is capable of surviving outside the mother's body if prenatal tests or other medical findings indicate a high risk that the foetus will be severely and irreversibly damaged or suffer from an incurable life-threatening ailment. Hence, access to full and reliable information on the foetus' health is not only important for the comfort of the pregnant woman but also a necessary prerequisite for a legally permitted possibility to have an abortion to arise.[43]

The Court had already established in *Tysiąc* v. *Poland* that 'the State is under a positive obligation to create a procedural framework enabling a pregnant woman to exercise her right of access to lawful abortion'.[44] Applying that principle to the narrower issue at hand, the ruling focused on the affirmative measures required to ensure the effective enjoyment of a domestic right, rather than establishing a free-standing Convention right to abortion on grounds of foetal abnormality: 'if the domestic law allows for abortion in cases of foetal malformation, there must be an adequate legal and procedural framework to guarantee that relevant, full and reliable information on the foetus' health is available to pregnant women'.[45] The inability to obtain a

[41] *R.R.* v. *Poland*, [188], citing *A, B and C* v. *Ireland*, [216].
[42] *R.R.* v. *Poland*, [196] (emphasis added).
[43] Ibid., [199].
[44] Ibid., [200], citing *Tysiąc* v. *Poland*, [116]–[124] (a case concerning obstacles to abortion on grounds of health risks for the pregnant woman, specifically the impact of child delivery on her eyesight).
[45] *R.R.* v. *Poland*, [200].

medical diagnosis of the foetus's condition within the time limit for lawful abortion deprived the applicant of an option afforded by the law.[46]

At the same time, the Court outlined the broader interests in prenatal testing, dismissing the Polish government's contention that access to prenatal genetic tests was tantamount to access to abortion; it noted that women sought access to such tests for various reasons: dispelling suspicions over foetal malformation, embarking on prenatal treatment where possible, giving the family time to prepare (including through counselling) for the arrival of a baby affected with an ailment; therefore, genetic tests could not be equated with encouraging pregnant women to seek abortion.[47]

The judgment remains heavily dependent on the domestic context at play. Since Polish law permitted abortion in cases of foetal malformation and entitled pregnant women to obtain information on the health of the foetus through genetic testing, the decision hinged on the flawed enforcement of the law and the 'striking discordance between the theoretical right to a lawful abortion in Poland ... and the reality of its practical implementation'.[48] The Court lamented the lack of effective mechanisms enabling an expectant mother to gain access to diagnostic services and to make an informed decision in light of the results.[49] It thus reached the conclusion that Polish authorities 'failed to comply with their positive obligations to secure to the applicant effective respect for her private life'.[50]

One important aspect of the implementation of the law is the positive obligation arising in relation to third-party action: 'States are obliged to organise the health services system in such a way as to ensure that an effective exercise of the freedom of conscience of health professionals in the professional context does not prevent patients from obtaining access to services to which they are entitled under the applicable legislation.'[51] This finding aligns with 'General Comment No. 22' (2016) of the Committee on Economic, Social and Cultural Rights, which highlighted the duty of States to ensure that the expectant woman's rights are not hindered by the ideological objections to abortion held by others, including by medical professionals.[52]

46 Ibid., [204].
47 Ibid., [205].
48 Ibid., [210].
49 Ibid., [209].
50 Ibid., [214].
51 Ibid, [206].
52 See 'General Comment No. 22' (2016), [14]: 'Unavailability of goods and services due to ideologically based policies or practices, such as the refusal to provide services based on conscience, must not be a barrier to accessing services. An adequate number of health-care

Admittedly, the *R.R.* v. *Poland* judgment does not go as far as establishing a Convention right to genetic testing and therapeutic abortion in case of foetal abnormality. A finding for the applicant did not require a judicial determination of this magnitude, unnecessarily straying into the controversial territory of abortion rights; this is an area of law where the Court has been notoriously deferential to municipal regulation, given the sensitive nature of the issues at stake.[53] However, *R.R.* v. *Poland* importantly stressed States' obligation to organise their health services so as to ensure that the exercise of freedom of conscience by health professionals did not prevent patients from obtaining access to services to which they were legally entitled. In addition, the *A, B and C* v. *Ireland* decision had already acknowledged that, by permitting abortion on grounds wider than risks to the mother's life, 'the majority of Contracting States have established a maternal-fetal legal balance in which a woman's interests in health and wellbeing can outweigh the fetus's in life'.[54] This arguably laid the foundations for the future judicial recognition of a right to terminate a pregnancy at least on the grounds of foetal abnormality, given its impact on the mother's psychological and emotional well-being. Moreover, in *R.R.* v. *Poland*, the Court cited the Council of Europe's 'Recommendation No. R (90) 13 on Prenatal Genetic Screening, Prenatal Genetic Diagnosis and Associated Genetic Counselling',[55] which promotes the adoption of legislation on genetic screening.[56] The decision could be seen as reinforcing a soft law recommendation by emphasising its human rights foundations.

Uncertainties remain, however, as to whether the scarcity of resources or training is an acceptable justification for the failure to secure access to genetic testing. In *R.R.* v. *Poland*, the Court appeared to make a theoretical concession *per a contrario* when it stressed that no technical obstacles existed in the case before it: 'it has not been argued, let alone shown, that at the material time genetic testing as such was unavailable for lack of equipment, medical

providers willing and able to provide such services should be available at all times in both public and private facilities and within reasonable geographical reach.'

53 See *A, B and C* v. *Ireland*; see further Carmen Draghici, *The Legitimacy of Family Rights in Strasbourg Case Law: 'Living Instrument' or Extinguished Sovereignty?* (Oxford: Hart, 2017) 166–173, and Carmen Draghici, 'The Strasbourg Court between European and Local Consensus: Anti-democratic or Guardian of Democratic Process?' (2017) *Public Law* 11–29, at 21–25.

54 See Rosamund Scott, 'Reproductive Health: Morals, Margin and Rights' (2018) 81(3) *Modern Law Review* 422–451, at 434.

55 Committee of Ministers of the Council of Europe, 'Recommendation No. R (90) 13 on Prenatal Genetic Screening, Prenatal Genetic Diagnosis and Associated Genetic Counselling', 21 June 1990.

56 *R.R.* v. *Poland*, [81].

expertise or funding'.[57] The Court recalled that 'the Convention does not guarantee as such a right to free medical care or to specific medical services', and it distinguished the case before it from previous rulings on positive obligations under Article 8 to afford access to certain healthcare services available.[58] Its emphasis was on the fact that no objective reasons had been adduced to justify the failure to carry out genetic tests without delay once suspicions as to the foetus's condition had arisen; instead, the delays had been caused by the doctors' reluctance to refer the patient for tests and also by 'a certain organisational and administrative confusion in the health system' in connection with costs and the provision of certain services.[59] The difficulties experienced by the applicant were therefore imputable to both individual liability and systemic problems. Despite the Court's understandable reluctance to impose costly obligations on States, it has been observed that 'it costs less to provide screening, diagnosis and termination than the medical and social care, special education and support for some children born with serious abnormality'.[60]

It is worth noting that, for the Court, the facts in *R.R.* v. *Poland* also disclosed a violation of Article 3 (prohibition of inhuman and degrading treatment) insofar as the applicant had been left in a state of anxiety and treated with disdain by medical professionals hostile to abortion; the determination of her access to genetic tests after the first scan indicating possible foetus malformation had been affected by stalling, confusion and lack of adequate counselling and information:

> For weeks she was made to believe that she would undergo the necessary tests. She was repeatedly sent to various doctors, clinics and hospitals far from her home and even hospitalised for several days for no clear clinical purpose. ... The Court finds that the determination of whether the applicant should have access to genetic testing ... was marred by procrastination, confusion and lack of proper counselling and information given to the applicant.[61]

The technical availability of diagnostic services and the applicant's entitlement to those services under domestic law were found to be aggravating circumstances.[62] The Court concluded that the applicant was 'shabbily

57 Ibid., [155].
58 Ibid., [198], citing *Nitecki* v. *Poland*, App. No. 65653/01, 21 March 2002; *Pentiacova and Others* v. *Moldova*, App. No. 14462/03, 4 January 2005.
59 *R.R.* v. *Poland*, [198].
60 Richards, 'Which Children Can We Choose', 213.
61 *R.R.* v. *Poland*, [153].
62 Ibid., [160].

treated by the doctors dealing with her case' and 'humiliated',[63] and that her suffering 'reached the minimum threshold of severity under Article 3 of the Convention'.[64] Interestingly, for the Court, the non-compliance with Article 3 stemmed not only from an omission, that is, the authorities' failure to regulate conscientious objection so as to enforce the applicant's rights against interferences by medical professionals based on their own moral preferences;[65] it was also due to active conduct amounting to degrading treatment:

> The Court notes that the applicant was in a situation of great vulnerability. … She was deeply distressed by information that the foetus could be affected with some malformation. … As a result of the procrastination of the health professionals …, she had to endure weeks of painful uncertainty concerning the health of the foetus, her own and her family's future and the prospect of raising a child suffering from an incurable ailment. She suffered acute anguish through having to think about how she and her family would be able to ensure the child's welfare, happiness and appropriate long-term medical care.[66]

Notwithstanding the narrow scope of the judgment (*existing* – but improperly implemented – domestic rights to prenatal testing and therapeutic abortion), the *R.R.* v. *Poland* ruling firmly established that access to prenatal diagnosis, critical to dispelling uncertainties over the health of the foetus, is an integral part of reproductive rights. Denial or procrastination of access to testing not only breaches privacy rights but may also amount to degrading treatment. Significantly, the judgment confirms that access to prenatal diagnosis, capable of identifying genetic disorders in a foetus and allowing the exercise of autonomous procreative choices, is not a purely domestic right.

The ECtHR's stance is strengthened by the jurisprudence developed under the ICCPR and the American Convention on Human Rights (ACHR). The UN Human Rights Committee (HRC) has found violations of the ICCPR in relation to the defective implementation of, and legal bans on, access to therapeutic abortion. In *Llantoy Huamán* v. *Peru*, the HRC criticised the restrictive interpretation by medical authorities of therapeutic abortion as

63 Ibid.

64 Ibid., [161].

65 The right to protection against third-party interference with the right to abort a foetus suffering from severe malformations was at stake in *B.B.* v. *Poland*, App. No. 67171/17, 18 October 2022 (anti-abortionist hospital director refusing to either have the abortion performed or refer to alternative facilities). However, the case was dismissed insofar as the applicant no longer had victim status after settling with the hospital for a substantial amount in compensation, which had discontinued her civil action in the Polish courts (see ibid., [48]–[56]).

66 *R.R.* v. *Poland*, [159].

inapplicable to a pregnancy involving an anencephalic foetus, insofar as it was not considered to endanger the woman's life and health.[67] In *Mellet* v. *Ireland* and *Whelan* v. *Ireland*, the HRC condemned the impossibility of legal abortion in circumstances where the congenital defects in the foetus were likely to result in its death *in utero* or shortly after birth (the grounds for termination being limited to cases of threat to the life of the woman).[68] The HRC emphasised the mental anguish suffered by the victim – who was already highly vulnerable after learning that her wanted pregnancy was not viable – when faced with the legal ban on the abortion of a fatally ill foetus, with the stigma associated with the criminalisation of abortion, with the trauma and expense of travelling to another country while carrying a dying foetus, and with the obstacles to information about her medical options and lawful abortion services overseas (due to the criminalisation of speech promoting abortion); overall, these acts and omissions violated the prohibition against cruel, inhuman or degrading treatment (Article 7 ICCPR).[69] The interference with the woman's decision not to continue her non-viable pregnancy was found to constitute an arbitrary interference in her privacy, in violation of Article 17 ICCPR, in that such a balance between protection of the foetus and the rights of the woman could not be justified.[70]

A similar approach was adopted in the inter-American system. In *Beatriz* v. *El Salvador*, the Inter-American Commission on Human Rights (IACmHR) condemned the absolute ban on abortion, which had compelled the victim to carry to term an anencephalic foetus, incapable of surviving more than a few hours after birth, despite the high risk to the mother's life and health.[71] For the IACmHR, the criminalisation of abortion was grounded in discriminatory stereotypes against women (based on women's reproductive role) and generated institutional violence against them, breaching their rights to life, personal integrity, private life, equality before the law, judicial protection and health.[72]

As regards the impact of bans on disseminating abortion information on reproductive choice, Cook et al. have noted that Strasbourg case law supports the claim that 'governments have positive duties to ensure access to information that is necessary for individuals to protect their health'.[73] They cite

67 See *Llantoy Huamán* v. *Peru*, Communication No. 1153/2003, 24 October 2005, [6.2]–[6.4].
68 *Mellet* v. *Ireland*, Communication No. 2324/2013, 31 March 2016; *Whelan* v. *Ireland*, Communication No. 2425/2014, 17 March 2017.
69 *Mellet* v. *Ireland*, [7.4]–[7.6]; *Whelan* v. *Ireland*, [7.5]–[7.7].
70 *Mellet* v. *Ireland*, [7.7]–[7.8]; *Whelan* v. *Ireland*, [7.8]–[7.9].
71 *Beatriz* v. *El Salvador*, Report No. 9/20, Case No. 13.378 (Merits), 3 March 2020.
72 Ibid., [205]–[206], [209]–[210], [215].
73 Cook et al., *Reproductive Health and Human Rights*, 210.

Open Doors Counselling v. *Ireland* to the effect that an injunction against the provision of information on abortion services creates a risk to the health of women seeking abortion at a later stage in their pregnancy.[74] The recent case law on therapeutic abortion in situations of foetal abnormality has developed the right of access to information that protects reproductive health, moving from information allowing the safe termination of pregnancies to the use of medical technology to avoid life-impairing conditions in the future progeny.

4.2.2 *Procedural Rights: Remedies in the Case of Delayed Access and Misdiagnosis*

A number of Strasbourg rulings have addressed the failure of medical professionals to conduct appropriate antenatal tests or to refer expecting women to antenatal testing where the law required them to do so (due to the mother's age and the increased likelihood of genetic abnormality) as well as cases of erroneous diagnosis (omitting to identify serious genetic defects in the foetus). In either situation, the expecting mothers were deprived of the opportunity to make an informed decision on the continuance of the pregnancy, and this was acknowledged in domestic proceedings. The complaints before the ECtHR related either to the lack of rigour in the conduct of domestic claims in negligence or to legal bars on instituting proceedings for compensation.

In 2005, the Grand Chamber pronounced on the retrospective application of a new legislative bar on claims for compensation by parents whose children's disabilities were undetected before birth due to the lack of appropriate medical tests. In *Draon* v. *France*[75] and *Maurice* v. *France*,[76] the applicants' children were born with severe congenital disabilities, which, due to medical negligence, had not been discovered in the course of prenatal medical examinations; the applicants had brought proceedings against the hospitals concerned. A new French law, introduced while those proceedings were pending, precluded them from claiming compensation for life-long 'special burdens' resulting from the children's disability. As a result, the level of compensation they were awarded was substantially lower.

In Strasbourg proceedings, the parties agreed that, based on the liability rules in force when the domestic claims were filed and the settled case law of

74 *Open Door Counselling and Others* v. *Ireland*, App. Nos. 14234/88; 14235/88, 29 October 1992, [77].

75 *Draon* v. *France* [GC], App. No. 1513/03, 6 October 2005.

76 *Maurice* v. *France* [GC], App. No. 11810/03, 6 October 2005.

administrative courts, the applicants had suffered prejudice directly caused by medical negligence and could expect to obtain compensation for damage, including the special burdens arising from their children's disability.[77] Consequently, the new bar amounted to an interference with the right to peaceful enjoyment of a 'possession'[78] within the meaning of Article 1 of Protocol No. 1 to the ECHR.[79] The Court accepted that this interference was in accordance with the law and recognised that national authorities were in principle better placed to decide 'what is in the public interest'.[80] However, it recalled that 'an interference with the peaceful enjoyment of possessions must strike a fair balance between the demands of the general interest of the community and the requirements of the protection of the individual's fundamental rights'.[81]

The assessment of proportionality hinged on the prior existence under domestic law of a right to a considerable sum of money payable as compensation for 'wrongful birth', hence the *deprivation of an asset* due to the repeal of an essential head of damage with retrospective effect, and without comparable financial support for parents under the revised welfare system.[82] Although the applicants were entitled to benefits under the new legislation, the amount was substantially lower than the asset lost (the amount to which previous liability rules entitled them) and inadequate to meet the costs associated with their children's disability.[83] Moreover, the compensation awarded to the applicants covered 'non-pecuniary damage and disruption to the applicants' lives, but not the special burdens arising from the child's disability throughout his life'.[84] The Grand Chamber held that the government's justification, alleging 'ethical considerations, equitable treatment and the proper organisation of the health service', 'could not … legitimise retrospective action whose result was to deprive the applicants, without sufficient compensation, of a

77 *Draon* v. *France*, [70].

78 Protocol 1 to the ECHR, Paris, 20 March 1952, in force 18 May 1954.

79 *Draon* v. *France*, [71].

80 Ibid., [73]–[77].

81 Ibid., [78].

82 See ibid., [82]: 'The French legislature thereby deprived the applicants of an existing "asset" which they previously possessed, namely an established claim to recovery of damages which they could legitimately expect to be determined.'

83 Ibid., [83]. The benefits available under the Law of 4 March 2002 were extended by new provisions introduced by the Law of 11 February 2005, which for the Court was an indicator of the respondent's recognition that the amount was not satisfactory. In addition, the Court lamented the uncertainties surrounding the level of compensation available under the 2005 Act (see ibid.).

84 Ibid., [84].

substantial portion of the damages they had claimed, thus *making them bear an individual and excessive burden*'.[85] The cost that the individual was required to bear was disproportionate in relation to the public interest aim pursued.[86]

Although the Court concluded that the retrospective application of the new law was in violation of Article 1 of Protocol No. 1, the finding applied only to proceedings which were pending when the law came into force.[87] Moreover, despite this positive development under Protocol 1, the approach to the Article 8 claims in *Draon* and *Maurice* was disappointingly deferential and failed to establish a broader principle of compensation for wrongful birth, capable of recognising the devastating consequences of diagnostic errors on autonomous family planning and the family's quality of life. The Court reiterated the subsidiary nature of the Convention system[88] and interpreted the Article 8 complaint to regard 'inaction by the State, which had not set up an effective system to provide compensation for special burdens arising from their child's disability'.[89] Framed in these terms, the issue was for the Court whether the measures in relation to disabled persons 'have anything to do with the applicants' right to lead a normal family life'.[90] The Court deemed it unnecessary to reach a definitive answer on the applicability of Article 8 to the claim, insofar as, even if it did apply, the situation complained of had not breached that provision.[91] More specifically, the new law was the product of 'comprehensive debate in Parliament', following consultations with the relevant stakeholders[92] (essentially the *Animal Defenders International* v. *The*

[85] Ibid., [85] (emphasis added).

[86] See ibid.: 'Such a radical interference with the applicants' rights upset the fair balance to be maintained between the demands of the general interest on the one hand and protection of the right to peaceful enjoyment of possessions on the other.' See also *Maurice* v. *France*, [93].

[87] See *Draon* v. *France*, [86]; *Maurice* v. *France*, [94]: '*In so far as it concerned proceedings pending on 7 March 2002*, the date of its entry into force, section 1 of the Law of 4 March 2002 therefore breached Article 1 of Protocol No. 1 to the Convention' (emphasis added). *N.M. and Others* v. *France*, App. No. 66328/14, 3 February 2022 (available only in French) found that parents were entitled to the level of compensation available when the medical mistake occurred, even if the law changed before they instituted proceedings.

[88] *Draon* v. *France*, [108]; *Maurice* v. *France*, [117].

[89] *Draon* v. *France*, [109]; *Maurice* v. *France*, [118].

[90] *Draon* v. *France*, [110]; *Maurice* v. *France*, [119].

[91] *Draon* v. *France*, [111]; *Maurice* v. *France*, [120].

[92] See *Draon* v. *France*, [112]; *Maurice* v. *France*, [121]: 'the French parliament, after consulting the various persons and interest groups concerned, decided to intervene to establish a new system of compensation for the prejudice sustained by children born with disabilities and their parents . . . These rules were the result of comprehensive debate in Parliament, in the course of which account was taken of legal, ethical and social considerations, and concerns relating to the proper organisation of the health service and the need for fair treatment for all disabled persons.'

United Kingdom position,[93] albeit not referenced), and it was within the wide margin of appreciation of the national legislature to decide whether it was best for the costs of caring for disabled children to be borne by social solidarity rather than through actions brought under the ordinary law of liability.[94]

The Court's Article 8 analysis revolves entirely around the issue of State support for disabled children, rather than addressing the obligation to protect against third-party negligence.[95] This is an unfortunate distortion of the claim. The Article 8 complaint arguably concerned the positive duty to prevent private-party negligence affecting a person's private and family life, through inter alia deterring financial sanctions. There is ample case law to establish obligations under Article 8 to prevent wrongful acts of third parties through appropriate legislation;[96] indeed, civil and criminal liability for negligence resulting in wrongful birth can act as an important behaviour modifier. In a Separate Opinion, Judge Bonnello also noted the discriminatory immunity given by the impugned law to medical practitioners working in one particular branch of medicine, in derogation from the internationally accepted norm of liability for harm caused to others through malice or negligence.[97] Although the judge cites this as an additional factor in assessing the proportionality of the interference with Article 1 of Protocol 1, it could be argued that relieving doctors from the consequences of their mistakes also debilitates the protection of Article 8 rights. The very core of that right is affected by a supervening law barring parents from obtaining compensation for damage from those negligently causing them to raise a disabled child, commensurate to the special burdens arising therefrom throughout their lives (not just during the child's minority).[98]

93 See *Animal Defenders International* v. *The United Kingdom* [GC], App. No. 48876/08, 22 April 2013, [114]–[115].

94 *Draon* v. *France*, [114]; *Maurice* v. *France*, [123]; see in particular the reliance on the margin: 'It is certainly not for the Court to take the place of the national authorities in assessing the advisability of such a system or in determining what might be the best policy in this difficult social sphere. This is an area where the Contracting States are to be recognised as enjoying a wide margin of appreciation.'

95 See *Draon* v. *France*, [115]; *Maurice* v. *France*, [124]: 'It cannot reasonably be claimed that the French parliament, by deciding to reorganise the system of compensation for disability in France, overstepped the wide margin of appreciation left to it on the question or upset the fair balance that must be maintained.'

96 See *X and Y* v. *The Netherlands*, App. No. 8978/80, 26 March 1985, [27]–[30], where the Court held that the effective protection of Article 8 rights was not satisfied by a civil remedy in relation to the sexual assault of a mentally handicapped girl; effective deterrence required criminal sanctions.

97 *Draon* v. *France*, Separate Opinion of Judge Bonnello, [6].

98 In addition to citing States' obligation to protect the interests of the family practically and effectively, the applicants in *Maurice* v. *France* complained that the rules introduced by the Law of 4 March 2002 constituted an arbitrary interference with their private and family life

While the *Draon* and *Maurice* rulings regrettably sidestepped the discussion of prospective parents' entitlement to protection against negligence affecting procreative rights, this returned prominently before the ECtHR in *A.K. v. Latvia*.[99] This case required it to address State obligations in relation to the negligent antenatal care given to women whose pregnancy presents the risk of congenital abnormality. The applicant, who was expecting her third child at the age of forty, alleged that her doctor did not refer her for an antenatal screening test, despite the fact that domestic law provided that all pregnant women over the age of thirty-five undertake that test, given the increased medical risks. The applicant subsequently gave birth to a daughter suffering from Down's syndrome and was denied any compensation in civil proceedings against the doctor for medical negligence. She argued that she had been denied adequate medical care, in that the antenatal screening test provided for by law would have indicated the risk of the foetus having a genetic disorder, allowing her to choose whether or not to continue the pregnancy.

The judgment treats the failure to refer a patient for antenatal screening tests and its inadequate judicial scrutiny in civil proceedings as a violation of the procedural limb of Article 8. This approach may have been inspired by the fact that, as the Court noted at the outset, the applicant did not claim that the domestic framework was inadequate to ensure the appropriate level of care to pregnant women; instead, she contended that the doctor had not observed the regulations and that domestic courts had failed to properly examine her claim for compensation.[100] The Court is yet to adjudicate a case where the complaint regards the lack of provision in domestic law for antenatal testing capable of detecting foetal abnormality. The *A.K. v. Latvia* dispute merely regarded the failure to enforce the law. Since legislation was in place to protect Article 8 rights, but its implementation was deficient, and hence the protection of the rights was ineffective, a substantive violation of Article 8 might have also been warranted.[101] It is worth noting, however, that the

because 'it prevented them from meeting their child's needs' (*Maurice* v. *France*, [109]). They submitted that the new law's considerations linked to improving the organisation of the health service – in particular the concern to avoid increases in insurance premiums for doctors and healthcare establishments – could not justify giving the latter immunity in respect of their negligent acts or omissions.

99 *A.K.* v. *Latvia*, App. No. 33011/08, 24 June 2014.

100 Ibid., [85].

101 The issue was also addressed in *Eryiğit* v. *Turkey*, App. No. 18356/11, 10 April 2018, a case concerning erroneous prenatal diagnosis (albeit not in relation to disability); the future parents had been told that they were expecting twins, and when the birth only resulted in one child, they believed that one baby had been stolen. The criminal investigation established that there had never been a second baby, but the proceedings for compensation lasted nearly twelve

majority of the Court chose to treat the case as a procedural violation of Article 8, as opposed to a violation of Article 6 (which was the preference expressed in a concurring opinion).[102] This choice is significant, because it recognises that the matter affected not only fair trial rights but also private and family life rights.

Indeed, this trend seems to take hold. *Ulusoy and Others* v. *Turkey* concerned the investigation of responsibility for severe disabilities allegedly caused to a child by inadequate prenatal and delivery care; although the applicants invoked Articles 3 and 6 ECHR, the Court, who remains the master of the characterisation of the case, invited the parties to make submissions as to whether there had been a violation of Article 8.[103] The finding of a violation of Article 8 in its procedural aspect consolidated – as part of the notion of respect for private life – the right to an effective investigation into allegations of gross fault in the provision of prenatal and delivery care.[104]

The A.K. v. *Latvia* judgment examined the conduct of proceedings against the doctor for negligence, to which, in the upper courts, the applicant had added the failings of the first instance court. The ECtHR found that 'the domestic courts' approach to the applicant's claim disclose[d] the appearance of arbitrariness', given 'the cumulative effect of the failings' in the conduct of proceedings, which meant that her claim that she had not received medical care as required by law for the protection of her interests had not been properly examined.[105] Albeit recognising the significant margin of appreciation left to States in this sensitive area of law, the Court noted several shortcomings in the domestic courts' assessment of the case, and in particular 'important factual discrepancies':[106] the judicial finding that the applicant was not in a risk category solely on account of her age, despite a domestic ordinance to the contrary; the lack of investigation of discrepancies in the medical records as to the date of commencement of the applicant's pregnancy and the time of her referral for a test; the disappearance of the applicant's medical records for several months during the criminal investigation, despite

years, a duration the Court rightly found excessive and unreasonable. The Court therefore found a violation of Article 8 in its procedural aspect in relation to proceedings undertaken by the parents. See in particular *Eryiğit* v. *Turkey*, [49], recalling that Article 8 obligations cannot be considered satisfied if the mechanisms of protection available in domestic law only exist on a theoretical level.

102 See A.K. v. *Latvia*, Separate Opinion of Judge Kalaydjieva.

103 *Ulusoy and Others* v. *Turkey*, App. No. 54969/09, 25 June 2019 (available only in French), [3], [60]–[64].

104 Ibid., [90]–[93], [116]–[117].

105 A.K. v. *Latvia*, [94].

106 Ibid., [88].

the legal obligation for doctors to keep and make records available promptly; the failure to consider the lack of reaction from the doctor, during subsequent appointments, to the applicant's absence from the alleged genetic test appointment; the refusal of one of the courts to take evidence from the applicant, allegedly unnecessary, although it had taken evidence from the doctor and there were factual inconsistencies; finally, the failure to examine the applicant's right to compensation in respect of non-pecuniary damage.[107] In light of these circumstances, the Court ascertained 'a violation of Article 8 in its procedural aspect'.[108] This decision must be welcomed. Although a dissenting opinion saw the Court acting 'as a fourth-instance national court',[109] if the Court refrains from taking a stance in the presence of serious procedural shortcomings, depriving a victim of redress, its review would be a token exercise.

Admittedly, all the aforementioned judgments condemned the lack of effective and timely access to accurate antenatal testing for disabilities, and an adequate remedy in case of interference with that right, in circumstances where domestic law already provided for such services. A total ban on access to prenatal diagnosis and therapeutic abortion has not been examined by the ECtHR. A large number of cases brought against Poland following a recent change in the law which restricts access to legal abortion on grounds of foetal defects are currently awaiting deliberation.[110] However, the following sections argue that a ban would be difficult to justify, on the basis of either the 'rights of others' or under the 'public morals' exception.

4.2.3 *The 'Expressivist' Objection: 'Rights of Others' and Proportionality*

In principle, the 'rights of others' justification for restrictions might be relevant to the debate on prenatal diagnosis and therapeutic abortion if one interprets permissive laws as tantamount to passing judgment on the worthiness of *existing* people with disabilities. Some view abortion on the grounds of the foetus's medical condition as 'sending a problematic message to other people (mainly the affected family members) with the same disability'.[111] Moral opposition to the availability of prenatal testing and selective abortion has also

[107] Ibid., [88]–[92].
[108] Ibid., [94].
[109] Ibid., Dissenting Opinion of Judge Mahoney, [1].
[110] *K.C.* v. *Poland*, App. No. 3639/21; *A.L.-B.* v. *Poland*, 3801/21 et al.; *M.L.* v. *Poland*, App. No. 40119/21, *M.B.* v. *Poland*, App. No. 5014/21, *K.B.* v. *Poland*, 1819/21, *I.Z.* v. *Poland*, 57338/21.
[111] Gilbar, 'Between Unconditional Acceptance and Responsibility', 322.

invoked 'the belief that a just society must appreciate and nurture the lives of all people, whatever the endowments they receive in the natural lottery'.[112]

The expressivist objection to prenatal diagnosis and therapeutic abortion conflates the value of individuals and the value of impairments; the view that impairments are undesirable does not equate with the view that individuals living with impairments (congenial or acquired) are undesirable. As John Gilliott pointed out, parents who choose against disability make a '*relative* judgment' that 'life without the condition is better than life with it', which is entirely different from saying that life with a genetic disorder is not worth living.[113] In a democratic, pluralist society, the law should not prohibit parents from holding and acting upon such belief. Moreover, Ruth Deech and Anna Smajdor have suggested that many parents may prefer not to have a child with a condition – for example, Down's syndrome – not only because of the impact on their own lives but also because the children may suffer from harassment, discrimination, the inability to lead an independent life and hence vulnerability to potential abuse.[114] The concern not to bring into the world children whose well-being would be at risk is not indicative of disparaging attitudes towards disabled people. While society should, of course, nurture all individuals once they are born, parents should not be compelled to accept the natural lottery with fatalistic resignation when they have the ability to influence it in the early stages of conception or gestation. The decision as to what disabilities make the future child's life and the parenting experience insufficiently rewarding is a personal – not a societal – one; in some cases (e.g. severe mental development arrest), the condition is such that no bonding can exist between the child and the parent, or the child exhibits aggressive behaviour. For instance, a child afflicted by the Lesch–Nyhan syndrome 'will suffer from limb spasms, and self-mutilation and aggressive behaviour, and will usually die in his teens'.[115] Jackson also challenged the assumption that the abortion of foetuses with disability sends a message that disabled people should not have

[112] Adrienne Asch, 'Prenatal Diagnosis and Selective Abortion: A Challenge to Practice and Policy' (1999) 89(11) *American Journal of Public Health* 1649–1657, reprinted in Helga Kuhse, Udo Schüklenk and Peter Singer (eds.), *Bioethics: An Anthology* (Chichester: John Wiley & Sons, 2016, 3rd ed.) 112–126, at 117.

[113] Gillott, 'Screening for Disability', ii22 (original emphasis).

[114] Ruth Deech and Anna Smajdor, *From IVF to Immortality: Controversy in the Era of Reproductive Technology* (Oxford and New York: Oxford University Press, 2007) 46–47.

[115] Emily Jackson, *Regulating Reproduction: Law, Technology and Autonomy* (Oxford: Hart, 2001), 245. Tay-Sachs is another example.

been born, insofar as predicated on 'some belief in the moral equivalence of a fetus and a person'.[116]

By seeking to limit one person's autonomy to avoid sending an unpleasant message to others, the expressivist objection to genetic selection also fails to recognise modern society's neutral acceptance of individual choice within the boundaries of the medically feasible. The availability of weight loss programmes and liposuction procedures does not send the message that overweight members of society are not (or are less) valued. Admittedly, obesity is not desirable on account of medical risks, but even in areas where no medical benefits justify choice, and individuals pursue mere preferences that they perceive as enhancing their well-being, the law does not preclude it, and in doing so, it does not convey any particular message. Surely the lawfulness of nose reduction and breast augmentation surgery does not suggest that society consider individuals without those features to be inferior. If one were to accommodate expressivist theories, people with the opposite traits might be offended by the fact that surgical procedures are offered to 'correct' them, implicitly conveying the message that their traits are judged as inaesthetic and undesirable, or that individuals born with such traits are less appreciated by society. Taken to its ultimate consequences, the expressivist objection would justify laws preventing parents from providing their child with prosthetic legs to improve the child's mobility and independence, lest this could be perceived as an offensive suggestion that individuals missing a limb are less valued. Decisions pertaining to private and family life are personal and self-referential; they are not a reflection on others. The fact that some people could misread the permissive approach of the law is not sufficient to justify restrictions on parental choice with far-reaching consequences.

Interestingly, it was noted that 'disability rights activists have challenged the use of language such as "abnormalities", "defects", and "risks" [in the way prenatal testing is presented] because they are normative and have built-in connotations', indirectly influencing pregnant women's decisions.[117] However, respect for reproductive health and procreative autonomy is not ensured if, out of deference to euphemism-prone political correctness, objective medical data are not accurately represented to prospective parents, allowing them to make informed decisions. Disability can entail deprivation of certain opportunities, and often hardship, both for children and their parents. This is recognised in international instruments intended to protect

116 Jackson, 'Abortion, Autonomy and Prenatal Diagnosis', 481.

117 Victoria Seavilleklein, 'Challenging the Rhetoric of Choice in Prenatal Screening' (2008) 23 (1) *Bioethics* 68–77, at 74.

the rights of people with disabilities and not to disparage them; such is, for instance, Article 1 of the UN Convention on the Rights of People with Disabilities: 'Persons with disabilities include those who have long-term physical, mental, intellectual or sensory impairments which in interaction with various barriers may hinder their full and effective participation in society on an equal basis with others.'[118]

More importantly perhaps, the rights *of others* are not sufficiently engaged by aspiring parents' ability to exercise choice. Some individuals' ability to choose for themselves and their future children should not be limited by fears of perceptions by others who are not directly affected, nor subordinated to the dominant views of the majority in society. To compel someone to forego the medical care capable of preventing life-long trauma simply for the sake of sparing the feelings of others who might be offended by that choice is a disproportionate infringement of fundamental rights. The lack of choice has dramatic, life-altering consequences for those immediately impacted by a legal ban on selective abortion. Whenever a conflict of interests arises, human rights analysis resolves it through a balance of the harms involved in (not) adopting a measure. The symbolic harm for existing disabled people, if selection is permitted, is outweighed by the harm for prospective parents if the law prohibits the choice of avoiding serious genetic illnesses or disabilities (i.e. the harm ensuing from physical, psychological, financial and opportunity costs). The unpleasantness of the idea of selection against genetic illness, even if magnified as 'harm', should be mitigated through civic education. Wilkinson has highlighted the distinction between 'the intended message and the message that is received (or perceived) by people with disabilities', stressing the importance of minimising the discrepancy between the two so as to allay concerns.[119] Glover has helpfully suggested that, to reduce the impact of genetic screening on the disabled, a clear signal needs to be sent about its purpose: 'To think that a particular disability makes someone's life less good is not one of the ugly attitudes [towards disability]. . . . The existence of doctors, hospitals, and pharmaceuticals is not an insult to the sick, just a sign of the platitude that illness impairs human flourishing.'[120] Jackson draws a useful parallel with the decision of a middle-aged woman not to continue a pregnancy: 'if a 48 year old woman decides to terminate an unexpected pregnancy, she is not presumed to be sending a message to all children with older mothers

[118] Convention on the Rights of Persons with Disabilities, 13 December 2006, in force 3 May 2008, UNTS vol. 2515 (p. 3).
[119] Wilkinson, *Choosing Tomorrow's Children*, 172–173.
[120] Glover, *Choosing Children*, 35.

that they should not have been born. Rather she has taken a decision about the course of her life that only she is equipped to make.'[121]

The alleged practical impact of prenatal tests on the disabled, such as the reduction of public expenditure on accessibility adjustments (e.g. ramps) or on medical research, is speculative and insufficient to qualify as harm (certainly not as greater harm when compared to the impact that a ban would have on parents). Jackson has pointed out that only very few types of disability can be avoided through genetic testing and therefore the impact on society at large is insignificant:

> Limiting access to prenatal tests, or to abortion after a positive result is unlikely to transform attitudes towards disability. Most diseases and disabilities are not the result of genetic abnormalities, but are instead caused by poverty, accidents, war or exposure to environmental hazards. . . . Hardly any illnesses or abnormalities could plausibly be eliminated by genetic screening.[122]

The concrete benefits for disabled people of prohibiting selective abortion are not demonstrated and certainly too remote to legitimise such an extreme interference with the expectant woman's rights to bodily self-determination and reproductive choice. Jackson has convincingly argued against the tyranny of intrusive restrictions of patient autonomy aimed at influencing public perceptions: 'Forcing a woman to continue an unwanted pregnancy to term in order to achieve a shift in social attitudes or in scientific priorities would represent a marked exception to the current trend in medical law of treating patient autonomy as the overriding consideration.'[123] Unless the adverse impact of a person's right to self-determination on others is of a certain magnitude, restrictions based on remote and indirect effects are disproportionate.

4.2.4 *'Public Morals' and Self-Determination*

For the same considerations of proportionality seen in relation to the 'rights of others', 'morals' is a feeble justification for barring abortion on foetal abnormality grounds. Strasbourg case law has accepted that decisions in the sphere of medical treatment or personal lifestyle that others find immoral cannot be restricted merely on the basis of the repugnance or condemnation of the majority. For instance, the majority's belief in the absolute sanctity of life does not prevail over a patient's right to refuse life-saving treatment. Indeed,

[121] Jackson, *Regulating Reproduction*, 98.
[122] Jackson, 'Abortion, Autonomy and Prenatal Diagnosis', 482.
[123] Ibid., 481.

autonomy extends to self-harming decisions.[124] As the ECtHR clarified in *Pretty* v. *The United Kingdom*: 'the ability to conduct one's life in a manner of one's own choosing may also include the opportunity to pursue activities perceived to be of a physically or morally harmful or dangerous nature for the individual concerned'.[125] To limit a woman's physical self-determination based on others' philosophical views on the moral status of the foetus is equally unacceptable. Moreover, the treatment of the woman as a mere vehicle for the foetus and the subordination of her bodily self-determination rights to the interests of the foetus would deprive her of agency and raise questions of human dignity. Cook et al. have highlighted the increasing international trend against the denial of abortion, based on its demeaning and discriminatory impact on women's rights:

> The term 'forced pregnancy' has emerged as a way of describing how women view denial of abortion services, equating such denial to the outrage of rape. Forced pregnancy was condemned by governments at the Beijing Fourth World Conference on Women as a violation of women's rights. The Committee on the Elimination of Discrimination against Women (CEDAW) has issued a General Recommendation on Women and Health that addresses the discriminatory dimensions of denial of abortion.[126]

Many authors view the concerns over women's rights as important not only when abortion is sought on health grounds. Nicolette Priaulx has argued that permitting abortion only on grounds of serious foetus abnormality is not satisfactory, because the 'additional emotional, financial and caring burden if she continues to care for the child' is not limited to cases of disability.[127] Moreover, the legal option of genetic testing does not lend itself easily to abuse. Jackson has pointed out that it is unlikely that prenatal testing can be offered as a routine and generalised procedure, firstly, because the procedure to obtain foetal tissue sample is invasive and involves a risk of miscarriage and, secondly, because it is impossible to test for all genetic diseases; in fact, the clinical team must know which condition they aim to detect (or screen for the most common conditions, such as cystic fibrosis).[128]

[124] See *Pretty* v. *The United Kingdom*, App. No. 2346/02, 29 April 2002, [63].
[125] Ibid., [62].
[126] Cook et al., *Reproductive Health and Human Rights*, 352.
[127] Nicolette Priaulx, 'Beyond Health and Disability: Rethinking the "Foetal Abnormality" Ground in Abortion Law', in Kirsty Horsey and Hazel Biggs (eds.), *Human Fertilisation and Embryology: Reproducing Regulation* (London: Routledge-Cavendish, 2007) 205–230, at 225.
[128] Jackson, *Regulating Reproduction*, 102–103.

It could be further argued that abortion restrictions are inconsistent with the priority given to the expectant woman' rights over foetal interests under the law on consent to medical treatment; she cannot be administered life-preserving medical treatment against her wishes even if her death also ends the life of the foetus. Nor can public authorities restrict the woman's lifestyle choices on the basis that they harm the foetus.[129] The decision not to carry the pregnancy to term may affect the sensitivities of those attaching moral value to any human tissue, but their unease, even if elevated to the status of 'public morals', is too remotely connected to justify the grave interference with the woman's self-determination and procreative rights.

4.3 PGD AND SCREENING FOR DISABILITY

4.3.1 *Embryo Selection in Human Rights Litigation*

Reportedly, each year nearly 8 million children worldwide are born with serious illnesses having a genetic cause.[130] These statistics are not unavoidable; procreative liberty arguably encompasses an individual's right to pre-empt, rather than treat, genetic illness in the offspring through recourse to PGD and the selection of healthy embryos.[131] There is, in fact, little basis for distinguishing, in moral terms, between medical therapy given to a child after birth (to cure, or manage the symptoms of, an illness) and antenatal medical intervention, allowing the child to be shielded against foreseeable diseases before it is born. In both cases, treatment is provided because the disease or disability reduces the child's quality of life and opportunities for development; the timing of such action, at the conception stage or after birth, should not be overmagnified. In some cases, PGD may be crucial for a couple's ability to procreate altogether; as Robertson has indicated, in the absence of PGD, many at-risk couples might forego reproduction rather than taking the chance

[129] See *Re F (In Utero)*.

[130] See Han Somsen, 'Regulating Human Genetics in a Neo-Eugenic Era', in Thérèse Murphy (ed.), *New Technologies and Human Rights* (Oxford: Oxford University Press, 2009) 85–127, at 88.

[131] The benefits of PGD are considerable. See Lisa Rubin and Aliza Phillips, 'Infertility and Assisted Reproduction Technologies: Matters of Reproductive Justice', in Joan Chrisler (ed.), *Reproductive Justice: A Global Concern* (Santa Barbara: Praeger, 2012) 173–199, at 186–187: 'In addition to the use of PGD to avoid heritable, single gene disorders (e.g., cystic fibrosis, sickle cell anemia, Tay-Sachs disease, spinal muscular atrophy) or (albeit less commonly) for immunologically compatible (i.e., Human Leukocyte Antigen [HLA] matched) sibling donors (i.e., "savior siblings"), PGD increasingly is being used for late-onset disorders with a genetic predisposition, such as hereditary breast/ovarian cancer (BRCA) or colon cancer (HNPCC) risk.'

of having a seriously ill child or terminating an affected pregnancy.[132] In such cases, the refusal of access to PGD and IVF raises significant concerns as to the effective protection of reproductive rights.

Although Strasbourg case law does not seek to harmonise medically assisted procreation laws,[133] the Court has shown readiness to act as an enforcer of domestic reproductive rights, especially in the presence of inconsistencies in domestic legislation. In *Costa and Pavan* v. *Italy*, the Court held that the prohibition of access to IVF and PGD for couples wishing to avoid the transmission of genetic diseases to their children, in circumstances where prenatal diagnosis and abortion were permitted, was a disproportionate interference with Article 8 rights.[134] The applicants – healthy carriers of cystic fibrosis – had one child to whom the disease had been transmitted and had terminated a subsequent pregnancy when the foetus was diagnosed with the disease. To avoid replicating this situation, they sought access to IVF and PGD allowing for the selection of healthy embryos. Under Italian law, IVF treatment and PGD were available only to infertile couples and to couples in which the male partner suffered from a sexually transmissible viral disease (such as HIV or hepatitis B and C);[135] the selection of embryos for eugenic purposes was, conversely, prohibited. The applicants invoked their Article 8 rights and complained that the law limited their options to starting a pregnancy by natural means and terminating it if the foetus tested positive for cystic fibrosis.

An essential contribution of the *Costa and Pavan* unanimous judgment is the Court's finding that the desire to have a healthy child is protected by Article 8:

> The applicants' desire to conceive a child unaffected by the genetic disease of which they are healthy carriers and to use ART and PGD to this end attracts the protection of Article 8, as this choice is a form of expression of their private and family life.[136]

The ECtHR agreed that the denial of access to reproductive technologies, in circumstances where these were available to other categories, amounted to an

[132] See John Robertson, 'Extending Preimplantation Genetic Diagnosis: The Ethical Debate. Ethical Issues in New Uses of Preimplantation Genetic Diagnosis' (2003) 18(3) *Human Reproduction* 465–471, at 467.

[133] See Chapter 2 on the ECtHR's approach to heterologous fertilisation and surrogacy.

[134] *Costa and Pavan* v. *Italy*, [71].

[135] Ibid., [58].

[136] Ibid., [57]. See also [65]: 'In order to protect *their right to have a child unaffected by the disease of which they are healthy carriers*, the only possibility available to them is to start a pregnancy by natural means and then terminate it if the prenatal test shows that the fœtus is unhealthy' (emphasis added).

interference with the applicants' right to respect for their private and family life.[137] The applicants did not dispute that the restriction pursued the protection of morals and of the rights of others,[138] and the Court accepted this without further analysis, although the specific aims listed are unconvincing: 'the concern to protect the health of "the child" and the woman, the dignity and freedom of conscience of the medical professions and the interest in precluding a risk of eugenic selection'.[139] Conversely, the measure failed the 'necessary in a democratic society' test, in that it did not protect the interests invoked by the respondent government as legitimate aims.

Firstly, Italian law allowed the applicants to terminate a pregnancy on medical grounds if the foetus was found to be affected by the disease.[140] The Court questioned the law's adequacy to protect the health of the mother, which was difficult to reconcile with the possibility of an abortion instead of PGD.[141] The Court pointed out 'the anxiety experienced by the first applicant, whose only hope of having another child, since she is unable to have recourse to PGD, carries the concomitant risk that the child will be born with the disease or the suffering inherent in the painful decision to undergo, as the case may be, an abortion on medical grounds'.[142] A law preventing healthy carriers of genetic diseases to use IVF and embryo screening services, while allowing abortion if the foetus was affected by the same diseases, was deemed intrinsically inconsistent; this inconsistency compromised the proportionality of the restriction and violated the prospective parents' Article 8 rights.[143]

Secondly, the Court acknowledged the different moral claim of the foetus when compared to the embryo, given the former's more advanced stage of development:

> [The Court] fails to see how the protection of the interests referred to by the Government can be reconciled with the possibility available to the applicants of having an abortion on medical grounds if the fœtus turns out to be affected by the disease, having regard in particular to the consequences of this both for

[137] Ibid., [58].

[138] Ibid., [59]. See further [61].

[139] Ibid., [61].

[140] Ibid., [60].

[141] Ibid., [62].

[142] Ibid., [66]. The Court also notes that the applicants had already terminated a pregnancy because the foetus was affected by the disease ([65]).

[143] See ibid., [64]: 'The Court cannot but note that the Italian legislation lacks consistency in this area. On the one hand it bans implantation limited to those embryos unaffected by the disease of which the applicants are healthy carriers, while on the other hand it allows the applicants to abort a fœtus affected by the disease.'

> the fœtus, which is clearly far further developed than an embryo, and for the parents, in particular the woman.[144]

The Court also questioned the justification based on eugenic selection and doctors' freedom of conscience and dignity: 'the Government have failed to explain how the risk of eugenic selection and affecting the dignity and freedom of conscience of the medical professions would be averted in the event of an abortion being carried out on medical grounds'.[145] The finding that therapeutic abortion and PGD are equally eugenic in nature, and hence banning one but not the other was arbitrary, was sufficient for the case at hand. One may query, however, why selection against catastrophic illness is problematic and its avoidance is a legitimate aim. In the case of procreative rights, the boundary between medical *needs* and *preferential* (eugenic) selection is not always clear-cut. Stefano Biondi has highlighted the illogical use of medically assisted reproduction in Italian law 'to treat infertility, but not to prevent the greater health impairments stemming from the birth of a disabled child, by [sic] the psycho-physical consequences of pregnancy termination or by [sic] the distress of having to make a tragic choice between these two options'.[146] There is no discussion in the *Costa and Pavan* judgment of the concern to avoid eugenic selection as opposed to eugenic abuse. For the Court's purposes, it was sufficient to note that abortion had the same result as embryo screening, except at greater costs to the parents, and hence the impugned measure was excessively intrusive and disproportionate.

As with the case law on prenatal diagnosis, the finding of a violation hinged primarily – albeit not exclusively – upon existing laws in the respondent State rather than upon autonomous ECHR rights, in particular the availability of abortion on grounds of diagnosed genetic disease. Although the judgment recognises that Article 8 protects the desire for a healthy child and the denial of embryo selection constitutes an interference with this right, what delegitimised the ban on PGD was the irrationality of an overall bioethical scheme requiring a couple to wait and abort the foetus on grounds of severe illness, but not allowing them to select healthy embryos:

> The applicants' complaint does not concern the question whether, taken alone, the ban … is compatible with Article 8 of the Convention.

[144] Ibid., [62].
[145] Ibid., [63].
[146] Stefano Biondi, 'Access to Medical-Assisted [sic] Reproduction and PGD in Italian Law: A Deadly Blow to an Illiberal Statute? Commentary to the European Court on [sic] Human Rights's [sic] Decision *Costa and Pavan* v. *Italy* (ECtHR, 28 August 2012, App. 54270/2010)' (2013) 21 *Medical Law Review* 474–486, at 486.

> The applicants complain of a lack of proportionality of such a measure given that Italian law does allow them to abort the foetus if it is affected by the disease of which they are carriers.[147]

The decision was also influenced, however, by the results of a comparative survey of thirty-two European States, which indicated that embryo screening on medical grounds was either permitted or not regulated in most States, whereas only an exiguous minority prohibited it.[148] In addition, in its review of the relevant international and comparative legal framework, the Court cited Article 12 of the Oviedo Convention on Human Rights and Biomedicine,[149] which allows PGD for the purposes of detecting genetic susceptibility to a disease, although it noted that Italy had not ratified this treaty.[150] This may suggest an incipient ECHR right to have recourse to PGD. Indeed, the Court has previously relied on international treaties, not always widely ratified ones, to establish new ECHR rights, regardless of whether the respondent was a signatory.[151] While the Court noted that the vast majority of ECHR States permit genetic selection (via prenatal and pre-implantation genetic diagnosis) aimed at avoiding a serious disease or disability,[152] it did not need to base the judgment *solely* on European consensus, given the less controversial ground of domestic incongruity. This does not invalidate the argument that Article 8 rights have evolved to encompass prospective parents' right to have recourse to the technologies available to safeguard their reproductive health, which includes, in line with the WHO definition, access to healthcare services providing couples with the best chance of having healthy infants.[153]

The Court did not embark upon the more ambitious task of establishing a 'right to a healthy child'; indeed, it dismissed the Italian government's contention that this was the right the applicant couple sought to assert and limited

[147] *Costa and Pavan* v. *Italy*, [60].

[148] Ibid., [29]–[32], [70]. Only two other States apart from Italy banned PGD, and one of them was considering a repeal of the ban.

[149] Council of Europe, Convention for the Protection of Human Rights and Dignity of the Human Being with Regard to the Application of Biology and Medicine, Oviedo, 4 April 1997, in force 1 December 1999, ETS No. 164.

[150] *Costa and Pavan* v. *Italy*, [21]–[23].

[151] See, e.g., the case law on the rights of children born out of wedlock to automatic recognition of their maternal affiliation and equal inheritance rights (*Marckx* v. *Belgium*, App. No. 6833/74, 13 June 1979); for a discussion of the Strasbourg Court's reliance on international treaties, often not widely ratified, under the 'consensus' doctrine, see Draghici, *The Legitimacy of Family Rights*, 117, 121, 402–404. The Court's willingness to endorse the principles of the Hague Convention on International Child Abduction in Article 8 proceedings is also illuminating; for references and further discussion see ibid., 279–289.

[152] See *Costa and Pavan* v. *Italy*, [29], [77].

[153] See Section 4.1.

the claim before it to the right to detect and prevent a specific and particularly serious disease in the offspring, rather than all medical conditions.[154] One might have preferred a broader condemnation of laws denying parents access to pre-emptive solutions against the transmission of serious hereditary diseases, which is in the interests neither of the parents nor of the resulting child (or indeed society as a whole, given the burdens associated with social solidarity and disability benefits, at the expense of provision for other rights such as education, fair trial or personal security). However, considering the wide margin of appreciation enjoyed by States in bioethical matters, a well-supported verdict upholding a narrow right was arguably more politic than a comprehensive finding of a right to a healthy child open to contestation. The Court, as an international tribunal, may understandably avoid acting as an intrepid vehicle for the assertion of a right to eugenic selection. Establishing the more limited right to choose PGD over therapeutic abortion advanced the human rights dimension of bioethical politics without calling into question the legitimacy of the judgment.

Significantly, the Court did not place domestic policies on access to PGD beyond the reach of international human rights supervision: 'While acknowledging that the question of access to PGD raises sensitivie [*sic*] moral and ethical questions, the Court notes that the solutions reached by the legislature are not beyond the scrutiny of the Court.'[155] To the extent that more European States offer IVF services with embryo pre-implantation screening, the scope of enforceable procreative rights is likely to widen, while the margin of appreciation reserved to States will continue to wane.

This emerging jurisprudence also suggests that, in future, Article 8 may expand to include access to more recent reproductive technologies, such as mitochondrial replacement techniques (MRTs), aimed at avoiding maternally inherited mitochondrial disease.[156] The novel challenge posed by MRTs from a human rights perspective is that, in addition to preventing genetic disease, they involve partial reliance on ovum donation (so as to allow the replacement of the affected mitochondria with healthy mitochondria) and hence what could be seen as split biological motherhood, although the third-party material used is a very small percentage of the genetic heritage of the child. In the UK, legal by virtue of the Human Fertilisation and Embryology

[154] *Costa and Pavan* v. *Italy*, [46]–[47].

[155] Ibid., [68].

[156] MRTs presuppose the alteration of the genetic make-up of an egg through a process involving third-party donation designed to prevent the transmission of serious mitochondrial disease to the child.

(Mitochondrial Donation) Regulations 2015,[157] MRTs were initially met with some resistance. The most troublesome objection in the public consultation leading up to the legalisation of this technique was that women in this situation have other options, such as adopting or resorting to IVF with donated ovum.[158] This, as Scott has rightly noted, amounts to the '*downgrading* of the interest which generates the need ... in having not only a child free from serious genetic disease but also to whom the woman, the future mother, is genetically related'.[159] As discussed in Chapter 2, the two alternatives to MRTs contemplated in the consultation misunderstand the fundamental right to a genetically related child and are wholly unsatisfactory.

The Strasbourg Court is yet to pronounce on any rights to resort to MRTs, and there is a certain danger that the centrality of the consensus doctrine in the analysis of reproductive autonomy cases will rein in the development of European human rights in this new and controversial area. As Scott has suggested, infertility issues and risks of genetic disease in the offspring only affect a minority, hence 'the likely influence of hostile preference in relation to the lawfulness of reproductive interventions and technologies'.[160] From this perspective, human rights challenges to the prohibition of new reproductive techniques present the same difficulty of other unpopular minority causes in Strasbourg litigation, such as assisted dying claims. The moral unease of unsympathetic majorities in the Council of Europe States might lead the Court to the deferral to domestic regulation.

4.3.2 *'Morals' and Individual Eugenic Pursuits*

The legitimacy of policies precluding eugenic selection was not discussed at length in *Costa and Pavan* v. *Italy* insofar as not challenged by the applicants. Had the complaint regarded a free-standing ban on PGD, rather than the illogical combination of the ban with therapeutic abortion, a more extensive analysis of the legitimate aims and proportionality of the interference would have been necessary.

[157] Adopted in the exercise of powers conferred by s. 3ZA(5) Human Fertilisation and Embryology Act 1990 – an amendment introduced by s. 3 Human Fertilisation and Embryology Act 2008.

[158] HFEA, *Mithocondria Replacement Consultation: Advice to Government* (March 2013), available at www.hfea.gov.uk/media/2618/mitochondria_replacement_consultation_-_advice_for_government.pdf, discussed in Scott, 'Reproductive Health', 449.

[159] Scott, 'Reproductive Health', 449 (original emphasis).

[160] Ibid., 450.

Notwithstanding the 'normalisation of IVF',[161] the use of PGD is still regarded with scepticism. Objections to human intervention at the early stages of procreation are variously inspired by aversion towards unnatural processes, 'playing God' concerns and eugenic scaremongering. As Glover has noted, eugenic selection tends to be accompanied by disapproval insofar as mistakenly linked with Nazi values, whereas the values guiding parents who wish to avoid genetic disability in their child are entirely different: they do not wish to cleanse society's gene pool of disabled people, nor do they deem them inferior; their choice is based on compassion for the potential child.[162] Respect for individual choice, shaped by the prospective parents' own experiences and expectations, bears no resemblance to a State-engineered programme on a societal scale. Somsen has suggested that 'the eugenic instincts of private individuals', 'as a cumulative of individually expressed preferences, could systematically damage the interests of carriers of undesirable alleles'.[163] It is unclear why the aggregate result of private utilisations of PGD, which may reduce disability in society by a small margin and not as a matter of State policy, should be seen as detrimental to existing carriers of diseases.

The idea that the State should have the monopoly on deciding which diseases entitle genetic selection and which are trivial eugenic pursuits is also questionable. As Gilbar wrote: 'arriving at a societal agreement about the definition of "significant risk" or the "seriousness" of a disease or disability seems impossible, so leaving the decision to the doctors and prospective parents ... may be the right policy, especially if the parents have already experienced having a child or a relative with a particular disease or disability'.[164] What constitutes an unacceptably low quality of life is a subjective evaluation, and since parents bear the responsibility of raising the children, as well as being in charge of decision-making as regards children's medical treatment, it needs to be deferred to them.

Objections to parents being able to predetermine the fate of their children and to avoid future children afflicted by genetic abnormality – the 'playing God' objection and its 'consumerism' variant[165] – are oblivious to the fact that

[161] Deirdre Madden, *Medicine, Ethics and the Law* (Haywards Heath: Bloomsbury, 2016, 3rd ed.) 249, noting that over 6.5 million children were born through IVF worldwide by 2016.

[162] Glover, *Choosing Children*, 28–29.

[163] Somsen, 'Regulating Human Genetics', 92.

[164] Gilbar, 'Between Unconditional Acceptance and Responsibility', 331.

[165] See David King, 'Why We Should Not Permit Embryos to Be Selected as Tissue Donors' (2003) 190 *Bulletin of Medical Ethics* 13–16, reprinted in Kuhse et al., *Bioethics*, 152–155, at 153: 'The increased technologisation of reproduction, and the use of technology to choose our children's characteristics, tend to make reproduction just another process for producing

the law already allows parents to decide for minor patients what an acceptable quality of life is, and hence to make life-and-death decisions for their children, accommodating the desire to avoid the harm suffered by children as a result of catastrophic disabilities.[166] The greater scepticism towards preventing disease in future children as opposed to consenting to active euthanasia or termination of life-sustaining treatment for existing children might be explained by the novelty of the ART field. On closer analysis, however, they both relate to the parents' ability to decide for their (existing/future) children that a certain life is not worth living or that one possible life is preferable to another. If anything, allowing/causing a child to die on that basis is a more drastic decision than avoiding conception, by not selecting the embryo for implantation; the latter also seems preferable to avoiding the birth, by terminating a pregnancy, given the foetus's further development.

Glover has also noted that genetic intervention against disability, aimed at promoting the child's chances of flourishing, is not dissimilar to other medical treatments parents seek for their children: 'We owe to our children other forms of medical treatment that they need, and gene therapy ... is not different.'[167] Indeed, he has suggested that there may be a parental duty to avoid life-impairing abnormalities: 'Where an obstacle to flourishing can be eliminated in a way that is not unreasonably burdensome, its removal is something we owe to our children.'[168] Since the desire to have a healthy child has been recognised as protected by the right to private and family life, State interferences cannot be justified by a blanket reference to eugenic risks or the undemonstrated assumption that all eugenic pursuits are to be seen as contrary to public policy.

consumer goods. Although the outputs of this process are undeniably human beings, by choosing their characteristics we turn them into things, just human-designed objects. Conversely, by taking this new power of selection/design over a key part of what constitutes those individuals, we elevate ourselves above them. This is part of what people mean when they talk about playing God.' This grossly overestimates the ability to influence the genetic make-up of future children. Moreover, on that basis, we are playing God every time we decide to procreate, as but for our will to do so, the child would not exist. The very existence of the child is entirely determined by the parent's volition – but this is biology, in its most natural and inevitable consequences, not some new-fangled self-arrogated superagency.

166 See, e.g., Neil Gorsuch, *The Future of Assisted Suicide and Euthanasia* (Princeton: Princeton University Press, 2006) 191–203 for a discussion (based on US and UK case law) of parents' right to refuse life-prolonging treatment for infant patients (subject to court scrutiny as to whether or not the decision remains within the range of debatable action).

167 Glover, *Choosing Children*, 61.

168 Ibid., 62.

4.3.3 *Genetic Manipulation and the 'Human Dignity' Rhetoric*

Another objection to selecting genes adduces that this is an unnatural process that affects human dignity. The rejection of all interventions seeking to modify human nature is problematic; probably no one would view living with an artificial limb or coronary bypass unnatural and, therefore, objectionable. Altering human nature to prolong and improve existence is already part of the contemporary human being's identity. Glover makes the interesting point that, before the development of modern reproductive technology, being born inside of the genetic mother's womb was seen as an essential characteristic of the human being, whereas 'now we do not think that children of surrogate mothers are not human'.[169] Buxton also notes that selecting the healthiest embryos 'is mirroring ... rather than interfering with Nature', in that 'many fertilised eggs never get as far as implanting into the womb'.[170] The shallowness of the argument based on what is natural is also patent in Robertson's observation that, 'if any interference with nature is inappropriate, ... any attempt to avoid reproduction or treat infertility would also be illegitimate'.[171] Contraception and circumventing infertility through ART are not natural processes, but their moral or legal permissibility is no longer in question. Respect for human rights is predicated on pluralism of life visions, and to impose on others deterministic fatalism in reproduction – requiring couples to resign to infertility and unwanted pregnancies – would be too narrow a view of the right (not) to reproduce.

From an ECHR perspective, 'human dignity' concerns could be accommodated under the 'protection of morals' justification for interferences with reproductive freedom. There are, however, notable difficulties with accepting that not only does 'human dignity' (an imprecise and subjective construct) constitute a legitimate aim, but curtailing human rights in its name is necessary and proportionate. As Deirdre Madden has explained, the concept of 'human dignity', albeit invoked in various international instruments (such as the Universal Declaration on Human Rights 1948 and the Universal Declaration on Bioethics and Human Rights 2005), is not defined, and 'it serves as a placeholder for whatever it is about human beings that entitles them to basic human rights and freedoms'.[172] Human dignity arguments

[169] Ibid., 84.
[170] Buxton, 'Unforeseen Uses of Preimplantation Genetic Diagnosis', 120.
[171] Robertson, *Children of Choice*, 153.
[172] Madden, *Medicine, Ethics and the Law*, 242.

should be used with caution for both doctrinal credibility and because of its potentially deleterious practical consequences for certain individuals. The notion of human dignity should not be invoked as a smokescreen, to subvert its meaning from the foundation of human rights to blanket reason for inhibiting them.

Roger Brownsword has clarified that, for those adhering to the 'dignitarian' view, which posits that 'human life should be protected and respected (from the point of conception onwards)',[173] 'the use of embryos at any stage compromises human dignity'.[174] However, without some gradation in the attribution of human dignity to human tissue capable of becoming a child, the rights of living persons risk being excessively curtailed in the name of future/potential human beings. That the embryo and the foetus have some moral status is unquestionable, whatever view one takes of human dignity, but the rights of sentient human beings, capable of feelings, occupy a superior position, not just on the technicality that they are the only genuine rights-bearers but also because they are the only ones susceptible of experiencing harm.

By the same token, if the notion of human dignity is applied indiscriminately to all forms of human tissue, as opposed to living persons, we arrive at paradoxical claims; for example, non-fertilised gametes have an entitlement to protection, and so discarding sperm is an affront to human dignity, since it does not allow the sperm to continue and materialise the potentiality for human life. Not all genetic material can have an equal claim to human dignity; otherwise contraception/family planning would have to be prohibited insofar as interfering with the potential of gametes to become a child. Madden has also drawn attention to the fact that 'there is no certainty that the fertilized egg will ever become an embryo, or that the embryo will become a foetus', and hence entities that have the potential to become human beings, subject to changes they may or may not undergo in order to develop the characteristics of personhood (i.e. intellect, will), should not be accorded the same rights as

[173] Roger Brownsword, 'Human Dignity, Ethical Pluralism, and the Regulation of Modern Biotechnologies', in Thérèse Murphy (ed.), *New Technologies and Human Rights* (Oxford: Oxford University Press, 2009) 19–84, at 25. See also 26–29 for the distinction between 'human dignity as empowerment' (i.e. the belief that humans have intrinsic dignity) and 'human dignity as constraint' (i.e. opposition to the commodification of the human body).

[174] Ibid., 75. Holm, 'Ethical Issues in Pre-implantation Diagnosis', 190, explained the ethical objection to all PGD by those who believe in the moral status of zygotes, in that the technique 'is aimed at detecting and destroying certain kinds of human zygotes'. The claim made in this chapter is not that zygotes are not entitled to protection but that human beings are entitled to greater protection.

actual human beings.[175] Querying the argument from potentiality, Jackson also notes that 'occasionally, a fertilised egg will even develop into a type of tumour known as a hydatidiform mole rather than a human embryo'.[176] However, Jackson supports the distinction between embryos and gametes: 'the embryo contains a new genetic code, so it is clearly a significant step further on in the process of becoming a person than a spermatozoa or an unfertilised egg'.[177] Moreover, Wicks has aptly noted that the 'preservation of human dignity' argument is incapable of justifying State regulation of reproduction, insofar as 'assisted reproduction does not seek to use the human body for gain, nor put a price upon it, nor make it the subject of a commercial transaction (any more than does medical assistance in other forms of reproduction)'.[178]

The other notable difficulty with the concept of human dignity as an all-purpose justification for the restriction of procreative rights is that it allows the views of the majority, unaffected by infertility or transmissible congenital diseases, to restrict the rights of those few individuals who need PGD for the fulfilment of parenthood aspirations. The ECHR is not subordinate to utilitarian justice. Individual rights cannot be limited excessively in pursuit of some common good, even assuming that there is a shared understanding of human dignity that would qualify as common good rather than majority prejudice. Even if the prohibition of genetic screening could be seen as pursuing the legitimate aim of protecting public morals, that would not suffice to account for the impact on the lives of couples suffering from serious hereditary diseases. A measure affecting a small number of individuals disproportionately can still constitute a breach of human rights. Brownsword has noted 'the tension between utilitarian promotion of the general good (where little or no attention is paid to the distribution of utility or disutility) and the constraints imposed if individual rights are to be respected'.[179] Bars on genetic

[175] Madden, *Medicine, Ethics and the Law*, 244–245. The author also points out that, to the extent that it relies on external intervention to lead to a pregnancy, by being transferred into a womb, the embryo is similar to unfertilised egg and sperm; see 246.

[176] Jackson, *Regulating Reproduction*, 226–227.

[177] Ibid., 228. Jackson further proposes an interesting comparison with the threshold for personhood at the end of life; see 229: 'If we say that someone is dead when they have lost the capacity for consciousness or sentience, then it might seem logical to say that the first appearance of the capacity for consciousness or sentience marks the beginning of a valuable human life.'

[178] Wicks, *The State and the Body*, 58.

[179] Brownsword, 'Human Dignity, Ethical Pluralism, and the Regulation of Modern Biotechnologies', 24.

testing and IVF could be seen as indirectly discriminatory against the categories needing them and likely to express a demand for them.

Nor is the precautionary principle sufficient to explain away the restriction, given the stakes for some individuals. Somsen has pointed out that the debate over human genetics can borrow from the WTO and EU case law regarding genetically modified organisms, in particular the principle that a measure cannot be justified on the basis of a purely hypothetical approach to risk and the fact that science can never provide absolute certainty that there will never be any risks.[180] He also points out that, from the perspective of a human rights review of the regulation of human genetics, 'precaution leads to arbitrariness and provides governments with a blank cheque for limiting individual liberties'.[181]

4.3.4 *PGD and Disability Rights Concerns*

Like prenatal diagnosis and therapeutic abortion, PGD has faced the expressivist objection. Glover has summarised the 'expressivist objection' to antenatal screening and pre-implantation diagnosis as follows: 'What attitudes towards disabled people do these programmes express, and what message do they send to people who already live with these conditions? What does it do to your sense of being a valued member of society to realize that there are people who go to great lengths to avoid the birth of someone like you?'[182] In response, he argued: 'there need be nothing wrong with the intention to have children with a better chance of flourishing as a result of not having a disability. ... People should not be prevented from choosing children with more rather than less potential for flourishing.'[183] The 'message of the law' basis for the denial of individual autonomy has also been raised in the context of assisted dying. In the literature and court proceedings, it was often adduced that the legalisation of assisted dying might send a message that life with certain critical impairments is not worth living; this argument confuses the State's ethical neutrality in allowing individual beliefs and choices with a State policy promoting a specific view on critical illness.[184] The unease with genetic choice for people living with disabilities is understandable, but the availability

[180] Somsen, 'Regulating Human Genetics', 100–102.
[181] Ibid., 115.
[182] Glover, *Choosing Children*, 4–5.
[183] Ibid., 34.
[184] See Carmen Draghici, 'Assisted Dying', in Ian Loveland (ed.), *Canadian and British Public Law in Comparative Perspective* (Oxford: Hart, 2021) 25–74, at 45–46.

of genetic testing – or PGD and IVF – simply endorses autonomous choice. It does not compel or encourage prospective parents to avoid disability.

It has been argued, on the other hand, that the process of expanding the number of medical conditions accepted by the law as sufficiently serious to justify PGD 'may lead society to show intolerance towards people with disabilities'.[185] This is an undemonstrated concern, as is the alleged danger that, as a result of an increase in PGD, 'people may become unwilling to accept children who are physically or mentally disabled'.[186] On the contrary, Buxton has noted that the argument that PGD encourages discrimination against existing disabled or seriously ill individuals 'is not borne out by studies of families who already have, and cherish, one child affected by a genetic disorder but wish to avoid the disease in future children'.[187]

Disability rights advocates have also attempted to accredit the idea that disability is not intrinsic but socially determined, in that it is created by the inadequate environment, with insufficient accommodations. According to Asch, 'most of the problems associated with having a disability stem from discriminatory social arrangements that are changeable, just as much of what has in the past made the lives of women or gays difficult has been the set of social arrangements they have faced'.[188] The analogy seems far-fetched and unhelpfully sugarcoating reality. Some conditions are so disabling that no adjustments can allow the individual to function well in society. The equal treatment and the recognition of the equal worth of people with disabilities should not translate into a hypocritical claim that disability is mere diversity and that being born with a disability is desirable.[189] Scott has highlighted this simple reality: 'No-one has an interest in acquiring mental or physical impairments.'[190] A person is not reducible to their illness, and the value attached to them does not detract from the fact that illness is, on any account, undesirable. This is not to say that a life with a serious disability is not worth living; rather,

185 Gilbar, 'Between Unconditional Acceptance and Responsibility', 335. See also Rubin and Phillips, 'Infertility and Assisted Reproduction Technologies', 187–188: 'For disability rights advocates, technologies such as PGD, as well as earlier prenatal diagnosis, have the potential to devalue the lives of individuals with genetic differences.'

186 Ruth Deech, 'Family Law and Genetics' (1998) 61(5) *Modern Law Review* 697–715, at 713.

187 Buxton, 'Unforeseen Uses of Preimplantation Genetic Diagnosis', 121.

188 Asch, 'Prenatal Diagnosis and Selective Abortion', 113–114.

189 See also Holm, 'Ethical Issues in Pre-implantation Diagnosis', 184: 'Despite the political correctness lobby and its attempt to force the view upon us that there are no disabled people but only differently abled people, there can be little doubt that some conditions are actually disabling in any realistically conceivable human society. It is disabling to be blind and deaf at the same time, and no amount of re-description can change that.'

190 Scott, 'Choosing between Possible Lives', 170.

assessed comparatively, a life free from impairments offers a better quality of life, and it is reasonable (and indeed natural) for parents to prefer it for their children. As Wilkinson has suggested: 'all other things being equal, when faced with a choice between creating a child with a higher quality of life and one with a lower (but nonetheless positive) quality of life, we ought to choose the one with the higher quality of life'.[191] Wilkinson has emphasised the distinction between the assessment of the disability and of the person with disabilities: 'There is nothing wrong with assigning a negative value to the functional impairment aspects of disability and this negative valuation of impairment does not entail and need not be accompanied by any negative valuation of the person with the impairment.'[192] He has also pointed out the absurd consequences of the expressivist argument: if we value disability as much as non-disability, this principle 'entails that we should not seek to cure people when they acquire disabilities, and certainly should not use public resources to do so, because this would suggest that disability is less valuable than non-disability'.[193]

Moreover, the interests of existing individuals with disabilities cannot be taken so far as to deny the interest of future individuals in the promotion of their health at the conception stage. Scott has convincingly argued that any 'offence' caused to disabled people by PGD selection is justified in cases where otherwise a child has no chance at a reasonable quality of life, or his/her impairments have a significant adverse effect on the parents' lives.[194] When all the rights at stake are put into balance, the rights of the future child and of his/her parents to a higher quality of life and the avoidance of emotional distress greatly outweigh any abstract interest that the disabled may have in restrictions promoting a different social message; the latter are much more indirectly affected by the law's approach to PGD. Since genetic screening techniques exist and greatly benefit future children and prospective parents, whereas the lack of choice has life-altering results, the burden is on the proponents of obstacles to PGD use to adduce compelling reasons, other than the discomfiture at speculative abstract implications of permissive laws. As with prenatal testing and therapeutic abortion – given the limited assistance of PGD against a small number of illnesses, as well as the non-congenital nature of many disabilities – the claim that PGD will reduce public

[191] Wilkinson, *Choosing Tomorrow's Children*, 97.
[192] Ibid., 166.
[193] Ibid., 163.
[194] Scott, 'Choosing between Possible Lives', 173.

investment in medical research and social adjustments for the disabled appears entirely unfounded.

4.4 THE RIGHT TO A BESPOKE CHILD?

4.4.1 *Social Sex Selection through PGD and Prenatal Testing*

While PGD is currently used for negative selection against serious impairments, other controversial uses include the choice of the baby's sex and preimplantation tissue typing for the purposes of creating a 'saviour sibling' for an existing sick child; there is also a vast speculative debate about its potential future use for the positive selection of certain preferential features.[195] Although positive selection inspires less sympathy for the parents, Robertson has noted that, 'because the embryo is so rudimentary in development, selection for less serious reasons should be less objectionable than screening of fetuses for those same reasons'.[196]

In some cases, sex selection may be motivated by a desire to avoid the transmission of a genetic disease inherited only by male or female offspring (e.g. certain forms of cancer but also late-onset illnesses). Since it targets illness, *medical* sex selection is governed by the same general considerations on PGD, examined in the previous sections. This section focuses on *social* sex selection, that is, selection for non-medical reasons, where the parents wish to achieve family balancing (already having numerous children of one sex), or make up for the loss of a deceased child of that gender, or simply exercise preference (especially when they need to choose from equally viable and healthy embryos the maximum number allowed for implantation). Gilbar has explained the usual roots of requests for sex selection: 'Parents who want to choose the sex of their fourth or fifth child may have good reasons. . . . They may want to experience bringing up a child of a different sex. . . . They may believe . . . [it] will enrich their familial relationship and family life and will contribute to the emotional development of their existing children.'[197]

While there is no international case law on this issue, in principle, social sex selection falls within the parents' autonomy rights. In relation to prenatal testing and abortion on the ground of the baby's sex, Jackson has noted that 'unease about sex-selective abortion does not justify derogating from the basic principle that a competent adult ought to be entitled to make her own

[195] On the distinction between negative and positive selection, see ibid., 163.
[196] Robertson, *Children of Choice*, 156.
[197] Gilbar, 'Between Unconditional Acceptance and Responsibility', 333.

decisions about what happens to her body'.[198] She further argues that the termination of female foetuses in certain cultures (e.g. India and other South Asian countries), based on the devaluation of women, cannot be cured through bans on abortion: 'Sex-selective abortion may be a particularly emotive symbol of entrenched sex inequality, but it makes little sense to tackle sex-selective abortion in isolation from the other social, economic and legal practices that devalue women's lives.'[199] Cook et al. have pointed out that many of the causes of devaluation of girl children (e.g. economic burdens associated with their marriage, lack of employment, etc.) are human rights violations in themselves, and 'to claim that prohibition of sex-based abortion is sufficient to remedy these human rights violations is unrealistic'.[200] These authors also make the interesting point that societal gender imbalance may be self-correcting in the long run: 'gross imbalance in birth rates between male and female children might over time create a scarcity value in girl children as potential brides and mothers of their children as to show prevailing sex-selection practices to be a short-lived phenomenon not justifying repressive laws'.[201]

While preference for sons might be typical of some parts of the world, it is also important to note that in European countries the demand for sex selection does not disclose embedded discrimination against women and does not pose a risk of gender imbalance in the population. Buxton has indicated that fears of societal gender imbalance are not borne out by empirical studies and case law; the overwhelming majority of families interviewed in a UK survey wished to be able to use sex selection in order to ensure an equal number of boys and girls in the family, rather than exercising a preference for one gender, and two couples notoriously litigating the right to sex selection in the UK sought embryo selection for family balancing reasons.[202] For the same considerations, Richards has similarly suggested that a change in the overall sex ratio of British society would be unlikely to occur if couples' preferences as to the sex of the children could materialise.[203] Savulescu and Dahl have also noted that, in the Western world, the demand for sex selection comes from couples who already have two or more children of the same sex and wish to have at least one child of the opposite sex; 'since their choice is simply based on the gender of already existing children, and not on the absurd assumption that one

[198] Jackson, 'Abortion, Autonomy and Prenatal Diagnosis', 479.
[199] Ibid., 487.
[200] Cook et al., *Reproductive Health and Human Rights*, 368.
[201] Ibid.
[202] Buxton, 'Unforeseen Uses of Preimplantation Genetic Diagnosis', 126–127.
[203] Richards, 'Which Children Can We Choose', 202.

sex is “superior” to another, the claim that these couples are making a sexist choice is an unjustified accusation’.[204] The family balance motivation and the comparable frequency of choices in favour of girls and boys mean that the practice of sex selection cannot be seen to contribute to gender discrimination in society.[205]

From a rights discourse perspective, restrictions on procreative autonomy in order to promote gender equality fail to achieve their goal. Evidence shows that the practice of male selection continues on the black market in countries where there is a gender bias, and it has been suggested that this will be the case as long as the roots of inequality remain unaddressed; moreover, women will adapt their reasons to request an abortion to fit the normative framework (in the same way that English patients do in relation to the well-being ground in the Abortion Act 1967).[206] Restrictions on the exercise of a right that are incapable of achieving the legitimate aim pursued breach ECHR obligations, as indicated by the Strasbourg Court in *B. and L.* v. *The United Kingdom*.[207] The same principle should arguably apply to measures obtaining trifling and incremental benefits for society and therefore too remotely connected with the legitimate goal pursued. Colin Farrelly has rightly pointed out that, even if equality and gender balance are important aims, this is not a sufficient reason to prohibit the non-medical use of PGD; in fact, ‘one must also make a compelling case that restrictions on reproductive freedom are reasonable means for pursuing these reasonable aims’.[208] John Harris has perceptively suggested that the correct approach is to allow sex selection and revise the policy if severe gender unbalance in the population or other unforeseen harms emerge.[209]

Gilbar has expressed concern that allowing social sex selection might open a floodgate.[210] It is not clear that opening a floodgate – that is, the possibility of requests for other specific traits – is either an ethical problem or a distinct

[204] Julian Savulescu and Edgar Dahl, ‘Sex Selection and Preimplantation Diagnosis: A Response to the Ethics Committee of the American Society of Reproductive Medicine’ (2000) *Human Reproduction* 1879–1880, reprinted in Kuhse et al., *Bioethics*, 141–143, at 142.

[205] Ibid.

[206] See Jackson, ‘Abortion, Autonomy and Prenatal Diagnosis’, 486–487.

[207] See *B. and L.* v. *The United Kingdom*, App. No. 36536/02, 13 September 2005, [38] (finding that a restriction on the marriage between former parents-in-law and children-in-law did not prevent the formation of intimate relationships and any ensuing confusion for children raised by the couple).

[208] Colin Farrelly, ‘Preimplantation Genetic Diagnosis, Reproductive Freedom, and Deliberative Democracy’ (2009) 34(2) *Journal of Medicine and Philosophy* 135–154, at 152.

[209] John Harris, ‘No Sex Selection Please, We’re British’ (2005) 31 *Journal of Medical Ethics* 286–288, at 288.

[210] Gilbar, ‘Between Unconditional Acceptance and Responsibility’, 333.

prospect in practice. Not many parents would face the costs, physical pain and medical risks (ova collection being an actual surgical procedure) in order to go through PGD and IVF just to secure a child of a certain sex or with eyes of a certain colour (if this were achievable). As Deech has noted, given the low chances of pregnancy from an IVF procedure (approx. 15 per cent), 'it is a procedure to be resorted to only by those who are very anxious indeed about the future health of their embryo and prepared to risk a much lower chance of becoming pregnant than would occur naturally, in order to avoid an inheritable disease'.[211] For Farrelly, considering the invasive and expensive nature of the procedures involved, it is unlikely that equality and gender balance would be compromised by permitting non-medical uses of PGD, and therefore it makes more sense to adopt a provisional permissive attitude and re-evaluate issues if there are significant changes in the costs of PGD and what it can achieve.[212]

Criticising the weight attached by the UK's Human Fertilisation and Embryology Authority to the widespread hostility to sex selection as a justification for its rejection, Harris has deftly stressed that the democratic presumption is that a practice should be allowed, unless the State can show that its prohibition is necessary to prevent harm, and a ban based merely on public opinion is 'to formalise the tyranny of the majority'.[213] He has also recalled that, in a liberal democracy, the majority is not allowed to decide what religion others are to follow, 'because we rightly regard such matters as issues of personal liberty and fundamental rights'.[214]

One of the objections to sex selection, according to a survey conducted in the UK, is that it is 'unnatural' and amounts to 'playing God'.[215] The outdatedness of this argument has been considered earlier in relation to PGD in general; suffice it to recall that a heart transplant is also unnatural and a way of playing God by extending life beyond natural possibilities. Nor are all things unnatural morally wrong and a valid reason to prohibit conduct; harm to society or resulting children would need to be proven. A further argument reported in the literature is that 'sex selection involves a diversion of (scarce and expensive) medical resources for nonmedical purposes'.[216] This is obviously inaccurate if the treatment is privately paid for. Any elective surgery can be seen as diverting from medical purposes, yet such procedures are not illegal; the extent to which

211 Deech, 'Family Law and Genetics', 698.

212 Farrelly, 'Preimplantation Genetic Diagnosis', 152–153.

213 John Harris, 'Sex Selection and Regulated Hatred' (2005) 31 *Journal of Medical Ethics* 291–294, at 294.

214 Ibid., 293.

215 Richards, 'Which Children Can We Choose', 201.

216 Ibid., 202.

they should be financed by public funds is debatable; however, as long as there is demand and supply of such services on the private market, a legal ban is unjustifiable on the basis of scarcity of resources.

No case has been recorded in Strasbourg case law (or indeed in the practice of other international human rights bodies) concerning sex selection, whether therapeutic or social. It is worth noting, however, that the Council of Europe, in Article 14 of the Oviedo Convention on Human Rights and Biomedicine, has taken a firm stand against non-therapeutic sex selection: 'The use of techniques of medically assisted procreation shall not be allowed for the purpose of choosing a future child's sex, except where serious hereditary sex-related disease is to be avoided.' This makes the prospects of successful litigation in Strasbourg asserting parents' right to choose the sex of the future child highly unlikely.

4.4.2 *Tissue Typing and the Creation of 'Saviour Siblings'*

Another controversial use of PGD is pre-implantation tissue typing for the purposes of creating a 'saviour sibling', that is, the selection of an embryo that is not only free from diagnosable diseases but also a potential cord blood stem cell donor for a seriously ill sibling.[217] The main objections against the saviour sibling phenomenon could be seen as pertaining to the 'protection of morals' (the principle against treating human beings as means) and 'rights of others' (the future child's emotional well-being). As Semon et al. have explained:

> The main ethical arguments against are that a child is being used as a treatment, hence breaching the Kantian imperative that a person should never be used as a means. Furthermore, how will the child feel when they are told that they were made for the purpose of saving a sibling?[218]

However, as Wilkinson has pointed out, 'in order to fall foul of the Kantian anti-instrumentalization principle, parents must treat children solely or merely as means'; moreover, 'the having of children for selfish reasons that are nothing to do with the interests of the (possible, future) child is ubiquitous'.[219]

[217] See Buxton, 'Unforeseen Uses of Preimplantation Genetic Diagnosis', 114–115. Buxton recalls the first known case, recorded in the USA in 2000, which allowed a young girl suffering from Fanconi's anaemia (a rare blood disease affecting the bone marrow) to receive a blood stem cell transplant from her brother's umbilical cord, with a remarkable health improvement.

[218] Sermon et al., 'Preimplantation Genetic Diagnosis', 1636.

[219] Wilkinson, *Choosing Tomorrow's Children*, 138. See also Richards, 'Which Children Can We Choose', 212: 'there are many other circumstances in which children are conceived for a wide variety of reasons, or inadvertently'. It has not been established that children of unplanned pregnancies feel unwanted.

A related moral objection is that against medical interventions carried out for the benefit of a third party rather than the patient; however, Merle Spriggs has noted that the objection is associated with invasive, risky or inconvenient procedures, whereas taking stem cells from the umbilical cord poses no risks or inconvenience to the baby.[220] Buxton also emphasises that, if a child is loved and valued, 'it is of no consequence that it is *also* a source of donor tissue'.[221] In addition, Buxton criticises the inconsistency of a legal system, on the one hand, allowing parents to terminate pregnancies if the foetus is not a correct tissue match but, on the other, preventing the use of PGD for tissue typing,[222] an argument reminiscent of the *Costa and Pavan* assessment of PGD prohibition coupled with the availability of abortion of foetuses suffering from cystic fibrosis. Also seemingly inspired by the need for ethical consistency is Robertson's claim that, if PGD is acceptable for the prevention of a serious genetic disease in the offspring, additional uses such as HLA matching with an existing sick child should also be deemed acceptable.[223] Robertson further argues that the parents' treatment of a child born as a saviour sibling is unaffected and no harm arises for the child:

> Although helping an existing child is a motivating factor in having an additional child, such a reason alone is not likely to make the parents ignore the needs of the new child. With stem cells available from umbilical cord blood no further intrusions on the new child will occur. Its birth might save the life of an existing, loved child, which would only increase its specialness. If the stem cell transplant fails, the parents will have a surviving child to love.[224]

On the other hand, criticism of PGD and HLA matching often targets the fact that it involves the intentional creation of embryos that will not be transferred to the uterus, despite being healthy, which raises the issue of the embryo's moral status. In this regard, Robertson et al. have pointed out that this occurs in all IVF procedures:

[220] Merle Spriggs, 'Is Conceiving a Child to Benefit Another against the Interests of the New Child?' (2005) 31 *Journal of Medical Ethics* 341–342, at 342.

[221] Buxton, 'Unforeseen Uses of Preimplantation Genetic Diagnosis', 121 (original emphasis).

[222] Ibid., 129.

[223] Robertson, 'Extending Preimplantation Genetic Diagnosis', 471. Interestingly, he supports most extensions of the use of PGD save for the selection of the sex of the first child.

[224] See ibid., 468: 'PGD has also been used to enable a family with a child with Fanconi anaemia to have another child who would serve as a source of haematopoietic stem cells obtained from that child's umbilical cord blood. . . . Without a stem cell transplant, the first child is likely to die. Non-sibling matches, even if available, are not nearly as safe and effective as sibling donations.'

> Even in basic IVF, as performed to help infertile couples have children, it is common practice to create more embryos than can be safely transferred to the uterus and to store or eventually discard the rest. This practice is accepted by most people (those with right-to-life views excepted) because it serves the important purpose of promoting pregnancy for infertile persons.[225]

Providing treatment to a sick child is no less worthy of protection than addressing infertility, and if the creation of embryos not destined to grow into a foetus is acceptable for the latter, then there is nothing intrinsically wrong with creating embryos that will not be selected for implantation because they are not a match. Moreover, as Robertson et al. convincingly argue, PGD for HLA matching 'does serve an important, life-affirming social purpose – that of saving the life of a child, reassuring parents that compatible stem cells are available, and preventing abortion'.[226]

Finally, the risk of abuse is sometimes invoked as an argument against tissue typing. David King draws attention to the potential use of the technique for less sympathetic causes: 'many people could benefit medically from matched tissue donation. ... How will we feel when the tissue recipient is not another child, but an adult, maybe a parent or a more remote family member?'[227] Apart from the fact that saving a human life should not be endearing only when a child is at stake, the problem of organ donation exists with independence from HLA typing; any time a child is conceived, he or she may be a potential kidney or bone marrow donor for a relative. Whether the procedure involving donation is authorised depends on the medical and judicial assessment of the case, based on the risks of harm to the donor, the wishes of the child and so on. In the debate over novel uses of PGD, the excessive emphasis on speculative fear of slippery slopes, however palatably packaged under the precautionary principle, risks limiting reproductive autonomy for no sound reason.

4.4.3 *Trait Selection, Genetic Enhancement and Misplaced Equalitarianism*

Jackson powerfully argues that 'it would be a mistake to restrict developments that can indubitably improve the lives of families that are at a risk of passing on debilitating genetic diseases in order to prevent the entirely speculative and

[225] John Robertson, Jeffrey Kahn and John Wagner, 'Conception to Obtain Hematopoietic Stem Cells', in Kuhse et al., *Bioethics*, 144–151, at 148.

[226] Ibid., 148–149. See also Robertson, 'Extending Preimplantation Genetic Diagnosis', 468: 'Creating and discarding embryos to provide donor cells for an existing child is not a trivial or frivolous use of embryos, and thus is consistent with the special respect that the nonright-to-life position accords to human embryos.'

[227] King, 'Why We Should Not Permit Embryos to Be Selected as Tissue Donors', 153.

inherently unlikely spectre of routine PGD for trivial behavioural traits'.[228] However, it is unclear whether procreative autonomy also extends to less compelling uses of PGD. At present, the ambition to use PGD in order to obtain a child with certain physical attributes, IQ level or artistic inclination remains confined to the realm of science fiction, despite vivid bioethical debates on the desirability of this practice.[229] If this were an option available to parents and they availed themselves of it, it would arguably be an acceptable exercise of their reproductive rights; in fact, it would not pose any risk of harm to those children, to existing children of the family or to anyone else in society. One possible limit would be the creation of embryos destined for destruction merely for the selection of preferential traits, without conferring any discernible benefit to the future child.

Although the 'playing God' objection is at its strongest when parents choose traits rather than avoiding illness, Richards rightly notes that it is difficult to justify the rejection of enhancement-oriented selection on the basis of its 'hyperagency' while at the same time accepting medical techniques 'to repair damaged bodies, to replace defective genes or select out the abnormal', which involve the same attempt to recreate nature.[230] Nonetheless, the pursuit of a child reflecting specific expectations is often referred to through 'the pejorative terminology of "designer babies", which implies the making of ethically unacceptable reproductive choices'.[231]

Even though intelligence, attractiveness and good moral character are not ascribable to one particular gene, and therefore embryo selection cannot guarantee such traits, more modest eugenic enterprises are possible, such as

[228] Jackson, *Regulating Reproduction*, 247.

[229] Ilana Löwy, 'ART with PGD: Risky Heredity and Stratified Reproduction' (2020) 11 *Reproductive Biomedicine & Society Online* 48–55, at 49, notes: 'Numerous articles in bioethics journals have discussed the risk of use of PGD for "enhancement" of qualities of future children, a risk which – to the author's knowledge – has not materialized to date. Even in countries where this approach is totally unregulated, there are no signs of the use of PGD to promote the birth of "designer babies"'. Richards, 'Which Children Can We Choose', 203, explains that there are no biomarkers available to allow the selection of high intelligence, physical attractiveness or a certain personality type: 'Differences in these characteristics depend on the outcome of very complex developmental systems involving interactions of many genes and all sorts of other elements in a system operating in variable environments.' For an overview of the types of enhancement potentially achievable through genetic technologies and related ethical problems, see Jonathan Anomaly, *Creating Future People: The Ethics of Genetic Enhancement* (New York and Abingdon: Routledge, 2020).

[230] Richards, 'Which Children Can We Choose', 204.

[231] Hazel Biggs, 'The Quest for a Perfect Child: How Far Should the Law Intervene?', in Kirsty Horsey and Hazel Biggs (eds.), *Human Fertilisation and Embryology: Reproducing Regulation* (London: Routledge-Cavendish, 2007) 1–14, at 12.

the US-based high-IQ sperm bank 'Repository for Germinal Choice' established in the 1970s.[232] Should donors, aspiring parents and the medical facility be prevented from this enterprise in the name of equality and aversion against anything eugenic? Information on the appearance of the donor (height, eye colour) is routinely disclosed by sperm banks, and the prospective parents can choose based on the preference for a physical attribute; preference for intelligence should not be treated any differently. The choice of gametes from a high-IQ male for insemination cannot be seen as different from the same choice in the context of natural reproduction (a partner is often chosen to procreate with for his or her intelligence); these are individual pursuits that do not harm others and are private choices as opposed to a State-orchestrated programme for the combination of individuals with high IQ to improve the species.

One objection in connection with trait selection is that it would create injustice by giving children born with ART-facilitated desirable traits an upper hand on other individuals. This argument is problematic. The human being is in constant pursuit of self-improvement. Virtually everyone strives to defeat the natural lottery of birth and achieve the best available version of themselves. Elective surgery to improve one's physical appearance is fairly common and neither contested nor banned. We also make relentless efforts to defy natural processes such as disease and ageing, through vaccination, prophylaxis and treatment, and this is generally considered to be a positive contribution of science and technology to human life and to society at large. Yet, moral objections are raised to seeking to alter some of these natural processes in our offspring *before* they commence, by improving genetic heritage rather than rectifying problems emerging after birth. The validity of the ethical distinction between what we currently and routinely do in an attempt to control nature and what ART has the potential to allow us to do is elusive. Rather, technological novelty in the sphere of human reproduction appears to be met with the instinctive fear of the unknown, and, as Somsen has observed, 'fear alone does not justify the elevation of the status quo as policy objective'.[233]

There may be, in addition, a certain reluctance to accept that the human being should be able to decide which life is preferable, by selecting the embryos for implantation based on their health and, possibly, traits. However, avoiding disease and extending life expectancy are seen as desirable objectives. If one has the technological ability to secure a healthier, longer or happier life for one's child through embryo selection at the conception stage rather than mitigating problems after the birth, exercising that option seems to

232 Gillian Douglas, *Law, Fertility and Reproduction* (London: Sweet and Maxwell, 1991), 202.
233 Somsen, 'Regulating Human Genetics', 87.

be eminently sensible. Nor should one be apologetic about aspiring towards improvement, either as an individual or as a society. The mere fact that health and education are recognised as human rights is already a powerful message that valuing health and the ability to learn is acceptable and need not be concealed. As Wilkinson has noted: 'there is nothing wrong with sending out the message that we ... prefer to create future populations with more rather than less health and welfare'.[234]

While the term 'eugenic' is often employed with derogatory anxiety, an important distinction was drawn by Glover in respect of gene selection between private choice and State-regimented agenda: 'We are right to be frightened by the dangers of any state eugenic programme. Positive choices of characteristics should be left to parents, subject to some possible "public-interest" regulation of the options available.'[235] According to Wilkinson, 'the main reason for thinking of "eugenics" as a negative moral term is that most people who use it in contemporary debates do so to express condemnation, and it is rare for people who support embryo selection to describe it as "eugenic"'.[236] Legal bars will always carry a negative connotation; thus, Article 3(2)(b) of the EU Charter of Fundamental Rights (protecting the right to the integrity of the person) enshrines 'the prohibition of eugenic practices, in particular those aiming at the selection of persons'. Without clear definitions and contextualisation, misunderstandings about eugenics are likely to be perpetuated.

Moreover, one would be hard-pressed to accept the distinction between non-relational good enhancement and positional enhancement, or the assumption that therapeutic selection is to be treated differently from enhancement;[237] for example, better health, although intrinsically desirable, is also a positional enhancement to the extent that it allows, say, mobility, which might be important in applying for a job, or indeed the ability to work long hours. Similarly, the assumption that height is necessarily a positional good is flawed; there are jobs for which height is desirable, and other jobs for which height plays no role or, indeed, it may be more convenient to be short

[234] Ibid., 181.

[235] Glover, *Choosing Children*, 87.

[236] Wilkinson, *Choosing Tomorrow's Children*, 158.

[237] For a definition of positional goods, see I. Glenn Cohen, 'What (If Anything) Is Wrong with Human Enhancement; What (If Anything) Is Right with It' (2013–14) 49 *Tulsa Law Review* 645–688 at 651: 'Absolute goods are desirable even if they became universally available, while positional goods are desirable only because others are deprived of them. Most traits, though, are mixes of positional and absolute goods, in that they are sought to confer positional advantage and because they have absolute benefit.'

(e.g. to be a ballerina). Enhancement sceptics also list appearance as a positional enhancement, but that presupposes that we all agree as to what is a better appearance, whereas aesthetical standards differ greatly. It is impossible to say for a couple who would like to choose traits such as blue eyes in their future child that they target a positional good, as their preference does not amount to objectively 'superior' traits. The assumption that certain traits are a relational good is, thus, an expression of prejudice. To legitimately restrict human rights, one needs more than mere speculation about what everyone perceives as desirable and an absolute advantage, and different traits arguably carry with them a different comparative advantage; certain jobs require physical strength, other jobs good memorisation skills, and so on. All individuals are valued precisely because of their different contributions to society, and therefore trait selection cannot be said to harm individuals with other skills. Human rights law provides protection for autonomous choice unless there is clear detriment to others.

Even for indubitably desirable traits, the concern that the use of genetic technology will engender inequalities between individuals is not a convincing objection against its use. As scholars have pointed out, human beings are already endowed differently in terms of physical strength, intellect or aptitudes, and natural inequality is not conducive to inequality of rights. In her critique of George Annas' thesis,[238] Fenton argues that the biological differences among human beings 'do not undermine the universality of human rights'; on the contrary, 'it is the very purpose of human rights to render all human individuals equal *regardless* of such differences'.[239]

Not only are physical, intellectual and aptitudinal inequalities unavoidable, but society does not seem to think that boosts to the immune system (vaccination), memory (lecithin pills, vitamins), body build (fitness programme, swimming pool) or beauty (elective surgery) go against social equality, albeit they are by no means equally available. As Robertson has pointed out, parents' discretion in rearing children already includes enhancing physical attributes and educational abilities through means not available to all (special tutors, training camps, orthodontia, administration of growth hormones), and there is no rationale to exclude prenatal enhancement from parental choice.[240] If the 'positional good' argument had any validity, middle-class parents would be

[238] George Annas, *American Bioethics: Crossing Human Rights and Health Law Boundaries* (Oxford: Oxford University Press, 2005), 37.

[239] Elizabeth Fenton, 'Genetic Enhancement: A Threat to Human Rights?' (2008) 22(1) *Bioethics* 1–7, at 6 (original emphasis).

[240] Robertson, *Children of Choice*, 164.

prevented from sending their children to expensive private schools because education is a positional advantage. To view any improvement in a child's life as harm to someone else on the basis of competitive advantage (i.e. harm to others who lag behind due to financial disparity) would be an unacceptable width of the notion of harm. Only active and direct harm to others ought to be seen as amounting to harm in a Millian sense and justify restriction upon individual autonomy.

Invoking distributive justice as an objection to the choice of traits, because enhancement is not financially available to all, is no different from saying that, given the unequal access to medical treatment for diseases, the law should prohibit it for all, to avoid people of limited means being disadvantaged when compared to wealthy people; if no medical treatment is available, everyone has the same chance, based on genetic lottery, to overcome illness or not. If society accepts that medical treatment must not be banned, although not everyone can afford it, genetic enhancement should also be permitted. Spurious radical equalitarianism blocks progress by requiring a race to the bottom. Running water and heating are not available everywhere, and downwards equalisation means those should be abolished too. It further means that the law could impose the standardisation of every asset available to purchase, for example, car size, so that, in case of collision, neither of the parties has a better chance of avoiding harm; equal access to road safety would justify banning large-sized cars such as SUVs. Overemphasised equality would also justify abolishing private property and banning high-end fashion, for example, by placing a cap on the price of clothes. Accepting equalitarianism as superior to human rights would also lead us to conclude that a criminal system based on fines for minor misdemeanours is morally wrong, because fines have little or no impact on rich citizens, whereas their full punitive force is felt by impecunious offenders; we would possibly have to concede that all crimes should be punished with deprivation of liberty, because only this would penalise everyone equally: unlike wealth, freedom is equally distributed. But then everyone would be worse off. In the same vein, if unequal access to a good is seen as justifying a ban on scarce goods, judicial remedies should be abolished, too, because access to court requires costly legal representation, and not everyone can obtain redress. Admittedly, there is always an initial stage when a new technology is expensive and may not be available to all. When they were first introduced, flatscreen TVs were a luxury many could not afford. The same occurred with personal computers and mobile phones. Today's society would be quite different if the development of communication technology had been obstructed by concerns that it gave an unfair advantage to some. Equality-driven objections to enhancement lead to absurd ramifications, depriving society as a whole of some of its most important achievements.

Similarly unconvincing is the objectification-of-the-child argument against trait selection, which views parents' ability to 'manufacture' children with desired traits as depriving children of agency. Parents make personal choices for their children in the early stages of their development, including on medical treatment, religious practice and educational pursuits, and this is not seen as affecting the child's agency. Rather, this is inherent in parental prerogatives, in turn an inevitable consequence of the fact that children lack the capacity to make certain decisions for themselves. Parents' right to mould the child's personality in accordance with 'their own religious and philosophical convictions', protected by Article 2 of Protocol 1 to the ECHR,[241] cannot be seen as 'commodifying' children, even though it is intended to satisfy the parents' expectations and preferences. Genetic interventions such as the choice of traits would be just another aspect of parents' endeavour to protect the child's welfare; as Robertson has suggested: 'Enhancement could be seen as an act of love and concern, rather than a narcissistic effort to make the child a product or commodity.'[242] Indeed, trait selection serves the same purpose as selection against disability, which is giving the child the best chance at a fulfilling life.[243] Glover aptly notes that the same rationale justifying selection against disability also legitimises genetic enhancement, namely the desire to allow children to flourish to the best of their potential: 'making some enhancements may add to flourishing as much as eliminating some disabilities'.[244] Wilkinson has also criticised the artificial nature of the distinction between negative and positive selection, insofar as the positive feature selected is the absence of the negative feature screened out, that is, 'selecting *out* low(er) intelligence ("negative eugenics") might be the same practice as selecting *in* high(er) intelligence ("positive eugenics")'.[245]

The concerns about the routine and/or frivolous use of PGD by aspiring parents also seem grossly exaggerated. As Buxton has pointed out: 'Given the

[241] See Art. 2 of Protocol 1: 'the State shall respect the right of parents to ensure such education and teaching in conformity with their own religious and philosophical convictions.'

[242] Robertson, *Children of Choice*, 166. See further 167: 'As long as they are safe, effective, and likely to benefit offspring, they would not more impermissibly objectify or commodify offspring than postnatal enhancement efforts.'

[243] See Glover, *Choosing Children*, 75–76: 'the case for reducing the incidence of disorders and disabilities is that they are obstacles to people having flourishing lives. … Those who want to defend the medical boundary need to say what is special about medical obstacles to flourishing. What makes them the only candidates for elimination by genetic choices?'

[244] Ibid., 36.

[245] Wilkinson, *Choosing Tomorrow's Children*, 157 (original emphasis).

limited availability, expense and low success rate of PGD, along with the lengthy and invasive nature of the treatment . . . it is highly unlikely that there will ever be much demand from individuals wanting to use the technique for "trivial" reasons.'[246] It should also not be assumed that everyone will want to predetermine the sex of the child, its height or the colour of its eyes; indeed, many parents do not wish to know the sex of the child before its birth, even though this is widely offered.

A more palatable equality-based argument is that States should endeavour to make access to ART more accessible by reducing its costs. The debate should not focus on banning trait selection but on whether genetic enhancement is so fundamental a good that it deserves public funding, in the interest of making it available to all. Since no such positive obligations exist at present in relation to medical treatment and educational opportunities, it is difficult to justify a claim to public funding for genetic enhancement; however, the same negative obligation currently governing parental choice of improvements through medical treatment and education should be recognised.

4.4.4 *'Intentional Diminishment': Future Children's Welfare as a Limit to Parental Choice*

The reverse aspect of parental choice concerns the (less likely) case of parents choosing to influence the child's genetic make-up in such a way as to have a child born with the same disability as them – a phenomenon known as 'intentional diminishment', by contrast with offspring enhancement. [247] The literature has reported the astounding case of a deaf lesbian couple in the USA selecting a man with hereditary deafness as sperm donor to deliberately conceive a deaf child.[248] Naturally, for people suffering from congenital disabilities, it is difficult to appreciate what future children are deprived of (someone born in a prison would not value freedom, and someone living before the discovery of electricity would not be frustrated by its absence). Those who never possessed the sense of hearing are unable to appreciate the wealth of experiences it offers (sounds of nature, music, human voices) and the way in which it facilitates everyday life (e.g. crossing the street); this is not a reason to deny the future child access to all this. As Benatar and Archard have

[246] Buxton, 'Unforeseen Uses of Preimplantation Genetic Diagnosis', 112.

[247] The term is borrowed from Robertson, *Children of Choice*, 170.

[248] See Merle Spriggs, 'Lesbian Couple Create a Child Who Is Deaf Like Them' (2002) 28 *Journal of Medical Ethics* 283. The author notes that not only did the couple go to great lengths to obtain a deaf child, but they also denied the child a hearing aid, which the doctors believed could help with learning English if used at an early age.

noted, the parents' interest in the child being a member of their linguistic community (which may include the sign language community) must be weighed against the children's interests in participating in the broader society in which they live; thus, if Spaniards in England not only taught their children Spanish but also prevented children from learning English, this would 'close off important options' for those children.[249]

Glover has defended the choice of the deaf lesbian couple claiming that their child was not harmed, because, had they used a different donor, a different child would have been born.[250] Applying this logic, a woman who knowingly has intercourse with a man suffering from a serious sexually transmissible disease – as a result of which the child is born, for example, HIV-positive – did not harm the child, as that particular child would never have been born. If Glover's analysis were correct, claims for 'wrongful birth' brought by the children themselves would need to fail.[251] Parents choosing the child to be born with a disability can be said to have harmed the child by choosing from among potential lives one with the challenges posed by a physical impairment and missing out on an enriching experience and opportunities; the pregnant woman's lifestyle can be said to harm the future child if it causes the foetus to be born with alcohol- or drug-related problems. The question in deciding if parental choice has harmed the child is not whether the child's life is so horrific that not being born would have been preferable, but whether the mother's conduct deliberately chose a less advantageous life for the child, or the 'but for' test. In the deaf lesbian couple's case, but for the women's choice of a sperm donor with hereditary deafness, the child would have had a chance to be born with all senses intact. Genetic choices – actions or omissions – can harm the future child just as much as abuse or negligence, during the pregnancy or after birth, resulting in permanent handicap.

Some bioethicists find it difficult to explain the moral wrongfulness of decisions affecting future children given that, but for those decisions, other people would have been born (better off but non-identical), and therefore

[249] David Archard and David Benatar, 'Introduction', in David Archard and David Benatar (eds.), *Procreation and Parenthood: The Ethics of Bearing and Rearing Children* (Oxford: Oxford University Press, 2010) 1–30, at 14.

[250] See Glover, *Choosing Children*, 23: 'Their son, Gauvin, has not been harmed by what they did. If they had not sought out a donor with hereditary deafness, they might have had another child who was not deaf. But Gauvin himself would not have existed.'

[251] See the recent decision of the UK High Court in *Toombes* v. *Mitchell* [2020] EWHC 3506 (QB), recognising that the child herself has a lawful claim for damages for personal injury arising from her disability where the congenital defect with which she was born is ascribable to the defendant's negligent medical advice (*in casu*, failure to advise the mother to take folic acid before her conception).

those precise children have not been harmed; this is known as the 'non-identity problem'.[252] It seems, however, that the question should not be whether the child has been harmed by being brought into existence with certain congenital conditions, by comparison with no existence at all, but whether any conscious decision of the parents has caused the child to experience a worse existence than through genetic lottery. A woman choosing to procreate with a male partner infected with HIV, or choosing a donor exclusively based on his hereditary disease, is harming the future child. An analogy may be drawn with decisions affecting the healthy development of the foetus: the fact that the foetus is better off being born with a disability than not being born at all does not detract from the moral wrongfulness of deliberate conduct causing the future baby to suffer. The pregnant woman who drinks affects the future child even if, but for the willingness of the alcoholic woman to carry the pregnancy to term, the child would not have been born. It also cannot be said that the midwife who delivers the baby, albeit negligently causing a neurological impairment for the rest of the child's life, did not harm the child because without her intervention the child would not have been born at all. As Deech and Smajdor note, for some the non-identity problem can be resolved by saying that 'the person has been harmed if, on balance, his or her life is not worth living', although 'the problem of quantifying suffering' 'yields no obvious answers'.[253] This approach, however, downplays the moral wrongfulness of deliberately depriving the child of a significantly better quality of life.[254] Robertson has more convincingly argued that 'the parents should have no greater right to produce that handicapping condition by prenatal genetic alteration just because they would not otherwise bring the child into the world'.[255] He also points out that 'not providing a cochlear implant that might overcome a mild form of congenital deafness' would constitute child

[252] Russell DiSilvestro, 'Reproductive Autonomy, the Non-identity Problem, and the Non-person Problem' (2009) 23(1) *Bioethics* 59–67, at 59–60, discussing Derek Parfit, *Reasons and Persons* (Oxford: Oxford University Press, 1984), 359. Robertson, *Children of Choice*, 170, refers to this as 'the paradox of harm and nonexistence', that is, the idea that it is in the best interests of a child to be created in a lesser form than not at all. See also David Boonin, *The Non-identity Problem and the Ethics of Future People* (Oxford: Oxford University Press, 2014).

[253] Deech and Smajdor, *From IVF to Immortality*, 50.

[254] Where concerns over the impact of procreative decisions on the welfare of the future child have been incorporated in human fertilisation legislation, the non-identity problem is largely superseded. For instance, the UK's Human Fertilisation and Embryology Act 2008 makes provision for licenced clinics to investigate the welfare of any child born as a result of ART, even though whichever child results from the treatment cannot be said to be worse off because of the authorisation of treatment.

[255] Robertson, *Children of Choice*, 171.

abuse, because 'the child would be denied a treatment for future functioning in society'.[256] Parental decisions affecting the child's normal development and flourishment – whether at the stage of conception, gestation or after birth – warrant public scrutiny and intervention.

The question thus arises whether procreative choices harming the child should be banned, in the same way that choices for living children can be restricted – from medical treatment to education, and from religion to corporal punishment. With natural intercourse, this would not be feasible (e.g. preventing the choice of a partner suffering from syphilis), but the welfare of the future child can be considered when offering ART. In general, the choice of donor should not be precluded, unless the donor is exclusively selected on grounds of hereditary disability or disease. However, in *Dickson* v. *The United Kingdom*, the Strasbourg Court has accepted, in principle, that the welfare of the future child, born to a father serving a long sentence in prison, could legitimately limit his right to reproduce.[257] Parental choice needs to be respected before and after conception/birth, but it must find a limit in the future child's welfare, and therefore it cannot extend to deliberate genetic diminishment. Article 24 of the UN Convention on the Rights of the Child, which recognises 'the right of the child to the enjoyment of the highest attainable standard of health',[258] includes an obligation to safeguard the child's health when placed at risk by his or her carers; arguably, this provision could be read to require States to also give the child the best prospects of a healthy life by offering protection against harm at the conception stage, where harm depends on the authorisation of medical assistance.

Trait selection aimed at improving the child's welfare cannot be seen as a selfish, consumerist choice; conversely, trait selection that sacrifices the child's welfare to the parents' convenience (e.g. to have a deaf child like them for better communication and belonging to the same community) breaches parental duties of care and is not worthy of protection. In the same way that courts can authorise treatment beneficial for the child despite the parents' opposition, as well as deny authorisation of treatment sought by the parent because it is deemed harmful to the child, prenatal choices need to remain subordinated to the 'best interests of the child' principle. There is a certain symmetry between, on the one hand, respect for parental prerogatives in

[256] Ibid.

[257] See *Dickson* v. *The United Kingdom* [GC], App. No. 44362/04, 4 December 2007. See further Chapter 2, Section 2.1.1.

[258] Convention on the Rights of the Child, New York, 20 November 1989, in force 2 September 1990, UNTS vol. 1577 (p. 3).

relation to child upbringing without tolerating child abuse and, on the other, respect for procreative choice without permitting exercises of discretion that result in harm for the future child.

4.5 CONCLUDING REMARKS

This chapter has argued that the development of international human rights law in Europe has laid the foundations for an emerging new right to a healthy child or, more accurately worded, a right to gain access to the available medical technologies so as to maximise the chances of having a child free from severe illness or disability. Naturally, limits to the realisation of this right are bound to arise from the availability of technology and public resources, as well as the limited number of illnesses and disabilities detectable through (pre-implantation or prenatal) genetic testing. Nevertheless, growing case law suggests that there is a strong negative component to this right: to the extent that a medical service facilitating the fulfilment of this right is available domestically (prenatal testing/PGD coupled with IVF), the ability to use it must not be unreasonably restricted by law or hindered in practice. This right has developed more slowly than other aspects of procreative freedom, such as the use of contraceptives or artificial insemination.[259] However, the ECtHR has now determined, in a unanimous landmark judgment, that the desire to have a healthy child is protected by Article 8 as an expression of private and family life.

This chapter has examined a number of objections to the use of scientific advances to improve reproductive health and autonomy. Some pertain to the 'morals' exception (the 'human dignity' objection to destroying/choosing among embryos, the Kantian objection to producing saviour siblings as a means to save another); some invoke the 'rights of others' (the expressivist argument against negative selection of embryos/foetuses and other disability rights concerns). All of these objections, albeit centred around reasonable aims, underplay the principle of proportionality. The competing interests adduced to restrict prospective parents' autonomy are of lesser magnitude when compared to the impact of the interference on those directly affected by it. Such are, notably, the unease of disabled people with State support for the pursuit of disability-free offspring, and the moral unease of sections of the public with genetic manipulation, in particular the negative selection of

[259] See Richards, 'Which Children Can We Choose', 218: 'we can see long historical struggles over the boundaries of "natural" reproduction, as in the case of contraception. It has taken almost a century to bring what was once called "artificial birth control" into the realm of everyday taken-for-granted social practice.'

embryos and foetuses. Restrictions to the exercise of autonomy are particularly difficult to justify in relation to PGD and embryo selection, given the different stages of development of the embryo and the foetus, respectively; it is the consensus of international human rights bodies that the degree of protection expected varies with the degree of development of human life. Restrictions motivated by abstract principles that have a concrete, deleterious impact on a person's life (inability to produce a healthy child, compulsion to raise a disabled or severely ill child) have no place in a liberal democratic society.

Admittedly, a general entitlement to the provision of prenatal testing or PGD has not yet been clearly established in European human rights law, insofar as the applications brought before the Strasbourg Court did not present an opportunity to address such rights dispositively. The cases have revolved, rather, around issues of access to prenatal testing guaranteed by domestic law (*R.R.* v. *Poland*), lack of adequate redress for erroneous prenatal diagnosis (*A.K.* v. *Latvia*; *Draon* v. *France*; *Maurice* v. *France*) or the restriction of PGD to certain categories of beneficiaries (*Costa and Pavan* v. *Italy*). However, the case law unequivocally confirms that the denial of access to ART aimed at securing a healthy child, whether in law or in practice, interferes with Article 8 rights and requires justification. Even in an area of wide State discretion such as bioethics, domestic legislation must be internally consistent; for example, banning PGD and the selection of healthy embryos, while allowing abortion on foetal abnormality grounds, is a disproportionate interference, in that it does not protect the rights of the prospective mother nor the dignity of health professionals (*Costa and Pavan*). Moreover, any domestic rights conferred with a view to ensuring respect for procreative choices, and specifically the right to pursue a healthy child – for example, genetic testing by default for women of a certain age (*A.K.* v. *Latvia*) – must not be theoretical and illusory. Significantly, they must encompass, inter alia, measures of protection against third-party interference, for example, medical staff hostile to abortion on grounds of foetal abnormality (*R.R.* v. *Poland*).

There is also increasing acceptance in international fora of the need for States to actively enable reproductive choices. As noted in the UNESCO's 'Explanatory Memorandum on the Elaboration of the Preliminary Draft Declaration on Universal Norms on Bioethics', 'respect for autonomy involves not just a respectful attitude but also respectful action'.[260] It is questionable whether the positive intervention required of State authorities extends to subsidised access to PGD, but where the technology is available, a ban is

[260] UNESCO, Explanatory Memorandum on the Elaboration of the Preliminary Draft Declaration on Universal Norms on Bioethics, 2005, SHS/EST/05/CONF.203/4, [61].

arguably unjustified. Negative selection through genetic testing is also strongly connected with the right not to reproduce (in circumstances other than those decided by each individual), a relationship expressly acknowledged in *R.R.* v. *Poland*. According to Strasbourg jurisprudence, the right not to reproduce is as important as the right to reproduce. *Evans* v. *The United Kingdom* firmly established the negative facet of reproductive autonomy when it upheld legislation allowing a person to withdraw consent to the use of embryos created with their genetic material up until the moment of implantation. If the destruction of embryos is justified by a person's right not to become a parent after they had a change of heart (the *Evans* scenario), it is also justified when it prevents compelling a person to become a parent in circumstances they reject (i.e. when having a child with disability is incompatible with the person's procreative aspirations). Moreover, Robertson has pointed out that, since individuals have a general right not to reproduce, because of the physical, psychological and social burdens of reproduction, so too there must be a right to reject reproduction because of the specific burdens that a particular reproductive outcome entails; this supports the right to make selection decisions through either embryo screening or prenatal testing.[261] Wilkinson has similarly noted that 'if we believe in the moral optionality of parenting in cases … where disability and disease are not at issue, then we should surely believe that the moral optionality of parenting applies a fortiori to cases … where the decision is whether or not to have a child with a serious genetic disorder'.[262] Under Article 8 ECHR, individuals have a right to decide whether their self-fulfilment requires having children, and this encompasses a right to decide if they are prepared to have children with disabilities.

As times and technologies evolve, human rights inevitably follow suit. Access to internet while in detention has become a human right,[263] although

[261] Robertson, *Children of Choice*, 152.

[262] Wilkinson, *Choosing Tomorrow's Children*, 182.

[263] In *Arslan and Bingöl* v. *Turkey*, App. Nos. 47121/06; 13988/07; 34750/07, 18 June 2019, the Court held that, by denying the use of a computer and internet access to prisoners, the Turkish authorities breached their right to education. Previously, access to websites had been accepted as subsumed under the right to freedom of expression (specifically the right to *receive* information). In *Kalda* v. *Estonia* (App. No. 17429/10, 19 January 2016), the ECtHR found that, while States are not obliged to grant prisoners access to internet, if a State is willing to allow prisoners access, it must give sufficient reasons for refusing access to specific websites. The right to receive was also found engaged when the State blocked access to certain websites, although applications failed for lack of 'victim' status (see *Akdeniz* v. *Turkey*, App. No. 20877/10, 11 March 2014); see Carmen Draghici and Lorna Woods, 'Killing Journalists Is Not Media Regulation: Private Rights, Collective Wrongs and the Impact of Impunity' (2019) 28 (2) *Transnational Law and Contemporary Problems* 263–306, at 272.

a few decades ago it would not have featured in anyone's pyramid of needs, let alone generate an enforceable claim. At present, parental autonomy can be said to include the right to choose to have a child without a *preventable* disability. Objections to the development of a right to a child free from preventable disabilities, which benefits the child, the family and society, are based on misconstrued non-discrimination concerns; they also appear inspired by an instinctive fear of changing the course of human life by allowing individuals to predetermine destinies. When access to genetic technology increases and costs decline, the recognition of the pursuit of healthy offspring as an essential component of procreative choice is likely to give rise to more prescriptive obligations under human rights law.

5

The Quest for Reproductive Equality

The Challenges of Sexual Orientation, Gender and Civil Status

5.1 REPRODUCTIVE RIGHTS BEYOND HETERONORMATIVITY AND COUPLEDOM

Non-traditional family units have gradually expanded their quest for the law's stamp of approval through international human rights adjudication. In particular, the European Court of Human Rights (ECtHR) and the former European Commission on Human Rights have examined requests concerning same-sex cohabitation and succession to tenancies,[1] the legal recognition of same-sex couples' familial association (whether through access to marriage or existing civil partnership regimes or the creation of an alternative institution),[2] challenges to the ineligibility of homosexual cohabitants for social benefits (such as the extension of sickness insurance to the partner[3] or survivor's exemption from inheritance tax)[4] due to the absence of avenues to formalise a committed long-term same-sex relationship, as well as applications targeting the higher financial liability for child support contributions for a non-resident parent living with a same-sex, as opposed to a heterosexual, new partner.[5] The UN Human Rights Committee has also been called upon to assess, through the lens of the International Covenant on Civil and Political Rights, same-sex couples' ineligibility for marriage;[6] the exclusion of long-term

[1] See *Röösli* v. *Germany*, App. No. 28318/95, 15 May 1996 (Commission); *Karner* v. *Austria*, App. No. 40016/98, 24 July 2003; *Kozak* v. *Poland*, App. No. 13102/02, 2 March 2010.

[2] See *Schalk and Kopf* v. *Austria*, App. No. 30141/04, 24 June 2010; *Vallianatos and Others* v. *Greece* [GC], App. Nos. 29381/09; 32684/09, 7 November 2013; *Oliari and Others* v. *Italy*, App. Nos. 18766/11; 36030/11, 21 July 2015; *Fedotova and Others* v. *Russia* [GC], App. Nos. 40792/10; 30538/14; 43439/14, 17 January 2023.

[3] See *P.B. and J.S.* v. *Austria*, App. No. 18984/02, 22 July 2010.

[4] See *Courten* v. *The United Kingdom*, App. No. 4479/06, 4 November 2008.

[5] See *J.M.* v. *The United Kingdom*, App. No. 37060/06, 28 September 2010.

[6] See *Joslin and Others* v. *New Zealand*, Communication No. 902/1999, 30 July 2002.

same-sex cohabitants, unable to opt into marriage, from economic entitlements associated with marital status;[7] as well as the prohibition of access to divorce proceedings for same-sex couples married abroad, in circumstances where divorce was available to parties in other unrecognised marriages (polygamous/underage marriages).[8] The issue of long-term same-sex cohabitees' right to a survivor's pension was raised equally under the American Convention on Human Rights.[9] In its advisory capacity, the Inter-American Court has also advanced the right of same-sex couples to equality before the law more broadly (establishing States' obligation to guarantee access to all the mechanisms available in domestic law, including marriage, to ensure the protection of the rights of families composed of same-sex couples without discrimination).[10]

Shared parenthood claims arose as a natural continuation of same-sex couples' incremental success in asserting a right to the formalisation of committed cohabitation. As Dorothy Greenfeld and Emre Seli have noted: 'in recent years a growing recognition of same-sex unions as culturally and socially acceptable has led inevitably to a parallel acceptance of such unions as a foundation for family'.[11] Pleas for a departure from heteronormativity in the understanding of conjugality[12] were followed by attempts to secure the recognition of two parents of the same sex, initially through step-parent adoption and subsequently through the acquisition of parental status for jointly planned children.[13]

7 See *Young* v. *Australia*, Communication No. 941/2000, 6 August 2003; X v. *Colombia*, Communication No. 1361/2005, 30 March 2007.

8 See C. v. *Australia*, Communication No. 2216/2012, 28 March 2017.

9 See *Duque* v. *Colombia*, Report No. 5/14, Case No. 12.841 (Merits), 2 April 2014. Some of the current LGBT claims in the inter-American system reflect concerns addressed a few decades ago in ECHR jurisprudence, for example, challenges to the criminalisation of homosexual activity in *Henry and Edwards* v. *Jamaica*, Report No. 400/20, Case 13.637 (Merits), 31 December 2020, and *T.B. and S.H.* v. *Jamaica*, Report No. 401/20, Case 13.095 (Merits), 31 December 2020; equal treatment in *Alvarez Giraldo* v. *Colombia*, Report No.122/18, Case No. 11.656 (Merits), 5 October 2018 (equal right to intimate visits in prison for lesbian inmates).

10 IACtHR, Advisory Opinion on Gender Identity, Equality, and Non-discrimination of Same-Sex Couples, OC-24/17 (2017).

11 Dorothy Greenfeld and Emre Seli, 'Assisted Reproduction in Same Sex Couples', in Mark Sauer (ed.), *Principles of Oocyte and Embryo Donation* (London: Springer-Verlag, 2013) 289–301, reprinted in Helga Kuhse, Udo Schüklenk and Peter Singers (eds.), *Bioethics: An Anthology* (Chichester: John Wiley and Sons, 2016, 3rd ed.) 74–85, at 74.

12 For a discussion of international claims to the formalisation of same-sex relationships and access to benefits associated with marriage/heterosexual cohabitation, see Carmen Draghici, *The Legitimacy of Family Rights in Strasbourg Case Law: 'Living Instrument' or Extinguished Sovereignty?* (Oxford: Hart, 2017) 187–223.

13 See Section 5.2.

Litigation in the Strasbourg Court has also seen the emergence of single-parent families by design, first in the context of foreign adoption,[14] and more recently in relation to procreation.[15] In fact, the advent of assisted reproduction treatment (ART) has made the choice to become a parent without being part of a couple, and more specifically a heterosexual couple, a scientific possibility. Insemination with donor sperm and the creation of embryos in vitro with donated gametes permit single women and women living with a partner of the same sex to start a family. In addition, surrogacy arrangements, based either on the artificial insemination of the surrogate mother (traditional surrogacy) or on ova donation and in vitro fertilisation (gestational surrogacy), allow single and homosexual men to become biological fathers. However, the law has accommodated these options only in a number of jurisdictions.[16] According to the Rainbow Index (Europe) 2022 published by the International Lesbian, Gay, Bisexual, Trans and Intersex Association (ILGA), in Europe fifteen States permit medically assisted insemination for homosexual couples, twenty-eight permit medically assisted insemination for singles, and automatic co-parent recognition in same-sex couples accessing fertility treatment is provided for in only ten States (Austria, Belgium, Denmark, Ireland, Malta, The Netherlands, Portugal, Spain, Sweden and the UK).[17] The purpose of this chapter is to inquire, in light of the judicial practice registered to date, whether there are any prescriptive obligations under international human rights law (and specifically under the European Convention on Human Rights [ECHR]) to allow single men and women or same-sex couples to have recourse to ART in the pursuit of parenthood aspirations.

This chapter will consider, on the one hand, if individuals seeking to become biological parents in the absence of a partner of the opposite sex, or of any partner at all, have arguable rights to the provision of medical assistance

[14] See *Wagner and J.M.W.L* v. *Luxembourg*, App. No. 76240/01, 28 June 2007 (discussed in Chapter 3, Section 3.3.2), where an adoptive mother successfully challenged the refusal of her country of origin – which only permitted adoption by couples – to recognise the foreign adoption. However, the basis for the decision was not an ECHR entitlement to sole adoption, but the need to protect de facto family life and the child's best interests. While *E.B.* v. *France* [GC], App. No. 43546/02, 22 January 2008, required States not to discriminate against prospective adopters based on, inter alia, their sexual orientation, there is no authority, to date, to suggest that a difference in treatment based on relationship status (predicated on the assumption that orphaned children are better off in two-parent households) violates Art. 8 taken together with Art. 14.

[15] See Section 5.4.

[16] In the UK, the law makes it possible for a child to have a second female parent (ss. 42–44 Human Fertilisation and Embryology Act 2008). Two same-sex parents (male or female) are also possible by virtue of parental orders following surrogacy arrangements (s. 54 Human Fertilisation and Embryology Act 2008).

[17] See ILGA Europe Rainbow Index 2022, available at www.ilga-europe.org/report/rainbow-europe-2022/ (accessed 23 November 2022).

to procreate. On the other hand, it will examine any rights flowing from joint same-sex parenthood projects and benefitting the partner who lacks biological ties with the child. It is, in fact, an immutable biological reality that a same-sex couple can only have common children genetically related to one member of the couple, even if both partners are fertile. Studies have shown that, in order to accommodate both partners' wish for a biological connection to the child, male couples using surrogacy sometimes prefer to have an equal number of donor eggs fertilised with each partner's sperm and two embryos, created with their respective gametes, transferred into the surrogate's womb, which can result in twins who are half-siblings.[18] Similarly, female couples sometimes resort to what is known as 'mutual IVF', whereby one of the partners contributes her ova to the creation of the embryos and the other carries the pregnancy and gives birth to the child;[19] this allows both women to form a connection, either genetic or gestational, with the child, although legal motherhood is ultimately allocated to one or the other depending on the applicable law.[20] From the viewpoint of same-sex family building, in which both partners wish to act as parents, but only one can contribute to the genetic make-up of the future child, granting access to biological parenthood through ART to one partner without recognising the legal parenthood of the other is unsatisfactory. Moreover, gaining legal parenthood in relation to a child – rather than limited guarantees for the stability of the family unit, for example, a residence/physical custody order or a parental responsibility/legal custody order (domestic terminology may vary) – is important to those concerned on multiple levels. As Fatemeh Ebtehaj has explained: 'kinship ties are central in the acquisition and circulation of material and symbolic resources, and in their transmission to future generations. Such resources include names, identity and cultural affiliation, property, and social status.'[21] The way in which public policy recognises kin relationships has a deep impact on selfhood, on the sense of belonging to a family and on perceptions of social acceptance. In their capacity as 'structurally infertile' couples,[22] same-sex couples have therefore aspired to emulate kin relationships not just in a functional sense but also in the eyes of the law.

[18] See Greenfeld and Seli, 'Assisted Reproduction in Same Sex Couples', 76.

[19] See ibid., 79.

[20] In the UK, s. 33(1) Human Fertilisation and Embryology Act 2008 treats the woman who carried the child as the legal mother (even if another woman's ova were used to produce the embryo).

[21] Fatemeh Ebtehaj, 'Introduction: Regulating Relationships?', in Fatemeh Ebtehaj, Bridget Lindley and Martin Richards (eds.), *Kinship Matters* (Oxford: Hart, 2006) 1–16, at 5.

[22] The term 'structural infertility' is borrowed from Michael Boucai, 'Is Assisted Procreation an LGBT Right?' (2016) *Wisconsin Law Review* 1065–1125, at 1110.

Single aspiring parents face comparable hurdles to achieving parenthood, in that they are unable to procreate without the law's authorisation of gamete donation and, for some, surrogacy (all men, as well as women who cannot carry a pregnancy). In jurisdictions where access to these techniques is available, but restricted to (married) couples, unless such policies are adequately justified, single persons may be unfairly excluded from reproductive treatment (i.e. from healthcare provision, as well as the enjoyment of measures of protection of private and family life). The discussion of civil status in this chapter will subsume cohabitation to marriage/civil partnership for the purposes of family formation. In fact, to the extent that it confers rights and obligations (including, in some jurisdictions, legal standing to apply for adoption or for an order vesting parenthood in the applicant following assisted reproduction with donor or surrogacy), cohabitation can also be seen in contrast with 'single' status. Given the somewhat different legal issues that access to parenthood raises for male couples, female couples and single aspiring parents, the chapter will address their respective positions separately. A common theme running through the following sections, however, is the spectre of discrimination in the enjoyment of reproductive rights on ground of sexual orientation, gender or civil status.[23]

5.2 ASSISTED CONCEPTION FOR SAME-SEX COUPLES

5.2.1 *Donor Insemination and the Recognition of the Second Female Parent*

Studies have shown that common motivations in all same-sex couples choosing assisted reproduction over adoption include the wish to raise a child from birth and have a biological connection; in addition, however, female couples often choose it due to one partner's desire to experience pregnancy and

[23] The principle of non-discrimination is firmly rooted in human rights law. Art. 14 of the European Convention on Human Rights and Fundamental Freedoms (ECHR), Rome, 4 November 1950, in force 3 September 1953, ETS No. 5, reads: 'The enjoyment of the rights and freedoms set forth in this Convention shall be secured without discrimination on any ground such as sex, race, colour, language, religion, political or other opinion, national or social origin, association with a national minority, property, birth or other status.' See also Protocol 12 to the ECHR, Rome, 4 November 2000, in force 1 April 2005, ETS No. 177; Art. 2(2) International Covenant on Economic, Social and Cultural Rights, New York, 16 December 1966, in force 3 January 1976, UNTS vol. 993 (p. 3); Art. 2(1) and Art. 26 International Covenant on Civil and Political Rights (ICCPR), New York, 16 December 1966, in force 23 March 1976, UNTS vol. 999 (p. 171); Art. 1(1) American Convention on Human Rights (ACHR), San José, 22 November 1969, in force 18 July 1978; Art. 2(1) African Charter on Human and Peoples' Rights, Banjul, 27 June 1981, in force 21 October 1986, O.A.U. Doc. CAB/LEG/67/3/Rev. 5.

childbirth.[24] Unlike male same-sex partners, generally female couples do not depend on the legal availability of surrogacy for gestation and only need gamete donation to be able to conceive. What further distinguishes the two sets of couples is that sperm donation and artificial insemination are less ethically controversial and technically complex than ova donation and embryo implantation. Relatedly, the assisted reproductive techniques (ARTs) required by female couples are not strictly reliant upon State support, and they are indeed difficult to prevent in practice through regulatory obstacles. In fact, two women can enter into an informal agreement with a man prepared to act as a sperm donor; the artificial insemination procedure does not necessitate expert medical assistance, nor does it have to be performed in a medical establishment.[25] Nevertheless, the couple's parenthood project remains dependent on the law's cooperation for the recognition of legal ties between the non-biological 'intentional' mother and the child. The legal recognition of the non-genetic mother has not only symbolic but also practical significance, from the viewpoint of both the child and the adults concerned:

> The legal sanction provided by second-parent adoption accomplishes the following: second-parent custody rights are protected should the legal parent die; protects second-parent rights to custody should the couple separate; establishes the requirement for child support from both if the couple separates, ensures the child's eligibility for health benefits from both parents; gives both parents the legal right to make medical decisions for their children; and creates the basis for financial security in the case of the death of either parent.[26]

The questions arising under international human rights law are (1) whether States are required to grant female couples access to donor insemination, followed by the recognition of parental status for the spouse/partner of the woman undergoing treatment, on the basis of a joint parenthood project ('access rights'); and (2) whether States have an obligation to accommodate family units created by female couples with a donor informally, without medical assistance, or abroad, within a permissive regulatory framework ('protection rights'). Subsidiary questions in relation to protection rights are (1) whether the ART-born child's welfare is better served by giving the child only one legal parent at birth (the biological mother) and (2) whether step-parent adoption is adequate to safeguard the child and the couple's interests.

[24] Greenfeld and Seli, 'Assisted Reproduction in Same Sex Couples', 81.

[25] For an example see *C.E.* v. *France*, App. No. 29775/18, 24 March 2022 (available only in French), discussed later.

[26] Greenfeld and Seli, 'Assisted Reproduction in Same Sex Couples', 80–81.

One common objection to permitting donor insemination for female couples is that it deliberately creates fatherless children, although the practical consequences for children's development or sense of identity are disputed. According to Lydia Bracken, 'there is a growing body of research that shows that the absence of a father does not impact negatively upon children in circumstances where they are raised by two loving mothers'.[27] Naturally, in jurisdictions allowing the treatment of single women with donor sperm and single-person adoption, the objection that creating fatherless children is inconsistent with the future child's welfare is insufficient to justify the exclusion of female couples from ART; other private or public interests pertaining to the attribution of legal parenthood or identity rights would have to be adduced. Similarly, if adoption by same-sex couples is permitted in a particular jurisdiction, the restriction of access to donor insemination and dual legal parenthood for female couples is more difficult to justify, although the analogy between adoption and assisted reproduction with donor has clear limitations. In fact, a distinction can be drawn between the benefits of the child-oriented liberalisation of adoption laws (maximising the available pool of adopters for existing children in need of a family) and the adult-oriented assisted reproduction legislation, which seeks to fulfil parenthood aspirations rather than address the problem of orphans and children taken into public care. Adoption and assisted reproduction with donor, albeit both being routes to non-biological parenthood, may be differently regulated to the extent that they serve different social purposes.

In respect of States' negative obligations, an active interference with a woman's reproductive autonomy may be said to arise if access to donor insemination is refused, compounded by prima facie discriminatory treatment if the refusal is based on her civil status or sexual orientation (e.g. if the law reserves treatment to women in a heterosexual relationship/marriage).[28] More difficult to establish is a positive obligation to enable the creation of legal ties between the woman's ART-born child and her female partner, with whom she intended to found a family. Particularly contentious is the obligation to recognise legal affiliation since birth, grounded in the couple's *intention* alone, as opposed to second-parent adoption, in which intention is corroborated by de facto *care* and the law ratifies and protects *existing family units*. This section will explore the extent to which international case law has accommodated either of these claims: access rights (to donor insemination and

[27] Lydia Bracken, *Same-Sex Parenting and Best Interests* (Cambridge: Cambridge University Press, 2020) 182.

[28] The position of single women is considered in Section 5.4.

parenthood for the non-genetic intentional mother) and/or protection rights (for the family life already created by a female couple and the child born to one of them through DIY artificial insemination with donor sperm or medically assisted insemination abroad).

Since the 1990s, the ECHR monitoring bodies have had an opportunity to consider the allocation of legal parenthood/parental authority for children conceived through artificial insemination with donor and raised by same-sex female couples. Initially, the Strasbourg position was ambivalent and largely deferential to States. In *Kerkhoven and Hinke* v. *The Netherlands*,[29] the Commission was called upon to consider a woman's alleged right to recognition as a parent in relation to the child born to her life partner through assisted fertilisation with donor sperm, in circumstances where both women had assumed a parental role since the child's birth. The Commission conceded that the impossibility of establishing legal ties between the child and the de facto carer could adversely affect the child's position in the event of her biological mother's death or the breakdown of the adults' relationship.[30] However, the Commission was not prepared to find a positive obligation for the State to afford parental rights to a woman who was not the child's biological mother.[31]

Much of the applicants' case hinged on the fact that the impugned Dutch legislation allowed a man to formally recognise a child as his own, whether or not the child was genetically related to him, thereby also gaining parental authority; conversely, a woman could not recognise a biologically unrelated child and establish legal ties with another woman's child, and there was, thus, no avenue for obtaining parental authority in relation to such a child. The applicants asked the Commission to find that the law discriminated on the basis of sexual orientation, since unmarried men could establish legal ties with non-biological children through the act of formal recognition. It was held that, 'as regards parental authority over a child, a homosexual couple cannot be equated to a man and a woman living together'.[32] The qualification 'as regards parental authority over a child' appears to emphasise that the decision was not based on a (negative) evaluation of same-sex cohabitation; rather, it accommodated fundamental assumptions about parenthood in Dutch society, namely that a child can only have one parent of each sex, consistent with

[29] *Kerkhoven and Hinke* v. *The Netherlands*, App. No. 15666/89, 19 May 1992 (Commission).

[30] Ibid., [1].

[31] Ibid.

[32] Ibid. The fact that the child had been born out of wedlock played no role in the analysis; indeed, the Commission referenced the earlier recognition in *Marckx* v. *Belgium* (App. No. 6833/74, 13 June 1979) that Art. 8 covered illegitimate families.

the reality of natural reproduction. The decision reveals an attachment to a biology-inspired parenthood paradigm rather than scepticism towards same-sex parenthood. In other words, the Dutch rule allowed a man to recognise a child who was otherwise fatherless, thereby restoring the natural parental dyad. The bar on the recognition by a woman of another woman's child stemmed from the fact that the mother's position was not vacant.

At the same time, although the Commission described the relationship between the parties as falling outside the scope of the notion of 'family life', it also indicated that the impugned legislation 'd[id] not prevent the three applicants from living together as a family'. This suggests that an *active* interference with the ability of the female cohabitants and the child born to one of them through ART might run counter to Convention rights. Because the regulation of parenthood and parental responsibility is concerned not only with the adults' rights but also with the superior interests of children born through assisted reproduction, the focus of the Strasbourg analysis understandably shifted away from the alleged discrimination aspect of the claim.

The broader understanding of the notion of 'family life' after *Schalk and Kopf* v. *Austria* in 2010,[33] which brought same-sex cohabitation within the sphere of 'family life', did not automatically trigger a reconsideration of parenthood; this notion remained anchored in the complementarity of one mother and one father, in accordance with natural procreation. The case of *Gas and Dubois* v. *France*,[34] decided in 2012, faced the Court again with the question of same-sex couples' right to joint parenthood for ART-born children. On this occasion, the Court held that two women who had cohabited for a long time, had formed a civil partnership and were bringing up together a child conceived by one of them by means of assisted reproduction constituted a family within the meaning of Article 8. In the couple's State of residence, medically assisted procreation using an anonymous donor was available only to infertile opposite-sex couples, and the applicants had resorted to treatment in Belgium. Significantly, the fact that the applicants' recourse to ART abroad was contrary to domestic law did not preclude a finding that Article 8 applied to the case. However, this finding appears inspired by the reality of childcare arrangements, rather than indicating support for intentional parenthood in female couples (although the parties were formal civil partners and long-term life partners at the time they planned to found a family). Indeed, in X v. *Austria*, the Court also found the notion of 'family life' applicable to a situation where a woman had raised her female partner's child from an early

[33] See *Schalk and Kopf* v. *Austria*, [94].

[34] *Gas and Dubois* v. *France*, App. No. 25951/07, 15 March 2012.

age, without having participated in the planning or conception of the child; in fact, the child had not been conceived with donor sperm and had been formally recognised by his father.[35]

Disappointingly, in *Gas and Dubois*, the Court accepted the respondent's argument that adoption by the other social parent would have the automatic effect of divesting the natural parent of her parental status, which ran against the child's interests.[36] Instead of querying the rationale of this automatism and the approach to sexual orientation in the regulation of step-parent adoption of donor-conceived children, the Court dismissed a complex debate on a technicality. For the Court, the fact that French legislation did not provide for ART for same-sex couples meant that the applicants' situation was not comparable to that of opposite-sex couples availing themselves of treatment and seeking the recognition of parental status for both members of the couple.[37] Consequently, the fact that adoption by the same-sex partner had the effect of depriving the mother of her own parental rights, in circumstances where adoption by a heterosexual partner left the mother's rights unaffected, did not breach Article 8. The Court could have arguably applied its reasoning in *Emonet* v. *Switzerland*:

> 'Respect' for the applicants' family life required that biological and social reality be taken into account to avoid the blind, mechanical application of the provisions of the law to this very particular situation for which they were clearly not intended. Failure to take such considerations into account flew in the face of the wishes of the persons concerned, without actually benefiting anybody.[38]

The factual similarity between the two cases is notable. In *Emonet*, a domestic rule entailed the automatic severance of the legal relationship between a

[35] See X *and Others* v. *Austria* [GC], App. No. 19010/07, 19 February 2013, [95]–[96]. The judgment found that a stable same-sex cohabiting couple and the child of one of the partners from a previous relationship that they raised jointly formed a family within the meaning of Art. 8 ([95]–[96]). The Court also concluded that the exclusion of a same-sex partner from second-parent adoption, while that possibility existed for unmarried different-sex partners, was not necessary for the protection of the traditional family or for the protection of the child's interests, and hence was discriminatory ([151]).

[36] *Gas and Dubois* v. *France*, [62].

[37] This analysis does not seem to distinguish between step-parent adoption for same-sex civil partners and same-sex couples' access to ART followed by the recognition of legal parenthood for both parties. A more helpful question would have been whether disallowing step-parent adoption legitimately sought to prevent same-sex couples from circumventing the bar on access to donor insemination. The discussion should also have addressed the distinction between parenthood *ab initio* and adoption – as they raise different identity issues – as well as between planned children and existing children, because of the different welfare concerns engaged.

[38] *Emonet* v. *Switzerland*, App. No. 39051/03, 13 December 2007, [86].

mother and her daughter as a result of the latter's adoption by the mother's male cohabitant; that rule was found to constitute an interference with the right to respect for family life. In fact, the blunt application of the rule divesting the birth parent of parenthood upon adoption by another did not serve the best interests of the adoptee (a dependent, disabled adult child requiring constant care and emotional support).[39] Analogously, in *Gas and Dubois*, the adoption order, which was sought to enable the two cohabitees and the child to become a family in the eyes of the law, had by default the effect of depriving the birth mother of parental status. By contrast with its position in *Emonet*, the Court accepted that the birth mother's loss of status was the necessary consequence of adoption by a female cohabitee, and hence the interference was justified. Consistency with its previous case law would have required the Court to ask why adoption by the mother's partner necessarily had that effect, as opposed to conferring parenthood on a further person. The apparent reason for the different outcome of these cases lies in the gender of the biological mother's partner. In *Emonet*, the male cohabitant's acquired fatherhood was not seen as intrinsically incompatible with the mother's natural parenthood. Conversely, in *Gas and Dubois*, the adoption order would have resulted in the child having two mothers (or two parents of the same sex, however designated on the birth certificate). The Court could have examined and possibly upheld the rationale of a rule precluding a child from having two mothers. By contrast, the uncritical acceptance of a legal automatism is unsatisfactory and could be explained perhaps by a desire to avoid that more difficult debate.[40]

Equally disappointing is the Court's conclusion that a measure restricting the availability of assisted insemination with donor to infertile heterosexual couples did not raise issues under Article 14 (non-discrimination in the enjoyment of Convention rights) insofar as the applicants, a same-sex couple, were differently situated:

> While French law provides that anonymous donor insemination is available only to heterosexual couples it also states that it is to be made available for therapeutic purposes only, with a view in particular to remedying clinically diagnosed infertility or preventing the transmission of a particularly serious

[39] See ibid., [80].

[40] See *Bonnaud and Lecoq* v. *France*, App. No. 6190/11, 1 March 2018 (available only in French), dismissing a – lesser – claim by a female couple for mutual parental responsibility in relation to their respective children conceived through donor insemination in Belgium. The Court agreed that the assessment by domestic courts of whether the couple met the domestic criteria for mutual delegation of parental responsibility did not disclose a difference in treatment based on sexual orientation; rather, the applicants had not established why the specific circumstances or the children's welfare required the delegation of parental responsibility for each other's child.

> disease. ... Hence, broadly speaking, anonymous donor insemination in France is confined to infertile heterosexual couples, a situation which is not comparable to that of the applicants.

The finding that same-sex couples and infertile heterosexual couples are differently situated is predicated on a narrow view of 'infertility' and of the 'therapeutic purposes' of ART, which overlooks the social infertility of all same-sex couples. While this view is, however, tenable, and it might obviate the need for a discussion of direct discrimination, one would have expected the Court to also consider the potential indirect discrimination embedded in the impugned law. In fact, by limiting donor insemination treatment to cases of infertility and inheritable disease, the law affected same-sex couples much more dramatically. The French assisted reproduction regime may have ultimately been found justified, but the absence of analysis weakens the ruling.

Additionally, the impossibility of adoption in relation to a same-sex civil partner's ART-born child also required further analysis, since legal parenthood following assisted reproduction was not an option. Instead, *Gas and Dubois* continued the oversimplifying approach to 'similarly situated' classes under Article 14 seen in *Manenc* v. *France*.[41] That case regarded the allocation of joint and survivor benefits to spouses, but not to couples having entered into a *Pacte Civil de Solidarité* (PACS). The decision relied on the different status and package of rights and obligations associated with marriage when contrasted to PACS, such as differences under succession and dissolution legislation. The Court was readily persuaded that all civil partners, whether of the same sex or the opposite sex, received the same – less favourable – treatment when compared to spouses (who were the sole beneficiaries of this measure). The analysis did not acknowledge that same-sex couples did not have the option to choose between marriage and civil partnership and, therefore, could not opt into a higher level of commitment in order to access greater benefits. This distinction was brushed away by the reiteration of the principle that eligibility for marriage, in particular the decision whether to extend this institution to same-sex couples, remained within each State's margin of appreciation. While the deference to States in the attribution of status is understandable, a more rigorous examination of the complaint ought to have started from recognising that the exclusion of civil partners from a family benefit, albeit apparently neutral (indeed, it did not target certain PACS specifically), affected same-sex couples with particular force.

The issue of whether the ECHR requires States not to discriminate on the basis of sexual orientation when regulating access to ART returned before the

[41] *Manenc* v. *France*, App. No. 66686/09, 21 September 2010 (available only in French).

Strasbourg Court in 2018 with *Charron and Merle-Montet* v. *France*.[42] The case presented the ECtHR with an opportunity to pronounce on the right of same-sex couples to receive ART, at least in jurisdictions recognising same-sex marriage. The complaint regarded the refusal of hospital authorities to accommodate a married female couple's request for medically assisted reproduction, on the basis that French legislation did not authorise the provision of this type of treatment for same-sex couples. Regrettably, the case was declared inadmissible under Article 35(1) for failure to exhaust domestic remedies.[43] According to the Court, the hospital's decision to reject the applicants' request for access to medically assisted reproduction had been an individual administrative decision, capable of being challenged and set aside on appeal for abuse of authority before the domestic administrative courts, which the applicants had not attempted to do; therefore, the applicants had not used a remedy available to them under domestic law (albeit with limited prospects of success).[44] Highlighting the importance of the subsidiarity principle in a procedural sense, the Court concluded that the applicants had failed to comply with the rule on the exhaustion of domestic remedies and the application could not be entertained.[45]

Nevertheless, the applicants' arguments in the *Charron and Merle-Montet* v. *France* case, relying on Article 8 (right to respect for private and family life) and Article 14 (prohibition of discrimination), as well as the submissions made by the European Centre for Law and Justice (ECLJ),[46] insightfully advanced the debate on the scope of same-sex couples' procreative rights. For the applicants, the situation of a same-sex female couple in relation to artificial insemination with donor was similar to that of a heterosexual couple in which the male is infertile; the refusal to provide treatment, therefore, discriminated against them on grounds of sexual orientation.[47] At the opposite end of the spectrum, the ECLJ's position was that surrogacy and all heterologous

42 *Charron and Merle-Montet* v. *France*, App. No. 22612/15, 16 January 2018.

43 See Art. 35(1) ECHR: 'The Court may only deal with the matter after all domestic remedies have been exhausted, according to the generally recognised rules of international law, and within a period of four months from the date on which the final decision was taken.'

44 See *Charron and Merle-Montet* v. *France*, [21]–[24], [29].

45 Ibid., [18], [30]–[31].

46 See Grégor Puppinck and Priscille Kulczyk, 'Written Observations Submitted to the European Court of Human Rights in the Case *Charron and Merle-Montet* v. *France* (N° 22612/15)', 12 June 2017, available at http://media.aclj.org/pdf/1-WRITTEN-OBSERVATIONS-Charron-and-Merle-Montet-v.-France.pdf (accessed 12 October 2022). The respondent government did not engage with the claimants' substantive submissions but opposed the lack of exhaustion of domestic remedies; see *Charron and Merle-Montet* v. *France*, [12]–[14].

47 *Charron and Merle-Montet* v. *France*, [10].

reproductive technologies amount to a violation of the child's rights under Articles 3 and 8 ECHR; in particular, heterologous fertilisation deliberately deprives the child of a father, which is a 'serious injustice contrary to the dignity and best interests of children and future generations'.[48] The ECLJ also contested the analogy with adoption proposed by the claimants, in that adoption aims to give the child a family, and a single-parent or same-sex family is 'the lesser evil' when compared to being an orphan; therefore, legislation allowing single-person/same-sex couple adoption, but restricting ART (which is concerned with giving a child to a family) to heterosexual couples, was not thought to be intrinsically inconsistent.[49]

After these missed opportunities for the re-evaluation of distinctions based on sexual orientation in the provision of ART, three recent cases have cast light on female couples' right to joint parenthood for existing ART-born children: *Honner* v. *France* in 2020[50] and *C.E. and Others* v. *France*[51] (two applications jointly decided in 2022 – *C.E. and Others* v. *France* and *A.E. and Others* v. *France*). In all these cases, the children had been born through assisted reproduction with donor sperm – either in overseas medical facilities (the *Honner* and *A.E.* situations) or with a friend's help in the country of residence (the *C.E.* case) to same-sex female cohabitees/civil partners, as part of a joint family project – and had been raised by the couple during the first few years of their lives, until the couple's separation. The approach of the Strasbourg Court to these petitions was to acknowledge the existence of family life between the child and the unrelated adult, on the basis of de facto close personal ties.[52] The Court placed particular emphasis on the child being 'the fruit of a parental project' between the two women, on their 'shared life' and on the commitment of the biological mother's partner to the child's rearing and education[53] (during a period of four-and-a-half years in *Honner*, and four and six years, respectively, in the cases conjoined in the *C.E.* judgment). In addition, the concept of 'private life' was also found to extend to emotional bonds developed between an adult and a child in circumstances other than the classic situations of kinship, these bonds pertaining to the individuals' life and social identity.[54] Importantly, the Court recognised that such bonds

48 Puppinck and Kulczyk, 'Written Observations', 8.

49 Ibid., 3.

50 *Honner* v. *France*, App. No. 19511/16, 12 November 2020 (available only in French).

51 *C.E. and Others* v. *France*, App. Nos. 29775/18; 29693/19, 24 March 2022 (available only in French).

52 See *Honner* v. *France*, [50]; *C.E. and Others* v. *France*, [49].

53 See *Honner* v. *France*, [51].

54 See *C.E. and Others* v. *France*, [53].

engage the child's privacy rights as well, affiliation being an essential aspect of identity.[55] Nevertheless, all the applications were ultimately unsuccessful, largely on account of the States' margin of appreciation in striking a fair balance between competing interests. That said, notable concessions were made in the analysis to the legal position of the applicants.

Before exploring those aspects in further detail, two essential distinctions must be noted between *Honner* v. *France* and *C.E. and Others*. The former concerned the denial of *contact* with the child based on case-specific circumstances, otherwise available under the French legal framework,[56] and it *opposed the private interests* of the former partners. The French courts had reversed the contact order due to the tense relationship between the adults, which rendered visitation exchanges traumatic for the child; the Strasbourg Court accepted that domestic courts had acted within their margin of appreciation and had motivated their decision, justifiably giving priority to the child's best interests.[57] By contrast, in *C.E. and Others* v. *France*, both requests sought *legal recognition of the relationship* between the child and the social parent, rather than mere contact, and *the private interests of the parties were in alignment*. Indeed, what is remarkable about the two more recent cases is the success of private ordering, notwithstanding the breakdown of the relationship; in fact, visitation and child support arrangements often require the intervention of courts following acrimonious breakups and the adults' inability to put the children's interests first. Moreover, while previous ART-related applications were brought to the ECtHR by cohabiting couples during the currency of their relationship, in *C.E.* the application was brought jointly by the former partners, and the biological mother also applied on behalf of the child to support the recognition of the social parent.[58] These amicable, child-

[55] Ibid., [53]–[54].

[56] The Court noted that French law allowed a person having developed de facto family ties with a child to apply for judicial orders in relation to the child, so as to secure the preservation of those ties (see *Honner* v. *France*, [58]–[59]). A similar conclusion was reached in *Bortolato* v. *Italy*, App. No. 35967, 10 January 2023, [21] (also regarding attempts to preserve the de facto ties with the children born through donor insemination to a lesbian partner after the couple's separation): Italian law afforded a possibility to persons having developed a familial bond with an unrelated child to maintain contact. As to the discrimination claim, adducing that it was not possible to recognise a child born through ART to a same-sex partner, the Court noted that the applicant had not sought to establish legal ties with the twins since birth, and that a male intended parent would also need either the consent of the biological parent or a judicial declaration of paternity ([25]).

[57] *Honner* v. *France*, [60]–[61].

[58] See *C.E. and Others* v. *France*, [2]. In the *A.E.* case, the former companion held shared parental authority rights and applied on behalf of the child on that basis (see [3]).

oriented private arrangements for financial support and contact post separation stand in stark contrast with the law's slow adaptability to such situations.

In terms of the assessment of the interference, *Honner* remains largely idiosyncratic. The *ratio decidendi* suggests that the outcome of the case was not influenced by the nature of the applicant's relationship to the child, and in particular the absence of genetic or legal ties. However, this invites a comparison with the general approach to private disputes over contact, typically in cases where the applicant complained about parental alienation and the authorities' failure to enforce contact after a hostile separation.[59] Although, in the early Strasbourg case law, the failure to grant or enforce contact in situations of strong opposition from the residential carer was seen as justified by the need to protect the child's welfare,[60] more recent case law has consistently indicated that States must take all practical measures to protect contact with the non-resident parent in the face of third-party obstructive behaviour.[61] While the *Honner* ruling examined the application as a matter of positive obligations to secure respect for family life,[62] it did not clarify whether intended parents of ART-born children who also acted as de facto carers are entitled to the same level of protection and standard of review in child proceedings as biological/legal parents. This involved a more nuanced discussion of what defines a parent and whether the female partner of the woman receiving assisted insemination with donor, whom the law does not recognise as a parent, has lesser rights. Also, nowhere in the judgment is there a reference to the child benefitting from continuing the relationship with the second parental figure (whether or not outweighed by the trauma caused by the unfriendly exchanges); rather, the interests of the mother's former civil partner are seen exclusively in opposition to those of the child.[63]

It is worth recalling that contact with a child is not exclusively a prerogative of parents. Non-parents with a close relationship with the child (e.g. relatives) can apply for visitation and are entitled to a fair trial. To that extent, the *Honner* judgment did not elucidate the expectations raised by the Convention

59 See Draghici, *The Legitimacy of Family Rights*, 266–279, on the ECtHR's treatment of private disputes over residence and contact arrangements.

60 See *Hendricks* v. *The Netherlands*, App. No. 8427/78, 8 March 1982 (Commission); *Jonsson* v. *Sweden*, App. No. 12495/86, 7 December 1987 (Commission).

61 See *Hokkanen* v. *Finland*, App. No. 19823/92, 23 September 1994; *Gudrun Hansen* v. *Turkey*, App. No. 36141/97, 23 September 2003; *H.N.* v. *Poland*, App. No. 77710/01, 13 September 2005; *Lyubenova* v. *Bulgaria*, App. No. 13786/04, 18 October 2011; *Cengiz Kılıç* v. *Turkey*, App. No. 16192/06, 6 December 2011; *Santos Nunes* v. *Portugal*, App. No. 61173/08, 22 May 2012; *Kuppinger* v. *Germany*, App. No. 62198/11, 15 January 2015.

62 *Honner* v. *France*, [52]–[57].

63 See ibid., [65]–[66].

in relation to same-sex parenthood in the context of medically assisted procreation. The *C.E. and Others* v. *France* judgment provided a direct examination of the specific issue of whether States must permit the creation of legal ties (through either adoption or a document attesting de facto enjoyment of civil status) between a woman and the child born through ART to her former same-sex companion and jointly planned and reared. The applications were assessed from the viewpoint of positive obligations to ensure effective respect for private and family life, insofar as they raised the issue of lacunae in French law.[64] The Court accepted that the respondent State enjoyed a wide margin of appreciation, given the ethical questions raised by the cases and the absence of European consensus on the establishment of a legal parent–child relationship between a child and the biological mother's former partner; at the same time, that margin was narrowed in relation to the children's claims, insofar as parent–child relationships engage an essential aspect of individual identity.[65]

As regards family life, the judgment noted that the applicants encountered no difficulties in conducting their family life after the couples' separation; indeed, the State had put in place legal instruments enabling the protection of their social ties (joint parental responsibility and shared custody arrangements, to which both parties consented); this was confirmed by the delay in the women's applications to formalise their relationship with the children (nine years lapsed between the couple's separation and C.E.'s application for adoption in the first case; four years between the dissolution of the civil partnership and A.E.'s application for a declaration of de facto enjoyment of status).[66] In addition, the law entitled family courts – where the child's best interests so required – to make arrangements concerning the relationship between a child and an unrelated person who had resided stably with the child, participated in the child's education, everyday care or accommodation, and had developed lasting emotional bonds with the child.[67] Consequently, the State had not failed in its obligation to guarantee effective respect for family life.[68]

Given the Court's focus on the personal circumstances of the applicants and the impact of the impugned measures on them, it did not address *in abstracto* the question of whether the law offered adequate protection to

64 See *C.E. and Others* v. *France*, [80]–[84], explaining both the Court's choice to examine the case from the angle of positive obligations (notwithstanding the common ground between the parties on the existence of an interference) and the scope of the analysis when compared to negative obligations. See further the discussion in Chapter 1, Section 1.2.

65 See *C.E. and Others* v. *France*, [85]–[89].

66 Ibid., [94]–[95].

67 Ibid., [95].

68 Ibid., [96].

intentional parents whose relationship broke down shortly after the child's birth and hence could not rely on long-term de facto ties through no fault of their own. It is also worth noting that, in all three cases involved in *C.E. and Others* and *Honner*, the long-term care of the children by the intentional non-genetic parents (several years) played a role in the Court's assessment of the quality of the effective bonds. It is not clear whether the relationship between ART-born children and their intentional mother is entitled to protection as soon as the latter starts undertaking an effective parental role, by analogy with the intended mother's position in foreign surrogacy cases.

From the standpoint of private life, the Court distinguished the applicants' position from that of intended parents of surrogacy-born children, who are legal parents in the jurisdictions where treatment was received.[69] The Court conceded, however, that genuine bonds of a filial nature had developed between the children and the mothers' companions, and the impossibility of securing the legal recognition of the parent–child relationship raised a serious issue in relation to the best-interests-of-the-child principle and children's privacy rights.[70] At the same time, it noted the legal mechanisms through which same-sex partners of the genetic mothers could acquire some of the rights associated with parenthood, albeit not parental status, in particular the exercise of joint parental responsibility, with the mother's consent[71] or through recourse to the courts if consent was not forthcoming.[72] The Court was satisfied that those mechanisms resembled, 'to a certain extent', the recognition of the relationship in the eyes of the law.[73] Finally, the judgment noted a recent development in French law, after the applications had been lodged with the Court, which benefitted the *A.E.* case, insofar as it allowed the retrospective recognition of affiliation for children born abroad to same-sex couples;[74] while the *C.E.* situation did not qualify, as conception had taken place in France through DIY artificial insemination, the option of adoption existed, at least after the child had reached majority.[75]

69 Ibid., [100]. This focus on the effective protection of de facto family life, however created, may have the potential to enforce the position of non-biological intended parents in future surrogacy cases and divert the attention from the alleged illegality of their conduct, excessively emphasised in *Paradiso and Campanelli* v. *Italy* [GC], App. No. 25358/12, 24 January 2017 (see Chapter 3, Section 3.3.2).

70 *C.E. and Others* v. *France*, [102]–[104].

71 Ibid., [105].

72 Ibid., [107].

73 Ibid.

74 Ibid., [108], [111].

75 Ibid., [112]. The court appears to be unclear as to whether the adoption while a minor would have been possible without extinguishing the biological mother's parental responsibility.

The timeframe chosen by the Court for the assessment of the impugned law – the Strasbourg decision date as opposed to the date of the applications – is peculiar (albeit already seen in *Schalk and Kopf* v. *Austria*), and it appears based on the view that States responding to the gradual evolution of behaviours and expectations in their society in bioethical matters, and having engaged in a process of reform, cannot be reproached for not doing so earlier, given the lack of European consensus.[76] This choice is negatively affecting the applicants at hand, who do not obtain relief for what might have been a lacuna in the law at the relevant time. However, it does benefit the Court's jurisprudence in general.[77] In fact, the finding that the State had not failed in its obligations was justified by the existence of legal avenues to secure the relationship between the child and the social mother, including routes to acquiring parental status, introduced by the time the case was heard in Strasbourg (retrospective recognition of parenthood for overseas ART-born children/adoption). This suggests, *a contrario*, that, at present, States who offer no mechanisms safeguarding the relationship between a woman and the child born to her (former) partner through ART during their cohabitation/civil partnership/marriage might fall short of Convention requirements.

Although the Court did not require States to grant parental status in such circumstances, *C.E. and Others* v. *France* appears to indicate that legal mechanisms conferring some of the rights associated with parenthood must be available to the non-genetic social parent, even in the absence of consent from the genetic parent and in situations of relationship breakdown. This is an important achievement for female couples' parenthood aspirations. The judgment, albeit concluding that the respondent State had met its positive obligations, is thus deceptively supportive of the advancement of same-sex couples' procreative rights. The acceptance that jointly planned and delivered same-sex parenthood engages both private and family life and the requirement for legislation to protect the relationship between the child and the non-genetic moral author of conception are noteworthy. Another important element is the

76 Ibid., [108]–[110].

77 There is a striking contrast between this approach and the one adopted in *S.H. and Others* v. *Austria* [GC], App. No. 57813/00, 3 November 2011 (discussed in Chapter 2, Section 2.2), where the Court measured the ECHR compatibility of the impugned decision against the ECHR standard applicable at material time (a decade prior to the ECtHR judgment): 'it is not for the Court to consider whether the prohibition of sperm and ovum donation at issue would or would not be justified *today* under the Convention. The issue for the Court to decide is whether these prohibitions were justified *at the time they were considered by the Austrian Constitutional Court*' (ibid., [84], emphasis added). In *C.E. and Others* v. *France*, the Court evaluates domestic law as it stood at the time of the Strasbourg decision, rather than the situation facing the applicants when they instituted proceedings.

Court's explicit reference to the value *to the child* of the relationship with the social parent, albeit not legally recognisable as a parent–child relationship.

A conspicuous limitation of the *C.E. and Others* judgment is that it only imposes obligations vis-à-vis parent–child relationships *already* established via ART (abroad or without medical assistance at home). By contrast, it does not require States to allow access to ART for same-sex couples seeking to found a family within the jurisdiction. By the same token, an important part of the rationale for the decision is based on the identity rights of *existing* children, which do not arise in relation to future children and hence cannot support access-to-ART claims. A parallel may be drawn with the Court's case law on parenthood following foreign surrogacy arrangements: while the relationship between a surrogacy-born child with the biological parent and the other intended parent must be protected, the legalisation of surrogacy is left entirely within the discretion of each State.[78] In *D. and B.* v. *Austria*, a discrimination claim in connection with access to donor insemination followed by joint custody was struck out after legislative reform extended eligibility to same-sex couples.[79] The Court did not clarify whether the reform responded to an ECHR obligation and if the pre-reform scheme was in breach of Article 14 read together with Article 8. It simply noted that the rights sought by the applicants were 'evolving rights with no European consensus established as yet' and therefore States 'enjoy a certain margin of appreciation in the timing of the introduction of legislative changes'.[80]

Interestingly, *C.E.* was the first purely domestic ART case, without a cross-border element, concerning the relationship with an existing ART-born child (as opposed to 'access' cases, e.g., *S.H. and Others* v. *Austria*). In fact, the child was the product of DIY artificial insemination in the country of residence, outside the framework of the law, that is, carried out with the help of a friend acting as donor, all parties agreeing that the women would co-parent the child. This distinguishes the *C.E.* case from the *A.E.* scenario (two women receiving treatment abroad, where the law offered the procreative assistance sought – essentially the *Gas and Dubois* v. *France* matrix); it also distinguishes it from the majority of surrogacy cases heard in Strasbourg to date.[81] Nonetheless, the Court did not hesitate to find Article 8 applicable in both foreign/legal and

78 See Chapter 2, Section 2.4, and Chapter 3, Section 3.3.1.

79 *D. and B.* v. *Austria*, App. No. 40597/12, 31 October 2017.

80 Ibid., [24].

81 *A.L.* v. *France*, App. No. 13344/20, 7 April 2022 (available only in French), and *H.* v. *The United Kingdom*, App. No. 32185/20, 31 May 2022, are rare examples of surrogacy-related complaints involving purely domestic situations.

domestic/'illegal'[82] situations of donor insemination and to require measures of protection for the private and family life of the adults and children concerned. This suggests that the Court might be prepared to uphold obligations in relation to the protection of de facto family life even where it is built outside a permissive legal regime, and possibly even going against express prohibitions.

A final aspect of the 2022 *C.E. and Others* v. *France* ruling worthy of notice is the approach to the alleged discrimination of children born through unregulated assisted reproduction with donor. The Court acknowledged the potential issues, under Article 8 alone or read in conjunction with Article 14, raised by the exclusion of children born in France from the new Bioethics Act, which allowed the (retrospective and prospective) recognition of affiliation between a child born overseas through ART and his/her mother's same-sex companion. However, the Court was hastily dismissive of that possibility, invoking the State's margin of appreciation (however narrow, given the best interests of the minors at stake) and a generic reference to a fair balance being achieved.[83] This analysis is unsatisfactory in its brevity. Once the Court had recognised (in the context of foreign surrogacy) that the best interests of the child require the identification at law of the persons responsible for his or her care and well-being,[84] one would have expected it to investigate whether French law discriminated against some children merely on the ground of their place/circumstances of conception or birth. The Court could have well found that the different treatment pursued a legitimate objective, such as deterring the use of ART by female couples in France, while accommodating, as a *fait accompli*, situations legally created abroad. Even so, the magnitude of the impact of this restriction on the child (and possibly the de facto carer as well) might have outweighed the public interest, unless alternative mechanisms falling short of legal affiliation were deemed sufficient to protect effective private and family life. The absence of any analysis merely on the basis that, in

[82] It is improper to speak of illegality in the case of DIY artificial insemination, because the conduct of the parties cannot be said to breach the law – rather, their arrangement falls outside the assisted reproduction framework and the 'donor' does not qualify as such. Conversely, in cases where the law explicitly prohibits surrogacy, informal surrogacy agreements are a breach of the law.

[83] *C.E. and Others* v. *France*, [113]–[114]. According to Greenfeld and Seli, 'Assisted Reproduction in Same Sex Couples', 83, the literature on same-sex couples and their children born through ART has some limitations (small sample size, predominantly white, urban, well-educated middle- to upper-class subjects); however, 'the consensus is that these families are doing well and that there are no significant differences in the psychological development in children raised by gay families compared to children raised by heterosexual parents'.

[84] See *C.E. and Others* v. *France*, [101].

the specific case before it, adoption had become an option after the child had turned eighteen does not assist with the assessment of the law at the material time and does not contribute to the general understanding of non-discrimination issues in relation to children born to same-sex couples outside a dedicated legal framework.

5.2.2 *The Complex Pathway to Fatherhood in Male Couples: Surrogacy and Ova Donation*

Biology rather than man-made law is the first obstacle to achieving equality in respect of reproductive rights. In fact, male same-sex couples wishing to found a family cannot do so through natural procreation. For such couples, access to assisted reproduction, in particular traditional surrogacy, or gestational surrogacy combined with ova donation, is the only route to attaining biological fatherhood. In its 'General Comment No. 22' (2016), the Committee on Economic, Social and Cultural Rights has highlighted that equality requires the acknowledgement of different reproductive needs: 'Substantive equality requires that the distinct sexual and reproductive health needs of particular groups, as well as any barriers that particular groups may face, be addressed.'[85] Barbara Stark has suggested that the legalisation of surrogacy can be seen as a way of ensuring gay couples' equal right to become a parent.[86] The question arises whether human rights law imposes or should impose any obligations on States to permit practices such as surrogacy agreements and ova donation for the treatment of individuals and couples dependent on them to procreate, inter alia, single aspiring fathers and male same-sex couples.

By contrast to sperm donation, ova donation raises significant ethical concerns;[87] it requires the patient to undergo the risks of an invasive surgical procedure (and of the preceding ovarian stimulation regime) without clinical benefit to herself, which may run counter to the bioethical principles of beneficence and non-maleficence. Further ethical concerns include the difficulty of obtaining genuine informed consent in circumstances where

[85] Committee on Economic, Social and Cultural Rights, 'General Comment No. 22 (2016) on the Right to Sexual and Reproductive Health (Article 12 of the International Covenant on Economic, Social and Cultural Rights)', E/C.12/GC/22, 2 May 2016, [24].

[86] Barbara Stark, 'Transnational Surrogacy and International Human Rights Law' (2011–12) 18 *ILSA Journal of International & Comparative Law* 369–386, at 380.

[87] Ova donation is much more complex than sperm donation and only became a medical possibility a hundred years after the first documented case of donor insemination, which dates back to 1884; see Emily Jackson, *Regulating Reproduction: Law, Technology and Autonomy* (Oxford: Hart, 2001) 165–166.

the risks to the egg donor are unknown and the donor is offered substantial compensation.[88] In addition, objections to any positive entitlement to ova donation can be raised on the basis of *ordre public* and the pre-eminence of the future child's best interests. For instance, it could be adduced that the deliberate creation of motherless children, as opposed to the adoption of abandoned minors by same-sex couples, is both against public policy and inconsistent with the child's welfare. However, for such an objection to avoid discriminatory undertones, the approach to deliberate single parenthood (whether one mother or one father) would have to be consistent.[89] It was, indeed, on this basis that *E.B.* v. *France* was primarily decided: a legal system allowing single-person adoption but not adoption by a single person in a same-sex relationship breached Article 8 taken in conjunction with Article 14 for lack of a cohesive approach to the child's best interests:

> Regarding the systematic reference to the lack of a 'paternal referent', the Court disputes not the desirability of addressing the issue, but the importance attached to it by the domestic authorities in the context of adoption by a single person. ... Her sexual orientation was consistently at the centre of deliberations in her regard and omnipresent at every stage of the administrative and judicial proceedings.[90]

A right to fatherhood for same-sex couples through medically assisted reproduction is not supported by the current state of international human rights law. Although this specific question was not before the ECtHR, in cases involving heterosexual couples, such as *S.H. and Others* v. *Austria* and *Mennesson* v. *France*,[91] the Court noted that ECHR States take different approaches to ova donation and surrogacy, and because of the sensitive ethical issues involved, it is not the Court's place to substitute its judgment to that of national legislatures. However, there is an argument to suggest that the blanket refusal of access to ova donation and surrogacy, not targeting same-sex couples

[88] See Lorna Marshall, 'Ethical Issues in the Evolving Realm of Egg Donation', in Leslie Francis (ed.), *The Oxford Handbook of Reproductive Ethics* (Oxford: Oxford University Press, 2017) 478–498, at 479–481. The objections to the practice of surrogacy advanced in the literature were addressed in Chapter 2, Section 2.4, and will not be discussed here.

[89] It is not the purpose of the present inquiry to enter into the debate of whether it is detrimental to children to be raised with only one gender model in the family, or on the contested significance of gender roles in today's society; these are outside the author's expertise. This chapter acknowledges different doctrinal positions on these issues, but draws the attention to the need for a consistent approach to children's psychological and educational needs to avoid unwarranted discrimination.

[90] See *E.B.* v. *France* [GC], [86]–[88].

[91] See *Mennesson* v. *France*, App. No. 65192/11, 26 June 2014, and the discussion in Chapter 2, Section 2.4.

specifically, may nonetheless have a greater impact on them. Consequently, there may be an unintended discriminatory aspect to it. As Boucai has pointed out,[92] unlike 'disparate treatment claims', which 'concern policies and practices that specifically disadvantage LGBT people', ART claims are 'disparate impact claims', that is, they 'concern policies and practices that do not single out LGBT people for unfavourable treatment but nonetheless affect them disproportionately relative to the population at large', because of their inability to have children through intercourse.[93] There is, to date, no authority on this argument from international litigation, but given the Strasbourg Court's general reluctance to engage with challenges to eligibility for ART treatment and its dismissal of claims based on Article 14 taken with Article 8 in other same-sex reproduction cases (e.g. *C.E. and Others* v. *France*), it is unlikely to gain traction in the short run.

The case of *A.L.* v. *France* tangentially touched upon the issue of fatherhood for same-sex couples. The applicant was in a relationship with another man and together had sought the services of a surrogate mother in order to have a child, in breach of domestic legislation. However, the Strasbourg case was merely concerned with the alleged breach of the genetic father's right to private life as a result of protracted court proceedings for challenging the paternity of the man to whom the surrogate had sold the child. There was no discussion in the judgment of a right for same-sex couples to become parents through ART (which domestic law did not permit) or of intentional parenthood. Rather, the focus of the judgment was on the excessive length of proceedings, which predetermined the outcome of the case, in that the child, aged six when the case was finalised, was likely to be harmed by the belated recognition of, and transfer to, the genetic father.[94]

The issue of same-sex couples and parenthood achieved via overseas surrogacy was before the ECtHR in *Valdís Fjölnisdóttir and Others* v. *Iceland*.[95] However, neither intended parent had genetic links to the child, and the decision revolved around family life arising from long-term care, under a foster care order. The Strasbourg treatment of the case echoed the approach to heterosexual couples in which neither parent has genetic ties to the child, seen in *Paradiso and Campanelli* v. *Italy*, except in the latter case the Court found that there had been insufficient time to create family life, given the

92 Boucai, 'Is Assisted Procreation an LGBT Right?', 1108.

93 Ibid., 1110.

94 Because the case concerns the recognition of genetic fatherhood in surrogacy cases, it was discussed in Chapter 2, Section 2.4; in fact, it does not add to the understanding of same-sex parenthood in male couples.

95 *Valdís Fjölnisdóttir and Others* v. *Iceland*, App. No. 71552/17, 18 May 2021.

immediate removal of the child by social services.[96] *Valdís Fjölnisdóttir* and *Paradiso and Campanelli* suggest that, regardless of the couple's sexual orientation, the Court does not uphold intentional parenthood in foreign surrogacy cases if neither member of the couple is a genetic parent.[97]

S.-H. v. *Poland* presented the Court with a case of overseas surrogacy commissioned by a male couple in which one of the partners was the genetic father.[98] However, the case is not susceptible to extrapolation due to the parties' unusual circumstances: the family ties and the children's nationality rights were recognised and adequately protected in two jurisdictions, including the family's place of residence, and the applicants sought recognition from a third jurisdiction – the place of birth of the biological father. The Court found Article 8 inapplicable to the Polish authorities' refusal to grant Polish nationality by descent to the twins born through surrogacy in the United States to a same-sex couple residing in Israel, where legal parent–child ties were recognised, although the intended biological father was a Polish-Israeli citizen.[99] While Polish law conferred Polish nationality on any child born to a Polish citizen, surrogacy was prohibited, and the American birth certificates, indicating two men as the parents, ran counter to basic principles of the Polish legal order; therefore, the commissioning genetic father could not be treated as the legal father.[100]

Even making allowance for the specific circumstances of the case, the ruling is not entirely convincing. Instead of focusing on the principled contention that all parents had to be able to pass on their nationality to the child, and that all children were entitled to acquire their biological parents' nationality, regardless of the mode of conception, the Court preferred a consequence-based approach. Arguably ill-suited to identity cases, this approach placed the burden on the applicants to demonstrate that the inability to acquire Polish nationality had sufficiently serious negative consequences for them.[101]

96 *Paradiso and Campanelli* v. *Italy* [GC], [185]–[215]. The reaction of domestic authorities in foreign surrogacy cases with no genetic links predetermines the Strasbourg outcome, because the Court's Art. 8 assessment depends on the length of the care and the consequential impact of uprooting the child on the child's welfare. So, too, does the couple's legal standing to bring proceedings on behalf of the child: foster carers have locus standi after years of cohabitation, while intended non-biological parents shortly after birth do not.

97 See the discussion in Chapter 3, Section 3.3.2.

98 *S.-H.* v. *Poland*, App. Nos. 56846/15 and 56849/15, 16 November 2021.

99 Ibid., [76].

100 Ibid., [24].

101 Ibid., [67]. The Court did not explain why a consequence-based approach was employed in relation to an identity rights case, which often has symbolic and emotive undertones. The Court relied on the test in *Denisov* v. *Ukraine* [GC], App. No. 76639/11, 25 September 2018, [110]–[114]: 'In cases where the Court employs the consequence-based approach, the analysis of the seriousness of the impugned measure's effects occupies an important place. . . . It is thus

The Court dismissed the claim that the measure hindered the family's potential relocation to Poland on account of Israel's difficult geopolitical situation, because no details of imminent plans had been presented.[102] It further reasoned that the children already had dual US-Israeli citizenship, and therefore the courts' refusal to sanction the acquisition of Polish citizenship had not rendered them stateless; nor had they encountered any practical difficulties in their country of residence (Israel) as a result of that decision.[103] While the Court conceded that the applicants must have experienced some obstacles as a result of not having Polish, and consequently European, citizenship, those were not deemed sufficient to cross the threshold of seriousness required for the application of Article 8.[104]

Interestingly, the Court distinguished the case from *Mennesson* v. *France*, where it had found that the lack of a possibility of recognition of the legal relationship between the child born through surrogacy abroad and the intended biological father violated the child's right to respect for private life, on the basis that 'this link is recognised in the country where the family resides'.[105] One might find this logic peculiar, as it is tantamount to saying that one State meets its obligations under the Convention simply because *another* State protects the rights claimed by the applicants. Admittedly, the Polish authorities' refusal to give effect to the foreign birth certificates had not left the children in a legal vacuum, insofar as the legal relationship with the biological father and citizenship rights were granted by Israel, the State of residence. However, in *Mennesson*, the existence of other countries recognising the legal parent–child relationship did not absolve France from its responsibilities; since Poland exercised effective jurisdiction over the children in relation to the acquisition of rights descending from the biological father's nationality, its failure to respect the children' identity rights should have been recognised. Equally paradoxical is the reference to the Directive 2004/38/EC, pursuant to which the applicants, as family members of an EU citizen, were entitled to reside in the territory of *another* EU Member State.[106] One would

an intrinsic feature of the consequence-based approach within Art. 8 that convincing evidence showing that the threshold of severity was attained has to be submitted by the applicant. ... Applicants are obliged to identify and explain the concrete repercussions on their private life and the nature and extent of their suffering, and to substantiate such allegations in a proper way.'

102 *S.-H.* v. *Poland*, [68].

103 Ibid., [69].

104 Ibid., [73].

105 Ibid., [71].

106 Ibid., [72].

be hard-pressed not to read, behind the Court's emphasis on practical detriment in *S.-H.* v. *Poland* and unconvincing attempt to distinguish from *Mennesson* v. *France*, the unease with confronting another distinction between the two cases: the commissioning couple's sexual orientation.

Regrettably, the claim brought on behalf of the children under Article 8 taken in conjunction with Article 14 – different treatment in the conferral of citizenship based on the parents' sexual orientation[107] – was superficially dismissed on the basis that Article 8 had not been found applicable. This position appears untenable. Article 14 jurisprudence has established that the 'significant detriment' test used for the assessment of Article 8 taken alone is not relevant to discrimination claims. In cases such as *Abdulaziz, Cabales and Balkandali* v. *The United Kingdom*, the Court had clarified that being excluded from a discretionary benefit, that is, a more favourable treatment not owed under the Convention, raises an Article 14 issue just as much as suffering a prejudice: 'The notion of discrimination within the meaning of Article 14 (art. 14) includes in general cases where a person or group is treated, without proper justification, less favourably than another, even though the more favourable treatment is not called for by the Convention.'[108] In *S.-H.* v. *Poland*, even if the conferral of nationality is seen as a privilege (as opposed to the refusal to grant nationality being a detriment), the less favourable treatment cannot be justified by the fact that it did not cause statelessness or significant practical difficulties.[109] Consequently, the claim under Article 14 read with Article 8 deserved further analysis.

Moreover, under Article 8 taken alone, the Court had placed the burden on the applicants to show significant disadvantage; in discrimination cases, a strict proportionality test is applied, placing the burden *on the State* to justify the need for differential treatment.[110] Any other children born to a Polish genetic father would have acquired Polish nationality by virtue of *jus sanguinis*. The applicant children had been treated less favourably owing to the indication of two parents of the same sex on their birth certificates. Albeit reiterated by the

[107] Ibid., [50].

[108] *Abdulaziz, Cabales and Balkandali* v. *The United Kingdom*, App. Nos. 9214/80; 9473/81; 9474/81, 28 May 1985, [82]. For a discussion, see Carmen Draghici, 'Equal Marriage, Unequal Civil Partnership: A Bizarre Case of Discrimination in Europe' (2017) 29(4) *Child and Family Law Quarterly* 313–334, at 318–319.

[109] *S.-H.* v. *Poland*, [66]–[75]. See in particular the principles at [66], where the Court framed the question as whether the refusal to recognise the legal relationship with the Polish father and hence to grant Polish nationality 'affected' the applicants' private life, 'thus rendering Article 8 applicable'. Clearly the Court uses the term 'affected' so as to mean 'negatively impacted' rather than merely 'engaged'.

[110] See Draghici, 'Equal Marriage, Unequal Civil Partnership', 315.

Court,[111] the fact that they resided abroad should not have been deemed relevant (certainly not dispositive), because foreign residence was not an impediment to the transmission of nationality to children of opposite-sex couples. This difference in treatment should have inspired a discussion of whether Polish law took a discriminatory approach to children born to same-sex commissioning couples through overseas surrogacy; the children's dual nationality reduced the practical significance of the inability to acquire Polish nationality, but did not obviate the need for a minimum standard in the legal treatment of all surrogate-born children. Nor is it clear that a less intrusive measure upholding Polish public policy values was unavailable, for example, recognising the relationship with the genetic father and the ensuing citizenship rights, without recognising the father's partner as a legal parent.

In the aftermath of the Grand Chamber's Advisory Opinion No. P16-2018-001, which confirmed the obligation to introduce an effective mechanism through which the non-genetic intended mother could establish parental ties with the surrogate-born child related to her husband,[112] it was suggested that the same approach must be extended to the non-genetic intended father in same-sex couples; otherwise, the State would fall foul of non-discrimination principles. Relying on the non-discrimination principles emerging from *Gas and Dubois* v. *France* and *X and Others* v. *Austria*,[113] Lydia Bracken argues that a non-genetic intended father is in a directly comparable position to a non-genetic intended mother, and therefore the same mechanism for recognition of legal ties to the child should be available to them.[114] However, the non-genetic intended mother has no rights herself (*Mennesson* v. *France* and the Advisory Opinion make it clear that the recognition of affiliation is *the child's* right); consequently, the non-genetic intended father cannot rely on Articles 8 and 14 to claim equal treatment.[115] Conversely, the case could be made that the surrogate-born child with two intended parents of the same sex

[111] *S.-H.* v. *Poland*, [69]–[71].

[112] 'Advisory Opinion Concerning the Recognition in Domestic Law of a Legal Parent–Child Relationship between a Child Born through a Gestational Surrogacy Arrangement Abroad and the Intended Mother', No. P16-2018-001, 10 April 2019; see Chapter 3, Section 3.3.1.

[113] *X and Others* v. *Austria* [GC], App. No. 19010/07, 19 February 2013.

[114] Lydia Bracken, 'The ECtHR's First Advisory Opinion: Implications for Cross-Border Surrogacy Involving Male Intended Parents (2021) 21(1) *Medical Law International* 3–18, at 16–17.

[115] To succeed, the complaint must show that they were denied a Convention right or a domestic entitlement having a connection with an ECHR right (e.g. adoption, parental leave allowance) on one of the grounds prohibited by Art. 14. See Draghici, 'Equal Marriage, Unequal Civil Partnership', 315–319, for a discussion of case law requiring ECHR-compatible regulation of (non-mandatory) domestic rights attached to ECHR rights.

is suffering discrimination (based on the circumstances of conception or on the gender of one of the intended parents) if the relationship is not recognised, where a child with two opposite-sex intended parents would have two legal parents. This debate has now been superseded by the *D.B. and Others* v. *Switzerland* judgment,[116] although interestingly the case was decided under Article 8 taken alone (upholding only the child's right to private life).[117]

The case of *D.B. and Others* v. *Switzerland* faced the Court directly with the regulation of the relationship between children born through foreign surrogacy to same-sex couples and the non-genetic intended fathers. The application concerned a Swiss same-sex couple who were registered partners and who had entered into a gestational surrogacy contract in the United States; while the parent–child relationship was established by a US court in relation to both of them, the Swiss authorities had only recognised the genetic father. In Strasbourg, it was held that the child's Article 8 rights had been breached as a result of the absolute impossibility under domestic law to achieve recognition of the parent–child relationship with the non-genetic intended father; in fact, step-parent adoption was initially open only to married couples, to the exclusion of registered partners, and a change in the law permitting adoption by a registered partner had intervened when the child was nearly eight years old.[118] Consequently, no route to securing the recognition of the parent–child relationship with the social father had been available for a substantial period of time. Withholding recognition of the lawfully issued foreign birth certificate insofar as it concerned the social father, without providing any alternative means of recognition, had not been in the best interests of the child and had amounted to a disproportionate interference with his right to respect for private life.[119] By contrast, as regards the adults'

[116] *D.B. and Others* v. *Switzerland*, App. Nos. 58817/15; 58252/15, 22 November 2022.

[117] Before *D.B. and Others* v. *Switzerland*, some conclusions could be inferred by analogy from *C.E. and Others* v. *France*. As discussed in Section 5.2.1, the ECtHR has intimated that Art. 8 requires States to protect the family life established by the ART-born child and the non-genetic social mother, based on the latter's committed relationship with the child's biological mother, the joint parenthood project and the effective care of the child. Consequently, an obligation was likely to arise to safeguard the relationship between the surrogate-born child and the intended/social father. Both types of situations involve third-party reproduction, a committed same-sex relationship and intentional parenthood; the type of ART used (gamete donation/ surrogacy) and the gender of the biological parent in a same-sex partnership are not sufficient to distinguish them for the purposes of establishing family life and identity rights for the child. However, in *C.E. and Others* the Court was satisfied that avenues such as step-parent adoption or the acquisition of parental responsibility suffice to protect the interests of the child and of the de facto family unit.

[118] *D.B. and Others* v. *Switzerland*, [87]–[90].

[119] Ibid., [89].

rights, the Court noted that the surrogacy arrangement had been contrary to Swiss public policy, and the limited practical difficulties the couple were likely to encounter in their family life in the absence of recognition of the relationship between the child and the social father remained within the limits of compliance with Article 8.[120] Importantly, the Court found the objection that surrogacy was contrary to public policy pertinent but not decisive in the evaluation of the child's rights; in fact, the parents' culpable conduct cannot detract from the primacy of the children's best interests.[121]

The *D.B. and Others* v. *Switzerland* ruling marks a notable departure from *C. and E.* v. *France*,[122] where the Court had made allowance for the gradual reform in the respondent's society; in particular, it was satisfied that, several years after the children's birth (when child C. was seven years old and the E. triplets were three), a legal avenue to establish filiation (step-parent adoption) had become available.[123] By contrast, in *D.B.* v. *Switzerland*, it was held that the respondent had overstepped its margin of appreciation by not making timely legislative provision for the recognition of the relationship between the surrogate-born child and the non-genetic father. For the Court, a lengthy period of non-recognition is not consistent with the best interests of the child, insofar as it places him in a situation of legal uncertainty as regards his identity in society and deprives him of the opportunity to live and develop in a stable environment.[124]

This judgment, rendered in 2022, suggests that the legal situation at the time of the child's birth (non-recognition of the relationship with the intended father) breached the Convention, which places the existence of that obligation around 2011 and calls into question the 2019 decision in *C. and E.* v. *France*. One might criticise the retrospective application of arguably more

[120] Ibid., [92]–[94].

[121] Ibid., [86].

[122] *C. and E.* v. *France*, App. Nos. 1462/18; 17348/18, 19 November 2019; see Chapter 3, Section 3.3.1.

[123] Ibid., [41]–[44].

[124] See *D.B. and Others* v. *Switzerland*, [88]. These principles were reiterated a month later in relation to the intended mother in *K.K. and Others* v. *Denmark*, App. No. 25212/21, 6 December 2022, [72]. A very similar case is pending before the Court in S.C. v. *Switzerland*, App. No. 26848/18: although the same-sex couple availed themselves of the intervening legal option of step-parent adoption for civil partners, they complain that the non-recognition of legal ties between the child and the intended father during the first three-and-a-half years of the child's life, during which the former was unable to exercise parental authority or transmit to the child his surname and nationality (the genetic father being French), was not consistent with the child's best interests. Moreover, they submit that the adoption process, which took twenty months, did not constitute a suitably prompt and effective mechanism for the creation of legal ties (per Advisory Opinion P16-2018-001).

recent standards,[125] which superimposed an obligation not crystallised at the material time. Judge Elósegui, partly dissenting, noted that at the relevant time (2011–18), Convention case law was governed by *Mennesson* v. *France*, which only required the recognition of legal affiliation with the biological father, and not by the 2019 Advisory Opinion (extending the obligation of recognition to the intended mother). It could be argued, however, that the Advisory Opinion did not change ECHR law, but merely ascertained the correct interpretation of Article 8 at the time; that standard may well have already existed before 2019. The fact that no Strasbourg pronouncement requiring the recognition of the genetic parent existed before *Mennesson* did not prevent the Court from finding a violation in that case. At the same time, the impact on the children in *Mennesson* (where neither parent was recognised and citizenship rights were in doubt) was such that the State ought to have been aware of the disproportionate impact of its restrictive measure; nor was France faced with a clash between its public policy tenets and the acknowledgement of two parents of the same sex. Many factors supported Switzerland's position in *D.B.*: the lesser practical impact on the child, the resistance in many ECHR States to altering the mother/father paradigm, the difficulty in ascertaining with precision at which point in time the obligation to recognise the social parent of the same sex as the genetic parent arose, but also the fact that, in 2018, Switzerland did reform the law. The Court could have found that Switzerland had acted within the margin of discretion afforded to it. In addition, the *D.B.* approach cannot be reconciled with the choice, in *C.E. and Others* v. *France*, to assess the complaint against the domestic law at the time of Strasbourg proceedings, as opposed to the law at the time the facts lamented in the complaint; this inconsistency is unfortunate for the development of the Court's case law on fast-evolving legal areas. Thus, a conclusion less open to challenge in *D.B.* might have been that ECHR standards at the time of the judgment (2022) included the right sought by the applicant, which, indeed, the respondent had afforded in 2018, but that during the first seven years of the child's life (2011–17) that new pan-European standard was not sufficiently established to warrant a finding of violation.

At the other end of the spectrum, another partly dissenting opinion would have wanted the Court to also ascertain a violation in respect of the child's

[125] See *D.B. and Others* v. *Switzerland*, Part-Dissenting Opinion of Judge Elósegui, [4]–[6]. The judge also found problematic the application of the Advisory Opinion to a State not party to Protocol 16; however, this is a more questionable objection: the Opinion expressed the Court's interpretation of a point of law arising under Art. 8 ECHR and one could only expect to find it applied in contentious proceedings. This is not to say that the Opinion was deemed 'binding'; indeed, it is not even binding for the State parties to Protocol 16.

Article 8 rights taken in conjunction with Article 14, a claim which the majority of the Court saw as raising no essential separate issue requiring examination.[126] For Judge Pavli, the child had suffered either direct discrimination or discrimination by association on account of his parents' sexual orientation; unlike children born to married parents in analogous circumstances, for the first seven-and-a-half years of his life, the applicant, born to a legally recognised couple of civil partners (ineligible for marriage), could not be adopted by one of his intended and de facto parents.[127]

Nonetheless, *D.B.* v. *Switzerland* ultimately aligned the Court's approach to children born to same-sex parents via foreign surrogacy to that established in the 2019 Advisory Opinion in relation to children born to heterosexual couples in the same circumstances; the latter was consolidated in contentious proceedings shortly after the *D.B.* judgment: *K.K. and Others* v. *Denmark*[128] found that the refusal to allow the intended non-genetic mother to adopt the children breached the children's Article 8 rights (joint custody and other measures of protection were insufficient to safeguard their interests).

5.3 TRANSGENDER PARENTHOOD AND CHILDREN BORN THROUGH ARTIFICIAL INSEMINATION

The allocation of legal parenthood for a child born through assisted reproduction with donor acquires a further layer of complexity when the non-biological intended parent is a transsexual. This issue was before the Court in *X, Y and Z* v. *The United Kingdom*[129] a few years after *Kerkhoven and Hinke* v. *The Netherlands*. The factual matrix contained one significant variation: the non-biological carer was a postoperative female-to-male transsexual partner. Unlike the mother's female partner in the previous case, he acted as a father figure, although the law at the material time did not permit gender reassignment and, therefore, his gender was female for all legal purposes. On this occasion, the Court did not hesitate to qualify the three applicants as a family within the meaning of Article 8. Albeit unexplained, the different evaluation in this case seems largely owed to the fact that the social reality involved a child and two parental figures apparently of opposite sex, mirroring biological reality. The couple did not function socially as a same-sex couple, and the

[126] *D.B. and Others* v. *Switzerland*, [101].
[127] Ibid., Part-Dissenting Opinion of Judge Pavli, [2]–[3].
[128] See Chapter 3, Section 3.3.1.
[129] *X, Y and Z* v. *United Kingdom* [GC], App. No. 21830/93, 22 April 1997.

resulting family unit thus conformed to heteronormative expectations, fitting without difficulty within the scope of Article 8.

Despite the more favourable approach at the Article 8 applicability threshold when compared to the earlier case involving a same-sex couple and an ART-born child, the *X, Y and Z* v. *The United Kingdom* judgment ultimately revolved around the lack of European consensus on transsexuality and parenthood, hence the difficulty of establishing positive obligations under the Convention:

> The Court observes that there is no common European standard with regard to the granting of parental rights to transsexuals … [nor] with regard to the manner in which the social relationship between a child conceived by AID and the person who performs the role of father should be reflected in law … the respondent State must be afforded a wide margin of appreciation.[130]

The Court arguably went further than necessary for the purposes of the case, in that it afforded the respondent State a wide margin of appreciation more generally in relation to the recognition of parental rights for 'the person who acts as a father', whether or not the situation was compounded by the discrepancy between the intended father's legal and apparent gender. The ruling also left within States' discretion the decision to exclude the transsexual partner who holds a gender recognition certificate and is legally classified as a male[131] from artificial insemination treatment together with the aspiring mother and the attribution of legal parenthood.

Less controversially, in *X, Y and Z* v. *The United Kingdom*, the Grand Chamber placed emphasis on the child's interests, which may justify curtailing the adults' rights, and on the lack of evidence as to how those rights were better safeguarded (which justified a precautionary approach in Strasbourg proceedings): 'at the present time there is uncertainty with regard to how the interests of children in Z's position can best be protected … and the Court should not adopt or impose any single viewpoint'.[132] Alice Margaria has noted the Court's insistence on the lack of genetic ties between X and Z in upholding the interference, despite having prioritised effective care over biology at the Article 8 applicability stage: 'the Court found it important to stress that,

[130] Ibid., [44].

[131] The law applicable at the material time allowed a male partner to be recognised as the legal father following treatment together with the child's mother (s. 28(3) Human Fertilisation and Embryology Act 1990).

[132] *X, Y and Z* v. *The United Kingdom* [GC], [51]. See also [47]: 'the Court considers that the State may justifiably be cautious in changing the law, since it is possible that the amendment sought might have undesirable or unforeseen ramifications for children in Z's position'.

while its earlier case law where Article 8 was read to require States to actively protect family life concerned ties existing between biological parents and their offspring, "Z was conceived by AID and is not related, in the biological sense, to X, who is a transsexual"'.[133] While this does not necessarily disclose an inconsistency on the value assigned to social ties, insofar as the applicability test is broader than the proportionality test, the ruling appears to be influenced by a traditional understanding of parenthood as genetic. Specifically, the Court views genetic parenthood as the only form of parenthood requiring protection through the establishment of legal affiliation and takes a more laissez-faire approach to the means for safeguarding non-genetic parenthood.

This is not to say, however, that the Court was prepared to condone any interference with the family life of the applicants. When assessing the proportionality of the interference, the Court considered the disadvantages suffered by the applicants as a result of the authorities' refusal to recognise X as Z's legal father; it reasoned that making a will could solve the problem of the child's lack of automatic inheritance rights upon intestacy, and that the child had British nationality by virtue of the connection with her mother.[134] In terms of Z's sense of identity and security within her family, the Court pointed out that nothing prevented X from presenting himself as Z's father and giving her his surname, as well as applying for a joint residence order, which also conferred shared parental responsibility.[135] The Court was perhaps unduly dismissive of the allegation of distress caused to Z whenever necessary to produce her birth certificate; it was satisfied that the use of the birth certificate in the UK was not common for administrative or identification purposes, and that neither Z nor third parties had to be informed of the reason for the absence of Z's name from the certificate.[136]

According to Ursula Kilkelly, 'the Court clearly considered that the case concerned how the law should treat transsexuals, rather than how it should recognise children's family ties'.[137] While the ruling seems indeed focused on the regulation of transsexualism, the Court dwells more on the child's identity and her need for stable family arrangements than on X's interests. The allegation of discrimination with respect to X's rights – since a person born male was able to register himself as the father following treatment with the

[133] Alice Margaria, *The Construction of Fatherhood: The Jurisprudence of the European Court of Human Rights* (Cambridge: Cambridge University Press, 2019) 56.

[134] *X, Y and Z* v. *The United Kingdom* [GC], [48].

[135] Ibid., [50].

[136] Ibid., [49].

[137] Ursula Kilkelly, 'Protecting Children's Rights under the ECHR: The Role of Positive Obligations' (2010) 61(3) *Northern Ireland Legal Quarterly* 245–261, at 253.

mother – was unfortunately dismissed as a restatement of the Article 8 submission.[138] Even if legal fatherhood following a joint reproductive enterprise was a discretionary domestic right, rather than corresponding to a Convention right, a discussion would have been desirable of whether States can legitimately distinguish, in the provision of ART, between persons who are born male (or have become legally male) and persons in the applicant's position. Since an important part of the Court's reasoning on Article 8 taken alone was devoted to the lack of European consensus on the new identity of transsexuals and the wide domestic margin of appreciation on its legal effects, the ruling was dominated by gender fluidity concerns and did not advance the understanding of intentional parenthood rights.

The wide discretion allowed to States as regards the means of protection of de facto family ties between ART-born children and their unrelated transsexual social parents in *X, Y and Z* v. *The United Kingdom* can be seen as largely superseded by the subsequent change of direction in the case law on transgender persons' right to the recognition of the acquired gender as the legal gender (*Christine Goodwin* v. *The United Kingdom*; *I.* v. *The United Kingdom*).[139] Once the legal gender is aligned with the social role, challenges in relation to ART for transgender persons are similar to those experienced by other prospective parents (e.g. access to treatment may be reserved to couples/married couples in their jurisdiction, or the non-biological intentional parent of a child born through donor insemination abroad may be entitled to acquire parental responsibility but not parental status).

5.4 SINGLE ASPIRING PARENTS: REDEFINING 'REPRODUCTIVELY CHALLENGED' CONDITIONS

Although the development of ART was a response to infertility problems, to reduce access to medical treatment to infertile couples would be insensitive to social challenges to reproduction and modern life pressures. Gillian Douglas has noted that 'there might be good reasons for permitting the fertile to have access'; for example, 'women who wish to delay childbearing in order to advance their careers could store their ova until they were ready for a career break, rather than risk experiencing the difficulties in conceiving associated with older women'.[140] A right to delay the pregnancy through ova cryopreservation may also be justified by the lack of a partner with whom to set up a

[138] Ibid., [53]–[56].

[139] See *Christine Goodwin* v. *The United Kingdom* [GC], App. No. 28957/95, 11 July 2002; *I.* v. *The United Kingdom* [GC], App. No. 25680/94, 11 July 2002.

[140] Gillian Douglas, *Law, Fertility and Reproduction* (London: Sweet and Maxwell, 1991) 119.

family at an age when fertility starts to decline, or to safeguard the option to procreate before undertaking medical treatment that impairs the capacity to produce oocytes. It could also be argued that, since the storage of semen before a man embarks upon treatment affecting his reproductive capacity is readily accessible, whereas ova collection and storage presuppose medical equipment and expertise, effective gender equality in the area of reproduction requires State support for women in these circumstances. Similarly, a right to assisted insemination with donor/surrogacy services may be rendered necessary by medical problems or the absence of a partner.

The availability of treatment allowing individuals to reproduce in more varied circumstances has shaped both private and social expectations. Indeed, it was remarked that 'the casting of involuntary childlessness . . . as *infertility* (a medical condition) is relatively recent and connected with the development of new technologies to assist reproduction'.[141] While international human rights law may be unable to micromanage the regulation of access to ART at this stage, consistency in the law is critical to avoiding discrimination; for example, if the law does not require a person to resign themself to having an infertile partner, incapable of supplying viable gametes of the opposite sex, it should also not require a single person to resign themself to the lack of a partner. Chapter 2 has discussed access to gamete donation as a means to simultaneously ensure respect for a person's decision to become a parent and for their choice of partner. Naturally, this can be seen as extending to the choice of no partner at all (whether deliberate or fortuitous). In fact, a general restriction on access to gamete/embryo donation penalises with particular force individuals who are not in a marriage, civil partnership or stable cohabitation (the latter category being often treated as a relevant status by laws defining eligibility for adoption or ART).[142] A measure reserving such treatment expressly to couples would, *a fortiori*, raise discrimination concerns based on civil status. It is also worth noting that medically assisted insemination for single women is permitted in twenty-seven out of the current forty-six Council of Europe Member States,[143] a sufficient majority, spread across all the geopolitical areas of the

[141] Lisa Rubin and Aliza Phillips, 'Infertility and Assisted Reproduction Technologies: Matters of Reproductive Justice', in Joan Chrisler (ed.), *Reproductive Justice: A Global Concern* (Santa Barbara: Praeger, 2012) 173–199, at 174 (original emphasis).

[142] See, for instance, in England and Wales, s. 144(4)(b) Adoption and Child Act 2002, defining a 'couple' eligible to adopt as 'two people (whether of different sexes or the same sex) living as partners in an enduring family relationship'.

[143] See ILGA-Europe Rainbow Index 2022. Russia also permits treatment for singles, although its practice has become less relevant for ECHR standards after its membership to the Council of Europe came to an end on 16 September 2022.

continent, to lend support to the finding that there is no pressing need to exclude this category from treatment.

Admittedly, the creation of one-parent families by design may face different objections, mostly based on the welfare of the child: the injustice of deliberately creating a fatherless/motherless child, the absence of a role model for one of the genders and the economic difficulties potentially faced by the family. The first objection would require robust evidence that the child is harmed by being given life in circumstances where he/she only knows[144] – and is raised by – one parent. Arguably, the quality of the care is much more important than the family structure: children can thrive in single-parent families while facing developmental challenges in two-parent families. Moreover, applying Derek Parfit's theory on reproductive choice,[145] future children are not harmed by the decision to conceive them unless their lives are so impaired as a result of that decision that they are not worth living; being raised by a single parent certainly does not have that effect. As regards the second objection (absence of parental referents of both genders), in jurisdictions permitting same-sex adoption and/or same-sex access to ART, obstacles to the creation of single-parent families would be arbitrary and discriminatory. As to the risk of poverty, if, in the context of natural reproduction, State policies do not encourage individuals to reproduce responsibly, according to their financial means, but provide assistance to single women who reproduce despite being unable to afford to raise the child, wealth cannot be a precondition for single women seeking to procreate through ART. Moreover, as Douglas has observed, the economic and psychological considerations underlying the opposition to one-parent families tend not to apply to ART-born children, who are carefully planned:

> Children from one-parent families might experience poverty, or the emotional trauma of their parents' relationship breaking up, but children who are born after assisted reproduction are arguably less likely to experience such problems, since their birth was planned when the parent was already settled into her life-style.[146]

To some extent, Strasbourg case law on the right to become a parent has evolved in time in a liberal direction, departing from the attachment to procreation as an extension of marriage and hence a prerogative of married couples. A few decades ago, in *X v. Belgium and The Netherlands*, the former European Commission on

[144] The identity of the donor may be known to the child (or become known in adulthood), depending on the relevant donor disclosure regulations/private agreements.

[145] See Derek Parfit, 'Rights, Interests, and Possible People', in Samuel Gorowitz et al. (eds.), *Moral Problems in Medicine* (Englewood Cliffs, NJ: Prentice Hall, 1976) 369–375, reprinted in Kuhse et al., *Bioethics*, 86–90.

[146] Douglas, *Law, Fertility and Reproduction*, 122.

Human Rights held that the 'right to found a family' guaranteed in Article 12 was premised on the existence of a couple; in fact, the rights to marry and to found a family are merged in a single provision in the Convention.[147] Additionally, in *M.* v. *Federal Republic of Germany*, a case regarding posthumous marriage, the Commission stressed that Article 12 only recognised rights to 'men and women of marriageable age'.[148] Since then, however, the interest in having a biological child and the right to use reproductive technologies to that end have been recognised as a component of Article 8 (see, e.g., *Dickson* v. *The United Kingdom*; *Evans* v. *The United Kingdom*; *S.H. and Others* v. *Austria*),[149] as well as being decoupled from the right to marry. In its more recent jurisprudence, the Court has abandoned the reference to Article 12 when it comes to procreation cases, and it examines parenthood claims under Article 8 as a matter of respect for private and family life. Therefore, the *individual* right to become a parent has acquired independent meaning, and a spouse (or life partner) is not a strict prerequisite for a parenthood project.

The surrogacy case law examined earlier concerned married couples and foreign arrangements, the effects of which the couples sought to have recognised in their country of residence. Single individuals aspiring to become parents through overseas surrogacy may have an analogous claim. If a single man wishes to have a biologically related child, the only medically feasible solution is to resort to traditional surrogacy or ova donation combined with gestational surrogacy. The option of traditional surrogacy increases the chances of the agreement failing due to the surrogate's attachment to her genetic child; there may be other reasons for the intended parents to prefer third-party donor's eggs (e.g. matching racial/ethnic/physical characteristics of the non-genetic intended parent, using a known donor whose attributes the parents would like to see transmitted to the child). Similarly, a single woman who produces viable oocytes but cannot carry a pregnancy to term, or whose health would be at risk as a result of the pregnancy or childbirth, needs to rely on surrogacy. The question arising is whether intentional human rights obligations, in particular under the ECHR, require States to permit such arrangements or recognise legal effects to arrangements lawfully entered into abroad.[150]

147 See X v. *Belgium and The Netherlands*, App. No. 6482/74, 10 July 1975 (Commission).

148 *M.* v. *Federal Republic of Germany*, App. No. 10995/84, 13 December 1984 (Commission).

149 *Evans* v. *The United Kingdom* [GC], App. No. 6339/05, 10 April 2007.

150 Domestic courts have been called upon to pronounce on these issues. In *Re Z (A Child) (No 2)* [2016] EWHC 1191 (Fam), the UK High Court held that the unavailability of parental orders for single persons using surrogacy (as opposed to being part of a couple) under ss. 54(1) and (2) of the Human Fertilisation and Embryology Act 2008 amounted to discrimination on ground of status and breached Art. 8 taken in conjunction with Art. 14 ECHR.

Recent case law has started to engage with these questions, albeit again from a child's rights perspective rather than as an access issue for the adult. In *Foulon and Bouvet* v. *France*,[151] it was held that the domestic authorities' refusal to transcribe birth certificates issued in India to surrogate-born children amounted to a violation of the children's right to private life. In both cases (jointly decided), the applicants were the biological fathers of children born as a result of agreements entered into with Indian surrogate mothers. According to the Indian birth certificates, the men were the legal fathers and the Indian surrogates were the legal mothers. Both men wished to have their paternity recognised in France, and the children were co-applicants. After mixed fate in the lower courts, the French Court of Cassation, invoking the circumvention of the domestic ban on surrogacy agreements, upheld the refusal to register the births as documented in the Indian birth certificates. Recognising the similarity with the *Mennesson* and *Labassee* cases, notwithstanding the absence of a heterosexual commissioning couple, the ECtHR found no basis to depart from its previous rulings and concluded that the measures did not violate the right to respect for family life of either the fathers or the children, but did violate the children's right to respect for their private life.[152] By implication, the Court's position indicates that, at least at present, Article 8 does not require positive measures of protection for the decision to become a parent when a person is entirely reliant on ART due to their civil status.

An opportunity to strengthen the rights of the single genetic parent in surrogacy arrangements presented itself with the French request for an Advisory Opinion on the recognition of a legal parent–child relationship between a child born through surrogacy abroad and the intended non-genetic mother. Addressing the question before it, the Court held that, in cases where domestic authorities have recognised the parent–child relationship between the surrogate-born child and the intended genetic father, the child's right to respect for his or her private life requires a legal avenue for the acquisition of parenthood by the intended non-genetic mother. However, in an *obiter dictum*, the Court further indicated that, if the embryo transferred into the surrogate was created with the intended mother's ova and donor sperm, the obligation to recognise the legal parent–child relationship between the child and the genetic mother arises *a fortiori*:

> Although the domestic proceedings do not concern the case of a child born through a gestational surrogacy arrangement abroad and conceived using the

[151] *Foulon and Bouvet* v. *France*, App. Nos. 9063/14; 10410/14, 21 July 2016.
[152] Ibid., [55]–[58].

> eggs of the intended mother, the Court considers it important to emphasise that, *where the situation is otherwise similar to that in issue in the present proceedings*, the need to provide a possibility of recognition of the legal relationship between the child and the intended mother applies with even greater force in such a case.[153]

While the Court envisaged a situation where both commissioning parents were also genetic parents,[154] it is illogical to maintain that the genetic mother has to be in a relationship with the genetic father in order for that obligation to arise. If *Foulon and Bouvet* v. *France* is not applied to single motherhood following overseas gestational surrogacy, the child's best interests are compromised. In fact, if the single woman returns with her genetic child to her country of residence and the authorities refuse to transcribe the foreign birth certificate due to their understanding of motherhood as gestational, the child is left an orphan and deprived of all the benefits attached to maternal affiliation (including economic and citizenship rights). Additionally, the resulting double standard would likely constitute discrimination against the children based on the gender of their commissioning parent (following, *mutatis mutandis*, the analysis of Judge Pavli in *D.B. v Switzerland*).

It is possible that the *obiter dictum* in the Advisory Opinion simply offered a minor variation to the matrix before it, rather than revealing scepticism towards single motherhood or a conservative attachment to gestational motherhood. Perhaps somewhat speculatively, Alice Margaria has suggested that, in *Evans* v. *The United Kingdom*, 'J's wish to resist fatherhood was taken seriously because the child would have been born and raised by a single mother and, as such, in an unconventional family unit'.[155] Although the Court found that the UK legislation would also have been ECHR-compliant had it allowed Ms Evans to use the embryos, it is quite possible that ART-founded single motherhood inspired a lower intensity of review when compared to the joint biological parenthood project in *Dickson*.[156] While *S.H. and Others* v. *Austria* found against the married couple, the claim regarded *heterologous* fertilisation, which is a significant departure from the conventional family based on marriage and biological descent.

[153] See Advisory Opinion No. P16-2018-001, [47] (emphasis added).

[154] The sentence 'the situation is otherwise similar to that in issue in the present proceedings' seems to suggest that the Court refers to a scenario where the genetic father has been recognised in domestic law as the legal father.

[155] Margaria, *The Construction of Fatherhood*, 69.

[156] *Dickson* v. *The United Kingdom* [GC], App. No. 44362/04, 4 December 2007.

The centrality of marriage and co-parenting in the judicial assessment of parenthood claims can also place the intended non-biological parent at a significant disadvantage, as recently illustrated by the *A.M.* v. *Norway* decision.[157] In this case, a couple had resorted to foreign surrogacy after separation, and only the intended father, genetically related to the child, was recognised in Norway as a legal parent with parental responsibility. Consequently, he had been able to exclude the intended non-genetic mother entirely from the child's life after a year and a half of de facto care, following disagreements about residence and parenting arrangements. One of the complaints regarded the lack of objective justification for treating the applicant differently from persons who were covered by the temporary Surrogacy Act 2013 on the transfer of parenthood for children born abroad by surrogate mothers, merely on the basis that she had not been married or living together with the child's father when the child was born (the interim Act required 'a shared wish to raise the child together').[158] As forcefully put by the Dissenting Opinion of Judge Jelić, the applicant had been discriminated against on the grounds of marital status based on a narrow and obsolete understanding of co-parenting:

> The notion of 'raising a child together' in the authorities' understanding is remote from the reality of family life and family constellations in the twenty-first century. A multitude of couples raise their children together while not living together, ranging from separated or divorced couples to families whose parents commute or simply decide to live apart while maintaining their romantic relationship. Under such circumstances, and provided both parents are involved, they are still regarded as raising their children together. There is thus no evidence that the concept of raising a child together implies the existence of a shared family home.[159]

Regrettably, although the Advisory Opinion No. P16-2018-001 had found that the child's right to respect for private life required the possibility of legal recognition of the non-genetic intended parent through an *effective* mechanism left at the State's discretion,[160] the *A.M.* v. *Norway* decision failed to assess

[157] *A.M.* v. *Norway*, App. No. 30254/18, 24 March 2022; see Chapter 3, Section 3.3.1.

[158] *A.M.* v. *Norway*, [140]. The majority judgment did not dispute the domestic interpretation of the Act nor the domestic court's conclusion that the applicant would not have qualified even if her case had fallen within the temporal scope of the Act ([145]).

[159] *A.M.* v. *Norway*, Dissenting Opinion of Judge Jelić, [40].

[160] See Advisory Opinion No. P16-2018-001, [54]: 'What is important is that *at the latest when*, according to the assessment of the circumstances of each case, *the relationship between the child and the intended mother has become a practical reality* . . ., *an effective mechanism* should exist enabling that relationship to be recognised. Adoption may satisfy this requirement

the genetic parent's insurmountable veto right as inconsistent with the effectiveness criterion. From the child's perspective as well as that of the intended parent, a legal mechanism wholly dependent on the biological parent's will, such as step-parent adoption, can be illusory. Moreover, since step-parent adoption is only available to formalised relationships (marriage, potentially registered partnerships), a mechanism requiring the intended parent to be married to the child's genetic parent discriminates against the former on the ground of civil status, and against the child on the ground of being born out of wedlock (or shortly after the intended parents' divorce).

Finally, hurdles raised by the civil status in accessing ART can include the free provision of treatment only to married couples. Naturally, a justiciable right to publicly funded fertility treatment seems unlikely to emerge in international human rights law. Courts have been reluctant to question decisions regarding resource allocation in healthcare and state benefits, seen as a prerogative for domestic authorities.[161] However, resource allocation issues are not beyond the Court's remit when the access criteria operate a difference in treatment potentially amounting to discrimination. The Court's case law on eligibility for welfare measures, such as child benefits and parental leave allowance, demonstrates that the principle of non-discrimination can bring economic claims within the purview of civil and political rights. In fact, ECHR jurisprudence has established that 'Article 14 comes into play whenever "the subject-matter of the disadvantage … constitutes one of the modalities of the exercise of a right guaranteed", or the measures complained of are "linked to the exercise of a right guaranteed"'.[162] In particular, *Okpisz* v. *Germany* shows that, although Article 8 does not impose any obligation to grant public assistance for childcare, those types of benefits cannot be dispensed on a discriminatory basis (e.g. residency status). Firstly, even if what is at stake is an advantage afforded under domestic law and not an ECHR entitlement, if it concerns an ECHR area, the discretionary advantages must conform to non-discrimination principles; specifically, 'by granting child benefits, States are able to demonstrate their respect for family life within

provided that the conditions which govern it are appropriate and the procedure enables a decision to be taken rapidly, so that the child is not kept for a lengthy period in a position of legal uncertainty as regards the relationship. It is self-evident that these conditions must include an assessment by the courts of the child's best interests in the light of the circumstances of the case' (emphasis added).

[161] See Atina Krajewska, 'Access of Single Women to Fertility Treatment: A Case of Incidental Discrimination?' (2015) 23(4) *Medical Law Review* 620–645, at 628–629.

[162] See *Petrovic* v. *Austria*, App. No. 20458/92, 27 March 1998, [28]; *Okpisz* v. *Germany*, App. No. 59140/00, 25 October 2005, [31].

the meaning of Article 8 of the Convention; the benefits therefore come within the scope of that provision'.[163] Secondly, the different treatment of aliens with regard to child benefits depending on whether or not they were in possession of a stable residence permit did not have a reasonable justification and breached Article 14 in conjunction with Article 8.[164] Similarly, in *Konstantin Markin* v. *Russia*, the Court found that the difference in treatment between male and female military personnel regarding rights to parental leave allowance, an economic benefit related to the right to respect for family life,[165] discriminated unjustifiably on the ground of gender and breached Convention rights.[166] By analogy, access to publicly funded fertility treatment is a means to support the right to make procreative choices and pursue the interest in having a biological child, and it must be granted without discrimination, whether express or implied (e.g. by defining infertility, for the purposes of eligibility for treatment, as requiring one year of unprotected intercourse, which for a single woman would presuppose unsafe and morally objectionable casual sex).[167]

Reproductive justice, including access to publicly funded fertility services without discrimination, might find its way into international litigation in a similar fashion. It is also worth recalling that non-discrimination grounds in international human rights law are not exhaustively defined; all human rights instruments reference 'other status'/'any other social condition'. Consequently, the prohibition on discrimination extends to 'single' status.

[163] *Okpisz* v. *Germany*, [32]. In *Petrovic* v. *Austria*, the Court accepted that the parental leave allowance paid by State 'is intended to promote family life and necessarily affects the way in which the latter is organised as, in conjunction with parental leave, it enables one of the parents to stay at home to look after the children' ([27]); moreover, 'by granting parental leave allowance States are able to demonstrate their respect for family life within the meaning of Art. 8 of the Convention; the allowance therefore comes within the scope of that provision' ([29]). However, there was no consensus in Europe on parental leave for fathers; indeed, few States contemplated it; the respondent had not overstepped its margin of appreciation ([35]–[43]).

[164] *Okpisz* v. *Germany*, [34]. See also *Weller* v. *Hungary*, App. No. 44399/05, 31 March 2005, [34].

[165] See *Konstantin Markin* v. *Russia* [GC], App. No. 30078/06, 22 March 2012, [130]: although Art. 8 does not require States to offer parental leave allowances, they 'promote family life and necessarily affect the way in which it is organised' and hence 'come within the scope of Article 8'; therefore, 'if a State does decide to create a parental leave scheme, it must do so in a manner which is compatible with Article 14 of the Convention'.

[166] See ibid., [143]: the reference to the traditional distribution of gender roles in society cannot justify the exclusion of men, including servicemen, from the entitlement to parental leave. . . . Gender stereotypes, such as the perception of women as primary child-carers and men as primary breadwinners, cannot, by themselves, be considered to amount to sufficient justification for a difference in treatment.'

[167] See Krajewska, 'Access of Single Women to Fertility Treatment', 635.

'Relationship status' rather than 'marital status' or 'civil status' is often the problem in domestic access to fertility treatment, especially that which is publicly funded. For instance, it was noted that, in English law, a woman seeking treatment with an unmarried partner is not excluded from funding, because protected characteristics under equality legislation encompass marital status, but being single, as opposed to unmarried, appears to be outside the boundaries of that notion.[168] The absence of 'relationship status' from the suspect grounds for differences in treatment under domestic legislation can be superseded in proceedings under international human rights treaties. Significantly, the Inter-American Court of Human Rights has recognised that access to ARTs in furthering the decision to become a biological parent affects a person's autonomy and identity not just as part of a couple but also on an individual basis:

> The decision to have biological children using assisted reproduction techniques forms part of the sphere of the right to personal integrity and to private and family life. In addition, the way in which this decision is arrived at is part of the autonomy and identity of a person, *in both the individual dimension and as part of a couple*.[169]

Consequently, as the Inter-American Commission on Human Rights reiterated in 2016, the ban on the use of IVF breaches the rights of '*all persons and/or couples*' under several provisions of the American Convention, namely Articles 5 (humane treatment), 7 (personal liberty), 11(2) (right to private and family life), 17(2) (right to raise a family) and 24 (equal protection of the law): 'This prohibition is an across-the-board ban affecting all persons and/or couples who require *in vitro* fertilization in order to follow through with their decision to have biological children.'[170]

5.5 THE DIFFERENT TREATMENT OF GENETIC MOTHERS IN RELATION TO SURROGACY ARRANGEMENTS

Despite notable advances towards the protection of surrogacy-based families,[171] the jurisprudence of the ECtHR seemingly permits gender-based

[168] Ibid., 644.

[169] *Artavia Murillo et al. ('In Vitro Fertilisation')* v. *Costa Rica*, Case No. 12.361, 28 November 2012, [272] (emphasis added).

[170] *Gómez Murillo and Others* v. *Costa Rica*, Report No. 1/15, Case No. 12.798 (Merits), 29 January 2015, [39].

[171] See Chapters 2 and 3 for a discussion of the ECtHR's approach to genetic and non-genetic commissioning parents, respectively.

inequality between genetic commissioning parents. In fact, it is now well established in ECHR case law that the relationship between children born through foreign surrogacy and their intended genetic fathers must be recognised in domestic law.[172] Conversely, the Court has been ambivalent on the child's legal affiliation with the genetic commissioning mother. The case of *D.* v. *France* conceded that Article 8 allows States to secure that relationship through less immediate mechanisms, such as step-parent adoption.[173] The ambiguous position in the Advisory Opinion No. P16-2018-001 on the modalities for the recognition of the genetic intended mother in foreign surrogacy arrangements (noted in the preceding section) only confirmed that problematic finding.

The *D.* v. *France* case required the Court to pronounce on whether the refusal to transcribe the details of the mother from the foreign birth certificate on suspicion of surrogacy, while the father's details benefitted from a presumption in favour of automatic recognition, amounted to unlawful discrimination.[174] In fact, the father was recognised by default, merely based on the foreign birth certificate, even in circumstances where the requested authorities suspected that the child had been born as a result of a surrogacy arrangement; conversely, the mother had to adopt the child,[175] and this was considered by the Court to be an effective and sufficient means of establishing maternal affiliation.[176] The disquieting result of the ruling is that it allows States to distinguish between the genetic commissioning parents based on their gender without reasonable justification. Unhelpfully, the paperwork initially submitted by the applicants in *D.* v. *France* had not indicated that the intended mother was the genetic mother;[177] nor did it contain a discrimination claim on her behalf,[178] and this new complaint was caught by the six-month time bar in Article 35(1).[179]

However, the Court's analysis in relation to Article 8 taken alone also casts light on its potential approach to a claim based on Article 14 taken in

[172] See *Mennesson* v. *France*; *Labassee* v. *France*; *C. and E.* v. *France*.
[173] *D.* v. *France*, App. No. 11288/18, 16 July 2004 (available only in French).
[174] Ibid., [74]. Chapter 2, Section 2.4, examined the applicants' claims based on Art. 8 taken alone and on Arts. 8 and 14 in relation to the child.
[175] See ibid., [35]–[38].
[176] See ibid., [70]; the contrast with the immediacy of recognition required in the case of biological motherhood in *Marckx* v. *Belgium* is striking and appears to disclose prejudice towards genetic, but not gestational, motherhood; this leads to significant concessions to the State.
[177] See *D.* v. *France*, [61].
[178] See ibid., [63].
[179] See ibid., [81]–[82].

conjunction with Article 8. In particular, the Court accepted unquestioningly the argument that the refusal to recognise the relationship between the surrogate-born child and the genetic commissioning mother sought to protect the rights of the child and of the surrogate. Similar concerns might be valid in a domestic case of disputed motherhood; conversely, the foreign certificate confirmed the success of the surrogacy arrangement and the relinquishment by the surrogate mother of all parental rights (or the existence of a final judicial determination that the baby must be handed over to the commissioning parents). The refusal to transcribe the mother's details as listed in the birth certificate cannot be, therefore, justified by the protection of the surrogate mother's interests. Nor can it be said to protect the child, because the gestational mother is uninterested in acting as a social parent (or precluded by the law governing the surrogacy arrangement from doing so), which means that the child is effectively motherless in the jurisdiction of destination, whereas it has a willing and capable genetic mother.

An important finding in *Mennesson* and *Labassee* was that the failure to transcribe the foreign birth certificates deprived children of the recognition of parentage in respect of a biological parent (the fathers in those cases), which was not in their best interests and inconsistent with their identity rights. Instead of upholding this principle in relation to both genetic parents, *D.* v. *France* improperly placed the genetic intended mother in the same position as the non-genetic intended mother (the *Mennesson/C. and E.* v. *France* situation), effectively treating the mother's biological ties with the child as irrelevant for the purposes of Article 8. While non-biological intentional motherhood is closer to the adoption of abandoned minors or step-children, the genetic mother contributed her gametes to conception to the same extent as the father, and neither of the two had a contribution to gestation. Moreover, for the child's private life, the biological reality – underpinning the child's identity – was that the intended mother was also her genetic parent. The Court ought to be prepared to find that the child's right to respect for family life – including the development of normal ties with both biological parents – is breached by the absence of legal recognition, as are the child's identity rights under the 'privacy' limb of Article 8. In fact, in the context of natural procreation, 'the Court's identity case law concerns both mothers and fathers, suggesting that the identity interest is equally important in both instances'.[180]

[180] Andrea Mulligan, 'Identity Rights and Sensitive Ethical Questions: The European Convention on Human Rights and the Regulation of Surrogacy Arrangements' (2018) 26(3) *Medical Law Review* 449–475, at 470, citing *Gaskin* v. *The United Kingdom*, App. No. 10454/83, 7 July 1989, and *Odièvre* v. *France* [GC], App. No. 42326/98, 13 February 2003.

There is no well-founded reason to depart from this principle in the case of children born through foreign surrogacy, especially since they have no effective or legal ties whatsoever with the surrogate mother.

The respondent's justification in *D. v. France* for the absolute presumption of accuracy of the father's details on foreign birth certificates and their automatic transcription in the domestic civil register, by contrast with a vetting procedure for the mother, is mystifying. According to the French government, the judicial scrutiny was rendered necessary by the fact that maternal affiliation could not be immediately verified in situations where the intended mother had not been the one giving birth.[181] However, paternal affiliation also escapes immediate verification by the mere fact of birth (indeed, it has always been the case that *pater incertus est*, even at a time that medical technology had not displaced the *mater semper certa* principle), and yet this was not deemed an obstacle to the recognition of the intended father's legal status. Had the law required proof of genetic parentage of both parents and subordinated the transcription of the foreign certificate to it, differential treatment concerns would not have arisen. Arguably, a procedure whereby the father is presumed such and the mother is registered subject to genetic proof would be a less disproportionate disparity of treatment. Conversely, the absolute presumption benefitting the father's parental status, in stark contrast with the obligation for the mother to adopt her own child as a step-parent, notwithstanding her equal genetic ties, cannot be seen as consistent with Article 14 taken together with Article 8. Article 14 also applies when the more beneficial domestic treatment (in this case, the automatic recognition of the father's legal status on the basis of a foreign civil registry document) is not mandated by Article 8, but voluntarily introduced by the State.

Equally disquieting in the *D. v. France* decision is the Court's intimation that *Mennesson* had not required the recognition of biological ties with the commissioning father through the transcription of the birth certificate, but through any suitable means. Since the commissioning mother is also not a legal parent, and hence step-parent adoption is not an option for the acquisition of fatherhood, it is unclear what mechanism the Court envisaged. If the immediacy of the transcription of the foreign birth certificate is not mandatory, States may presumably declare surrogate-born children entering the jurisdiction abandoned; even if the genetic parents are considered eligible and preferential adopters, treating the child as an orphan upon entering the

[181] See *D. v. France*, [77]. The biological ties between the mother and the child are devalued by the Court's view of the situation of surrogacy-born children as 'analogous' to that of unrelated prospective adoptees towards whom the woman forms a parental project.

jurisdiction leaves the child in a temporary legal vacuum for the period of time required to complete adoption proceedings, a situation condemned in *Marckx* v. *Belgium*.[182] The risks entailed by placing the child in a legal limbo include, in case of intervening death of one or both commissioning parents, the forfeiture of rights to which their parentage otherwise entitled them, inter alia, inheritance rights, which goes against the child's rights to respect for private and family life. It is, in fact, well established that family life extends to patrimonial rights based on kinship.[183] In its attempt to rationalise the finding of non-discrimination in *D.* v. *France* by second-guessing the meaning of *Mennesson*, the Court therefore ended up watering down the progress previously achieved in developing the rights of surrogate-born children. One can only surmise that the Court wished to avoid upholding a discriminatory regime, differentiating between genetic commissioning parents based on their gender, while also avoiding requiring France to change its legislation in a sensitive area.

It is also worth noting that, in *D.* v. *France*, the step-parent adoption route was opened to the genetic mother only because the father's legal status was already recognised and they had an ongoing marital relationship. If States are no longer required to transcribe the father's details even where he is ascertained to be the genetic father, the mother's step-parent adoption option falls away. The vetting procedure then becomes similar to adoption by strangers, which is a distortion of biological reality. In addition, if the commissioning couple's relationship breaks down and step-parent adoption requires the father's consent as the legal parent, the genetic mother is left without protection, and so is the child in respect of his/her relationship with one of the genetic parents. An inequitable situation may thus arise whereby the intended mother's rights are subjected to a veto right afforded to the intended father; problematically, the father may have an interest in raising obstacles to the adoption so that a new female partner may adopt the child. Finally, since, until the adoption is finalised, the mother has no right to contact, the father is enabled by the law to engage with impunity in parental alienation; this fails to

182 See *Marckx* v. *Belgium*, [37]: 'There is thus a risk that the establishment of affiliation will be time-consuming and that, in the interim, the child will remain separated in law from his mother. This system resulted in a lack of respect for the family life of Alexandra Marckx who, in the eyes of the law, was motherless from 16 to 29 October 1973.'

183 See ibid., [52]: 'Family life does not include only social, moral or cultural relations, for example in the sphere of children's education; it also comprises interests of a material kind, as is shown by, amongst other things, the obligations in respect of maintenance and the position occupied in the domestic legal systems of the majority of the Contracting States by the institution of the reserved portion of an estate (réserve héréditaire).'

safeguard not only the mother's but also the child's rights against third-party interference. The acceptance of step-parent adoption as a suitable alternative to the immediate recognition of maternal affiliation in respect of a biological child discriminates against the mother on ground of gender and fails to secure respect for the child's private life. It also discriminates against *unmarried* women resorting to overseas surrogacy, alone or as part of a couple, on the grounds of civil status; this is all the more problematic since *Foulon* v. *France* confirmed that single men who father children abroad through surrogacy arrangements are to be recognised as the legal parents upon return (based on their genetic link and the child's identity rights).

These are the paradoxical results of a ruling excessively concerned with accommodating policy objections. *D.* v. *France* operates a gender-based distinction between parents without a reasonable and objective justification, as well as granting different privacy rights to surrogate-born children depending on whether their commissioning parent is male or female. Both intended parents are in the same situation: their genetic material was used for IVF treatment resulting in the embryo implanted into the surrogate's body (a woman who did not wish to be treated as the mother and was not treated as the mother pursuant to the applicable law in the jurisdiction where the treatment took place), and they both embarked upon treatment with the intention to become parents. If the ECtHR does not require a free-standing route for the recognition of genetic motherhood, which does not depend on the marriage to the genetic father, a single man will be able to resort to surrogacy abroad and be recognised as the legal father in his country of residence, whereas a woman resorting to gestational surrogacy abroad as well as her biological child may be left without protection. The inequity, from the mother's perspective, is compounded by the fact that the genetic mother's contribution to medically assisted conception is much more onerous than the father's: ova extraction is an invasive surgical procedure and hormonal treatment is administered to increase fertility; the commissioning mother is, therefore, much more directly involved in the treatment than the commissioning father.[184]

Allowing States to refuse the recognition of parental status to the genetic commissioning mother (and possibly father, if the U-turn from *Mennesson* in *D.* is to be followed) has further repercussions on the surrogate-born child, depending on the effects of adoption orders in the jurisdiction in question. As an example, in English law, an adopted person cannot marry their adoptive

[184] See Chapter 2, Section 2.1.2, on *Evans* v. *The United Kingdom* and the unfairness of the veto right given to the male progenitor of embryos once an assisted reproduction procedure is underway, with substantially greater costs to the woman.

parent, but there is no bar on marrying an adoptive sibling, grandparent or uncle;[185] this suggests that adoption only creates a legal tie analogous to natural procreation between the child and the parent rather than a full integration into the extended family. More generally, adoption can be inadequate in recognising the child's links with other close relatives (e.g. grandparents), a ramification condemned in *Marckx* v. *Belgium* as incompatible with the child's Article 8 rights.[186] The Court noted in that judgment:

> 'Respect' for a family life so understood implies an obligation for the State to act in a manner calculated to allow these ties to develop normally. . . . Yet the development of the family life of an unmarried mother and her child whom she has recognised may be hindered if the child does not become a member of the mother's family and if the establishment of affiliation has effects only as between the two of them.[187]

The adoption route for a genetic parent is consequently unsatisfactory from the viewpoint of the child' identity rights and the normal development of ties with the extended family. To deny surrogacy-born children the full extent of recognition as a member of their biological family would be to grant them lesser rights in relation to establishing kinship, merely on the grounds of their conception; this would be an unmitigated breach of their rights under Article 8 read in conjunction with Article 14.

5.6 CONCLUDING REMARKS

In recent years, the ECtHR's case law has recognised the need to protect *existing* family ties created by singles and same-sex couples through donor insemination and surrogacy, whether through overseas treatment or domestically outside a regulatory framework (*X, Y and Z* v. *The United Kingdom*; *Foulon and Bouvet* v. *France*; *C.E. and Others* v. *France*; *D.B.* v. *Switzerland*; Advisory Opinion P-16-2018-001). This stance builds on the well-established Strasbourg approach to 'family life' as defined by close personal ties (and hence the obligation to safeguard de facto family units), on the understanding of privacy as encompassing identity rights, and on the priority given to the child's best interests, even when this compels States to sanction a *fait accompli*.

[185] See s. 1 and Part 1, Schedule 1 of the Marriage Act 1949 for the relationships caught by the nullity bar.

[186] See *Marckx* v. *Belgium*, [45]–[47].

[187] Ibid., [45].

By contrast, there is no authority in support of a right to accommodate *planned* ART-based families involving gamete donation and/or surrogacy. The right to respect for the decision to become a parent remains narrowly construed, as a right to protection against active interferences from the State, which may include the denial of access to homologous assisted fertilisation (*Dickson* v. *The United Kingdom*), a technique only benefitting heterosexual couples. However, where States allow third-party reproduction (which *S.H.* v. *Austria* deferred to States), the exclusion of certain categories (such as single persons or same-sex couples) will require justification. Indeed, the case law developed under the ACHR has recognised that single persons are entitled to have recourse to IVF in order to have a biological child (*Artavia Murillo* v. *Costa Rica*; *Gómez Murillo* v. *Costa Rica*).

Moreover, States continue to enjoy considerable latitude in deciding the modalities through which family life must be protected, so as to reconcile the private interests at stake with other interests in society. Although, in *C.E. and Others* v. *France*, the Court did not require the conferral of parental status to the intentional parent of children born to female couples through donor insemination, nor access to step-parent adoption, it acknowledged the reality of the family bonds between the child and the non-biological parent and the need to protect those through effective legal mechanisms (such as an order for shared parental authority with the child's biological mother). Importantly, the Court did not differentiate between children born overseas through a lawful artificial insemination procedure with donor and those born out of unauthorised, informal assisted insemination within the jurisdiction.

In relation to surrogacy, the case law does not afford any preferential treatment to opposite-sex married couples. In all foreign surrogacy rulings, the interference with the adults' Article 8 rights is seen justified by their foreknowledge of the inopposability of the parent–child legal ties created abroad in their country of habitual residence. *D.B.* v. *Switzerland* equalised the position of male couples and heterosexual couples when it comes to the recognition of parenthood following foreign surrogacy; although the rights of the adults were not upheld, the rights of the children to the certainty of their identity and to being raised in a stable environment were found to apply regardless of the gender of the unrelated intended parent; the principle expressed in the 2019 Advisory Opinion in relation to the opposite-sex spouse of the genetic father was thus extended to the same-sex registered partner. The judgment also removed the ambiguity as regards the acceptable routes to the recognition of the relationship between the child and the non-genetic commissioning parent, by clarifying that legal affiliation is required by the protection of the child's identity rights (whether established through registration at birth or adoption), whereas lesser mechanisms, such as shared custody and wills, are unsatisfactory.

Recent case law has, therefore, seen progress in relation to single or homosexual male commissioning parents for whom surrogacy is the only route to biological parenthood, albeit from the child's rights perspective. As seen in Chapter 2, the same applies to heterosexual commissioning couples: the adults benefit indirectly from the children's right to legal recognition of the relationship (*Mennesson* v. *France*; *Labassee* v. *France*; *Laborie* v. *France*). The case of *Foulon and Bouvet* v. *France* confirmed that there is no difference between the position of single genetic commissioning fathers and those who resort to overseas surrogacy as part of a heterosexual couple (the *Mennesson* scenario). In both cases, the refusal to grant legal recognition to the parent–child relationship violates the child's privacy rights under Article 8. While there are no decided applications brought by single commissioning mothers, both Article 8 taken alone and Article 8 taken in conjunction with Article 14 have the potential to support such claims in future litigation, at least through the prism of children's rights. *D.* v. *France* and the Advisory Opinion No. P16-2018-001, albeit concerned with heterosexual couples and not requiring the transcription of the foreign birth certificate insofar as the mother's name is concerned, indicated that a prompt and effective route to establishing legal ties between a genetic mother and her surrogate-born child must exist, although not necessarily identical to the one offered to the genetic father.

There remains thus a gap in protection against gender-based discrimination in procreative matters in the treatment of the genetic commissioning mother in surrogacy arrangements entered into by couples. To date, the case law has established (*Mennesson*, *Labassee*, *D.* v. *France*) that the genetic commissioning father must be recognised as the legal father.[188] The position on the genetic commissioning mother has been much more ambivalent, and the Court has accepted that step-parent adoption is a satisfactory means of protecting the rights of those concerned, without any distinction between genetic and non-genetic commissioning mothers. This not only makes the commissioning mother's relationship with the child dependent on that with the commissioning father, but it also deprives surrogate-born children of their kinship rights on the maternal side: identity rights, as well as patrimonial and citizenship rights (while the latter two can be restored through adoption, they are placed at risk

[188] *D.* v. *France* intimated that *Mennesson* did not specifically require the transcription of the birth certificate establishing the genetic commissioning father as the father, but it appears to be an after-thought designed to give States more latitude in relation to commissioning genetic mothers – the new issue before the Court.

throughout the duration of the proceedings). As noted in a Separate Opinion in an intentional parenthood case, European law has lagged behind social and scientific developments:

> By entering a surrogacy arrangement abroad which practice is not lawful in their own State, an intended parent embarks on a legally precarious journey ... the journey is particularly precarious for non-biological parents and *even genetic (not gestational) mothers*, in relation to whom *the law has not kept apace either of social reality or of science.*[189]

The understanding of filiation as presupposing two parents of the opposite sex remains prevalent in Europe, and the Convention interpretation suggests that States can legitimately continue to adhere to it. Thus, the protection to which non-conventional family units are entitled does not necessarily extend to the legal recognition of affiliation between the child and the non-genetic social parent; an alternative route to creating legal ties, such as step-parent adoption, is equally satisfactory (*D.B.* v. *Switzerland*). While the allocation of parental authority and the right to contact with a child after separation from the biological parent are likely to give rise to successful Article 8 claims (following the principles in *Honner* v. *France* and *C.E.* v. *France*), an obligation for State authorities to record two parents of the same sex in the births register may clash with fundamental societal beliefs and attract deference in international proceedings (as seen in *S.-H.* v. *Poland*).

As regards the ECtHR's Article 14 methodology, non-discrimination case law in the area of assisted reproduction continues to be influenced by formalistic categorisations that oversimplify the distinctions between same-sex and opposite-sex couples in terms of law and biology. This influences a key question at the core of the Article 14 analysis, namely whether the applicants can compare themselves to a category receiving more advantageous treatment:

> Article 14 (art. 14) does not prohibit distinctions in treatment which are founded on an objective assessment of essentially different factual circumstances and which, being based on the public interest strike a fair balance between the protection of the interests of the community and respect for the rights and freedoms safeguarded by the Convention.[190]

[189] *A.M.* v. *Norway*, Concurring Opinion of Judge O'Leary, [23].

[190] See 'Belgian Linguistics Case', App. Nos. 1474/62 et al., 23 July 1968, 'The Law', 'The Six Questions', [7]. For an application to succeed, the Court must be satisfied not only that the complaint falls within the scope of a substantive ECHR provision, and that the reason for the alleged discrimination is a ground covered by Art. 14, but also that the applicants' situation is comparable to that of the class treated more favourably and the difference in treatment is not reasonably and objectively justified.

For instance, the finding in *Gas and Dubois* that homosexual civil partners were similarly situated to heterosexual civil partners, but not to spouses (insofar as marriage confers a special status), led the Court to conclude that the ineligibility for step-parent adoption of an ART-born child did not discriminate on the basis of sexual orientation. That finding overlooked an important distinction: opposite-sex couples having elected civil partnership over marriage and same-sex partners, only eligible for civil partnerships, do not pertain to the same category; opposite-sex couples had the option to intermarry and assume further legal obligations in order to be eligible for step-parent adoption. The situation of same-sex couples in relation to assisted reproduction would have warranted at least an exploration of potential indirect discrimination aspects.

The notion of 'indirect discrimination' is clearly established in international case law and concerns neutrally formulated provisions (i.e. measures not distinguishing based on a suspect ground, such as gender or sexual orientation) which in practice have 'disproportionately prejudicial effects on a particular group', as noted by the ECtHR in *Hugh Jordan* v. *The United Kingdom*.[191] A similar definition can be found in the practice of the UN Human Rights Committee in the interpretation of Article 26 ICCPR (equality before the law and non-discrimination), specifically in *Althammer* v. *Austria*.[192] Whether the measure (in *Gas and Dubois*, the bar on step-parent adoption in civil partners) is justified, despite the impact on a particular category (same-sex civil partners, ineligible for marriage), by outweighing competing rights and interests, may be open to interpretation, but the use of unsuitable comparators and the dismissal of Article 14 claims without proper analysis merely avoid tackling the substantive debate.

Access to gamete and embryo donation, the legalisation of surrogacy services and the allocation of parenthood to intentional, non-genetic parents are not the only controversial measures potentially required by substantive procreative equality. The notion of respect for the decision to become a genetic parent may expand so as to encompass the right to make use of an artificial

[191] See *Hugh Jordan* v. *The United Kingdom*, App. No. 24746/94, 4 May 2001, [154].

[192] See *Althammer* v. *Austria*, Communication No. 998/2001, 8 August 2003, [10.2]. The Committee also distinguished between the scope of Art. 14 (non-discrimination in the enjoyment of a Convention right) and the broader protection under Art. 26 ICCPR: 'The Committee on earlier occasions has already decided that the independent right to equality and non-discrimination embedded in article 26 of the Covenant provides a greater protection than the accessory right to non-discrimination contained in article 14 of the European Convention' ([8.4]).

womb, at present only explored speculatively in the literature.[193] Whereas all prospective parents may benefit from this technique, given the risks of pregnancy and childbirth, it would be particularly significant for women who can produce gametes but cannot carry a pregnancy to term, as well as for individuals/couples biologically unable to gestate – single men and male same-sex couples. This would obviate the need to resort to surrogacy, with the ensuing dependency upon the surrogate mother, in terms of both her lifestyle choices during the pregnancy that may harm the foetus (e.g. alcohol consumption) and her cooperation to transfer the baby after birth (in jurisdictions allowing her to renege on the agreement). Ruth Deech and Anna Smajdor have also pointed out the feminist perspective discrediting possible objections to the use of artificial wombs: 'it seems that there is an injustice in the fact that if a man wants to father a child he can do so without undergoing the pains and risks of gestation and childbirth. However, a woman cannot. If we can use technological means to redress this balance, why should we hesitate?'[194] The idea of ectogenesis can thus be seen as a matter of reproductive equality, between men and women but also between heterosexual and homosexual couples.

Naturally, should the successful use of artificial wombs become a reality, any actionable access rights would have to consider the equitable distribution of resources in society. Several questions emerge in that respect. Should ectogenesis be subsidised by the State even when it is merely elective (i.e. there is no infertility issue, either biological or social, and no particular health risk other than those normally associated with pregnancy and childbirth)? If the State supports one's decision to become a parent by offering financial support in relation to any number of children born through natural gestation, on what basis can financial support be denied to individuals who need an artificial womb to become parents (as opposed to public assistance to defray childcare costs)? Should there be a cap in the financial resources offered to an individual in relation to procreation (either childcare or ART), if the public budget cannot satisfy all needs? Is recourse to ectogenesis a type of medical treatment less worthy of support than the one sought by couples who reproduce with the knowledge of high risks of severe illness or disability in their

[193] On technical prospects and ethical aspects of ectogenesis, see Seppe Segers, 'The Path toward Ectogenesis: Looking beyond the Technical Challenges' (2021) 22(1) *BMC Medical Ethics* 59.

[194] Ruth Deech and Anna Smajdor, *From IVF to Immortality* (Oxford: Oxford University Press, 2007) 98.

offspring, which will require substantial State funding after birth? Ultimately, the question raised by any procreative treatment – against the background of finite resources in society and the traditional postnatal welfare support – is this: what entitles a person's decision to become a parent to greater protection than that of another, whether at the conception, gestation or rearing stage?

Conclusions

The new reproductive technologies have not been unreservedly welcomed in the scholarship and law-making fora around the world. On the contrary, 'their tendency to press the limits of nature and transform definitions of family'[1] has inspired scepticism in many quarters. Support for 'the right of persons to use technology in pursuing their reproductive goals'[2] has been matched by staunch adherence to procreation as 'a personal act between a man and a woman'.[3] Against the background of this mixed reception, the book has explored the human rights justifications for the use of scientific advances in biomedicine to achieve individual self-fulfilment through parenthood. While adopting a normative perspective, the book has highlighted the contribution of international case law, most notably from the European Court of Human Rights (ECtHR), to the development of procreative rights as a matter of positive law.

Certainly, human rights treaties were not designed to address complex bioethical conundrums. Indeed, many technological advances examined in this book were beyond contemplation at the time of the adoption of the European Convention on Human Rights (ECHR). Despite the evolutive interpretation of ECHR provisions by the Strasbourg Court, its capacity to shape international bioethical standards has been questioned. Richard Ashcroft has argued that the ECHR 'is not a specifically "bioethical"

1 Lisa Rubin and Aliza Phillips, 'Infertility and Assisted Reproduction Technologies: Matters of Reproductive Justice', in Joan Chrisler (ed.), *Reproductive Justice: A Global Concern* (Santa Barbara: Praeger, 2012) 173–199, at 173–174.

2 John Robertson, 'The Presumptive Primacy of Procreative Liberty', in Tom Beauchamp et al. (eds.), *Contemporary Issues in Bioethics* (Boston: Wadsworth Cengage Learning, 2014) 245–251, at 251.

3 *S.H.* v. *Austria* [GC], App. No. 57813/00, 3 November 2011, Separate Opinion of Judge De Gaetano, [2].

instrument, and the coherent development of any principles is hampered by the employment of the margin of appreciation in the regulation of biomedicine';[4] therefore, 'expecting bioethics to arise out of the European Convention jurisprudence is a mistake'.[5] Nevertheless, the recent Strasbourg case law examined in this book suggests that doubts over the ability of human rights methodology to respond to bioethical issues might be misplaced.

Section C.1 of this concluding chapter distils the extensive jurisprudence analysed in the foregoing pages into a brief catalogue of established rights, synthesising the key contributions of international law to procreative freedom. Section C.2 collects cross-chapter observations on the methodological and extrajudicial obstacles to the further development of reproductive rights to date. Finally, Section C.3 offers some reflections on claims not yet upheld in international litigation, but which the evolving social perceptions and legislative practice in Europe and beyond may in the future bring within the purview of human rights law.

C.1 THE CONTRIBUTION OF INTERNATIONAL CASE LAW TO THE DEVELOPMENT OF PROCREATIVE RIGHTS

This section focuses on positive international human rights law, primarily legal developments under the ECHR, insofar as very few claims have addressed assisted reproductive treatment (ART) in other treaty-based human rights systems. The argument advanced here is that several rights associated with procreative choice have been affirmed *de lege lata*, and notwithstanding their non-absolute nature, they can have a tangible impact on the domestic regulation of ART. In fact, it is currently undisputed that Article 8 ECHR protects every person's *right to respect for the decision to become (and not to become) a genetic parent*, which is encompassed in the notion of privacy, as well as the *right of couples to conceive a child and to make use of medically assisted procreation to that end*, such a choice being recognised as an expression of private and family life.[6] Specific applications of these principles include a couple's *access to artificial insemination* and the *ability to use*

[4] Richard Ashcroft, 'Could Human Rights Supersede Bioethics?' (2010) 10(4) *Human Rights Law Review* 639–660, at 655.

[5] Ibid., 656.

[6] See *Evans* v. *The United Kingdom* [GC], App. No. 6339/05, 10 April 2007, [71]; *Dickson* v. *The United Kingdom* [GC], App. No. 44362/04, 4 December 2007, [66]; *S.H. and Others* v. *Austria* [GC], [82]; *Knecht* v. *Romania*, App. No. 10048/10, 2 October 2012, [54]; *Lia* v. *Malta*, App. No. 8709/20, 5 May 2022, [39]; *Pejřilová* v. *The Czech Republic*, App. No. 14889/19, 8 December 2022, [42].

embryos created with their gametes for implantation. The refusal of artificial insemination facilities concerns the aspiring parents' private and family lives, which notions incorporate the right to respect for their decision to become genetic parents.[7] In the same vein, the joint parental project of a couple who wish to have a child by making use of assisted procreation using their own embryos is an intimate aspect of the couple's private life and hence protected by Article 8.[8] Access to IVF is a further ramification of the right to use ART, although eligibility criteria remain within the State's discretion.[9] A total ban on the use of IVF was before the Inter-American Court of Human Rights (IACtHR) and deemed in breach of the obligation to grant couples access to the necessary techniques to resolve reproductive health problems, acknowledging that infertility is a disability.[10] Additionally, the notion of private life protects the right to respect for the decision to become a parent more broadly, not necessarily in a biological sense (recourse to gamete donation and surrogacy also evidencing a genuine intention to become parents), as well as prospective parents' personal development through the role of parents.[11]

These are, admittedly, qualified rights; while restrictions in the access to ART have been analysed as active interferences with the prospective parents' rights, requiring justification under Article 8(2),[12] in practice these new rights can be readily outflanked by State interests. Alice Margaria has noted that, although Strasbourg case law has made steps towards bringing Article 8 in line with medical advances and new ways of creating families, 'the "updating" effects do not go beyond the Court's first stage of review – concerning the applicability of Article 8 – and, therefore, are not reflected in the content of the obligations imposed by that provision on States'.[13] It would be inaccurate to suggest, however, that these rights never prevail over State interests, or that their recognition is merely symbolic and inconsequential. Albeit infrequently, they form the basis for a finding of violation, which demonstrates their potential to change the scope of international obligations. For instance, the indiscriminate refusal to grant access to artificial insemination facilities to

7 *Dickson* v. *The United Kingdom* [GC], [66].

8 *Knecht* v. *Romania*, [54]; *Nedescu* v. *Romania*, App. No. 70035/10, 16 January 2018, [70].

9 *Lia* v. *Malta*, [60].

10 *Artavia Murillo et al. ('In Vitro Fertilisation')* v. *Costa Rica*, Case No. 12.361, 28 November 2012, [289], [293].

11 *Paradiso and Campanelli* v. *Italy* [GC], App. No. 25358/12, 24 January 2017, [163]; *Nedescu* v. *Romania*, [67].

12 See, e.g., *Pejřilová* v. *The Czech Republic*, [47], and the general discussion on the classification of the alleged obligations in Chapter 1, Section 1.2.2.

13 Alice Margaria, *The Construction of Fatherhood: The Jurisprudence of the European Court of Human Rights* (Cambridge: Cambridge University Press, 2019) 53.

prisoners was found to violate Article 8.[14] So, too, were the authorities' delays in returning a couple's cryopreserved embryos seized from a clinic, depriving them of the possibility of having another child.[15] In future, a different balancing exercise may see procreative rights take priority over other interests in a wider range of circumstances, especially if the European consensus assessment changes. To date, the Court has maintained a cautious approach in relation to controversial techniques, such as ova donation, sperm donation for heterologous IVF, posthumous insemination, posthumous use of cryopreserved embryos and surrogacy arrangements. In fact, the refusal to grant prospective parents access to these techniques (or to recognise their parental status when achieved abroad through such techniques) was found to lie within the States' margin of appreciation.[16]

Nonetheless, while the lack of success of claims regarding access to third-party and posthumous treatment remains unmitigated, new and concrete obligations have been established in relation to existing parent–child relationships arising from proscribed reproductive methods. Remarkably, *a right for children born through overseas surrogacy to the recognition of legal ties with the genetic intended father* was derived from the child's identity rights, given the importance of biological parentage as a component of identity.[17] Concerns for the surrogate-born child's private life have also generated an *obligation to provide a prompt, effective mechanism for creating legal ties between the non-genetic intended parent and the child* (e.g. step-parent adoption).[18] In fact, children's best interests require the legal identification of the persons responsible for raising them, enabling them to live and develop in a stable environment,[19] and hence the recognition of the parent–child relationship legally established abroad, *at the latest when that relationship has become a practical reality*.[20] The absolute impossibility of establishing legal ties between the

[14] *Dickson* v. *The United Kingdom* [GC], [84]–[85].

[15] *Nedescu* v. *Romania*, [72].

[16] See *S.H. and Others* v. *Austria* [GC], [115] (ova donation, sperm donation for IVF); *Pejřilová* v. *The Czech Republic*, [62] (fertilisation with the deceased husband's frozen sperm); *Mennesson* v. *France*, App. No. 65192/11, 26 June 2014, [94] (legal ties between commissioning parents, one of whom genetic, and children born through foreign surrogacy).

[17] See *Mennesson* v. *France*, [100].

[18] 'Advisory Opinion Concerning the Recognition in Domestic Law of a Legal Parent–Child Relationship between a Child Born through a Gestational Surrogacy Arrangement Abroad and the Intended Mother', Request No. P16-2018-001, 10 April 2019; *C. and E.* v. *France*, App. Nos. 1462/18; 17348/18, 19 November 2019, [39]–[41] (acknowledging that the case fitted the Advisory Opinion matrix).

[19] Advisory Opinion P16-2018-001, [42].

[20] Ibid., [52].

surrogate-born child and the intended father for a long period of time constitutes a disproportionate interference with the child's private life.[21] Moreover, even cumulatively, means of protection of the relationship with the intended parent falling short of legal affiliation, such as arrangements relating to residence and parental authority, place children in a position of legal uncertainty as regards their identity in society.[22] Importantly, the case law has explicitly extended the application of these principles beyond the heterosexual couple; the same obligations arise in the case of *single commissioning genetic fathers*[23] and *same-sex commissioning couples in which one is a genetic parent*.[24]

The success of Strasbourg applications for the recognition of legal affiliation brought by children born through foreign surrogacy is explained, on the one hand, by the understanding of identity as covering genetic identity (biological ties with a parent), social identity (social ties with the other intended and de facto parent) and national identity (the belonging to the community and full citizenship rights) and, on the other, by the treatment of the interests of the child as the Court's paramount consideration. The origins of this stance, going beyond the international standard ('primary consideration', as codified chiefly in the UN Convention on the Rights of the Child (UNCRC)),[25] were questioned in a recent Dissenting Opinion:

> It is an intriguing feature in the Court's case-law that the phrase referring to the child's interests as 'paramount' is regularly cited, notwithstanding the fact that this is not the standard adopted in the special international law instrument in the field of children's rights. It is well known that according to Article 3 § 1 of the UNCRC, the requirement is that in all actions concerning children, whether undertaken by public or private social welfare institutions, courts of law, administrative authorities or legislative bodies, the best interests of the child shall be a primary consideration. The latter standard is also the one enshrined in the EU Charter of Fundamental Rights (Article 24 § 2).[26]

[21] *D.B. and Others* v. *Switzerland*, App. Nos. 58817/15; 58252/15, 22 November 2022, [89].

[22] Advisory Opinion P16-2018-001, [40]; *D.B. and Others* v. *Switzerland*, [88]; *K.K. and Others* v. *Denmark*, App. No. 25212/21, 6 December 2022, [72].

[23] *Foulon and Bouvet* v. *France*, App. Nos. 9063/14; 10410/14, 21 July 2016.

[24] *D.B. and Others* v. *Switzerland*.

[25] See Art. 3 Convention on the Rights of the Child, New York, 20 November 1989, in force 2 September 1990, UNTS vol. 1577 (p. 3).

[26] *K.K. and Others* v. *Denmark*, Joint Dissenting Opinion of Judges Kjølbro, Koskelo and Yüksel, [93]. The dissenters were concerned that the effect of this stricter test is 'to practically eliminate altogether, in substance, the margin of appreciation available to the Contracting States' ([88]), excluding 'general policy considerations' from the regulation of 'delicate and complex matters of family law' ([109]).

Another progressive feature of ART case law is *the protection of the fait accompli* under Article 8, including an obligation to *ensure respect for de facto family life created through reproductive means inconsistent with, or not provided for, domestic legislation*. While permitting ECHR States to outlaw and discourage third-party reproduction, the Court remains concerned to protect social bonds already created, for instance, between a child born through donor insemination abroad and the same-sex partner of his/her biological mother, in circumstances where domestic law does not recognise the legal affiliation between the child and the social mother.[27] In such cases, the Court has also found breaches of the adults' rights where the conduct of State authorities affected the continuance of those bonds. Thus, the refusal to grant the social mother post-separation contact with the donor-conceived child failed to meet the positive obligation to ensure effective respect for private and family life.[28]

Conversely, the absence of avenues for the acquisition of parenthood by the social parent in relation to donor-conceived children was not seen as exceeding States' margin of appreciation.[29] Although, unlike surrogacy, undergoing donor insemination with a view to raising a child with a same-sex partner was not depicted as an egregious circumvention of domestic law (there are no references to the parents' unlawful or 'fraudulent' conduct),[30] the Court has afforded less protection in such cases: it did not require the recognition of affiliation but accepted that the State met its positive obligations as long as mechanisms for the protection of the de facto ties existed (e.g. shared parental authority, arrangements for alternate residence/contact after the couple's separation).[31] While both surrogacy and donor insemination are heterologous techniques involving a genetic parent and a joint parenthood project,[32] only in surrogacy cases is the child's identity seen to require the

[27] See *Honner* v. *France*, App. No. 19511/16, 12 November 2020 (available only in French); *C.E. and Others* v. *France*, App. Nos. 29775/18; 29693/19, 24 March 2022 (available only in French); *Callamand* v. *France*, App. No. 2338/20, 7 April 2022 (available only in French).

[28] *Callamand* v. *France*, [44]–[45].

[29] See *C.E. and Others* v. *France*, concluding that the respondent had not failed in its obligation to guarantee effective respect for the private and family life existing between a woman and the child born to her former companion through donor insemination. See also *Bonnaud and Lecoq* v. *France*, App. No. 6190/11, 1 March 2018, where the ECtHR agreed with domestic courts that shared parental responsibility by lesbian partners for their respective donor-conceived children was not required by the children's welfare or the circumstances of the case.

[30] Contrast with *D.B.* v. *Switzerland*, [92] (the ECtHR agreed with the domestic courts' assessment that recourse to foreign surrogacy in order to circumvent the domestic prohibition constituted fraudulent conduct).

[31] See *C.E. and Others* v. *France*, [94]–[95], [105].

[32] The comparison here is with cases of surrogacy in which only one commissioning parent is a genetic parent (the majority of surrogacy cases before the ECtHR).

establishment of parent–child ties with the non-genetic intended parent. The explanation appears to lie in the existence of legal ties between both commissioning parents and the surrogate-born child in the foreign jurisdiction (where the birth took place and parenthood was legally transferred); in fact, the Court has distinguished the two situations on that basis.[33]

Another important right upheld in Strasbourg case law is the right to influence reproductive outcomes, during pregnancy and at the conception stage. Firstly, the ECtHR has recognised the right of the expectant woman to avail herself of *timely prenatal tests for the detection of foetal disability*, so as to make an informed decision on the continuance or termination of the pregnancy, as provided for by domestic law.[34] Although the Court acts as an enforcer of already available domestic rights, the ruling contributes to the consolidation of a right to informed procreative choice under the ECHR. Several pending cases will face the Court squarely with the question of whether a ban on abortion on grounds of foetal defects is compatible with the Convention.[35] This will give the Court an opportunity to align its position on therapeutic abortion with that of the inter-American bodies and the UN Human Rights Committee.[36] The significance of informed reproductive choice is reinforced by the recognition of a *right to compensation for wrongful birth*. The Court found States in violation of Article 8's procedural limb where domestic courts showed arbitrariness in proceedings for compensation for medical negligence resulting in wrongful birth (failure to refer a patient at risk of foetal abnormality for antenatal screening).[37] Secondly, the ECtHR has recognised that *the desire to conceive a healthy child* is protected by Article 8; consequently, it has upheld the *right of healthy carriers of serious genetic illnesses* to use the medical options available to that end, notably PGD, allowing them to *screen embryos against genetic illness* rather than becoming parents in circumstances inconsistent with their wishes or having to resort to a more traumatic therapeutic abortion.[38]

[33] *C.E. and Others* v. *France*, [102].
[34] See *R.R.* v. *Poland*, App. No. 27617/04, 26 May 2011.
[35] *K.C.* v. *Poland*, App. No. 3639/21; *A.L.-B.* v. *Poland*, App. Nos. 3801/21 et al.; *M.L.* v. *Poland*, App. No. 40119/21; *M.B.* v. *Poland*, App. No. 5014/21; *K.B.* v. *Poland*, App. No. 1819/21; *I.Z.* v. *Poland*, App. No. 57338/21.
[36] See Chapter 4, Section 4.2.1. Note, however, the focus on *fatal* foetal abnormality in those cases.
[37] *A.K.* v. *Latvia*, App. No. 33011/08, 24 June 2014.
[38] *Costa and Pavan* v. *Italy*, App. No. 54270/10, 28 August 2012, [57].

C.2 OBSTACLES TO THE DEVELOPMENT OF PROCREATIVE RIGHTS IN INTERNATIONAL LAW

The breadth of States' margin of appreciation in assisted reproduction cases is a first major obstacle to the development of prescriptive obligations. In fact, that margin is wide when there is no European consensus on the relative importance of a right or the means best to protect it, especially where it conflicts with other rights and interests, and in sensitive areas involving ethical or moral judgment.[39] The regulation of assisted reproduction is thus viewed as the province of domestic legislatures:

> The Court's task is not to substitute itself for the competent national authorities in determining the most appropriate policy for regulating matters of artificial procreation, in respect of procedures to be followed or authorities to be involved and to what extent, especially since the use of IVF treatment continues to give rise to sensitive moral and ethical issues against a background of fast-moving medical and scientific developments. It is why, in such a context, the Court has considered that the margin of appreciation to be afforded to the respondent State is a wide one.[40]

At the same time, where a particularly important facet of an individual's existence (e.g. the ability to conceive a child)[41] or identity (e.g. establishing biological parentage)[42] is at stake, the margin allowed to the State will be restricted. In practice, the scope of discretion resulting from these two criteria, pulling in opposite directions, usually tips the balance in favour of the State.

For instance, although the surrogate-born child's right to establish affiliation benefits the entire family, genetic parents' rights are trumped by public policy objections against the recognition of foreign acts and by the State's interest in disincentivising the use of surrogacy by its citizens abroad. Consequently, applications brought by the parents in surrogacy cases almost invariably fail. Exceptionally, a genetic father was successful in Strasbourg when complaining about the length of paternity proceedings after the surrogate sold the baby to another couple, which predetermined the case to his detriment; however, the violation stemmed from the father's procedural rights under Article 8, rather than the acknowledgement of a right to establish paternity for the child

[39] See, e.g., *Lia* v. *Malta*, [59]–[60] (specifically in relation to IVF treatment).

[40] *Pejřilová* v. *The Czech Republic*, [43], consolidating principles laid down in *X, Y and Z* v. *The United Kingdom* [GC], App. No. 21830/93, 22 April 1997, [44]; *Evans* v. *The United Kingdom* [GC], [81]; *S.H. and Others* v. *Austria* [GC], [97].

[41] See *Dickson* v. *The United Kingdom* [GC], [85].

[42] See *S.H. and Others* v. *Austria* [GC], [94]; *Mennesson* v. *France*, [77].

conceived through unlawful domestic surrogacy.[43] Problematically, even in the context of *lawful* domestic surrogacy, and despite examining an application brought by the child, the Court proved reluctant to interfere with the State's regulation of parenthood: it was satisfied that the surrogacy regime was ECHR-compliant insofar as the child's family life with the intended parents was protected (through residence and parental responsibility arrangements), and it refused to require the allocation of parenthood to the intended genetic father.[44] An irrebuttable presumption of paternity in favour of the gestational surrogate's husband, a man biologically unrelated to the child and not acting in a parental role, arguably fails to strike a fair balance. Against the background of legal avenues for children born through natural intercourse to align their paternal affiliation with genetic and social reality, it also discriminates on grounds of conception and ought to be found outside any reasonable margin of appreciation.

A further obstacle to the development of procreative rights, specifically women's rights, is the *understanding of motherhood as primarily gestational*, which results in an *ambiguous treatment of the genetic commissioning mother in surrogacy cases*. Indeed, she paradoxically appears to be treated like intended non-biological parents, in relation to whom a mere 'possibility of recognition' through a mechanism chosen by the State must be available,[45] even though the surrogate is not a genetic parent, did not intend to act as a parent at the time of conception and never acted as a social parent. This places genetic intended mothers at a disadvantage in surrogacy cases, as well as penalising the child in respect of their maternal affiliation; in fact, the refusal to register the genetic intended mother in accordance with the foreign birth certificate exposes both the mother and the child to the risks of (step-parent) adoption, in particular delays in establishing affiliation (with an impact on, e.g., inheritance rights in case of unforeseen death) and potentially intractable difficulties in case of relationship breakdown in the parental couple.[46] Since neither commissioning parent has a gestational relationship with the child, and they both enjoy an equal genetic link, the child's identity, to which genetic parentage is a key component, should require the recognition of legal ties with both parents on the same footing. To avoid any suggestion that it

[43] See *A.L.* v. *France*, App. No. 13344/20, 7 April 2022.

[44] See *H.* v. *The United Kingdom*, App. No. 32185/20, 31 May 2022.

[45] See Advisory Opinion P16-2018-001, [47]; *D.* v. *France*, App. No. 11288/18, 16 July 2004, [51]–[54].

[46] *A.M.* v. *Norway*, App. No. 30254/18, 24 March 2022, illustrates the extreme consequences of making legal motherhood dependent on step-parent adoption (the case regarded a non-genetic intended mother).

condones differences in treatment between commissioning parents based on their gender, when faced with a first claim by a genetic mother, the Court unhelpfully read down its previous rulings on the obligation to recognise the genetic intended father, reinterpreting them to require the creation of legal ties through any means, not necessarily the transcription of the foreign birth certificate.[47]

Human rights law may have to tackle more complex reproductive arrangements in the future, such as the use of mitochondrial DNA and babies with 'two mothers'; recent scientific developments have permitted two women to be genetically related to a child, albeit one of them in a negligeable proportion, insofar as most of the genetic information in a cell is contained in its nucleus.[48] Women with genetic abnormalities in their mitochondrial DNA are thus able to avoid transmitting those abnormalities (causing illness or even death) if the nucleus is removed from the mother's fertilised egg and inserted into an empty egg cell donated by a woman whose mitochondrial DNA is healthy.[49] A more flexible approach to motherhood will have to prevail if rights-respectful solutions are to be found in the allocation of parental status.

The development of individual procreative autonomy is also hindered by unuttered assumptions about marriage and family foundation. Thus, non-genetic intended parents benefit indirectly from the finding that respect for the surrogate-born child's private life requires the recognition of legal ties with both commissioning parents; however, this is all contingent upon the social parent's marriage to the biological parent.[50] *The dependence of intentional parenthood upon marriage* makes the position of the non-genetic parent precarious if the genetic parent decides to exclude her/him from the child's life.[51] The Strasbourg Court's acceptance of legal schemes allowing the genetic parent to veto the acquisition of parenthood by the other party to the joint parental project, who is also a legal parent in the jurisdiction where the child was born, and who acted as a de facto carer after the child's birth, endorses an ill-balanced vision of intentional parenthood and a 'situation unfairly penalising individuals biologically unable to procreate'.[52] A recent complaint provided the Court with an opportunity to revisit this position; the case regarded the absence of a legal mechanism enabling the social father to

47 *D.* v. *France*, [45]–[49].

48 See Ruth Deech and Anna Smajdor, *From IVF to Immortality: Controversy in the Era of Reproductive Technology* (Oxford and New York: Oxford University Press, 2007) 158.

49 Ibid., 159.

50 See *C. and E.* v. *France* (where the intended mothers were the genetic fathers' wives).

51 See *A.M.* v. *Norway*.

52 Ibid., Dissenting Opinion of Judge Jelić, [46].

maintain contact with the child born to his former partner through donor insemination, after living with the child during the first four years of her life and fulfilling a parental role.[53] While the Court recalled the positive obligation to protect de facto family life, it was satisfied – considering the State's wide margin of appreciation – that a public body had requested an investigation and contact had been found incompatible with the child's welfare due to the adults' acrimonious relationship.[54]

The dependence of legal parenthood on marriage and genetic parenthood in one member of the couple means that *intentional parenthood is not recognised in the absence of legal ties between the child and either of the commissioning parents*,[55] although family life more broadly is acknowledged in case of long-term care under a foster-parenting arrangement.[56] To that extent, the Court's case law adheres to a notion of ART anchored in biological parentage (and addressing partial infertility in the couple). Double gamete donation, expanding the ways in which humankind can reproduce in a manner more akin to adoption, seems to remain outside the ambit of Article 8.

Procedural limits to the application of the 'best interests' principle have further restricted the expansion of procreative rights. The Court treats the child's best interests as paramount *when the child is the alleged victim*, rather than every time domestic decisions affect the child. Thus, the Court *merely takes the child's interests into consideration when the commissioning parents lack locus standi to submit claims on behalf of the child*.[57] When the adults are the applicants, despite the use of the 'child's best interests' rhetoric, the Court does not treat them as paramount or even a primary consideration, allowing public policy to prevail.[58] This unwarranted distinction in the application of a key principle, based on a procedural detail, denies equal protection to children whose carers do not have legal standing to defend their rights.[59]

53 *Carbonai* v. *Italy*, App. No. 9825/21, 29 November 2022 (available only in French); see, similarly, *Bortolato* v. *Italy*, App. No. 35967/19, 10 January 2023, and *Aspisi* v. *Italy*, App. No. 44453/19, 14 February 2023 (available only in French), concerning same-sex female couples.

54 *Carbonai* v. *Italy*, [15]–[22].

55 *Paradiso and Campanelli* v. *Italy* [GC]; *Valdís Fjölnisdóttir and Others* v. *Iceland*, App. No. 71552/17, 18 May 2021.

56 *Valdís Fjölnisdóttir and Others* v. *Iceland*, [62].

57 *Paradiso and Campanelli* v. *Italy* [GC], [87].

58 See ibid., [215], finding that the domestic courts had struck a fair balance in removing the child from the commissioning parents based on the assessment that he would not suffer grave or irreparable harm from the separation.

59 See ibid., [86] (noting that the complaints raised on behalf of the child had been dismissed by the Chamber for lack of locus standi), [135] (distinguishing the case from *Mennesson* v. *France*/*Labassee* v. *France*, App. No. 65941/11, 26 June 2014, where the complaints were

Most inequitably, *legal standing in Strasbourg in foreign surrogacy cases is determined by the respondent's law*: the commissioning parents – that is, the legal parents under the law of the State where the child was conceived and born – are not permitted to represent the child's interests because the alleged perpetrator of violations does not recognise them as parents.[60] Given the principle of sovereign equality of States (in consequence of which, in an international court, the law of one State cannot be superior to that of another) and the Court's jurisdiction to entertain complaints regardless of the alleged victim's nationality or residence, the quality of legal parent in any State ought to allow submissions on behalf of the child to be heard. A recently communicated case will see the Court grapple with a new legal standing question in relation to foreign surrogacy: whether the surrogate mother of a child whose intended father was not recognised as a second parent can claim victim status.[61]

Another obstacle to the expansion of aspiring parents' rights is *the abstract application of the 'best interests' principle to potential future children*. When applied to an existing child, the best interests principle usually benefits the intended/social parents in foreign surrogacy and donor insemination cases.[62] Conversely, when applied *in abstracto* to hypothetical children, their best interests – including a right to know one's biological parents (part of a person's identity) and to be raised by one's birth parents (*per* Article 7 UNCRC) – are invoked to refuse gamete donation (i.e. the allocation of parenthood to individuals unrelated to the child) as well as posthumous conception.[63] These should not be seen, however, as insuperable objections. The *pater est* presumption and the institution of adoption suggest that the notion of parent

also successfully raised on behalf of the children). In *A.M.* v. *Norway*, the intended mother only applied on her behalf, possibly because of the Court's stance in *Paradiso and Campanelli*, rather than seeking to rely on her legal parenthood in the USA.

60 See *Paradiso and Campanelli* v. *Italy* [Chamber], App. No. 25358/12, 27 January 2015, [48]–[49], on the representation of children before Convention institutions, denying the applicants such possibility due to the lack of biological ties and the child's new identity following adoption proceedings under Italian law. There is no discussion of the international relevance of the couple's parental status under Russian law.

61 *S.C.* v. *Switzerland*, App. No. 26848/18. The surrogate mother is a co-applicant together with the same-sex couple and the child.

62 For an exception, see *Honner* v. *France* (post-separation contact refused insofar as the acrimonious exchanges were detrimental to the child).

63 See *Pejřilová* v. *The Czech Republic*, [59], accepting that the refusal to allow a widow's artificial insemination with the deceased husband's frozen gametes also served to protect 'the right of the unborn child to know his parents'. See also the respondent's successful submission in *S.H. and Others* v. *Austria* [GC], [70] that the ban on ova donation 'was intended to protect the child's welfare by ensuring the unambiguous identity of the mother'.

can have a broad meaning, not strictly associated with genetic ties, especially in the context of marriage to the child's genetic parent. While, admittedly, the adults' equality and privacy rights may be outweighed by the well-being of the future child, one needs to query whether the future child is actually harmed by having a non-genetic parent by design. Berge Solberg has criticised the application of the child welfare principle, borrowed from adoption, to procreation choices, insofar as in ART cases 'the child at risk does not exist' and the child is not 'better off not coming into existence';[64] rather, he supported the alignment of ART with all human reproduction (i.e. the reality that people do not reproduce for the sake of the potential child, but for their own sake) by de-emphasising the welfare principle in policy deliberations and by focusing on the 'intentions to become functional parents' and on the feasibility of the parental project.[65]

Another problematic trait of ECHR case law is *the accommodation of State sovereignty by downplaying the principles of 'effective protection' and 'best interests'*. In relation to surrogacy, the Court expressly stated that it regards as legitimate under Article 8(2) the domestic authorities' *wish to reaffirm the State's exclusive competence to recognise a legal parent–child relationship*.[66] Attempts to make concessions to State sovereignty often see the Court dilute the requirements for the effective protection of de facto family life/best interests of the ART-born child: for example, identity rights were deemed adequately protected where the child 'ha[d] not been wholly deprived of a legal relationship with' the genetic father;[67] the fair balance test was satisfied where the child's separation from his de facto carers did not cause 'grave or irreparable harm';[68] the child's sense of identity was not considered impaired by the non-recognition of affiliation because the mother's male transgender partner 'was not prevented in any way from acting as [her] father in the social sense'.[69] States are thus allowed to prioritise their public policy and sovereign law-making powers at the expense of children's rights, in a way reminiscent of the Strasbourg approach to immigration cases; in fact, interferences with children's rights stemming from immigration control measures against their

64 Berge Solber, 'Getting beyond the Welfare of the Child in Assisted Reproduction' (2009) 35(6) *Journal of Medical Ethics* 373–376, at 373.
65 Ibid., 376.
66 *Paradiso and Campanelli* v. *Italy* [GC], [177]; *A.M.* v. *Norway*, [124].
67 *H. v. The United Kingdom*, [46].
68 *Paradiso and Campanelli* v. *Italy* [GC], [215].
69 *X, Y and Z* v. *The United Kingdom* [GC], [50].

parents are not viewed as excessive as long as obstacles to relocating abroad are not 'insurmountable'.[70] The margin of appreciation appears particularly wide when aspiring parents resort to surrogacy domestically, and hence do not enjoy the title of parent in any other jurisdiction. In cases regarding purely domestic regulation, as opposed to rules of recognition of foreign acts, the State's choice from among several candidates at parenthood is allowed to prevail.[71]

Relatedly, *in cases with a cross-border element*, the ECtHR regrettably *accommodates the respondent's sovereign decision-making powers at the expense of ethical diversity, conflating illegality and conflict of laws*.[72] It is widely accepted, both in Strasbourg judgments and by commentators, that surrogacy tourism entails some illegal conduct. Andrea Mulligan has noted that the Grand Chamber's ruling in *Paradiso* 'appears to protect the entitlement of Member States to take robust action to deal with an illegal surrogacy arrangement after the child is born'.[73] It seems important to distinguish illegal domestic arrangements from legal overseas arrangements; their recognition concerns a conflict-of-laws dilemma, not clamping down on unlawful acts. Moreover, on occasion, the Court has commended the respondent for permitting its citizens to resort abroad to medical services not available domestically, a compromise seen as indicative of the law's proportionality (e.g. assigning paternity/maternity according to the wishes of parents having successfully used heterologous fertilisation abroad, notwithstanding the domestic ban).[74] There is no reason to treat procreative tourism differently when it

[70] See *Rodrigues da Silva and Hoogkamer* v. *The Netherlands*, App. No. 50435/99, 31 January 2006, [39]; *Omoregie and Others* v. *Norway*, App. No. 265/07, 31 July 2008, [66]; *Useinov* v. *The Netherlands*, App. No. 61292/00, 11 April 2006. For a discussion, see Carmen Draghici, *The Legitimacy of Family Rights in Strasbourg Case Law: 'Living Instrument' or Extinguished Sovereignty?* (Oxford: Hart, 2017) 343–353.

[71] See *K.K.* v. *Denmark*, [74], distinguishing the case from situations in which other persons are claiming parentage in relation to an assisted reproduction process, which alludes to the discussion of *H.* v. *The United Kingdom* (at [69]).

[72] There are numerous references to the illegality of the commissioning parents' conduct in *Paradiso and Campanelli* v. *Italy* [GC], [131], [199], [204], [211], [214] and so on.

[73] Andrea Mulligan, 'Identity Rights and Sensitive Ethical Questions: The European Convention on Human Rights and the Regulation of Surrogacy Arrangements' (2018) 26(3) *Medical Law Review* 449–475, at 468.

[74] See *S.H. and Others* v. *Austria* [GC], [114]: 'the Court also observes that there is no prohibition under Austrian law on going abroad to seek treatment of infertility that uses artificial procreation techniques not allowed in Austria and that in the event of a successful treatment the Civil Code contains clear rules on paternity and maternity that respect the wishes of the parents'. See also *A, B and C* v. *Ireland* [GC], App. No. 25579/05, 16 December 2010, [241]: '*having regard to the right to travel abroad lawfully for an abortion* with access to appropriate information and medical care in Ireland, the Court does not consider that the

involves the lawful use of surrogacy according to the law of the forum. The portrayal of foreign surrogacy as illegal conduct is also at odds with the Court's reliance on the legal status attained by commissioning parents abroad in order to reject the analogy between surrogacy and donor insemination cases (in which legal parenthood was not established in any jurisdiction).[75]

Finally, another concession made to State sovereignty is the '*Schalk and Kopf* approach'[76] to assessing ECHR conformity, that is, the conclusion that, *considering intervening measures of protection, albeit not available at the material time, the respondent cannot be reproached for not having introduced reform earlier.*[77] This is apparently explained by the Court's reluctance to penalise States at the vanguard of protection of a particular right, having introduced reform at the end of a gradual process in society and the law. By contrast, in other cases, the Court avoids a finding of violation by declaring that it *applies the ECHR standards at the time of the domestic decisions*, even if the effects for the victims are still ongoing, *refusing to pronounce on the ECHR standards at the time of Strasbourg deliberations.*[78] Rarely, the Court goes too far in the opposite direction by retrospectively applying very recent ECHR standards, not crystallised at the time of the facts in the complaint.[79] This inconsistency in the temporal framework for assessment of compliance with the Convention ought to be carefully reconsidered in future judgments.

C.3 THE PROSPECTS OF EMERGING PROCREATIVE RIGHTS IN INTERNATIONAL JURISPRUDENCE

International litigation, particularly in the Strasbourg Court, has demonstrated the capacity of human rights discourse to adapt to the new challenges posed by developments in human reproduction. Having considered, in the previous sections, the cluster of procreative rights upheld to date and the roots of slow

prohibition in Ireland of abortion for health and well-being reasons ... exceeds the margin of appreciation' (emphasis added).

75 See *C.E. and Others* v. *France*, [102].

76 See *Schalk and Kopf* v. *Austria*, App. No. 30141/04, 24 June 2010, [105]–[106].

77 *C.E and Others* v. *France*, [110]; *D. and B.* v. *Austria*, App. No. 40597/12, 31 October 2017, [24].

78 *S.H. and Others* v. *Austria* [GC], [84], viewing the issue before the Court as limited to whether the prohibitions 'were justified at the time they were considered by the Austrian Constitutional Court', and not 'whether the prohibition of sperm and ovum donation at issue would or would not be justified today under the Convention'.

79 See *D.B. and Others* v. *Switzerland*, Part-Dissenting Opinion of Judge Elósegui, [4]–[6], challenging the retrospective attribution of responsibility for ECHR standards not yet established at the material time.

advances in other areas of ART, this final section will examine possible new trajectories for international case law. A noteworthy aspect of ECHR jurisprudence is that the Strasbourg position on heterologous procreative techniques[80] and non-genetic surrogacy[81] changed after the respondent governments referred the dispute to the Grand Chamber, a mechanism which appears to put pressure on the Court to restore State discretion. Indeed, the same back-pedalling was visible in relation to the display of the crucifix in classrooms according to a long-standing national tradition (the Grand Chamber[82] overturning the Chamber decision pursuant to which this practice violated the parents' right to respect for their religious convictions).[83] The stark contrast between the two sets of rulings on gamete donation and non-genetic surrogacy demonstrates the fluidity of the balancing exercise in sensitive areas and its potential for change. Progressive Chamber decisions, albeit reversed by the Grand Chamber, can predict future developments in Strasbourg jurisprudence, subject to a larger number of ECHR States liberalising assisted reproduction laws.

Future developments in surrogacy tourism cases ought to include the *child's right to know and establish ties with the non-genetic moral author of conception irrespective of the breakdown in the couple's relationship*. While the means of recognition of legal ties with the non-genetic intended parent were left to States, the Court should take the next opportunity to clarify that an adoption mechanism which is conditional upon the continuing approval of the genetic parent is not satisfactory, especially where the non-genetic parent has already acted as a social parent at the start of the child's life. Mulligan has persuasively argued that, for surrogate-born children, 'the relationship to the intended parent should be captured by the Article 8 right to identity'.[84] Currently, this only applies to the intended parent who is married to, and continues to enjoy the support of, the genetic parent.[85] The notion of identity in ECHR jurisprudence is already broader than the mere reference to genetic origins; in the case of children placed in public care, it includes access to the social services records documenting their upbringing.[86] Similarly, children

80 See the comparison in Chapter 2 between *S.H. and Others* v. *Austria* [Chamber], App. No. 57813/00, 1 April 2010, and *S.H. and Others* v. *Austria* [GC].

81 See the comparison in Chapter 3 between *Paradiso and Campanelli* v. *Italy* [Chamber] and *Paradiso and Campanelli* v. *Italy* [GC].

82 See *Lautsi and Others* v. *Italy* [GC], App. No. 30814/06, 18 March 2011.

83 See *Lautsi and Others* v. *Italy* [Chamber], App. No. 30814/06, 3 November 2009.

84 Andrea Mulligan, 'Identity Rights and Sensitive Ethical Questions', 472.

85 See *D.B. and Others* v. *Switzerland*; *K.K. and Others* v. *Denmark*.

86 *Gaskin* v. *The United Kingdom*, App. No. 10454/83, 7 July 1989.

born through heterologous reproductive techniques should be recognised the right to information about their personal history, including knowledge of both individuals responsible for their genesis. In fact, the non-biological intended mother's role as 'the instigator of the pregnancy'[87] places her at the origin of conception.

Moreover, *where neither commissioning parent has genetic ties with the child*, since there is no other candidate at the child's parenthood and effective care, *the child's 'right to know and be cared for' by his/her parents under Article 7 UNCRC*[88] *should be construed as referable to the moral authors of conception*, that is, the persons who have 'intentional and causative responsibility for the birth of the child'.[89] Indeed, to treat donors and surrogates as parents, despite their State-endorsed arrangements with the commissioning parents, would be to coerce them into involuntary parenthood. Nor is the child's welfare better served by the vacancy of parenthood and by being brought up in public care. The case law on non-genetic surrogacy makes allowance for intentional parenthood, in that it does not treat the commissioning parents' position as a mere situation of de facto care (by contrast with foster carer rulings).[90] However, in those cases, Article 8 safeguards are not available as soon as the parties' effective family life is established; a genuine intention to conceive a child, coupled with de facto parenting, becomes constitutive of 'family life' only after a considerable period of time.[91]

The case law could also be more receptive to the notion of *parenthood as acted-upon intention to create life, corroborated by de facto care, in donor insemination cases*. There seems to be no valid reason for treating intended parents differently depending on the type of heterologous procreative method used, in particular whether the child was conceived abroad through surrogacy (in which case the ECtHR requires the creation of legal ties with both parents) or through assisted insemination with donor (in which case means of protection falling short of a parent–child relationship are deemed sufficient).

87 Rachel Cook, 'Donating Parenthood: Perspectives on Parenthood from Surrogacy and Gamete Donation', in Andrew Bainham, Shelley Day-Sclater and Martin Richards (eds.), *What Is a Parent? A Socio-Legal Analysis* (Oxford: Hart, 1999) 121–136, at 135.

88 See Art. 7(1) UNCRC: 'The child . . . shall have . . ., as far as possible, the right to know and be cared for by his or her parents.' On the interpretation of Art. 7(1) UNCRC as applicable to genetic parents, see Carmen Draghici, 'Unplanned Fatherhood Is Not Sperm Donation: An Unduly Moralistic Approach to Natural Fathers in ECHR Case Law' (2022) 2 *Child and Family Law Quarterly* 123–147, at 138.

89 Mulligan, 'Identity Rights and Sensitive Ethical Questions', 471.

90 See *Moretti and Benedetti* v. *Italy*, App. No. 16318/07, 27 April 2010.

91 See *Paradiso and Campanelli* v. *Italy* [GC], [151]–[157]; *Valdís Fjölnisdóttir and Others* v. *Iceland*, [62].

Two recent applications will give the Court an opportunity to align its jurisprudence on donor insemination with that on surrogacy, insofar as the intended parents were also named as legal parents on the foreign birth certificates,[92] and hence the distinction drawn between the two situations on the basis of parenthood abroad lapses.

Another desirable future development is the protection of the right to *respect for biological parentage in all ART cases, whether foreign or domestic, lawful or unlawful*. One must salute the ECtHR's readiness to require States prohibiting surrogacy to recognise parent–child relationships arising from lawful foreign surrogacy arrangements. However, while the child's privacy rights have been upheld, the adults are only accidental beneficiaries: it is on child welfare grounds, and not in the name of procreative rights, that the State of residence is expected to create legal ties between the surrogate-born child and the genetic parent. Aspiring parents' rights ought to be equally upheld, based on the reality of genetic and social ties and the intention to found/expand a family. Moreover, a dimension so far missing from the case law on intentional parenthood is the instrumental role of gamete donation/surrogacy in safeguarding the right to become a parent of the *fertile* member of the couple. Additionally, the right *not* to become a parent,[93] in particular the right not to be coerced into acting as a donor and the right to protection against unauthorised uses of one's genetic material,[94] justifies a finding of violation in cases where surrogacy legislation allows the gestational surrogate to assert her own parental title. In fact, prospective parents entering surrogacy arrangements do not agree to donate their gametes for the surrogate's reproduction.[95]

Furthermore, the case law should *elevate the interest in having a healthy child from idiosyncratic findings of violation to an explicit ECHR right*. In fact, decisions upholding the right to resort to medical technologies in order to control reproductive outcomes are largely dependent on the domestic legal system of reference. The ECtHR has thus found violations of Article 8 where domestic law already afforded access to prenatal testing and to therapeutic abortion but, in practice, access was hindered. The Court is yet to establish unambiguously that expecting parents are entitled to prenatal testing and

[92] See *Nuti* v. *Italy*, App. No. 47998/20; *Dallabora and Others* v. *Italie*, App. No. 23142/21 (donor insemination in female same-sex couples). In *Dallabora*, both the parents and the children are applicants, giving the Court an opportunity also to revisit adults' rights in ART cases.

[93] See *Evans* v. *The United Kingdom* [GC], [71], [90].

[94] See *Pejřilová* v. *The Czech Republic*, [52], [59].

[95] See *Johnson* v. *Calvert*, 5 Cal. 4th 84 (1993), 93.

reproductive choice as a matter of ECHR rights. Similarly, the right to use PGD in order to avoid the transmission of a serious hereditary illness was upheld in circumstances where selective abortion was (incongruously) available; this may lead to the paradoxical conclusion that a State not offering either PGD or abortion on grounds of foetal abnormalities is ECHR-compliant. A future case might provide the Court with an opportunity to refine its position and cement the right of prospective parents at risk of transmitting genetic illnesses to resort to PGD, regardless of whether abortion is an option. That, for centuries, humankind lacked the capacity to avert severe congenital disabilities in offspring does not make the choice of a healthy child less deserving of respect than other reproductive decisions. Given the direct and far-reaching impact of restrictions on procreative autonomy on the parents, they cannot be justified by the unease with novel genetic techniques of a large section of the population (likely unaffected by the problems addressed by PGD). Rubin and Phillips have also noted that, while 'the "designer-baby" rhetoric conjures up notions of eugenics, with images of elite parents selecting physically and intellectually superior children', research shows that parents using PGD wish to prevent the suffering and premature death of their children, and not choose desired traits.[96]

A next step for human rights jurisprudence, potentially prompted by the principle of non-discrimination, is to *domesticate access to ART*. ECHR case law has safeguarded parent–child relationships created abroad and has accepted that a ban on heterologous reproduction was proportionate, inter alia, because there was no impediment to travelling abroad to permissive jurisdictions.[97] This position ought to be revisited if the ECtHR is to promote reproductive justice. For the IACtHR, a ban on IVF, forcing infertile couples to travel abroad for treatment, amounts to indirect discrimination on grounds of economic status.[98] Interestingly, a case pending before the ECtHR claims the medical costs related to having an abortion on grounds of foetal abnormality abroad, owing to a domestic ban.[99]

Non-discrimination in access to ART may also bring economic claims – for example, free provision of ART services – within the ambit of the ECHR, notwithstanding the notorious difficulty in mounting a case for specific healthcare access conditions, given the dependency of services on public

96 Rubin and Phillips, 'Infertility and Assisted Reproduction Technologies', 186.
97 *S.H. and Others* v. *Austria* [GC], [114]–[115].
98 *Artavia Murillo et al.* v. *Costa Rica*, [303].
99 See *I.Z.* v. *Poland*, App. No. 57338/21.

resources. Challenges to the allocation of ART services are already starting to make their way through domestic courts, the scholarship and the ECtHR. In the UK, the lack of access of single women to publicly funded fertility treatment was denounced as discriminatory.[100] In a recent case in Northern Ireland, a same-sex couple challenged the lack of access to publicly funded fertility services (IVF with donor ova) where the prospective surrogate was voluntarily sterile.[101] A thought-provoking Strasbourg application under Articles 8, 12 and 14 ECHR, struck out following the parties' friendly settlement, concerned the dismissal of a claim, brought against the insurance company by a man whose reproductive function was impaired by a road accident, for medical expenses for his wife's IVF.[102] The refusal of sick leave on account of pregnancy-related complications to a woman who had undergone IVF shortly before taking up employment was found in breach of Article 14 taken in conjunction with Article 1 of Protocol 1.[103] Further pecuniary aspects of reproductive freedom are likely to be placed before the Court.

The number of Strasbourg applications regarding procreative rights is on the rise,[104] some of them presenting the Court with rather novel claims. For instance, while, so far, complaints have sought to assert the right of the intentional parent to establish legal ties with the ART-born child, a recently communicated case will require the Court to pronounce on the opposite situation: the claim by a child conceived through IVF with donor gametes and her mother that their rights were breached by domestic decisions permitting the intended father to disclaim paternity after divorce, reneging on the

[100] See Atina Krajewska, 'Access of Single Women to Fertility Treatment: A Case of Incidental Discrimination?' (2015) 23(4) *Medical Law Review* 620–645.

[101] See *Re JR176(2)* [2022] NIKB 21. For the High Court, there had been no difference of treatment and, even if that was the case, it was justified, primarily because a very wide margin had to be afforded to the State. While a well-founded reason might exist to consider a woman who has undergone voluntary sterilisation ineligible for public funding for IVF to further her own parenthood plans, when the funding is sought to enable a male couple to have a child, that justification lapses; in a jurisdiction not permitting commercial but only altruistic surrogacy, and given the emotional and legal intricacies of traditional surrogacy, this regulatory framework penalises structurally infertile couples.

[102] *Ristevska and Ristevski* v. *Former Yugoslav Republic of Macedonia*, App. No. 54344/07, 2 July 2013.

[103] *Jurčić* v. *Croatia*, App. No. 54711/15, 4 February 2021.

[104] Several claims have been brought against Italy in relation to the refusal to transcribe the full details of the birth certificates of children lawfully conceived through surrogacy abroad, by both heterosexual and homosexual couples; see *Modanese* v. *Italie*, App. No. 59054/19; *Bini and Others* v. *Italy*, App. No. 12109/20; *B.K. and Others* v. *Italy*, App. No. 45426/21; *Bonzano and Others* v. *Italy*, App. No. 10810/22; *Corona and Others* v. *Italy*, App. No. 29038/20, *Andrisani and Others* v. *Italy*, App. No. 2738/21, *C.B.* v. *Italy*, App. No. 47196/21.

parental project and leaving the child fatherless.[105] Additionally, some concerns emerging in relation to step-parent adoption in same-sex couples will likely transfer to ART cases, for example, the alleged right to a birth certificate template not disclosing the lack of biological link with the second female parent.[106] It is also worth noting the Court's warning that the issue of gamete donation 'must be kept under review',[107] and that in relation to 'evolving rights', such as the establishment of legal ties between an intended parent and the child born to his/her partner through donor insemination, States retain 'a *certain* margin of appreciation in the *timing* of the introduction of legislative changes'.[108] The margin will grow narrower as the practice of Council of Europe States becomes more convergent. Despite the regulatory hesitations (and indeed errors) accompanying any new socio-legal phenomenon, the expansion of parenthood through ART is an irreversible process. Upcoming legal cases can reinforce the notion that, to achieve the full realisation of procreative rights, technology must be embraced as an ally rather than being cast off as a foe.

[105] See *A. and B.* v. *France*, App. No. 12482/21; the intended father successfully annulled his recognition of parentage, in circumstances where the embryo had been transferred into the mother's uterus after the institution of divorce proceedings but before the divorce was granted.

[106] In *S.W. and Others* v. *Austria* (App. No. 1928/19, 6 September 2022), the complainants alleged that the refusal to issue a post-adoption birth certificate indicating both the biological mother and her same-sex partner as mothers was discriminatory, insofar as the indication of mother/parent and father/parent on the birth certificate revealed that one of them was an adoptive parent, whereas heterosexual parents did not face this problem. The same issue may arise in connection with the registration of the non-genetic intended parent in the case of surrogacy-born children.

[107] See *S.H. and Others* v. *Austria* [GC], [118]: 'Even if it finds no breach of Article 8 in the present case, the Court considers that this area, in which the law appears to be continuously evolving and which is subject to a particularly dynamic development in science and law, needs to be kept under review by the Contracting States.'

[108] *D. and B.* v. *Austria*, [24] (emphasis added).

Select Bibliography

Achmad, Claire, 'Children's Rights to the Fore in the European Court of Human Rights' First International Commercial Surrogacy Judgments' (2014) 6 *European Human Rights Law Review* 638–646.

Allan, Sonia, 'The Surrogate in Commercial Surrogacy: Legal and Ethical Considerations', in Paula Gerber and Katie O'Byrne (eds.), *Surrogacy, Law and Human Rights* (London: Routledge, 2015) 113–143.

Andorno, Roberto, 'Global Bioethics and Human Rights' (2008) 27(1) *Medicine and Law* 1–14.

Annas, George, *American Bioethics: Crossing Human Rights and Health Law Boundaries* (Oxford: Oxford University Press, 2005).

Anomaly, Jonathan, *Creating Future People: The Ethics of Genetic Enhancement* (New York: Routledge, 2020).

Archard, David, and Benatar, David, 'Introduction', in David Archard and David Benatar (eds.), *Procreation and Parenthood: The Ethics of Bearing and Rearing Children* (Oxford: Oxford University Press, 2010) 1–30.

Asch, Adrienne, 'Prenatal Diagnosis and Selective Abortion: A Challenge to Practice and Policy' (1999) 89(11) *American Journal of Public Health* 1649–1657, reprinted in Helga Kuhse, Udo Schüklenk and Peter Singer (eds.), *Bioethics: An Anthology* (Hoboken: John Wiley & Sons, 2016, 3rd ed.) 112–126.

Ashcroft, Richard, 'Could Human Rights Supersede Bioethics?' (2010) 10(4) *Human Rights Law Review* 639–660.

'The Troubled Relationship Between Bioethics and Human Rights', in Michael Freeman (ed.), *Law and Bioethics* (Oxford: Oxford University Press, 2008) 31—51.

Bainham, Andrew, 'Whose Sperm Is It Anyway?' (2003) 62(3) *Cambridge Law Journal* 566–570.

Baker, Robert, 'Bioethics and Human Rights: A Historical Perspective' (2001) 10 *Cambridge Quarterly of Health & Ethics* 241–252.

Bartholet, Elizabeth, *Family Bonds: Adoption and the Politics of Parenting* (Boston, MA: Houghton Mifflin, 1993).

Beauchamps, Tom, and Childress, James, *Principles of Biomedical Ethics* (Oxford: Oxford University Press, 2019, 8th ed.).

Beaumont, Paul, and Trimmings, Katarina, 'Surrogacy before the European Court of Human Rights', in Jens Scherpe, Claire Fenton-Glynn and Terry Kaan (eds.), *Eastern and Western Perspectives on Surrogacy* (Cambridge: Intersentia, 2019) 331–354.

Biggs, Hazel, 'The Quest for a Perfect Child', in Kirsty Horsey and Hazel Biggs (eds.), *Human Fertilisation and Embryology: Reproducing Regulation* (London: Routledge-Cavendish, 2007) 1–16.

Biondi, Stefano, 'Access to Medical-Assisted [sic] Reproduction and PGD in Italian Law: A Deadly Blow to an Illiberal Statute? Commentary to the European Court on [sic] Human Rights's [sic] Decision *Costa and Pavan v Italy* (ECtHR, 28 August 2012, App. 54270/2010)' (2013) 21 *Medical Law Review* 474–486.

Bomhoff, Jacco, and Zucca, Lorenzo, 'The Tragedy of Ms Evans: Conflicts and Incommensurability of Rights, *Evans* v *the United Kingdom*, Fourth Section Judgment of 7 March 2006, Application No 6339/05' (2006) 2(3) *European Constitutional Law Review* 424–442.

Boonin, David, *The Non-identity Problem and the Ethics of Future People* (Oxford: Oxford University Press, 2014).

Boucai, Michael, 'Is Assisted Procreation an LGBT Right?' (2016) (6) *Wisconsin Law Review* 1065–1125.

Bracken, Lydia, 'The ECtHR's First Advisory Opinion: Implications for Cross-Border Surrogacy Involving Male Intended Parents' (2021) 21(1) *Medical Law International* 3–18.

Same-Sex Parenting and Best Interests (Cambridge: Cambridge University Press, 2020).

Brännmark, Johan, 'Respect for Persons in Bioethics: Towards a Human Rights-Based Account' (2017) 18 *Human Rights Review* 171–187.

Braude, Peter, Pickering, Susan, Flinter, Frances, and Mackie Ogilvie, Caroline, 'Preimplantation Genetic Diagnosis' (2002) 3(12) *Nature Reviews: Genetics* 941–953.

Bridge, Stuart, 'Assisted Reproduction and the Legal Definition of Parentage', in Andrew Bainham, Shelley Day-Sclater and Martin Richards (eds.), *What Is a Parent? A Socio-Legal Analysis* (Oxford: Hart, 1999) 73–88.

Brownsword, Roger, 'Human Dignity, Ethical Pluralism, and the Regulation of Modern Biotechnologies', in Thérèse Murphy (ed.), *New Technologies and Human Rights* (Oxford: Oxford University Press, 2009) 19–84.

Brudney, Daniel, 'Is Health Care a Human Right?' (2016) 37 *Theoretical Medicine and Bioethics* 249–257.

Burley, Justine, 'The Price of Eggs: Who Should Bear the Costs of Fertility Treatments?', in John Harris and Søren Holm (eds.), *The Future of Human Reproduction: Ethics, Choice, and Regulation* (Oxford: Clarendon Press, 1998) 127–149.

Buxton, Jess, 'Unforeseen Uses of Preimplantation Genetic Diagnosis: Ethical and Legal Issues', in Kirsty Horsey and Hazel Biggs (eds.), *Human Fertilisation and Embryology: Reproducing Regulation* (London: Routledge-Cavendish, 2007) 109–134.

Cohen, Alma, Dehejia, Rajeev, and Romanov, Dmitri, 'Financial Incentives and Fertility' (2013) 95(1) *Review of Economics and Statistics* 1–20.

Cook, Rachel, 'Donating Parenthood: Perspectives on Parenthood from Surrogacy and Gamete Donation', in Andrew Bainham, Shelley Day-Sclater and Martin Richards (eds.), *What Is a Parent? A Socio-legal Analysis* (Oxford: Hart, 1999) 121–136.

Cook, Rebecca, Dickens, Bernard, and Fathalla, Mahmood, *Reproductive Health and Human Rights: Integrating Medicine, Ethics, and Law* (Oxford: Oxford University Press, 2003).

Coussirat-Coustère, Vincent, 'Famille et Convention Européenne des Droits de l'Homme', in Paul Mahoney and Rolv Ryssdal (eds.), *Protection des droits de l'homme: la perspective européenne. Mélanges à la mémoire de Rolv Ryssdl* (Cologne: Carl Heymanns, 2000) 281–307.

de Jong, Antina, Dondorp, Wybo, de Die-Smulders, Christine, Frints, Suzanne, and de Wert, Guido, 'Non-invasive Prenatal Testing: Ethical Issues Explored' (2010) 18 *European Journal of Human Genetics* 272–277.

Deech, Ruth, 'Family Law and Genetics' (1998) 61(5) *Modern Law Review* 697–715.

Deech, Ruth and Smajdor, Anna, *From IVF to Immortality: Controversy in the Era of Reproductive Technology* (Oxford/New York: Oxford University Press, 2007).

DiSilvestro, Russell, 'Reproductive Autonomy, the Non-identity Problem, and the Non-person Problem' (2009) 23(1) *Bioethics* 59–67.

Douglas, Gillian, *Law, Fertility and Reproduction* (London: Sweet and Maxwell, 1991).

'The Intention To Be a Parent and the Making of Mothers' (1994) 57 *Modern Law Review* 636–741.

Draghici, Carmen, 'Adoption and the European Court of Human Rights: From *Laissez-Faire* to Judicial Law-Making', in Lina Panella and Ersiliagrazia Spatafora (eds.), *Studi in onore di Claudio Zanghì* (Turin: Giappichelli, 2011) 255–282.

'Assisted Dying', in Ian Loveland (ed.), *Canadian and British Public Law in Comparative Perspective* (Oxford: Hart, 2021) 25–74.

'Equal Marriage, Unequal Civil Partnership: A Bizarre Case of Discrimination in Europe' (2017) 29(4) *Child and Family Law Quarterly* 313–334.

The Legitimacy of Family Rights in Strasbourg Case Law: 'Living Instrument' or Extinguished Sovereignty? (Oxford: Hart, 2017).

'Putative Fathers in English Law: A Human Rights Perspective', in Stephen Gilmore and Jens Sherpe (eds.), *Family Matters: Essays in Honour of John Eekelaar* (Cambridge: Intersentia, 2022) 595–609.

'The Strasbourg Court between European and Local Consensus: Anti-democratic or Guardian of Democratic Process?' (2017) *Public Law* 11–29.

'Unplanned Fatherhood Is Not Sperm Donation: An Unduly Moralistic Approach to Natural Fathers in ECHR Case Law' (2022) 2 *Child and Family Law Quarterly* 123–147.

Draghici, Carmen and Woods, Lorna, 'Killing Journalists Is Not Media Regulation: Private Rights, Collective Wrongs and the Impact of Impunity' (2019) 28(2) *Transnational Law and Contemporary Problems* 263–306.

Ebtehaj, Fatemeh, 'Introduction: Regulating Relationships?', in Fatemeh Ebtehaj, Bridget Lindley and Martin Richards (eds.), *Kinship Matters* (Oxford: Hart, 2006) 1–16.

Erdman, Joanna, 'Abortion in International Human Rights Law', in Sam Rowlands (ed.), *Abortion Care* (Cambridge: Cambridge University Press, 2014) 244–250.

Farrelly, Colin, 'Preimplantation Genetic Diagnosis, Reproductive Freedom, and Deliberative Democracy' (2009) 34(2) *Journal of Medicine and Philosophy* 135–154.

Fenton, Elizabeth, 'Genetic Enhancement: A Threat to Human Rights?' (2008) 22(1) *Bioethics* 1–7.

Finch, Janet, 'Kinship as "Family" in Contemporary Britain', in Fatemeh Ebtehaj, Bridget Lindley and Martin Richards (eds.), *Kinship Matters* (London: Hart, 2006) 295–306.

Francis, Leslie, 'Is Surrogacy Ethically Problematic?', in Leslie Francis (ed.), *The Oxford Handbook of Reproductive Ethics* (Oxford: Oxford University Press, 2017) 388–406.

Gallus, Nicole, 'La procréation médicalement assistée et la jurisprudence de la Court européenne des droits de l'homme', in Nicole Gallus (ed.), *Droit des familles, genre et sexualité* (Limal: Anthemis, 2012) 203–225.

Gerber, Paula and O'Byrne, Katie, 'Souls in the House of Tomorrow: The Rights of Children Born via Surrogacy', in Paula Gerber and Katie O'Byrne (eds.), *Surrogacy, Law and Human Rights* (London: Routledge, 2015) 81–112.

Gilbar, Roy, 'Between Unconditional Acceptance and Responsibility: Should Family Ethics Limit the Scope of Reproductive Autonomy?' (2009) 21(3) *Child and Family Law Quarterly* 309–335.

Giles, Jessica and Lee, Simon, '*Parrillo* v *Italy*: Is There Life in the European Court of Human Rights?' (2016) 5(1) *Oxford Journal of Law and Religion* 162–167.

Gillott, John, 'Screening for Disability: A Eugenic Pursuit?' (2001) 27(suppl. 2) *Journal of Medical Ethics* ii21–ii23.

Glover, Jonathan, *Choosing Children: Genes, Disability, and Design* (Oxford: Oxford University Press, 2006).

Gorsuch, Neil, *The Future of Assisted Suicide and Euthanasia* (Princeton: Princeton University Press, 2006).

Greenfeld, Dorothy and Seli, Emre, 'Assisted Reproduction in Same Sex Couples', in Mark Sauer (ed.), *Principles of Oocyte and Embryo Donation* (London: Springer-Verlag, 2013) 289–301, reprinted in Helga Kuhse, Udo Schüklenk and Peter Singer (eds.), *Bioethics: An Anthology* (Hoboken: John Wiley & Sons, 2016, 3rd ed.) 74–85.

Harris, David, O'Boyle, Michael, Bates, Ed, and Buckley, Carla, *Harris, O'Boyle & Warbrick: Law of the European Convention on Human Rights* (Oxford: Oxford University Press, 2014, 3rd ed.).

Harris, David, O'Boyle, Michael and Warbrick, Colin, *Law of the European Convention on Human Rights* (London: Butterworths, 1995).

Harris, John, 'No Sex Selection Please, We're British' (2005) 31 *Journal of Medical Ethics* 286–288.

'Sex Selection and Regulated Hatred' (2005) 31 *Journal of Medical Ethics* 291–294.

Herring, Jonathan, *Family Law* (Harlow: Pearson, 2021, 10th ed.).

Hevia, Martín and Constantin, Andrés, 'Gendered Power Relations and Informed Consent: The *I.V.* v. *Bolivia* Case' (2018) 20(2) *Health and Human Rights Journal* 197–203.

Holm, Søren, 'Ethical Issues in Pre-implantation Diagnosis', in John Harris and Søren Holm (eds.), *The Future of Human Reproduction: Ethics, Choice, and Regulation* (Oxford: Clarendon Press, 1998) 176–190.

Hurst, Hannum, *Rescuing Human Rights: A Radically Moderate Approach* (Cambridge: Cambridge University Press, 2019).

Hurst, Palmer and Hurst, Christina, 'Baby Steps: The European Court of Human Rights Moves Closer to Protecting the Unborn in *Parrillo v. Italy*' (2015) 2 *Journal of Global Justice and Public Policy* 155–163.

Iliadou, Marianna, 'Surrogacy and the ECtHR: Reflections on *Paradiso and Campanelli v Italy*' (2018) 27(1) *Medical Law Review* 144–154.

Jackson, Emily, 'Abortion, Autonomy and Prenatal Diagnosis' (2000) 9(4) *Social and Legal Studies* 467–494.

Regulating Reproduction: Law, Technology and Autonomy (Oxford: Hart, 2001).

Khazova, Olga, 'Some Reflections on a European Court Case: *Nazarenko* v. *Russia*', in Jens Scherpe and Stephen Gilmore (eds.), *Family Matters: Essays in Honour of John Eekelaar* (Cambridge: Intersentia, 2022) 612–621.

Kilkelly, Ursula, 'Protecting Children's Rights under the ECHR: The Role of Positive Obligations' (2010) 61(3) *Northern Ireland Legal Quarterly* 245–261.

King, David, 'Why We Should Not Permit Embryos to Be Selected as Tissue Donors' (August 2003) 190 *Bulletin of Medical Ethics* 13–16, reprinted in Helga Kuhse, Udo Schüklenk and Peter Singer (eds.), *Bioethics: An Anthology* (Hoboken: John Wiley & Sons, 2016, 3rd ed.) 152–155.

Knowles, Lori, 'The Lingua Franca of Human Rights and the Rise of a Global Bioethic' (2001) 10 *Cambridge Quarterly of Healthcare Ethics* 253–263.

Krahn, Timothy and Wong, Sophia, 'Preimplantation Genetic Diagnosis and Reproductive Autonomy' (2009) 19 *Reproductive BioMedicine Online* 34–42.

Krajewska, Atina, 'Access of Single Women to Fertility Treatment: A Case of Incidental Discrimination?' (2015) 23(4) *Medical Law Review* 620–645.

The Lancet Global Health, 'Infertility: Why the Silence?' (2022) 10(6) *Lancet Global Health* e773.

Lind, Craig, '*Evans* v *United Kingdom*: Judgments of Solomon – Power, Gender and Procreation' (2006) 18(4) *Child and Family Law Quarterly* 576–592.

Löwy, Ilana, 'ART with PGD: Risky Heredity and Stratified Reproduction' (2020) 11 *Reproductive Biomedicine & Society Online* 48–55.

MacCallum, Fiona, 'Parenting Genetically Unrelated Children: A Comparison of Embryo Donation and Adoption', in Kirsty Horsey and Hazel Biggs (eds.), *Human Fertilisation and Embryology: Reproducing Regulation* (London: Routledge-Cavendish, 2007) 135–154.

Mackenzie, Robin, 'Beyond Genetic and Gestational Dualities: Surrogacy Agreements, Legal Parenthood and Choice in Family Formation', in Kirsty Horsey and Hazel Biggs (eds.), *Human Fertilisation and Embryology: Reproducing Regulation* (London: Routledge-Cavendish, 2007) 181–203.

Maclean, Alasdair, 'Magic, Myths, and Fairy Tales: Consent and the Relationship between Law and Ethics', in Michael Freeman (ed.), *Law and Bioethics* (Oxford: Oxford University Press, 2008) 111–135.

Madden, Deirdre, *Medicine, Ethics and the Law* (Haywards Heath: Bloomsbury, 2016, 3rd ed.).

Margaria, Alice, *The Construction of Fatherhood: The Jurisprudence of the European Court of Human Rights* (Cambridge: Cambridge University Press, 2019).

'Parenthood and Cross-Border Surrogacy: What Is "New"? The ECtHR's First Advisory Opinion' (2020) 28(2) *Medical Law Review* 412–425.

Marshall, Lorna, 'Ethical Issues in the Evolving Realm of Egg Donation', in Leslie Francis (ed.), *The Oxford Handbook of Reproductive Ethics* (Oxford: Oxford University Press, 2017) 478–498.

Mignot, Jean-François, '"Simple" Adoption in France: Revival of an Old Institution (1804–2007)' (translation by Peter Hamilton) (2015) 56(3) *Revue française de sociologie* 365–394.

Moffitt, Robert, 'The Effect of Welfare on Marriage and Fertility', in Robert Moffitt (ed.), *Welfare, the Family, and Reproductive Behaviour: Research Perspectives* (Washington, DC: The National Academies Press, 1998), 50–97.

Mouliarova, Ekaterina, 'The Legal Recognition of Surrogacy in Russia' (2019) 11(1) *Italian Journal of Public Law* 393–433.

Mulligan, Andrea, 'Identity Rights and Sensitive Ethical Questions: The European Convention on Human Rights and the Regulation of Surrogacy Arrangements' (2018) 26(3) *Medical Law Review* 449–475.

'Reproductive Rights under Article 8: The Right to Respect for the Decision to Become or Not to Become a Parent' (2014) 4 *European Human Rights Law Review* 378–387.

Murat, Pierre, 'Filiation et vie familiale', in Frédéric Sudre (ed.), *Le droit au respect de la vie familiale au sens de la Convention européenne des droits de l'homme* (Brussels: Némésis-Bruylant, 2002) 161–208.

Nelson, Erin, *Law, Policy and Reproductive Autonomy* (Oxford: Hart, 2013).

Ngwena, Charles, 'Inscribing Abortion as a Human Right: Significance of the Protocol on the Rights of Women in Africa' (2010) 32(4) *Human Rights Quarterly* 783–864.

Parfit, Derek, *Reasons and Persons* (Oxford: Oxford University Press, 1984).

'Rights, Interests, and Possible People', in Samuel Gorowitz et al. (eds.), *Moral Problems in Medicine* (Englewood Cliffs: Prentice Hall, 1976) 369–375, reprinted in Helga Kuhse, Udo Schüklenk and Peter Singers (eds.), *Bioethics: An Anthology* (Hoboken: John Wiley and Sons, 2016, 3rd ed.) 86–90.

Plomer, Aurora, 'A Foetal Right to Life? The Case of *Vo* v *France*' (2005) 5(2) *Human Rights Law Review* 311–338.

Priaulx, Nicolette, 'Beyond Health and Disability: Rethinking the "Foetal Abnormality" Ground in Abortion Law', in Kirsty Horsey and Hazel Biggs (eds.), *Human Fertilisation and Embryology: Reproducing Regulation* (London: Routledge-Cavendish, 2007) 205–230.

Richards, Martin, 'Which Children Can We Choose? Boundaries of Reproductive Autonomy', in Shelley Day-Sclater, Fatemeh Ebtehaj, Emily Jackson and Martin Richards (eds.), *Regulating Autonomy: Sex, Reproduction and Family* (Oxford: Hart, 2009) 197–221.

Robertson, John, *Children of Choice: Freedom and the New Reproductive Technologies* (Princeton: Princeton University Press, 1994).

'Extending Preimplantation Genetic Diagnosis: The Ethical Debate – Ethical Issues in New Uses of Preimplantation Genetic Diagnosis' (2003) 18(3) *Human Reproduction* 465–471.

'The Presumptive Primacy of Procreative Liberty', in Tom Beauchamp, LeRoy Walters, Jeffrey Kahn and Anna Mastroiani (eds.), *Contemporary Issues in Bioethics* (Boston: Wadsworth Cengage Learning, 2014, 8th ed.) 245–251.

Robertson, John, Kahn, Jeffrey, and Wagner, John, 'Conception to Obtain Hematopoietic Stem Cells' (2002) 32(3) *Hastings Center Report* 34–40, reprinted in Helga Kuhse, Udo Schüklenk and Peter Singer (eds.), *Bioethics: An Anthology* (Hoboken: John Wiley & Sons, 2016, 3rd ed.) 144–151.

Rosenblum, Amanda, Horvat, Lucy, Siminoff, Laura, Prakash, Versha, Beitel, Janice and Garg, Amit, 'The Authority of Next-of-Kin in Explicit and Presumed Consent Systems for Deceased Organ Donation: An Analysis of 54 Nations' (2012) 27(6) *Nephrology Dialysis Transplantation* 2533–2546.

Rubin, Lisa and Phillips, Aliza, 'Infertility and Assisted Reproduction Technologies: Matters of Reproductive Justice', in Joan Chrisler (ed.), *Reproductive Justice: A Global Concern* (Santa Barbara: Praeger, 2012) 173–199.

Sabatello, Maya, 'Posthumously Conceived Children: An International and Human Rights Perspective' (2014) 27 *Journal of Law and Health* 29–67.

Sándor, Judit, 'Bioethics and Basic Rights: Persons, Humans, and Boundaries of Life', in Michel Rosenfeld and András Sajó (eds.), *The Oxford Handbook of Comparative Constitutional Law* (Oxford: Oxford University Press, 2012) 1142–1164.

Savulescu, Julian and Dahl, Edgar, 'Sex Selection and Preimplanation Diagnosis: A Response to the Ethics Committee of the American Society of Reproductive Medicine' (2000) 15(9) *Human Reproduction* 1879–1880, reprinted in Helga Kuhse, Udo Schüklenk and Peter Singer (eds.), *Bioethics: An Anthology* (Hoboken: John Wiley & Sons, 2016, 3rd ed.) 141–143.

Scherpe, Jens, 'Medically Assisted Procreation: This Margin Needs to Be Appreciated' (2012) 71(2) *Cambridge Law Journal* 276–279.

Scott, Rosamund, 'Choosing between Possible Lives: Legal and Ethical Issues in Preimplantation Genetic Diagnosis' (2006) 26(1) *Oxford Journal of Legal Studies* 153–178.

'Reproductive Health: Morals, Margin and Rights' (2018) 81(3) *Modern Law Review* 422–451.

Seatzu, Francesco, 'The Experience of the European Court of Human Rights with the European Convention on Human Rights and Biomedicine' (2015) 31(81) *Utrecht Journal of International and European Law* 5–16.

Seavillelein, Victoria, 'Challenging the Rhetoric of Choice in Prenatal Screening' (2008) 23(1) *Bioethics* 68–77.

Segers, Seppe, 'The Path toward Ectogenesis: Looking beyond the Technical Challenges' (2021) 22(1) *BMC Medical Ethics* 59.

Sermon, Karen, Van Steirteghem, André and Liebaers, Inge, 'Preimplantation Genetic Diagnosis' (2004) 363(9421) *Lancet* 1633–1641.

Sloan, Brian, 'Unmarried Fathers and the Frustration of Family Life' (2011) 70(2) *Cambridge Law Journal* 314–317.

Solberg, Berge, 'Getting beyond the Welfare of the Child in Assisted Reproduction' (2009) 35(6) *Journal of Medical Ethics* 373–376.

Somsen, Han, 'Regulating Human Genetics in a Neo-Eugenic Era', in Thérèse Murphy (ed.), *New Technologies and Human Rights* (Oxford: Oxford University Press, 2009) 85–127.

Sperling, Daniel, 'Law and Bioethics: A Right-Based Relationship and Its Troubling Implications', in Michael Freeman (ed.), *Law and Bioethics* (Oxford: Oxford University Press, 2008) 52–78.

Spriggs, Merle, *Autonomy and Patients' Decisions* (Boulder: Lexington Books, 2005).

'Is Conceiving a Child to Benefit Another against the Interests of the New Child?' (2005) 31 *Journal of Medical Ethics* 341–342.

'IVF Mixup: White Couple Have Black Babies' (2003) 29 *Journal of Medical Ethics* 65.

'Lesbian Couple Create a Child Who Is Deaf Like Them' (2002) 28 *Journal of Medical Ethics* 283.

Stack Jr, John, 'Judicial Policy-Making and the Evolving Protection of Human Rights: The European Court of Human Rights in Comparative Perspective' (1992) 15(3) *West European Politics* 137–155.

Staff Wilson, Mariblanca, *Derechos sexuales y derechos reproductivos: parte esencial de los derechos humanos* (Panamá: Instituto de la Mujer, Universidad de Panamá, 2010).

Stark, Barbara, 'Transnational Surrogacy and International Human Rights Law' (2011–12) 18 *ILSA Journal of International & Comparative Law* 369–386.

Steiner, Eva, '*Odièvre* v *France*: Desperately Seeking Mother – Anonymous Births in the European Court of Human Rights' (2003) 15(4) *Child and Family Law Quarterly* 425–448.

Thomasma, David, 'Proposing a New Agenda: Bioethics and International Human Rights' (2001) 10 *Cambridge Quarterly of Healthcare Ethics* 299–310.

Tobin, John, 'To Prohibit or Permit: What Is the (Human) Rights Response to the Practice of International Commercial Surrogacy?' (2014) 63(2) *International & Comparative Law Quarterly* 317–352.

van der Sloot, Bart, 'Between Fact and Fiction: An Analysis of the Case-Law on Article 12 of the European Convention on Human Rights' (2014) 26(4) *Child and Family Law Quarterly* 397–420.

Wade, Katherine, 'The Regulation of Surrogacy: A Children's Rights Perspective' (2017) 29(2) *Child and Family Law Quarterly* 113–131.

Weisfeld, Glenn and Weisfeld, Carol, 'Marriage: An Evolutionary Perspective' (2003) 23(suppl. 4) *Neuro Endocrinology Letters* 47–54.

Wicks, Elizabeth, *The State and the Body: Legal Regulation of Bodily Autonomy* (Oxford: Hart, 2016).

Wilkinson, Stephen, *Choosing Tomorrow's Children: The Ethics of Selective Reproduction* (Oxford: Oxford University Press, 2010).

Zampas, Christina and Gher, Jaime, 'Abortion as a Human Right: International and Regional Standards' (2008) 8(2) *Human Rights Law Review* 249–294.

Index